KT-389-183

The Postcolonial Exotic

Travel writing, it has been said, helped produce the rest of the world for a Western audience. Could the same be said more recently of *postcolonial writing*?

In *The Postcolonial Exotic*, Graham Huggan examines some of the processes by which value is attributed to postcolonial works within their cultural field. Using varied methods of analysis, Huggan discusses both the exoticist discourses that run through postcolonial studies and the means by which postcolonial products are marketed and domesticated for Western consumption.

Global in scope, the book takes in everything from:

- the latest 'Indo-chic' to the history of the Heinemann African Writers series;
- the celebrity stakes of the Booker Prize to those of the US academic star system;
- Canadian multicultural anthologies to Australian 'tourist novels'.

This timely and challenging volume points to the urgent need for a more carefully grounded understanding of the processes of production, dissemination and consumption that have surrounded the rapid development of the postcolonial field.

Graham Huggan is Professor of English at the University of Munich. His publications include *Territorial Disputes: Maps and Mapping Strategies in Contemporary Canadian and Australian Fiction* (1994), and *Peter Carey* (1996).

The Postcolonial Exotic

Marketing the margins

Graham Huggan

London and New York

First published 2001
by Routledge
11 New Fetter Lane, London EC4P 4EE

Simultaneously published in the USA and Canada
by Routledge
29 West 35th Street, New York, NY 10001

Routledge is an imprint of the Taylor & Francis Group

© 2001 Graham Huggan

Typeset in Goudy by Taylor & Francis Books Ltd

Printed and bound in Great Britain by TJ International Ltd,
Padstow, Cornwall

British Library Cataloguing in Publication Data
A catalogue record for this book is available from the British
Library

Library of Congress Cataloging in Publication Data
Huggan, Graham.
The postcolonial exotic : marketing the margins/Graham Huggan.
Includes bibliographical references and index.
1. English fiction–Minority authors–History and criticism. 2. Fiction–
Appreciation–English-speaking countries–History–20th century. 3. Fiction–
Publishing–English-speaking countries–History–20th century. 4. English
fiction–20th century–History and criticism. 5. Commonwealth fiction
(English)–History and criticism. 6.Multiculturalism in literature. 7.
Decolonization in literature. 8. Ethnic groups in literature. 9. Exoticism in
literature. 10. Booker Prize–History. 11. Canon (Literature). 12.
Postcolonialism. I. Title.
PR120.M55 H84   2001
823'.91409–dc21   00-045937

ISBN 0–415–25033–1 (hbk)
ISBN 0–415–25034–X (pbk)

Contents

Preface

When creative writers like Salman Rushdie are seen, despite their cosmopolitan background, as representatives of Third World countries; when literary works like Chinua Achebe's *Things Fall Apart* (1958) are gleaned, despite their fictional status, for the anthropological information they provide; when academic concepts like postcolonialism are turned, despite their historicist pretensions, into watchwords for the fashionable study of cultural otherness – all of these are instances of the *postcolonial exotic*, of the global commodification of cultural difference that provides the subject for this book. *The Postcolonial Exotic* is, in part, an examination of the sociological dimensions of postcolonial studies: the material conditions of production and consumption of postcolonial writings, and the influence of publishing houses and academic institutions on the selection, distribution and evaluation of these works. The book aims to address some of these sociological issues, inquiring into the status of postcolonial literatures – postcolonialism itself – as a cultural commodity, and exploring the relations between contemporary postcolonial studies and the booming 'alterity industry' that it at once serves and resists. The book is a study, in other words, of the varying degrees of complicity between local oppositional discourses and the global late-capitalist system in which these discourses circulate and are contained. The charge of complicity is of course hardly a new one, and might easily lend itself to the type of reductionist thinking that practitioners of postcolonial studies have always been eager to avoid. Suggestions, for example, that postcolonialism is primarily a form of academic careerism, or that the success of postcolonial products is merely a function of their viability as commodities on the global market, are recent cases in point – indications, perhaps, of the current intellectual backlash against postcolonial studies which, whether conducted from Left or Right, aims to cast serious doubt on, even to discredit, the field. Yet as an academic field postcolonial studies has always been more conflicted, and usually more finely nuanced, than its critics will admit. Its methods, although by no means unified, will no doubt continue to be misrecognised – and strategically homogenised – by those possibly self-serving critics who call for the latest paradigm shift.

Nonetheless, there remains a case to be made that postcolonial studies has yet to account for the often rapid transformations within its own discursive field. And one of those transformations has been its increasing *institutionalisation* as a recognised field of academic research across the English-speaking world. Postcolonial studies, it could be argued, has capitalised on its perceived marginality while helping turn marginality itself into a valuable intellectual commodity. Meanwhile, postcolonial writers, and a handful of critics, have accumulated forms of cultural capital that have made them recognised – even celebrity – figures despite their openly oppositional stance. As Kwame Anthony Appiah has suggested provocatively, the best known among this highly diverse body of writers and thinkers operate as latter-day culture brokers, 'mediating the international trade in cultural commodities of world capitalism at the periphery' (Appiah 1992: 149). Appiah's suggestion, while contestable, raises several pertinent questions about postcolonial modes of production/consumption that are central to the concerns of this book. What are the various mediating roles of postcolonial writers/thinkers, and to what extent is their capacity as mediators a function of their recognised status? To what degree is the recognition – the cultural capital – of postcolonial writing bound up in a system of cultural translation operating under the sign of the *exotic*? What role do exotic registers play in the construction of cultural value, more specifically those types of value (re)produced by postcolonial products and (re)presented in postcolonial discourse? How are these exoticisms marketed for predominantly metropolitan audiences – made available, but also palatable, for their target consumer public? How, within this process, do *post*colonial writers/thinkers contend with *neo*colonial market forces, negotiating the *realpolitik* of metropolitan economic dominance? How has the corporate publishing world co-opted postcolonial writing, and to what extent does the academy collaborate in similar processes of co-optation?

This book seeks to address, if hardly to answer, these various questions, operating in the spirit of informed and, inevitably, *interested* critique. It will be said, no doubt, that the book itself is complicit in the phenomena it attempts to critique. This is of course true – to some extent. The book is certainly not written – and how could it be? – from some Archimedean point of objective inquiry; it, too, seeks to benefit from the cultural capital that accrues to the postcolonial field. Nor is the book designed to score points off its rivals or to claim the moral high ground; rather, it aims to analyse (meaning also to historicise) some of the legitimising processes surrounding postcolonialism: processes which obviously help to consolidate the field as a bona fide area of international scientific inquiry, but are also instrumental in *commodifying* it as an object of – mostly metropolitan – consumption. (Within this dual context, it is highly ironic that the charge of complicity, while still frequently favoured by postcolonialism's fiercest adversaries, has itself become a standard commodity that shapes critical attitudes and responses to the field.) The book's own critical analysis takes in two distinct but interrelated exoticist discourses: first, those that traverse postcolonial texts and are implicated in them – exoticism in its anthropological, touristic and multicultural forms – and, second, those that pertain to the academic field of postcolonial studies – the exoticisms implicit in postcolonialism as an oppositional discursive field.

The introductory chapter begins by critically examining current definitions of the postcolonial. While postcolonial literatures may be simply defined as those English-language writings which have emerged from the former colonies of the British Empire, the term 'postcolonial' clearly has a wider valency. On one level, it refers to an ongoing process of 'cultural embattlement' (Suleri 1992b): postcolonialism, in this context, denotes an 'index of resistance, a perceived imperative to rewrite the social text of continuing imperial dominance' (Huggan 1996: 3). On another level, though, the term also circulates as a token of cultural value; it functions as a sales-tag in the context of today's globalised commodity culture. The chapter attempts to account for this constitutive split within the postcolonial, the entanglement of its ostensibly anti-imperial ideologies within a global economy that often manipulates them to neo-imperial ends. Taking its cue from the materialist critiques of Aijaz Ahmad and Arif Dirlik, but without endorsing their wholesale rejections, the chapter teases out the distinction between *postcolonialism* and *postcoloniality*. The first of these concerns largely localised agencies of resistance, the second refers to a global condition of cross-cultural symbolic exchange. Working from the premiss that postcolonialism and postcoloniality are inextricably interconnected, the chapter goes on to assess the impact of postcolonial writing in the global marketplace. More specifically, it draws on the sociology of Bourdieu and the anthropology of Appadurai and Foster to address the cultural commodification of postcolonial writing; the exotic appeal attributed to putatively 'marginal' literatures and cultures; and the problem of translation for a multiply (dis)located audience. The chapter eventually develops toward a definition of the cultural field of the postcolonial exotic. Within this field, exoticism may be understood conventionally as an aestheticising process through which the cultural other is translated, relayed back through the familiar. Yet in a postcolonial context, exoticism is effectively *repoliticised*, redeployed both to unsettle metropolitan expectations of cultural otherness and to effect a grounded critique of differential relations of power.

The following chapters exemplify the use of some of these unsettling techniques, as well as assessing the extent to which postcolonial tactics of resistance are dependent, though not exclusively, on metropolitan modes of production and consumption. Chapter 1 is the first of a four-part unit centring on so-called Third World literatures/cultures (Africa, the Caribbean, India, Sri Lanka and Pakistan). Chapters 1 and 2 explore the construction of 'non-Western' peoples, cultures and locations; Chapters 3 and 4 the exoticisation of marginal groups in the Western metropoles. No attempt is made at coverage here – always an illusion in a field of these dimensions. As throughout this book, the guiding principle is one of illustrative selection. No doubt, the selection process will yield a few surprises, such as the relative scarcity of material on what, from a Western touristic perspective, might probably be seen as two of the world's foremost 'exotic' sites – the Caribbean and the South Pacific. As will be seen, however, the book is ultimately less interested in exploring the specific geopolitics of exoticism than in examining the general mechanics of exoticist representation/consumption within an increasingly globalised culture industry (the alterity industry) and a transnationally conceived academic field (postcolonial studies).

Chapter 1 focuses on instances of the anthropological exotic in African writing. Beginning with an inquiry into Western constructions of African literature, the chapter goes on to consider Western anthropology's investment in the exotic and the returns this investment brings in (Europhone) African writing. The chapter explores the link, that is, between the ethnographic dimensions of African literatures and the role Africa has historically played as a profitable source for the marketing of cultural otherness. To establish this link, the chapter reopens the vexed debate between those who support anthropologically informed readings (Miller) and those who see them as a reinforcement of Eurocentric interpretive paradigms (Amuta). It then proceeds to examine three examples of counter-ethnographic – *strategically* exotic – African narratives: Chinua Achebe's *Things Fall Apart* (1958), an oblique if cutting satire on nineteenth-century cultural primitivism; Yambo Ouologuem's *Le devoir de violence* (1968), a searing critique of the anthropological quest for cultural authenticity; and Bessie Head's *The Collector of Treasures* (1977), a subtle exploration of the inside/outside dialectic of cross-cultural analysis. In each case, exoticist myths, reinforced rather than dispelled by anthropology, are turned back explicitly or implicitly on the voyeuristic Western observer/reader. The chapter closes by bridging the gap between exoticist elements *in* African writings and the perceived exoticism *of*

African writing as it is marketed and distributed for Western audiences. More particularly, it considers the ambivalent role played by the Heinemann African Writers Series, arguing that the Heinemann company, the world's leading publisher of English-language African writing, has been both a valuable promoter of cross-cultural understanding and an ironic purveyor of exoticist modes of cultural representation.

Chapter 2 focuses, similarly, on the Western consumption of 'non-Western' products. Its emphasis is on the consumption, literalised in Rushdie's gastronomic imagery, of India as exotic spectacle. It begins, accordingly, by addressing some recent examples of this 'spectacularising' process – the plethora of commemorative products and events, many of them British/European, surrounding India's fiftieth-year anniversary celebrations. Highlighted here are three highly mediated anniversary events: the publication of the special '50 Years of Independence' edition of the magazines *Granta* and *The New Yorker*; the appearance of the anthology, *The Vintage Book of Indian Writing*, rushed out to coincide with Golden Jubilee year; and the staging of an ambitious commemorative academic conference, 'India: 50 Years After', in Barcelona. The chapter argues that these events have functioned to some extent as aesthetic diversions, drawing attention away from the political achievements of independence and toward a carefully packaged, sanitised view of India as consumer product. Ostensibly meant as tributes to Indian independence, events such as these have ironically tended to reconfirm British/European dependence on a steady supply of 'exotic' Indian goods. The chapter goes on to analyse the reception of three of the most commercially successful Indo-Anglian novels of the last two decades – Salman Rushdie's *Midnight's Children* (1981), Vikram Seth's *A Suitable Boy* (1993) and Arundhati Roy's *The God of Small Things* (1997) – suggesting that, while these writers have capitalised on the 'politico-exotic' appeal of their novels (Brennan 1997), they have also succeeded in sustaining a *critique* of exoticism in their work. This critique is located in each case in forms of cultivated exhibitionism: the deliberately exaggerated hawking of Oriental(ist) wares by a narcissistic narrator (Rushdie); the consciously melodramatic combination of Indian romance and political intrigue (Seth); the overwrought staging of a tragic tale of illicit cross-caste love (Roy). The ironic self-consciousness of these novels might be seen as another form of strategic exoticism, designed as much to challenge as to profit from consumer needs; but it might also be seen as precisely the commodity form – the symbolic capital – on which their writers have made their reputations as reader-friendly, but also wryly sophisticated, Indo-Anglian novelists.

Chapter 3 continues the dialogue between Britain/Europe and South Asia by assessing the work of Rushdie alongside that of V.S. Naipaul and

Hanif Kureishi. These writers, although all longstanding British citizens, have frequently been perceived either as marginal or as coming from other places (India, the Caribbean, Pakistan). The chapter shows how Rushdie, Naipaul and Kureishi, despite their obvious ideological differences, have responded in kind by *staging* marginality in their works. The term 'staged marginality', adapted from the work of Dean MacCannell, denotes the process by which marginalised individuals or minority groups dramatise their 'subordinate' status for the imagined benefit of a majority audience. Staged marginality, far from being a form of necessary self-subordination, may function in certain contexts to uncover and challenge dominant structures of power. The chapter then goes on to analyse instances of staged marginality in Rushdie's *The Satanic Verses* (1988), Naipaul's *The Enigma of Arrival* (1987) and Kureishi's *The Buddha of Suburbia* (1990), with some reference also to Kureishi's screenplays for Stephen Frears' films. In Rushdie's and Kureishi's cases, the staging of marginality involves a strategic redeployment of commercialised forms of the exotic ('ethnic' TV shows, popular costume dramas, etc.); in Naipaul's, it cuts through romanticised perceptions of former imperial relations, recasting master–servant roles in a nominally postcolonial context. The chapter ends by considering further the contradictory status of Rushdie, Naipaul and Kureishi as 'celebrity minority' writers, assessing the extent to which their success has been linked to commodified perceptions of cultural marginality, and showing how all of them, in strategically staging marginality for their mainstream audience, explore their own ironic relation to majoritarian notions of British national culture.

Chapter 4 provides another perspective on the 'mainstreaming' of postcolonial literature by considering the promotional role of the Booker company, sponsor for over thirty years of the prestigious Booker Prize. The Booker award has tended to favour postcolonial writers – writers either based in countries of the former British Empire (Africa, the Caribbean, South Asia, Canada, Australia, New Zealand) or belonging to minority communities (Afro-Caribbean, South/east Asian) in Britain. Is Booker's promotional push the sign of a new transnational era in which writers increasingly demonstrate the global proportions of the English language; or is it rather the strategy of a multinational corporate enterprise that seeks alternative markets in order to expand its own commercial horizons? A discrepancy certainly exists between the Booker's postcolonial winners and the company's high colonial background in the Caribbean sugar trade. The chapter teases out further contradictions in Booker McConnell's chequered history, going behind the scenes of one of the world's top literary prizes and critically reassessing its role in the democratisation of literary taste. The chapter goes on to discuss the privileging of colonial

history, more specifically *Indian* history, in the three decades of the Booker
Prize. It argues that 'Raj revivalism' (Rushdie 1991e) has figured
prominently in the work of previous winners, even if the Raj itself is often
held up to ridicule or revisionist critique. Foregrounded here are the
prizewinning novels of J.G. Farrell and Paul Scott, published in the 1970s,
and their later postcolonial variants, among them Michael Ondaatje's *The
English Patient* (1992). The chapter argues that the Booker Prize, in
rewarding the work of these admittedly disparate writers, suggests a
continuing desire for metropolitan control born in part of 'imperialist
nostalgia' (Rosaldo 1993). The rehearsal of colonial history, projecting
both backward in time and outward in space, offers up nostalgic visions of
India (and other former colonies) as exotic sites; the *resistance* to such
nostalgia that is obviously exercised by many of the writers is effectively
recuperated by an 'otherness industry' that banks its profits on exotic
myths. The chapter closes by reconsidering the ambivalent nature of
Booker plc: at once a valuable sponsor of international English literatures
and a latter-day patron of the arts promoting culturally 'othered' goods.

Chapters 5, 6, 7 and 8 shift their location to settler cultures (particularly Canada and Australia), whose claims to postcolonial status are
weakened by their continuing records of 'internal colonialism' (Hutcheon
and Richmond 1990). How, these chapters ask, have Canada and
Australia sought in different ways to engage in a process of cultural
decolonisation? The most effective attempt has arguably been the move
to *multiculturalism*, as exemplified in government-sponsored projects to
celebrate ethnic diversity, and to forge a common future for a racially
mixed national community whose different groups are still encouraged to
sustain themselves on their own distinctive past. Is multiculturalism a
genuine attempt to move toward greater interethnic tolerance – toward a
more equitable society in which different groups are awarded equal
recognition – or is it a smokescreen that hides the continuing privilege of
the dominant culture, and that defuses the ethnic tensions that threaten
to divide the nation? Following the lead of writers who reject the 'ethnic'
label foisted upon them, Chapter 5 develops a critique of Canadian and
Australian multiculturalisms, showing that a discrepancy exists between a
democratic 'politics of recognition' (Taylor 1994) and an aestheticisation
of ethnic difference that creates, at worst, 'boutique xenophobia'
(Papaellinas 1992). The chapter initially focuses on the controversies
surrounding the books of Neil Bissoondath (in Canada) and Helen
Darville-Demidenko (in Australia), using these debates to shed light on
the contemporary merchandising of multicultural products. It then
proceeds to analyse two successful films, Stephan Elliott's *Adventures of
Priscilla, Queen of the Desert* (1994) and Atom Egoyan's *Exotica* (1994).

Both films are self-consciously exoticist in their spectacularisation of sexual/ethnic difference and in their ironic portrayal of the exoticised body as a 'forbidden' fetish object. Each film also comments on the surveillance and containment of nominally transgressive desire in societies which, for all their claims to multicultural diversification, are still beset by fears and fantasies surrounding the figure of the ethnic other. The chapter concludes by arguing that multiculturalism's celebratory 'rainbow' visions can easily be appropriated to recycle profitable exotic myths: about the threatening sexual/ethnic other as an object of dangerous erotic desire; and about the availability of society's others as a source of commercial spectacle.

Chapter 6 furthers the debate on the viability of 'ethnic' products by focusing on autobiographical works by writers from Australian Aboriginal communities. Why, the chapter asks, are autobiographical texts so often marketed as unmediated expressions of the lived authenticity of ethnic experience? And why has authenticity become such a popular marketing strategy in autobiographies by *women* writers, particularly from minority cultures? The chapter examines the argument first put forward in Australia by Susan Hawthorne that ethnic/Native autobiographies, particularly by women, are implicated in a Western metropolitan 'politics of the exotic' (Hawthorne 1989). This argument is developed by looking at a number of paratextual features (jacket blurbs and designs, editorial comments and notes, glossaries, etc.) in selected autobiographies by Australian Aboriginal women (Morgan, Ward, Langford Ginibi, Nannup, Huggins and Huggins, etc.). These features indicate a conflict between the recuperative packaging of autobiography and the life-narratives of Native women who resist, or resite, Western representational codes. The chapter closes by arguing, not for a dismissal of authenticity, but for a greater understanding of the different, possibly incompatible, uses to which it is put. Authenticity emerges both as a self-validating identitary category and as a consumer-oriented strategy to consolidate Western power by alleviating white-liberal guilt.

Chapter 7 suggests a further connection between discourses of the authentic and ideas of 'uncontaminated' travel that are reinforced by touristic myths. More specifically, the chapter looks at the operations of the 'tourist gaze' (Urry 1990) in contemporary Canadian and Australian fiction, focusing on a number of relatively recent 'tourist novels' which conduct their mostly white, often disillusioned Western protagonists on a series of unenlightening, sometimes catastrophic, Asian quests. The novels (by Janette Turner Hospital, Gerard Lee, Inez Baranay and several others) adopt a largely ironic approach to East–West clichés and cultural stereotypes. The tourist gaze is transformed, if not annulled, in a series of dubious Eastern settings that defy Western expectations while debunking Orientalist myths (Said 1978). The chapter ends by considering how the reversibility of the tourist gaze may be used to defamiliarise Western national narrative by resituating conventional exoticist paradigms of dislocation and transplantation in a domestic space.

Chapter 8 considers yet another form of exoticism, celebrity glamour, by looking at the critical industry surrounding Margaret Atwood, by far Canada's best-known living writer. The chapter analyses instances of global 'Atwood mania' while assessing the construction of Atwood as a representative national figure. The question of the representative writer is addressed by looking at institutionalised patterns of reception, both inside and outside Canada; at the place of Atwood's writings within not one but multiple canons (Canadian, North American feminist, utopian/dystopian, etc.); and, in more detail, at the history of the Margaret Atwood Society, founded in the mid 1980s in the United States. The chapter argues that the special status apparently being accorded to Atwood is due in part to the perception of Atwood herself as an intellectual celebrity. But it is also due to the malleability of her public image, as well as the diversity of her writings – a perceived flexibility that has allowed her to fill many different, often seemingly contradictory, roles.

The concluding chapter essays a short institutional history of postcolonial studies, beginning with the establishment of Commonwealth Literature in England in the mid 1960s and ending with the meteoric rise of postcolonial theory in 1990s America. The chapter considers the role played by the academy in legitimising marginal products and in helping writers accumulate cultural capital within the postcolonial field of production (Bourdieu 1993). It also attempts to account for some of the apparent ironies implicit in the current institutionalisation of postcolonial theory at Western universities, particularly in the United States. One of these ironies is that several of its best-known – in certain cases, 'star' – practitioners are conspicuously privileged academics working in the metropolitan centres; another is that its self-consciousness, its seemingly increasing involutions, might be seen as being at odds with its emancipatory social goals; and a third is that its speculative, potentially totalising abstractions risk reinforcing the very otherness that it wishes to call in question. Postcolonial theory, it might be said uncharitably, exhibits and to some extent manipulates its status as an intellectual commodity, providing at worst a pretext for continued cultural ignorance (Suleri 1992a). But it is also clear that, like other branches of theory, it asks some searching questions; and that those questions are certainly relevant, if not directly applicable, to everyday social concerns. This book seeks in the end, then, to defend the intellectual projects of postcolonial studies, and to honour the work of the many writers and scholars who are involved; but at the same time, it sees that work as bound up in a late-capitalist mode of production – a mode in which such terms as 'marginality', 'authenticity' and 'resistance' circulate as commodities available for commercial exploitation, and as signs within a larger semiotic system: the postcolonial exotic.

The emphasis of this book is on narrative, for the most part fiction; its restricted scope does not allow for the treatment of other potentially exotic forms (painting and sculpture, drama, poetry, music). These forms and their relation to the field invite a more extensive analysis; as it is, the book represents little more than a preliminary study, a speculative prolegomenon to the sociology of postcolonial cultural production. Its 'case studies' have been gathered over several years in different places, with most of the research being done at Harvard and, more recently, the University of Munich. My special thanks go out to my student research assistants at both universities – particularly Daryn David, Hugh Eakin, Yukun Harsono, Lynn Lee, Elisabeth Reber, Ann Seaton and Hanna Schwenkglenks – without whose help the book, already slow in the making, could not have been completed. Thanks also to the editors and publishers of the following journals and books for their permission to reprint material that had previously appeared in a different form: *Studies in the Novel* (Introduction and Chapter 4); *Comparative Literature* (Chapter 1); *Ariel* (Chapter 2); *Australian Studies* (Chapter 6); *Canadian Literature*, *Westerly* and *Australian Literary Studies* (Chapter 7); *Mainz Anglistentag Proceedings*: publisher WVT Verlag, Trier (Conclusion). Some of the initial work on exoticism in the introduction is taken from my essay in Daniel Clayton and Derek Gregory's collection *Colonialism, Postcolonialism and the Production of Space* (Blackwell, forthcoming); thanks to both editors and the publisher for permission to reprint material here. Parts of Chapters 3 and 5 are based on conference papers, initially delivered at the annual Zaragoza literary/cultural studies conference and later published by The University of Zaragoza/Grupo Milán and Rodopi; thanks to the publisher, the editors and, not least, the conference organisers, especially Isabel Santaolalla and Dolores Herrero. Valuable feedback on the concept of the postcolonial exotic was provided, courtesy of Ulrich Broich, Peter Hughes, Anton Kirchhofer and Allen Reddick at graduate colloquia at the Universities of Munich and Zurich, respectively. My thanks finally, as always, to those who initiated me into the field of postcolonial studies some ten or so years ago, especially Diana Brydon, Bill New, Craig Tapping and Helen Tiffin. This book, dedicated to them, is in part a personal reckoning with a field that has always excited me – and probably always will.

Introduction

Writing at the margins: postcolonialism, exoticism and the politics of cultural value

Postcolonialism in the age of global commodity culture

The trouble with postcolonialism

Critiques of postcolonialism have intensified over the last decade, by no coincidence the decade that has also brought postcolonial studies to prominence as an institutionalised academic field. Postcolonial studies, though never fully accepted within the academy, has become distinctly fashionable; 'postcolonial' is a word on many people's lips, even if no one seems to know quite what it means. Like other commodified terms used largely for academic purposes, postcolonialism has taken full advantage of its own semantic vagueness. Like its sister term, postmodernism, it has yielded a cache of definitions, each of these recognised as provisional, as if in anticipation of the next to come.[1] It would be simple, but also simplistic, to be cynical about this definition industry which, in an era of academic overproduction, has helped to keep people in careers; the fact remains that postcolonialism, for all its definitional – not to mention methodological – inconsistencies, has provided a catalyst for some of the most exciting intellectual work to be seen today. To ask 'what is postcolonialism?' appears, in any case, to be less productive than to ask some such other question as 'what can postcolonialism *do*?'. Bart Moore-Gilbert, in his recent survey *Postcolonial Theory* (1997), puts the case for postcolonial criticism as 'a more or less distinct set of reading practices ... preoccupied principally with analysis of cultural forms which mediate, challenge or reflect upon ... relations of domination and subordination' (Moore-Gilbert 1997: 12). These relations, continues Moore-Gilbert, 'have their roots in the history of modern European colonialism and imperialism', but they also 'continue to be apparent in the present era of neocolonialism' (12). While this is as good a working definition as any, it still leaves room for doubt. For as Moore-Gilbert himself recognises, it is far too broad and still too narrow: too broad in the obvious sense that too much time and space is covered, too narrow in that it excludes other, possibly related oppositional practices. The trouble with postcolonialism, when seen as a broad-based critical method, is that it risks being collapsed into a catch-all 'metaphor for cultural embattlement' (Suleri 1992b). At best, this inclusiveness provides the grounds for fruitful alliances (between colonial-discourse analysts and feminists, for example, or between more traditional New Literatures critics and radical scholar-activists in ethnic/minority fields); at worst, it affords a rationale for the kind of intellectual tourism that meanders dilettantishly from one place to another in search of ill-thought goals.

Is postcolonial studies to be seen, then, as a form of wayward eclecticism, inviting cross-cultural comparison but with insufficient cultural knowledge, or claiming historical method but without a clear grasp of historical facts? Certainly, the tendency among postcolonial critics to sacrifice cultural and historical specificity to the blandishments of abstract theory has not gone unnoticed. Anne McClintock, for example, finds the term postcolonial 'prematurely celebratory' (McClintock 1992: 88), while Ella Shohat sees its academic consecration as raising doubts about 'its ahistorical and universalizing deployments' (Shohat 1992: 99). Aijaz Ahmad, its fiercest critic, notes its conscription to a transhistorical narrative of colonialism, with the result that 'everyone gets the privilege, sooner or later, of being colonizer, colonized and postcolonial – sometimes all at once' (Ahmad 1995b: 31). These critiques, while by no means unfounded, are often remarkable for their own strategic misreadings: in McClintock's case, the perverse insistence that the multiple perspectives of postcolonial criticism are reducible to a single term that 're-center[s] global history around the … rubric of European time' (McClintock 1992: 86); or in Shohat's, the confident but mistaken assertion that postcolonial criticism, in positioning former colonies in relation to an imperial 'centre', 'assumes that white settler countries and emerging Third World nations broke away from the "center" in the same way' (Shohat 1992: 102); or in Ahmad's, the puzzling accusation that postcolonial treatments of history are 'reserved almost exclusively for the [Indian-based] Subaltern Studies group, whatever that group at any given point may be' (Ahmad 1995b: 30).

These generalised attacks are sometimes vulnerable to the identical criticisms – of homogenisation and lack of historical nuance – that their proponents are so keen to level. They might be seen, in this sense, as examples of the type of academic one-upmanship that is so common in the lively debates surrounding postcolonial criticism and, particularly, theory today. It has arguably become more fashionable to attack postcolonialism than to defend it – a sign, perhaps, rather less of the conceptual inadequacies of postcolonial studies than of its increasing commodification as a marketable academic field.[2] Critiques of postcoloni-alism, after all, add to the currency of postcolonial discourse: hence the paradox that postcolonial studies prospers even as its methods are called in question; that while the field grows rich on its accumulated cultural capital, it is recognised by an increasing number of its opponents as intellectually bankrupt (Huggan 1997b).

Nonetheless, these opponents have succeeded in raising a number of legitimate doubts about the field. Not least among these doubts is the suspicion that the potential for anti-colonial resistance within postcolonial studies might be limited largely to the effectiveness of its own discursive manoeuvres. To posit the indirect link between textual resistance and oppositional politics is one matter; to substitute the one for the other is, of course, a different thing. The problem resides for some in an abiding preference for poststructuralist methodologies, which are seen to run the risk either of theorising day-to-day struggles out of existence or of under-mining the intellectual basis for adversarial solidarity and group support.[3] This seems an over-narrow view of poststructuralism's critical capabilities; nevertheless, the danger exists that a rarefied critical/theoretical conscious-ness might end up turning the specific realities of social struggle into an infinite spiral of indeterminate abstractions.

There are signs in recent postcolonial criticism that the love-affair with poststructuralism might be over; and that locally produced theories and methods might prove in the end to be more productive than the reliance on Euro-American philosophical trends and habits of thought. One of the ironies, it could be said, of a particular kind of postcolonial criticism has been its articulation of anti-European sentiments by European conceptual means (Mukherjee 1990). This irony has been compounded by the tendency to privilege Europe as a frame of cultural reference, as the primary producer of the discourses against which postcolonial writers/thinkers are aligned. This 'counterdiscursive' approach (Tiffin 1987) now seems to have fallen out of favour, being seen somewhat inaccurately as a predominantly reactive model or as subscribing to the very binaries (e.g. 'Europe and its Others') it seeks to resist. A dissonance remains, however, between the democratic ideal of 'postcolonial culture' and the hyperproduction of 'postimperial criticism' in Europe and, above all, the United States (W. Mitchell 1992). W.J.T. Mitchell spells out the problem:

> [T]he most important new literature is now emerging from the former colonies of the Western empires – from (for instance) Africa, South

America, Australia, New Zealand; the most provocative new criticism is emanating from research universities in the advanced industrial democracies, that is, from the former 'centers of the Empire,'
Europe and the United States.

(Mitchell 1992: 14)

As Mitchell himself recognises, this view of affairs is oversimplified: 'It is
surely wrong to say that cultural "raw materials" are coming from the
colonies to be turned into "finished products" by the critical industries of
empire' (Mitchell 1992: 17). The globalisation of cultural production
within the so-called New World Order argues against such simple
formulae of metropolitan exploitation. All the same, it seems worth
questioning the neo-imperialist implications of a postcolonial liter-
ary/critical industry centred on, and largely catering to, the West. English
is, almost exclusively, the language of this critical industry, reinforcing the
view that postcolonialism is a discourse of *translation*, rerouting cultural
products regarded as emanating from the periphery toward audiences who
see themselves as coming from the centre. The metropolitan locations of
the major publishing houses (London and New York, for example) lend
strength to this view, as does the increasing number of foreign-language
texts from the 'non-West' available in translation. What is this postcolonial industry that turns out translated products for metropolitan
consumers in places like London and New York? And why does this
industry seem to privilege a handful of famous writers (Achebe, Naipaul,
Rushdie); why does it devote so much time and attention to its three
celebrity critics (Bhabha, Said, Spivak)?

Postcolonialism and postcoloniality

One possible explanation for this apparent hierarchy of postcolonial
writers/thinkers can be sought via Pierre Bourdieu's influential notion of
cultural capital. Cultural capital, says Bourdieu, is always unevenly
distributed; it circulates within a symbolic economy of cultural value that
is configured in a series of interlocking hierarchical structures. Cultural
capital – to elaborate – is transmitted, acquired and accumulated through
a complex process of legitimation negotiated through the interactions
between the producers and consumers of symbolic goods. This struggle for
legitimation takes place within designated fields of cultural production.
The literary field of cultural production

is the site of [continuing] struggles in which what is at stake is the
power to impose the dominant definition of the writer and therefore

to delimit the population of those entitled to take part in the struggle
to define the writer.

(Bourdieu 1993: 42)

The fundamental stake in these literary struggles

> is the monopoly of literary legitimacy, i.e., *inter alia*, the monopoly of
> the power to say with authority who are authorized to call themselves
> writers; or, to put it another way, it is the monopoly of the power to
> consecrate producers or products (we are dealing with a world of
> belief and the consecrated writer is the one who has the power to
> consecrate and to win assent when he or she consecrates an author or
> a work – with a preface, a favourable review, a prize, etc.).
>
> (Bourdieu 1993: 42)

The writer himself/herself is only one of several 'agents of legitimation' –
others might include booksellers, publishers, reviewers and, not least,
individual readers and 'valuing communities' (Frow 1995). These agents
are all contenders in the struggle to validate particular writers; and the
writers themselves vie for the right to attain and, in turn, confer
recognition and prestige (Huggan 1997a).

Bourdieu's model has been attacked for its over-schematised distinctions and, in particular, for its attempt to fix the class positions of
different consumer publics.[4] The model is useful, nonetheless, in
suggesting how postcolonial writers/thinkers operate within an overarching, if historically shifting, field of cultural production. The postcolonial
field of production, like other such fields, occupies a site of struggle
between contending 'regimes of value' – in John Frow's definition,
'mechanisms that permit the construction and regulation of value-
equivalence' (Frow 1995: 144; also Appadurai 1986: 4, 14–15). Yet such is
the battle between its two principal regimes of value that the field as a
whole might best be seen as constitutively split. These two regimes of
value can be referred to here by the terms *postcolonialism* and *postcoloniality*. Little attempt has so far been made in the history of postcolonial
criticism to distinguish between these two terms, even though some
critics (Ella Shohat, for instance) have recognised the need for clarifica-
tion. Postcolonialism, Shohat suggests in an endnote to her seminal essay
'Notes on the "Post-Colonial" ' (1992), might well need to be differentiated from the global condition of postcoloniality it sets out to document
and critique. Shohat's suggestion, a provocative one, can be teased out
here as follows, in part by comparing the better-known distinction
between postmodernism and postmodernity.[5]

Postcolonialism's regime of value relates to an ensemble of loosely connected oppositional practices, underpinned both by a highly eclectic methodology of 'cultural embattlement' (Suleri 1992b) and by an aesthetic of largely textualised, partly localised resistance. Postcolonialism, understood this way, becomes an anti-colonial intellectualism that reads and valorises the signs of social struggle in the faultlines of literary and cultural texts. Postcolonialism, in this sense, obviously shares some of *postmodernism's* relativistic preoccupations – with textual indeterminacy, the crisis of meaning, the questioning of the unitary subject, and so on. Yet it does not, or at least does not aim to, share postmodernism's somewhat irresponsible lack of commitment, its self-regarding obsession with play, or its Eurocentric frame of reference. Postcoloniality, on the other hand, is largely a function of *postmodernity*: its own regime of value pertains to a system of symbolic, as well as material, exchange in which even the language of resistance may be manipulated and consumed. Postcoloniality, in its function as a regime of cultural value, is compatible with a worldwide market whose power now 'extends over the whole range of cultural production' (Harvey 1989: 45). Postcoloniality, put another way, is a value-regulating mechanism within the global late-capitalist system of commodity exchange. Value is constructed through global market operations involving the exchange of cultural commodities and, particularly, culturally 'othered' goods. Postcoloniality's regime of value is implicitly assimilative and market-driven: it regulates the value-equivalence of putatively marginal products in the global marketplace. Postcolonialism, by contrast, implies a politics of value that stands in obvious opposition to global processes of commodification. Yet a cursory glance at the state of postcolonial studies at Western universities, or at the worldwide marketing of prominent postcolonial writers like Salman Rushdie, is enough to suggest that these two apparently conflicting regimes of value are mutually entangled. It is not just that postcolonialism and postcoloniality are at odds with one another, or that the former's emancipatory agenda clashes with the latter's; the point that needs to be stressed here is that postcolonialism *is bound up with* postcoloniality – that in the overwhelmingly commercial context of late twentieth-century commodity culture, postcolonialism and its rhetoric of resistance have themselves become consumer products.[6]

This is not simply to collapse postcolonial intellectual work to the logic of the market. Nor is it to suggest, as Arif Dirlik does somewhat intemperately in his essay 'The Postcolonial Aura' (1994), that the postcolonial is above all a marker of academic success: of the increasing cultural capital built up by self-designated postcolonial intellectuals in the universities of the West, especially the United States. It is, however, to suggest that these ostensibly *anti*-colonial writers/thinkers are all working, some of them conspicuously, within the *neo*colonial context of global commodity culture. The distinction is no doubt too sharp; to see commodity culture as necessarily compromising and/or imperialistic would be as absurd as to see all postcolonial writers/thinkers as heroic agents of liberation. Nonetheless, as postcolonial scholars such as Gayatri Spivak have attested, there is a constant need for vigilance to neocolonial structures of power. Speaking of the contemporary metropolitan reward-system for 'oppositional' intellectual projects, Spivak warns that:

> arguments from culturalism, multi-culturalism and ethnicity, however insular and heteromorphous they might seem from the great narra-tives of the techniques of global financial control, can work to ob-scure such separations in the interests of the production of a neo-colonial discourse. Today the old ways, of imperial adjudication and open systemic intervention cannot sustain unquestioned legitimacy. Neo-colonialism is fabricating its allies by proposing a share of the centre in a seemingly new way (not a rupture but a displacement): disciplinary support for the conviction of authentic marginality by the (aspiring) elite.
>
> (Spivak 1990a: 222)

Spivak's conception of postcoloniality as a deconstructive condition in which the postcolonial critic/teacher 'says "no" to the "moral luck" of the culture of imperialism while recognizing that she must inhabit it, indeed invest it, to criticize it' (Spivak 1990a: 228) is very different from the one I am proposing here. All the same, her work is useful in showing how the value-coding systems surrounding terms such as 'marginality', 'resistance', 'the postcolonial' itself, enter into conflict. Negotiating one's position within these regimes of value requires careful strategy:

> [T]he specificity of 'post-coloniality' ... can help us to grasp that no historically (or philosophically) adequate claims can be produced in any space for the guiding words of political, military, economic, ideo-logical emancipation and oppression. You take positions in terms not of the discovery of historical or philosophical grounds, but in terms of reversing, displacing, and seizing the apparatus of value-coding.
>
> (Spivak 1990a: 228)

Spivak recognises that part of the problem resides in taking up *localised* positions within the *global* framework of multi- and transnational corporate enterprise. This local-global dialectic has recently become a central talking-point in debates about postcolonialism and its role within the public sphere.

Postcolonialism and globalisation

As Stuart Hall points out in his essay 'When Was the "Post-Colonial"? Thinking at the Limit' (1996b), postcolonial critics have generally been reluctant to analyse their own positions, and the position of their field, within global-capitalist networks; this in spite of the fact that the operations of global capitalism are 'either implicitly assumed or silently at work in the underpinning assumptions of almost all ... post-colonial critical work' (Hall 1996b: 258). Reductive assaults by orthodox Marxists on postcolonialism's complicity with global market forces have not helped matters; as Hall scornfully remarks of Arif Dirlik's contention that 'postcoloniality serves capitalism's cultural requirements', and that 'postcolonial critics are, in effect, unwitting spokespersons for the new global capitalist order' (Hall's own paraphrases),

> This is a conclusion to a long and detailed argument of such stunning (and, one is obliged to say, banal) reductionism, a functionalism of a kind which one thought had disappeared from scholarly debate as an explanation of *anything*, that it reads like an echo from a distant, primeval era.
>
> (Hall 1996b: 258–9)

Hall's dismissal is perhaps unfair given Dirlik's relatively modest thesis that while 'postcolonial critics have engaged in valid criticisms of past forms of ideological hegemony, [they] have had little to say about its contemporary figurations' (Dirlik 1994: 356). Dirlik's argument, in brief, is that postcolonial critics' insistence on the value of the local has hindered them from analysing 'the ways in which totalizing structures [i.e. world capitalism] persist in the midst of apparent disintegration and fluidity' (Dirlik 1994: 356).[7] The problem with this argument, as Hall recognises, is that it repeatedly lapses into a tirade against the collective body of postcolonial intellectuals, who cover up their implication in 'a global capitalism of which they are not so much victims as beneficiaries' (Dirlik 1994: 353), and whose emancipatory agenda 'projects upon the past the same mystification of the relationship between power and culture that is characteristic of the ideology of global capitalism of which it is a product' (347). One notices again here the strategic homogenisation of postcolonialism – 'postcolonial critics', 'postcolonial intellectuals', 'the postcolonialist argument' – that allows its opponents to tar its highly diverse practitioners with the same wide-sweeping brush. One notices also the tendency to *equate* postcolonialism and postcoloniality – as if the discourse of resistance could automatically be seconded to the global condition of capitalism 'in whose interests it actually serves' (Dirlik 1994).

Yet if Dirlik is unduly dismissive, his critique should not be so easily dismissed. He is surely right to suggest that the local emancipatory imperatives of *some* postcolonial criticism tend to obscure the larger containing 'rhythms of globalization' (During 1992: 343); he is also right that *some* self-designated postcolonial intellectuals, notably in the United States, have reaped rich benefit from what we might uncharitably call the 'syndicated oppositionality' of their work. And his conclusion that 'postcoloniality is the condition of the intelligentsia of global capitalism' (Dirlik 1994: 356), while self-confessedly overgeneralised, is symptomatic of the dis-ease felt by many postcolonial scholars in face of the global machinery of cultural commodification. A characteristic response is that of Kwame Anthony Appiah, who, after stoutly defending the ethical value of postcolonial cultural criticism, still feels obliged to point out, in terms that closely resemble Dirlik's, that '[p]ostcoloniality is the condition of what we might ungenerously call a comprador intelligentsia: of a relatively small, Western-style, Western-trained, group of writers and thinkers who mediate the trade in cultural commodities of world capitalism at the periphery' (Appiah 1992: 149; see also Preface). Postcolonialism, to repeat, is bound up with postcoloniality; but to admit as much is not to 'sell out' to pernicious capitalist causes, it is rather to interrogate and strategise one's own position within the institutional parameters of the postcolonial field.

Two of these positions, both self-consciously globalist, are worth examining here: *worldliness* and *cosmopolitanism*. The former of these is most closely associated with the work of Edward Said. For Said, worldliness mobilises a combination of scholarship and politics in the service of global community; it acknowledges that 'intellectual and scholarly work from the peripheries, done by either immigrants or visitors, both of whom are generally anti-imperialist, is not simply the work of individuals, but mainly an extension into the metropolis of large mass-scale movements' (Said 1990: 30). Said's focus is on the inevitable, and for him desirable, hybridisation of postcolonial metropolitan culture, as can be seen in those 'surprising new configurations on the cultural map' that provide evidence of 'adversarial internationalization in an age of continued imperial structures' (Said 1990: 31). This view has the advantage of promoting transnational solidarities in an age of cultural fragmentation and the mass-dispersal of people, goods and ideas. Yet in his self-conscious privileging of global *metropolitan* culture, Said appears to exclude those who have no access – or at least no easy access – to the world's metropolitan centres. (One notices a similar privileging in the work of Salman Rushdie, for whom the city is the *locus classicus* of intercultural productivity and fermentation – see particularly *The Satanic Verses*.)[8] The most devastating attack on Said's concept of worldliness is in Aijaz Ahmad's coruscating *In Theory* (1992): a tinderbox of a book, written from an old-school Marxist perspective, where the sparks fly in a number of distinguished academic faces. In his chapter on Said, Ahmad takes particular umbrage at Said's assertion that 'our philological home' is neither the writer nor the nation, but the world (Said, qtd in Ahmad 1992: 217). Ahmad's response to this is characteristically vehement:

> Rarely in the latter half of the present century has one come across so unabashed a recommendation that the world, especially the 'Orient' – Palestine, Algeria, India – and indeed all the races, white and black, should be *consumed* in the form of those fictions of this world which are available in the bookshops of the metropolitan countries; the condition of becoming this perfect consumer, of course, is that one frees oneself from stable identities of class, nation, gender. Thus it is that sovereignty comes to be invested in the reader of literature, fully in command of an imperial geography. ... This is the imperial geography not of the colonial period but of late capitalism: commodity acquires universality, and a universal market arises across national frontiers and local customs, while white trade joins black trade. When cultural criticism reaches this point of convergence with the universal market, one might add, it becomes indistinguishable from commodity fetishism.
>
> (Ahmad 1992: 217, Ahmad's italics)

Ahmad is no doubt too eager, by turning Said's ideas against himself, to convert him into an apologist for the universal capitalist cause; but his criticism is valid insofar as it draws attention to the commodifying processes by which generalised cultural differences are manufactured, disseminated and consumed. Ahmad is also acute in his analysis of the fetishisation of cultural otherness that allows metropolitan readers to exercise fantasies of unrestricted movement and free will. More will need to be said about this fetishising process, which turns the literatures/cultures of the 'non-Western' world into saleable exotic objects. For the moment, suffice to say that the global concerns of postcolonialism meet in Said's work with a different kind of globalism – the postcoloniality of the universal market. The well-intentioned desire for 'adversarial internationalization' – for the fashioning of global solidarities in the continuing anti-imperial struggle – must contend with the power of a market that seeks, in part, to contain such oppositional gestures. The choice here may be not so much whether to 'succumb' to market forces as how to use them judiciously to suit one's own, and other people's, ends. The worldly reader/writer, like Spivak's canny cultural critic, may find himself/herself inhabiting the culture of imperialism in order to criticise it (Spivak 1990b: 228).

The ambivalence inscribed in worldliness also emerges in cosmopolitanism, a hotly debated term in the new cultural vocabulary of globalisation. Cosmopolitanism, for those who defend it, is a synonym for cultural tolerance and for the 'reciprocal interconnectedness' (Robbins 1993) that signifies an open, liberal-pluralist worldview. For its critics, such as Timothy Brennan, the term conceals as much as it reveals, operating as a cover for new forms of ethnocentrism or as a mystification of the continuing asymmetries of power within inclusive conceptions of global culture. Brennan, perhaps predictably, sees postcolonial studies as subscribing to the unexamined expansiveness that he associates with the cosmopolitan view. Echoing earlier critiques of the totalising tendencies of postcolonial studies, Brennan sees it as having led to 'a specious mastery of the whole, or a series of procrustean maneuvers to find a level of abstraction where difference is graspable' (Brennan 1997: 27). Cosmopolitanism (of which Saidian worldliness is a variant) allows the postcolonial critic to mediate between the world and the individual subject:

> With an almost allegorical resonance in the centers of imperial power, a dialectic within the field expresses itself most acutely in cosmopolitanism. An emphasis on the world is accompanied by an emphasis on identity and the subject by calling them forth as alleviating counterpoints. In this mixture of the specific and the broad, the need, I would argue, is for the opposite: a rethinking of the indigenous in the context of an intellectual generalism.
>
> (Brennan 1997: 27)

For Brennan, postcolonial studies not only embraces cosmopolitan principles; it is also complicit in the preferential treatment of cosmopolitan writers – especially novelists. Brennan, in an astonishing list, sees these novelists as modelling themselves 'on nostalgia for "democracy" as a vision of pluralist inclusion' (Brennan 1997: 38); as playing intermediary roles as 'outside' cultural commentators within the metropolis; as rejecting or at least ironising the liberation movements of the decolonisation era; and as joining 'political sarcasm [to] ironic detachment [in] a cosmic, celebratory pessimism' (Brennan 1997: 41). This type of formula fiction, to which Brennan later attaches the label 'politico-exotic', is, one might well imagine, more the object of suspicion than of admiration for most postcolonial critics. But Brennan surely has a point in drawing attention to the value-codings – the specific processes of *certification* – that underlie postcolonial authors' emergence into the public sphere. Postcoloniality meets cosmopolitanism in a variety of carefully managed products, packaged for easy consumption as a readily identifiable global corpus. Examples of this – and they are abundant – include:

> the new mammoth multicultural anthologies designed as textbooks for undergraduate teaching; ... highly publicized first novels by younger authors writing, often experimentally, about their own care- fully nurtured marginalities in a sort of highbrow mimicry of the testimonial; [and] ... book review[s by] critics who by name or accent or place of birth command an immediate and often suspicious authority over the new literatures under review.
>
> (Brennan 1997: 47–8)

As Brennan's examples suggest, this collaborative industry marshals a large number of legitimising agents, from multinational publishing companies which prepare 'large-market textbooks for a postnational curriculum' (Brennan 1997: 48) to individual buyers who pick up the latest ethnic autobiography to expand their own cultural horizons. The link clearly exists between postcoloniality as a global regime of value and a cosmopolitan alterity industry whose products are geared, in part, for educational use. This industry, invested on a large scale in the commodifi- cation of cultural difference, arguably belongs to what the art historian Deborah Root calls – deliberately turning the metaphor – a late-capitalist 'cannibal culture' of appropriative consumption. Root is far too keen to see consumerism as a necessary evil, and the global marketing of cultural difference as a latter-day version of imperialist plunder. Recent studies in the ideology of consumption suggest a *range* of available options for both the producers and consumers of culturally 'othered' goods. As Arjun Appadurai has recently argued, global processes of commodification may engender new social relations that operate in *anti*-imperialist interests, empowering the previously dispossessed (Appadurai 1996: esp. chaps 5 and 9).[9] While it would be a drastic simplification to suggest that postcolonial writers/thinkers are 'trapped' in commodity circuits, and that postcoloniality is the descriptive term for this condition of entrapment – the time has surely come to set aside the myth of commodity culture as some vast imperialist conspiracy sucking in its unwary victims – it would be fair to say that the globalisation of commodity culture has confronted postcolonial writers/thinkers with the irresolvable struggle between competing regimes of value. This struggle, I have been suggesting, plays itself out over the value of *cultural difference*. Under the sign of the postcolonial, cultural difference is politicised: it reveals through its representations the traces of unequal relations of power (Bhabha 1992). Yet, as the process of commodification clearly illustrates, cultural difference also has an aesthetic value, a value often measured explicitly or implicitly in terms of the *exotic*. To return for a moment to Brennan's examples, it seems quite clear that the value of the latest multicultural anthology or ethnic autobiography has something to do with the exotic appeal of these culturally different products. But what, exactly, is exotic about them? How is their exoticism coded, and in whose interests does it serve? To answer these questions, we need first to go back to the history of exoticist representation, and to trace exoticism's development from a privileged mode of aesthetic perception to its contemporary status as a global mode of mass consumption.

Exoticism in the margins

Exoticism as a system

Although the word 'exotic' currently has widespread application, it continues – possibly because of this – to be commonly misunderstood. For the exotic is not, as is often supposed, an inherent *quality* to be found 'in' certain people, distinctive objects, or specific places; exoticism describes, rather, a particular mode of aesthetic *perception* – one which renders people, objects and places strange even as it domesticates them, and which effectively manufactures otherness even as it claims to surrender to its immanent mystery. The exoticist production of otherness is dialectical and contingent; at various times and in different places, it may serve conflicting ideological interests, providing the rationale for projects of *rapprochement* and reconciliation, but legitimising just as easily the need for plunder and violent conquest.[10] Exoticism, in this context, might be described as a kind of semiotic circuit that oscillates between the opposite poles of strangeness and familiarity. Within this circuit, the strange and the familiar, as well as the relation between them, may be recoded to serve different, even contradictory, political needs and ends. As Stephen Foster has argued, the exotic functions dialectically as a *symbolic system*, domesticating the foreign, the culturally different and the extraordinary so that the 'phenomena to which they … apply begin to be structured in a way which makes them comprehensible and possibly predictable, if predictably defiant of total familiarity' (Foster 1982/3: 21). Exoticism is, in one sense, a control mechanism of cultural translation which relays the other inexorably back again to the same (Bongie 1991; Wasserman 1994); but to domesticate the exotic fully would neutralise its capacity to create surprises, thereby integrating it 'into the humdrum of everyday routines' (Foster 1982/3: 21–2). Thus, while exoticism describes the systematic assimilation of cultural difference, ascribing familiar meanings and associations to unfamiliar things, it also denotes an expanded, if inevitably distorted, comprehension of diversity which effectively limits assimilation 'since the exotic is … kept at arm's length rather than taken as one's own' (Foster 1982/3: 22). As a system, then, exoticism functions along predictable lines but with unpredictable content; and its political dimensions are similarly unstable, for the ideology it implies always 'stops short of an exhaustive interpretation' (Foster 1982/3: 22).

Exoticism describes a political as much as an aesthetic practice. But this politics is often concealed, hidden beneath layers of mystification. As a technology of representation, exoticism is self-empowering; self-referential even, insofar as the objects of its gaze are not supposed to look back (Root 1996: 45). For this reason, among others, exoticism has proved over time to be a highly effective instrument of imperial power. And its effectiveness can be measured, in part, by the occlusion of underlying political motives. The wonder beheld in exotic peoples, as Stephen Greenblatt demonstrates in his book on New World conquest, may precede their violent subjugation; the exotic splendour of newly colonised lands may disguise the brutal circumstances of their gain (Greenblatt 1991: esp. chap. 3). The exoticist rhetoric of fetishised otherness and sympathetic identification masks the inequality of the power relations without which the discourse could not function. In the imperial context, as Jonathan Arac and Harriet Ritvo have suggested, this masking involves the transformation of power-politics into *spectacle*. If imperialism, as they define it, is 'the expansion of nationality', then exoticism is 'the aestheticizing means by which the pain of that expansion is converted into spectacle, to culture in the service of empire' (Arac and Ritvo 1991: 3). A similar point is made by Edward Said in his study *Culture and Imperialism* (1993). For Said, exoticism functions in a variety of imperial contexts as a mechanism of aesthetic substitution which 'replaces the impress of power with the blandishments of curiosity' (Said 1993: 159). Said's formulation is characteristically elegant if, in this case, slightly inaccurate; for it is not that exotic spectacle and the curiosity it arouses replaces power, but rather that it functions as a decoy to *disguise* it.

Studies like Arac and Ritvo's and, to a lesser extent, Said's focus on nineteenth-century exoticisms and, more particularly, on the concealment of imperial authority through exotic spectacle. The plethora of exotic products currently available in the marketplace suggests, however, a rather different dimension to the global 'spectacularisation' of cultural difference. Late twentieth-century exoticisms are the products, less of the expansion of the nation than of a worldwide *market* – exoticism has shifted, that is, from a more or less privileged mode of aesthetic perception to an increasingly global mode of mass-market consumption. The massification of exotic merchandise implies a new generic form of exoticism, 'suitable for all markets and at the limits of its own semantic dispersion' (Gallini 1996: 219).[11] It also entails a reconsideration of the conventional exoticist distinction between the (imperial) 'centre' and the 'peripheries' on which it depends. As Roger Célestin remarks in the concluding chapter to his historical study of exoticist representation, *From Cannibals to Radicals* (1996),

> Center and Periphery are increasingly conflated in our present … [The] new movement of goods and capital, [the] new, diffuse origin of products, is accompanied by massive movements of population lead- ing to the hybridization of culture itself. When Juan Goytisolo writes that 'it is no longer necessary to take the plane for Istanbul or Mar- rakesh in search of exoticism, [that] a little stroll in the streets is enough,' he is referring to those millions of 'Peripherals' who have made their way to the Center. The presence of these 'exotics' in the West is not a result only of the internationalization and acceleration of economic flows; their arrival is also the result of the crumbling of imperial centers that created affinities that must be reckoned with in the postcolonial era.
>
> (Célestin 1996: 220)

Yet as Célestin recognises, this arrival of the exotic in the 'centre' cannot disguise the inequalities – the hierarchical encodings of cultural difference – through which exoticist discourses and industries continue to function. Reconstituted exoticisms in the age of globalisation include the trafficking of culturally 'othered' artifacts in the world's economic, not cultural, centres. These 'new' exotic products (African statues, Pacific Island necklaces, Indonesian batiks, and so forth) are characterised, not by remoteness but by *proximity* – by their availability in a shop or street-market or shopping-mall somewhere near you (Huggan 1994b: 24). Some advocates of globalisation might contend that this has become a two-way process, as desirable European products make their way to 'the most exotic and strange lands [*sic*], demonstrating the global extension and craving of the market' (Gallini 1996: 220). Others might claim that global processes of cultural hybridisation and transculturation signal the limits of the 'Center's exclusive control of the means of representation on a planetary level' (Célestin 1996: 221). Exchange, however, at both literal and symbolic levels is always uneven, as are the structures of economic development that underpin the global circulation of designated 'exotic' goods. It is not just, as Célestin claims, that 'in the postcolonial period the West is becoming increasingly the reader of the products of its own colonialism' (Célestin 1996: 220); rather, the West is *consuming* these products in an economic climate in which, to paraphrase Ahmad, the colonialisms of the past are perhaps less significant than the imperialisms of the present (Ahmad 1992: 222). What is clear, in any case, is that there are significant continuities between older forms of imperial exoticist representation and some of their more recent, allegedly postcolonial, counterparts. Two of these continuities, themselves interlinked, can be examined here: these are the *aesthetics of decontextualisation* and *commodity fetishism.*

In his excellent introduction to a collection of anthropological essays, *The Social Life of Things: Commodities in Cultural Perspective* (1986), Arjun Appadurai writes of the prevalent 'diversion of commodities from their original [cultural] nexus' (Appadurai 1986: 28). One of the best examples of this diversion, for Appadurai, is in 'the domain of fashion, domestic display, and collecting in the modern West' (28):

> In the logic of found art, the everyday commodity is framed and aestheticized ... [V]alue, in the art or fashion market, is accelerated or enhanced by placing objects and things in unlikely contexts. It is the aesthetics of decontextualization (itself driven by the quest for novelty) that is at the heart of the display, in highbrow Western homes, of the tools and artifacts of the 'other': the Turkmen saddle-bag, Masai spear, Dinka basket. In these objects, we see not only the equation of the authentic with the exotic everyday object, but also the aesthetics of diversion [whereby] diversion is not only an instrument of the decommoditization of the object, but also of the (potential) intensification of commoditization by the enhancement of value attendant upon its diversion.
>
> (Appadurai 1986: 28)

Appadurai argues that the search to domesticate and attribute value to exotic objects depends to some extent on their removal from their original cultural/historical context. The aesthetics of decontextualisation is also at work in so-called 'ethnic' and/or 'tribal' products whose authenticity is a function of their cultural dislocation. Examples of such products might include Native art and designs in Western households, World Music (largely catering to Western metropolitan listeners) and, more contentiously perhaps, Third World literature in English. As Deborah Root comments sardonically, 'the cultures from which [these] aesthetic or ceremonial forms are obtained are usually deemed more interesting … more authentic and exotic by those who are doing the taking, usually the politically or economically dominant societies' (Root 1996: 70). Exoticism is bound up here, not just in the perception of cultural difference but in the sympathetic identification with supposedly marginal cultural groups. Yet this urge to identify, as manifested in patterns of consumption, often comes at the expense of *knowledge* of cultures/cultural groups other than one's own. At its most extreme, exoticism's aesthetics of decontextualisation can end up sanctioning cultural ignorance; as Tzvetan Todorov notes, 'Knowledge is incompatible with exoticism, but lack of knowledge is in turn irreconcilable with praise of others; yet praise without knowledge is precisely what exoticism aspires to be. This is its constitutive paradox' (Todorov 1993: 265). Postcolonial cultural criticism, and the postcolonial industry at large, are by no means innocent of these exoticist manoeuvres. The current academic fetishisation of cultural otherness might be seen as a case in point; as Sara Suleri warns in her book *The Rhetoric of English India* (1992a) – itself arguably subject to similar criticisms (Brennan 1997: 57):

> While alteritism begins as a critical or theoretical revision of a Euro-centric or Orientalist study of the literatures of colonialism, its indiscriminate reliance on the centrality of otherness tends to replicate what in the context of imperialist discourse was the familiar category of the exotic.
>
> (Suleri 1992a: 12)

Critics (one cannot help noticing that Suleri pins the blame here, rather unfairly, on *Anglo-American* critics) run the risk of 'rendering otherness indistinguishable from exoticism, and of representing "difference" with no attention to the cultural nuances that differentiation implies' (Suleri 1992a: 12).[12] Such critics tend instead to 'reify questions of cultural misapprehension until "otherness" becomes a conceptual blockage that signifies a repetitive monumentalization of the academy's continuing fear of its own cultural ignorance' (Suleri 1992a: 12).

That exoticist discourses are more likely to mystify than to account for cultural difference has been noted by several critics, notably Christopher Bongie in his groundbreaking study *Exotic Memories* (1991). As Bongie notes, via Freud and Bhabha, fetishistic representations of an exotic other tend to repress the very cultural differences they are designed to reaffirm. Fetishism, in substituting a spiritual presence for a physical absence, has the effect of disavowing difference in the pursuit, instead, of unattainable ideals.[13] Clearly, fetishism plays a crucial role in colonialist fantasy-structures, which draw on the relationship between the exotic and the erotic to set up narratives of desire for, and partial containment of, the culturally 'othered' body (Bhabha 1983, 1994d). My focus here, however, will be on another variant of fetishism – *commodity* fetishism – within the contemporary order of postcolonial cultural production.

Commodity fetishism, according to the classic Marxian formulation, describes the veiling of the material circumstances under which commodities are produced and consumed.[14] In conveying both the allure of the commodity (through mystification) and the illusion of the severance of the finished work from its process of production, commodity fetishism links up with earlier forms of exoticist representation, arguably becoming the postmodern version of exoticist mystique. Now, it has become something of a cliché to speak of postmodernism in terms of commodification: Fredric Jameson, for instance, in his massive study on the subject, calls postmodernism the consumption, not just of commodities but of 'sheer commodification as a process' (Jameson 1991: x). In Western postmodern culture, commodity fetishism is not just rampant; it is the spirit of the age, a symptom of the ubiquitous 'aestheticization of the real' (Jameson 1991: x). Such postmodernist mantras, one might have thought, deserve to be treated with some suspicion, not least because they run the risk of celebrating the consumerism they are ostensibly critiquing, and of blanketing a diverse world with a universal late-capitalist creed.[15] If postmodernism, as Jameson suggests, represents the cultural logic of late capitalism, then that logic, however pervasive, will be highly variable in its effects. This is where postmodern theorists and postcolonial critics have tended to part company, with sometimes mutual accusations of universalising concepts, a crucial lack of local knowledge, and insufficient historical facts.[16] It is easy to understand why postcolonial writers/thinkers should be resistant to glib assertions of a global culture unified in the pursuit of consumer goods. For all that, it seems that postcolonialism needs a greater understanding of the commodifying processes through which its critical discourses, like its literary products, are disseminated and consumed.

In this context, Ahmad is quite right to draw attention to the connection between postcolonial cultural criticism (specifically, Said's) and the metropolitan marketing of exotic (by implication, Third World) literary texts. Said's appeal, however well-intentioned, to the worldly reader to 'think and experience with Genet in Palestine or Algeria, with Tayeb

Salih as a black man in London, with Jamaica Kincaid in the white world, with Rushdie in India and Britain' (qtd in Ahmad 1992: 217) certainly creates an impression of the *interchangeability* of highly discrepant cultural/historical experiences. It also suggests that access to these experiences is through the *consumption* of literary works by much-travelled writers who are perceived as having come from, or as having a connection to, 'exotic' places. And finally, it implies that these works, themselves the products of divergent histories, are to be consumed as if the philological world that they belong to were the *same*. These three aspects of commodity fetishism – mystification (or levelling-out) of historical experience; imagined access to the cultural other through the process of consumption; reification of people and places into exchangeable aesthetic objects – help these books and their authors acquire an almost talismanic status.

This status, I would argue, runs counter to the postcolonial imperative to demystify 'foreign' cultures and, ultimately, to show the constructed nature of discourses about culture itself. Said has played as important a role as any in this collective enterprise, as have the writers that he cites here (Kincaid and Rushdie are good examples). The postcolonial, as Said understands it, is an overtly politicising, implicitly *de*-exoticising category that demands an analysis of the material conditions surrounding textual production and representation. Ahmad's critique, in contrast, uncovers postcolonial/Third World texts as exotic objects, circulating within a metropolitan-regulated economy of commodity exchange. Moreover, Ahmad suggests that postcolonial criticism/critical theory *also* functions as a commodity; and that criticism like Said's, implicitly converging with 'the universal market', puts itself in danger of 'becom[ing] indistinguishable from commodity fetishism' (Ahmad 1992: 217). Why the contradiction? It is not enough to say, though it is clearly true, that Ahmad's argument is overstated, and that he is reliant on a partial understanding (in both senses of the word) of Said's work. One need only go to the local bookstore and check the packaging of Kincaid's and Rushdie's novels to see the kind of commercial 'third-worldism' to which Ahmad is ironically alluding here. One need only consider the hypercommodified status of the 'multicultural' or 'Third World' writer, or of literary categories such as magical realism or – often conflated with it – the Latin American 'Boom' novel. One need only look at the reception of works from Amos Tutuola's *The Palm-Wine Drinkard* (1952) to, more recently, Arundhati Roy's *The God of Small Things* (1997), to recognise the prevalence of the word 'exotic' as a marker of metropolitan commercial appeal. To conscript the criticism of Said to this blatantly commercial alterity industry is, in one sense, to do him and other postcolonial writers/thinkers a considerable disservice. But in another, it is to recognise that these writers/thinkers are not only subject to, but also actively manipulate, exoticist codes of cultural representation in their work. Exoticist spectacle, commodity fetishism and the aesthetics of decontextualisation are all at work, in different combinations and to varying degrees, in the production, transmission and consumption of postcolonial literary/cultural texts. They are also at work in the metropolitan marketing of marginal products and in their attempted assimilation to mainstream discourses of cross-cultural representation (Orientalism, neo-primitivism, native authenticity, and so on). If exoticism has *arrived* in the 'centre', it still *derives* from the cultural margins or, perhaps more accurately, from a commodified discourse of cultural marginality. How is value ascribed to, and regulated within, the cultural margins? What is the role of exoticism in putatively marginal modes of production and representation? What happens when marginal products, explicitly valued for their properties of 'resistance', are seconded to the mainstream as a means of reinvigorating mainstream culture? These questions are at the heart of postcolonial cultural politics; they also help us understand the dialectical processes of estrangement and familiarisation that are embedded in the valorised discourses of cultural otherness and difference today.

The value of marginality

In contemporary cultural theory, marginality is often given a positive value, being seen less as a site of social exclusion or deprivation than as a locus of resistance to socially imposed standards and coercive norms. As the African-American cultural critic bell hooks defiantly puts it:

> Marginality [is a] central location for the production of a counter-hegemonic discourse that is not just found in words but in habits of being and the way one lives ... [Marginality is] a site one stays in, clings to even, because it nourishes one's capacity to resist. It offers the possibility of radical perspectives from which to see and create, to imagine alternatives, new worlds.
>
> (hooks 1990: 341)

This view is echoed frequently by many postcolonial writers/thinkers, for whom marginality represents a challenge to the defining imperial 'centre' or a transvaluation of the lived or remembered experience of oppression. The embrace of marginality is, above all, an oppositional discursive strategy that flies in the face of hierarchical social structures and hegemonic cultural codes. This strategy is self-empowering, not just because it takes strength from opposition, but because it conceptualises the transformation of the subject's relationship to the wider world. The by now orthodox postcolonial/poststructuralist deconstruction of the opposition between a monolithic 'centre' and its designated 'margins' envisages the possibility of multiple centres and productively 'intersecting marginalities' (Ashcroft *et al.* 1989: 104). The subject – or so the argument runs – moves in a world no longer defined by fixed (op)positions but by a syncretic network of shifting, mutually transforming alliances and interconnections. Taken to its extreme, this syncretic model dispenses with the 'centre' altogether, leaving the 'marginal' to become 'the formative constituent of reality' (Ashcroft *et al.* 1989: 104). In such a case,

> [d]iscourses of marginality such as race, gender, psychological 'normalcy', geographical and social distance, political exclusion, intersect in a view of reality which supersedes the geometric distinction of centre and margin and replaces it with a sense of the complex, interweaving, and syncretic weaving of experience.
>
> (Ashcroft *et al.* 1989: 104)

Utopian theorising such as this aims at recuperating marginality in order to challenge, and work toward dissolving, imperial structures, modes of vision and habits of thought. It appropriates the discourse of imperial incorporation in order to set up its own transformative agenda and work toward its own emancipatory social goals. A well-known variant on this is the 'Third Space' theory of Homi Bhabha, where minority groups in the metropoles – marginals *within* the centre – adumbrate a third rhetorical space that disrupts and destabilises centralised authority. For Bhabha, it is the instability and incommensurability of this space which gives it liberating potential, opening the way 'to conceptualizing an *inter*national culture, based not on the exoticism of multiculturalism or the diversity of cultures, but on the inscription and articulation of culture's hybridity' (Bhabha 1994c: 38, Bhabha's italics).[17] It would be easy enough to raise objections to these rarefied versions of liberationist theory, which run the risk of being seen both as presuming to speak for the underprivileged and as daring to make intellectual capital out of their material disadvantage. Such objections might themselves be accused, though, of committing a common category error: that of assuming an unmediated, non-dialectical correspondence between necessarily abstracted *theories* of marginality and the historically authenticated *experiences* of socially marginalised groups (Young 1990: 163). ('Experience' is conceptually mediated, 'theory' is historically inflected; if postcolonial critics are agreed on anything, it is that theory and practice are dialectically interrelated.)

A further difficulty arises, however, with the *commodification* of marginality. As Russell Ferguson points out in his introduction to a collection of critical essays, *Out There: Marginalization and Contemporary Cultures* (1990),

> Counternarratives of all kinds ... constantly enter 'mainstream' culture. ... The vital, independent cultures of socially subordinated groups are constantly mined for new ideas with which to energize the jaded and restless mainstream of a political and economic system based on the circulation of commodities. The process depends on the delivery of continual novelty to the market while at the same time alternative cultural forms are drained of any elements which might challenge the system as a whole.
>
> (Ferguson *et al.* 1990: 11)

Surprisingly, Ferguson reads this mediated exchange between the 'exotic' and the 'mainstream' (his own categories) as beneficial, for '[in] any system based on consumption, new products and new styles must be perpetually supplied' (11). The easy assumption that cultural rejuvenation can be brought about merely by the influx of new commodities is worrying enough; more worrying still is the tacit acceptance that these commodities be politically disarmed so as not to damage the dominant system. Ferguson does not define the exotic, although he chooses better than he knows. For the exotic is the perfect term to describe the domesticating process through which commodities are taken from the margins and reabsorbed into mainstream culture. This process is to some extent reciprocal; mainstream culture is always altered by its contact with the margins, even if it finds ingenious ways of looking, or of pretending to look, the same. Exoticism helps maintain this pretence; it acts as the safety-net that supports these potentially dangerous transactions, as the regulating-mechanism that attempts to manoeuvre difference back again to the same. Exoticism posits the lure of difference while protecting its practitioners from close involvement (Todorov 1993). To define the margins can thus be seen as an exoticising strategy: as an impossible attempt to dictate the terms and limits of intercultural contact, and to fix the value-equivalence of metropolitan commodity exchange. To keep the margins exotic – at once threateningly strange and reassuringly familiar – is the objective of the mainstream; it is an objective which it can never fail to pose, but which it can never reach. For if metropolitan society (which, as Ferguson observes, is the primary contact-zone for exchanges between the mainstream and the margins) thrives on the commodifica-tion of marginality, it also recognises, without fully controlling, the changes taking place within its midst. Contemporary forms of exoticism are arguably misrecognitions of these changes – attempts to ensure the availability of the margins for the mainstream, and through this process to 'guarantee' the mainstream, keeping it out of harmful reach.

A similar point can perhaps be made about the institutionalisation of marginality in the Western academy, often under the rubric of postcolonial (cultural) studies. When marginality, as Gayatri Spivak has noted, comes with the seal of academic approval, this may only help to commodify it, at the university and elsewhere in society (Spivak 1991: 154). As is often the case with Spivak, this is a partly autobiographical statement: as an 'economic migrant' relocated from Calcutta, Spivak is referring among others to *herself* when she speaks of 'the upwardly mobile exmarginal [teacher], justifiably searching for validation' (Spivak 1991: 154).[18] Spivak's concept of the 'exmarginal' is, of course, partly self-ironic – elsewhere she has spoken of the 'luxuries' of academic self-marginalisation (Spivak 1985: 121). One is tempted to add that 'exmarginality' is just as much of a luxury; caught up in the ostensibly survivalist politics of academic position-taking, it represents a conscious strategy for professional success. Yet if Spivak is well aware of the consequences of her own celebrity, she is equally conscious of the pitfalls of institutional success. Her most subtle essay on the subject is the ambitiously titled 'Poststructuralism, Marginality, Postcoloniality and Value' (1990a), where she analyses the investment of contemporary literary studies in 'revolutionary' cultural critique. With characteristic brio, Spivak sees marginality as an *advantageous* subject-position, to be manipulated for maximum leverage within the postcolonial academic field. At the same time, she is anxious that the uncritical endorsement of marginality might play right into the hands of a 'neo-colonial education system' wishing to assimilate it for its own interests (Spivak 1990a: 223). Spivak, like several of her peers, fears the conscription of marginality into the service of an educational establishment designed to reassure the metropolitan élite (see also Suleri 1992a; Minh-ha 1989). It is not that Spivak rejects marginality *per se* but that she rejects it as *exotic* – as a vehicle for patronising views of minority representation and recruitment in the academy and, above all, as a legitimising category for palatable versions of cultural otherness in society at large.

This self-consciously moralistic view is shared by, among others, Trinh T. Minh-ha, who upbraids those affluent Westerners who see the 'exotic' Third World as a source of exploitable public entertainment; and by Timothy Brennan, who chastises those among his university colleagues who refer to the latest postcolonial job-opening as 'the "exotic" position, by which they mean exotic not as in *does* but as in *is*' (Brennan 1997: 115,

Brennan's italics). What is common to these objections is the belief that exoticist discourse is complicit with the essentialist labelling of marginalised racial/ethnic groups. Exoticism effectively hides the power relations behind these labels, allowing the dominant culture to attribute value to the margins while continuing to define them in its own self-privileging terms. What is more, the value it ascribes is predominantly *aesthetic*: marginality is deprived of its subversive implications by being rerouted into safe assertions of a fetishised cultural difference. Marginality is defined, that is, not only in terms of what, or who, is different but in the extent to which such difference conforms to preset cultural codes. Exoticism's 'aesthetics of diversity' (Segalen 1978) is manipulated for the purpose of channelling difference into areas where it can be attractively packaged and, at the same time, safely contained. What is at work here is a process, commodified of course, of *cultural translation* through which the marginalised other can be apprehended and described in familiar terms.

What do I mean here by cultural translation? I mean, not so much a process of convergence, mutual intellection and cross-fertilisation – that moving *between* different linguistic/cultural registers that Walter Benjamin takes to be the task of the translator – but rather the superimposition of a dominant way of seeing, speaking and thinking onto marginalised peoples and the cultural artifacts they produce. Eric Cheyfitz, in his book *The Poetics of Imperialism* (1991), associates this view of translation with the classical trope of *translatio imperii* (see also W. Mitchell 1992). Through *translatio imperii*, Cheyfitz explains, the civilisation of an empire founded on Western Christian values could be transferred onto those barbarians who could not speak the empire's language. Within this context, the imperial mission became from its beginnings one of translation: the other was to be translated into the master code of empire through the agency of an 'eloquent orator' who understood the empire's workings (Cheyfitz 1991: 112). The legacy of the *translatio* carries over into the neo-imperial present, re-emerging in the diplomacy of, say, US foreign policy and in the various, often covert ways in which the West continues to speak for others while only speaking to itself.

How can this imperialist legacy of translation be contested? Tejaswini Niranjana, in her poststructuralist-inflected study *Siting Translation* (1992), affirms the need to deconstruct the notion of translation, recovering its potential as a strategy of resistance (Niranjana 1992: 6). For Niranjana, the postcolonial project involves a process of 'disruptive retranslation'. The postcolonial subject, interpellated, already exists in a state of translation, 'imaged and re-imaged by colonial ways of seeing' (Niranjana 1992: 6). The task of the translator here is not to retrace the original – to reproduce the finer lineaments of an unblemished precolonial culture – but rather to intervene as a means of 'inscrib[ing] heterogeneity, warn[ing] against myths of purity and showing origins as always-already fissured' (Niranjana 1992: 186). The argument is abstract, but Niranjana supplies examples. She draws attention, for instance, to the work of the Indian-based Subaltern Studies group, which sees its primary task as to retranslate colonial historiography, uncovering beneath its folds a hidden history of resistance. She also cites the rhetorical sleight of hand of the 'non-Western' translator, whose work undoes the certainties of colonial translation, contesting the view that the 'foreign' world must submit, in time, to English.[19]

This last point is also taken up by Gayatri Spivak in her essay 'The Politics of Translation' (Spivak 1993c). Like Niranjana, Spivak views translation in terms not of containment but of dispersal. Translators must be alert to the shifting sands, the *rhetoricity*, of language; if they are not, then they risk merely adding another block to the 'neocolonialist construction of the non-West' (Spivak 1993c: 181). Spivak cites as an example the current boom in Third World translations into English:

> In the act of wholesale translation into English there can be a be-trayal of the democratic ideal into the law of the strongest. This happens when all the literature of the Third World gets translated into a sort of with-it translatese, so that the literature by a woman in Palestine begins to resemble, in the feel of its prose, something by a man in Taiwan.
>
> (Spivak 1993c: 182)

The homogenising tendencies of such generic Third World translations beg the larger question of audience and, more specifically, audience expectation. What are the laws of supply and demand that govern the global cultural marketplace? Could it be that Third World texts are tailored to please their (mostly) First World audience, or that the Third World is marketable only insofar as it can be translated?[20] Such a view seems unduly cynical, but as I have already suggested, a remarkable discrepancy exists between the progressiveness of postcolonial thinking and the rearguard myths and stereotypes that are used to promote and sell 'non-Western' cultural products in and to the West (Huggan 1994b). This holds true for Third World texts that are written in languages other than English and are then translated for the benefit of a monolingual readership; but it also seems valid for texts that were written originally in the English language but that emanate, or are perceived as emanating, from cultures considered to be different, strange, 'exotic'.

In the latter case, the issue seems to be primarily one of cultural representation. Are postcolonial writers persuaded to represent their respective cultures, and to translate those cultures for an unfamiliar metropolitan readership? To what extent does the value ascribed to them and attributed to their writing depend on their capacity to operate, not just as *representers* of culture but as bona fide cultural *representatives*? And is this representativeness a function of their inscription in the margins, of the mainstream demand for an 'authentic', but readily translatable, marginal voice?[21] These speculative questions yield no immediate or obvious answers. Postcolonial writers/thinkers, it could be said, are both aware of and resistant to their interpellation as marginal spokespersons, institutionalised cultural commentators and representative (iconic) figures. What is more, they make their *readers* aware of the constructedness of such cultural categories; their texts are metacommentaries on the politics of translation, on the power relations that inform cross-cultural perception and representation. Postcolonialism might thus be said to exist within the hybrid spaces opened up by cultural translation; it attests not to the transparency or accessibility of different cultural representations but, on the contrary, to the incommensurability – the untranslatability – of culture itself (Bhabha 1992). This argument, although a strong one, is possibly too idealistic. After all, postcolonial writers/thinkers, however vehemently some of them might wish to deny it, still remain subject to powerful forces of metropolitan mediation. They may still be seen, in spite of themselves, as more or less reliable commentators, and as both translators and exemplars of their own 'authentically' exotic cultures. (Note that exoticism functions here as in both 'does' *and* 'is' – Brennan 1997: 115.) In this sense, it is perhaps less accurate to think of them as cultural translators than as *culture brokers* mediating the global trade in exotic – culturally 'othered' – goods (Appiah 1992: 149). Kwame Anthony Appiah, whose formulation this is, sees the trade as being negotiated from the margins, but it surely makes more sense to see it as being conducted from the '*centre*'. The most successful postcolonial writers/thinkers, it could be argued, are those, like Achebe or Naipaul or Rushdie, who have proven adept at manipulating the codes of metropolitan *realpolitik* (Huggan 1994b: 24; 1997a: 428). They are latter-day 'eloquent orators' with first-hand knowledge of the empire's workings, but who use that knowledge to challenge, not endorse, imperial codes (Cheyfitz 1991). Brennan would no doubt call these writers 'cosmopolitan' in sensibility, meaning not so much that they are, or present themselves as, socially mobile and multiply affiliated as that they respond to and creatively rework metropolitan demands for cultural otherness in their work. Ironically, literary cosmopolitanism has as much to do with the misprision of *national* or *continental* cultures – Achebe, say, as a Nigerian or, more commonly, an 'African' writer; Naipaul as a chronicler of Trinidad or, more usually, 'the Caribbean' – as it does with the promotion and certification of a shared international/transnational outlook. It is interesting to see how many of the writers who think of themselves as global migrants are repositioned as 'native informants' for their original (natal) cultures.[22] Cosmopolitanism, in this sense, creates a conflicted politics of value through which writers are simultaneously rewarded for their democratic worldview and for their emplacement within set hierarchies of metropolitan cultural taste.

As Brennan admits, such writers do not *have* to respond in certain ways to metropolitan dictates; they are not *forced* to give in to a set of 'doctrinal demands for the "third-world" writer' (Brennan 1997: 36). However, the chances are that at some point they will be encouraged to do so, and that they may be rewarded – sometimes handsomely – for their ability to conform to the predetermined 'geopolitical-aesthetic' rules (Brennan 1997: 36). Difference thus risks dissolving in alternative kinds of sameness, in a process of homogenisation which nonetheless remains incomplete. This process, I would argue, bespeaks a new-found form of the exotic: difference is appreciated, but only in the terms of the beholder; diversity is translated and given a reassuringly familiar aesthetic cast. It would be foolish to suggest that all postcolonial writers/thinkers are equally bound up in this system, or that they respond to metropolitan demand, itself unstable, in uniform ways. (To suggest as much would ironically be to perpetuate a further 'exoticist fallacy', either by mystifying the distinction between postcolonial and Third World writing, or by essentialising one or other of these terms, or by conflating different kinds of audience.) Postcolonial cultural production is profoundly affected, but not totally governed, by commodification; it is frequently, but not invariably, subject to the fetishisation of cultural difference; it is increasingly, but by no means irredeemably, institutionalised in Western commercial and educational systems; its value is certainly shaped, but not rigidly determined, by its contact with the global market. It is something of a solecism perhaps to say that postcolonialism exists in the margins, when the best-known writers and thinkers are obviously operating in the mainstream. Still, it would be fair to say that it is validated, if not uniquely, by its insertion in discourses of marginality that are immediately local, but also potentially global, in their effects. And this means that exoticism, itself a discourse of the margin, must be confronted, incorporated into works that challenge – often looking to subvert – metropolitan mainstream cultural codes. The confrontation and incorporation of exoticist discourse(s) in postcolonial writing forms the principal subject of the remaining chapters in this book. But before going on to analyse some of these case studies in more detail, the book still needs a working definition for its main concept, the postcolonial exotic.

Toward a definition of the postcolonial exotic

The postcolonial exotic, I have been suggesting, occupies a site of discursive conflict between a local assemblage of more or less related oppositional practices and a global apparatus of assimilative institu- tional/commercial codes. More specifically, it marks the intersection between contending regimes of value: one regime – postcolonialism – that posits itself as anti-colonial, and that works toward the dissolution of imperial epistemologies and institutional structures; and another – postcoloniality – that is more closely tied to the global market, and that capitalises both on the widespread circulation of ideas about cultural otherness and on the worldwide trafficking of culturally 'othered' artifacts and goods. This constitutive tension within the postcolonial might help explain its abiding ambiguity; it also helps us better understand how value is generated, negotiated and disseminated in the postcolonial field of cultural production. The regime of postcolonialism, according to Patrick McGee, implicitly 'reads against the grain of value' (McGee 1992: 16); it interrogates the institutional processes by which value is acquired, exchanged and transmitted, ideally working toward what Edward Said calls the 'transvaluation of value' itself (Said 1986; also McGee 1992: 17). Postcolonialism, it could be said, acknowledges the contingency of value (Herrnstein Smith 1984, 1988); it recognises the need to critique value as a fixed or seemingly permanent presence; to see evaluation as a process subject to historical change and ideological manipulation; and to accept that value is 'transitive – that is to say, value for somebody in a particular situation – and is [therefore] always culturally and historically specific' (Eagleton and Fuller 1983: 76). Part of postcolonialism's regime of value appears to lie in the very *resistance* to value; or at least in the opposition to universalising codes of evaluation that assert the 'intrinsic' meaning or 'transhistorical' worth of literary/cultural texts. Value is constituted, rather, as a 'site of institutional struggle – a struggle over such issues as authorship, authenticity, and legitimacy, which involves several different but interconnected levels of mediation' (Huggan 1997a: 412).

So if postcolonial literary/cultural works, on one level, articulate forms of *material* struggle – the ongoing battle for emancipation, the continuing attempt to dismantle imperialist institutions and dominating structures – this struggle might also be extended to these works' *symbolic* power. Bourdieu's emphasis on the symbolic production of the literary work is important here. As Bourdieu points out, the value of literary (and other cultural) works is often generated through structures of belief:

> The sociology of ... literature has to take as its object not only the material production but also the symbolic production of the work, i.e. the production of the value of the work or, which amounts to the same thing, of belief in the value of the work.
>
> (Bourdieu 1993: 37)

Here, however, postcolonialism comes into conflict once again with postcoloniality; for while postcolonial works and their authors gain currency from their perceived capacity for anti-imperialist resistance, 'resistance' itself emerges as a commodified vehicle of symbolic power. The same might be said for much of the cultural vocabulary of postcolonial criticism. As Julia Emberley points out in the context of the critical reception of contemporary Native (Canadian/American) women's writing,

> [T]he society of the spectacle has ... displaced questions of political economy into a postcolonial discourse in which images, re-presentations, 'authenticities,' and 'the experience of marginality' circulate as the currency of exchange. ... The material administered and exchanged in the process of subjecting Native people to colonial historization no longer exists in the form of supplies or European commodities. In postcolonial discourse it is their symbolic value as textual commodities that is being exchanged.
>
> (Emberley 1993: 163, 109)

Emberley is too quick to see, and dismiss, postcolonialism as a hegemonic discourse that ironically contributes toward the containment and surveillance of its subaltern subjects. However, it is certainly true that the terms in which many postcolonial debates are currently being conducted – 'resistance', 'authenticity', 'marginality', and so on – circulate as reified objects in a late-capitalist currency of symbolic exchange. The postcolonial is thus constructed as an object of contestation between potentially incompatible ideologies, political factions and interest groups. The complex politics of value surrounding the postcolonial field of production clearly cannot be limited to the latest market rulings for commodity exchange. (In any case, as Arjun Appadurai argues, commodities 'constantly spill beyond ... specific regimes of value, [so that] political control of demand is always threatened with disturbance' (Appadurai 1986: 57).) Notwithstanding, postcolonial products function, at least in part, as cultural commodities that move back and forth within an economy regulated largely by Western metropolitan demand (Appadurai 1986). This economy functions on a symbolic, as well as a material, level; it is regulated, that is, not only by the flow of material objects (books, films, videotapes, etc.), but also by the institutional values that are brought to bear in their support (Huggan 1997a).

To accuse postcolonial writers/thinkers of being lackeys to this system is, as I have repeatedly suggested, to underestimate their power to exercise agency over their work. It may also be to devalue the agency, both individual and collective, of their *readers*, who by no means form a homogeneous or readily identifiable consumer group. Postcolonial literatures in English – to make an obvious point – are read by many different people in many different places; it would be misleading, not to mention arrogant, to gauge their value only to Western metropolitan response.[23] And it would be as difficult to distinguish a single reading public as to identify its location, in part because readers of postcolonial works are part of an increasingly diasporised, transnational English-speaking culture, but most of all because literary/cultural audiences all over the world are by their very nature plural and heterogeneous. Such audiences, according to John Frow, are composed of several different 'valuing communities' whose boundaries are necessarily porous and whose interests are far from evenly matched (Frow 1995: 142–3; also Huggan 1997a: 429). Audiences, says Frow, arguing in part against Bourdieu, are never fixed; 'valuing communities', similarly, cannot be conceptualised 'in terms of self-contained positional identities' (Frow 1995: 154) – the value ascribed to a literary work is never the more or less direct expression of a social group. This labile view of audience suggests that the attempt to locate and affix the social positions of 'valuing communities' is always likely to be chimerical; it also guards against the narrow identification of 'target' audiences or, more specifically in this case, the monumentalisation of a metropolitan readership, implied or not, for postcolonial texts. Postcolonial texts, as previously stated, are more subject than most to diasporic mediation; their readerships are highly likely to be multiply dislocated and dispersed (Radhakrishnan 1996). What is more, such texts often tend to *dramatise* these dislocations and dispersals, commenting ironically on the material conditions under which they are produced, distributed and consumed. I shall suggest here, following Frow, that postcolonial readerships, like audiences in general, are part of a wider semiotic apparatus of value-coding: one which is irreducible to a single set of standards or criteria governing reading, and which negotiates instead between intersecting 'discursive formations' (T. Bennett 1990) and 'evaluative regimes' (Appadurai 1986). Frow sums it up succinctly:

[N]either texts nor readers have an existence independent of [specific social] relations; … every act of reading, and hence every act of ascribing value, is specific to the particular regime that organizes it. Texts and readers are not separable elements with fixed properties but 'variable functions within a discursively ordered set of relations' [Bennett] … and apparently identical texts and readers will function quite differently within different regimes. … The concept of regime [implies] that no object, no text, no cultural practice has an intrinsic or necessary meaning or value or function; and that meaning, value, and function are always the effect of specific (and changing, change-able) social relations and mechanisms of signification.

(Frow 1995: 145)

To see postcolonial cultural production in terms of its own regimes of value (e.g. postcolonialism versus postcoloniality) is to open the way for historical and, not least, *institutional* critique. How does postcolonial discourse function within a network of changing 'social relations and mechanisms of signification'? How has the postcolonial come to acquire an increasingly commodified status; how is the cultural capital that accrues to it apportioned and controlled? How is value generated in the postcolonial field of production? All of these questions have to do, directly or indirectly, with the *politics of value* that governs commodity exchange within a more or less regulated field. Arjun Appadurai names some of the forms that this politics can take: 'the politics of diversion and of display; the politics of authenticity and of authentication; the politics of knowledge and ignorance; the politics of expertise … and connoisseur-ship' (Appadurai 1986: 57). What is interesting about these categories is that they have almost direct equivalents in the postcolonial field: 'the politics of diversion and of display' (the spectacle of cultural difference); 'the politics of authenticity and of authentication' (the construction of native authenticity, the marginal voice, the representative writer); 'the politics of knowledge and ignorance' (alterism, the fetishisation of the other); 'the politics of expertise … and connoisseurship' (aestheticisation, mechanisms of professional legitimation). Many of these categories, as we have seen, also belong to discourses of the exotic. What this homology suggests is that the postcolonial exotic is not itself a diversionary tactic but a dilemma that is very much central to the postcolonial field. And that dilemma might be posed as follows: is it possible to account for cultural difference without at the same time mystifying it? To locate and praise the other without also privileging the self? To promote the cultural margins without ministering to the needs of the mainstream? To construct an object of study that resists, and possibly forestalls, its own

cation? The postcolonial exotic is the name that one might
this dilemma, a name that accompanies the emergence of
postcolonial studies as an institutional field. The postcolonial exotic can
be either a contradiction in terms (for postcolonialism) or a tautology (for
postcoloniality). It is many different things at once: a mechanism of
cultural translation for the English-speaking mainstream and a vehicle for
the estrangement of metropolitan mainstream views; a semiotic circuit in
which the signs of oppositionality are continually recoded, circulating
alternately as commodities within a late-capitalist, neo-imperialist
symbolic economy and as markers of anti-imperialist resistance in an age
of 'adversarial internationalization' (Said 1990); a reminder, generally, of
the contradictions inscribed in the contemporary alterity industry and a
warning-sign, specifically, to those who invoke otherness to disguise their
fear of cultural ignorance (Suleri 1992a); a self-obsessed unfurling of
fetishistic spectacles, lures and distractions and a self-critical unveiling of
the imperialist power-politics that lurks behind aesthetic diversion
(Mason 1996; Rousseau and Porter 1990).

The question remains: what is it possible for postcolonial writ-
ers/thinkers to *do* about the postcolonial exotic? Some of them might wish
to disclaim or downplay their involvement in postcolonial theoretical
production, or to posit alternative epistemologies and strategies of cultural
representation (Ahmad 1992; Boyce Davies 1994). Others might wish to
'opt out' of, or at least defy, the processes of commodification and
institutionalisation that have arguably helped create a new canon of
'representative' postcolonial literary/cultural works. Still others, however,
have chosen to work within, while also seeking to challenge, institutional
structures and dominant systems of representation. These writers/thinkers
– in very different ways – have recognised their own complicity with
exoticist aesthetics while choosing to manipulate the conventions of the
exotic to their own political ends. The following chapters in this book
provide examples of what we might call 'strategic exoticism': the means
by which postcolonial writers/thinkers, working from within exoticist
codes of representation, either manage to subvert those codes ('inhabiting
them to criticize them', Spivak 1990a), or succeed in redeploying them for
the purposes of uncovering differential relations of power. Exoticism, after
all, remains an at best unstable system of containment: its assimilation of
the other to the same can never be definitive or exhaustive, since the
'collision between ego's culture and alien cultures' (Mason 1996: 147) is
continually refashioned, and the effects that collision produces may
unsettle as much as reassure, dislodge authority as much as reconfirm it
(Bhabha 1994d). 'Strategic exoticism' is an option, then, but as we shall
see, it is not necessarily a way out of the dilemma. Indeed, the self-

conscious use of exoticist techniques and modalities of cultural representation might be considered less as a response to the phenomenon of the
postcolonial exotic than as a further symptom of it. There will be plenty
other symptoms to chart here; for the postcolonial exotic is, to some
extent, a pathology of cultural representation under late capitalism – a
result of the spiralling commodification of cultural difference, and of
responses to it, that is characteristic of the (post)modern, market-driven
societies in which many of us currently live.

1 African literature and the anthropological exotic

This chapter begins with the deceptively simple question: what is African literature? The question immediately begs another: African literature *from which region?* 'African literature', after all, already conveys a fiction of homogeneity that smacks of 'sanctioned ignorance' (Spivak 1993a: 279); as if the vast literary and cultural diversity of one of the world's largest continents could be arrogantly reduced to a single classificatory term. And another: African literature *in which language?* For African literature – as a body of texts written by authors of African origin, as well as an object of academic study in Africa and various parts of the so-called First World – largely means literature in English, French and other European languages, along with a smattering of the large corpus of vernacular works often little known outside of Africa, and many of which remain untranslated for a Euro-American audience unlikely to be conversant with any African language. This suggests the view of African literature as primarily an export product, aimed at a largely foreign audience for whom the writer acts, willingly or not, as cultural spokesperson or interpreter. This view is of course simplistic, overlooking as it does the geographical complexities of audience formation (local, metropolitan, trans/national, diasporic, etc.), as well as the intricate nexus of related historical reasons for the primacy of European languages in the development of African literature as a recognised literary/cultural field. These reasons would have to include – at the very least – the predominance of local oral traditions across the African continent; the specific role played by European missionaries and, to a lesser extent, government teachers and administrators in setting up and promoting print culture; the more general ideological importance of literature and the literary text for the colonial enterprise; both the short- and long-term effects of European-language education on African writers and thinkers, who now comprise by and large a cosmopolitan, internationally trained intellectual élite (Appiah 1992); the historical function of English, among other European languages, as a regional interethnic lingua franca, as well as a status-enhancing inter- or transnational medium of communication and exchange; the deployment of Europhone African literatures as ideological weapons in the independence struggles and in the continuing critical reassessment of African national cultures in the post-independence era; the emergence of African studies as a viable subject in the Euro-American academy, often presided over by African scholars who have left – in some cases, have been forced to leave – Africa for fairer politico-economic shores; and perhaps most of all, the yawning disparity in material conditions of production and consumption between Africa and the post-industrial First World, especially Europe and America – a situation that has led to metropolitan publishers and other related patrons (commercial sponsors, institutionally based reviewers and accreditation agencies, and so on) being granted a virtual stranglehold, not only over the distribution, but also to some extent the *definition*, of African literature as a cultural field.[1]

All of this suggests that African literature, to some extent a hopeful child of the independence movements, is also imbricated with larger patterns of structural underdevelopment governing the global knowledge industry (Altbach 1975; Soyinka 1990). It also suggests the unequal state of affairs that arises when:

> a hybrid poetics comes into being, combining elements from the historically dominated system (the African one) with elements from the historically dominant one (the English [European] one), and acting as a constraint on the production of literature within the dominated system, while it leaves the dominant system relatively unaffected.
>
> (Lefevere 1983: 101)

As André Lefevere argues in his 1983 essay on the historiography of African literature, African writers are often caught between the desire to achieve recognition – and the financial rewards that come with it – with a wider audience and their awareness of the constraints this might place on their writing and the ways in which it is received. The danger exists, for example, of the edges of a certain, unmistakably politicised kind of writing becoming blunted by a coterie of publishers and other marketing agents anxious to exploit it for its 'exotic' appeal. So much is clear from the three obviously exasperated comments that follow, which indicate the formulaic patterns into which Western publishers have often seemed to want to assimilate African literary works. The first of these is from the Nigerian writer Obi Egbuna, who in a 1974 interview complains:

> What I resent is that once you go to a university and write in English, somebody comes along, like a talent scout from a London publishing house, and asks 'Why don't you just write something for us?' And he expects you to write just like the African author he has published before. So there he is, defining for you what you should do.
>
> (Egbuna, in Lindfors 1974: 17, also qtd in Lizarríbar 1998: 111)

The second, a year earlier, comes from the then President of the Ghana Association of Writers, Atukwei Okai, who laments the fact that if:

> you [the writer] set out to print anything on your own, the printing costs will stagger you. If you manage to print, the distribution difficulties will blow your mind. If you give your stuff to a local publisher, you will sympathize so much with his problems that you may not write again. … So all our best work … appears first to an audience which either regards us like some glass-enclosed specimen … or like an exotic weed to be sampled and made a conversation piece … or else we become some international organization's pet.
>
> (Okai 1973: 4)

And the third, also in the 1970s, comes from another Nigerian writer, Kole Omotoso, who, bitterly invoking the memory of the Western literary 'discovery' of his countryman Amos Tutuola in the early 1950s, conjures up the Tutuolan image of a 'headless triangle' comprising '[n]ative writer, foreign publisher and foreign audience' (Omotoso 1975: 252).

These commentaries, now three decades old, are indicative of a mounting resentment among many of the first generation of post-independence African writers that their political views were being consistently diluted – or simply ignored – even as their economic interests were, on the whole, adequately served. This consensus view was to find support in S.I.A. Kotei's ground-breaking study of the parlous state of the African book trade, *The Book Today in Africa* (1981), a work which currently needs to be brought up to date, and which has certainly not been bettered since.[2] While a systematic study like Kotei's is unavailable for the 1990s, there is little evidence to suggest that the situation for African writers has improved. Many more have found their way into print, to be sure, but most of these with foreign publishers (Heinemann, Longman, etc.), and a workable infrastructure for publishing in Africa – recently dubbed, in a devastating phrase, a 'bookless society' (Zell 1992) – can still hardly be said to exist.[3] If anything, the patronage systems that underpinned the emergence of African literature in the decades leading up to and immediately following independence have been consolidated, with the latest 'discoveries' often being skilfully, if not always seamlessly, assimilated to recognisable market trends.

One of the trends through which African literature has been filtered and has acquired a certain market value relates to a phenomenon that might best be described as the *anthropological exotic*. The anthropological exotic, like other contemporary forms of exoticist discourse, describes a mode of both perception and consumption; it invokes the familiar aura of other, incommensurably 'foreign' cultures while appearing to provide a modicum of information that gives the uninitiated reader access to the text and, by extension, the 'foreign culture' itself. Thus, the perceptual framework of the anthropological exotic allows for a reading of African literature as the more or less transparent window onto a richly detailed and culturally specific, but still somehow homogeneous – and of course readily marketable – African world. Anthropology is the watchword here, not for empirical documentation, but for the elaboration of a world of difference that conforms to often crudely stereotypical Western exoticist paradigms and myths ('primitive culture', 'unbounded nature', 'magical practices', 'noble savagery', and so on). The anthropological exotic might be seen in some sense as exploiting the exotic tendencies already inherent within anthropology, a discipline that even some of its own practitioners have seen as displaying a 'predilection for purveying exotica ... [and for choosing] the most exotic possible cultural data ... [and] the most exotic possible readings' for its own research (Keesing 1989: 460).[4] Yet anthropology, in the sense I am using it here, is less about the ideological groundrules of disciplinary practice than about the mobilisation of a series of metaphors for the reading and writing of 'foreign cultures'. To what extent does African literature deploy, however ironically, these anthropological metaphors? Is it justifiable to read African literature in this (pseudo-)anthropological manner; and what might be some of the implications of such anthropological readings?

It is helpful, before addressing these questions, to turn attention to a longstanding critical debate over the merits and demerits, the viability or not, of anthropological approaches to African literature. The opposing sides of the debate may be represented here by two of the most respected and theoretically informed among contemporary Africanist scholars, Chidi Amuta and Christopher L. Miller. Amuta, in his influential study *The Theory of African Literature* (1989), is dismissive of what he calls Africanist critics' 'unmediated obsession with cultural anthropology' (Amuta 1989: 22). For Amuta, this obsession marks the transition from 'outright colonialist criticism to the faintest recognition of the specific socio-cultural character and historical determination of African literature by critics of African literature' (Amuta 1989: 22). Not surprisingly,

Amuta lists a number of well-known Euro-American critics among the culprits; but equally well-known African scholars, too, are subjected to withering critical scrutiny: Biodun Jeyifo and Wole Soyinka, for instance, peremptorily labelled 'ethno-critics', whose criticism performs the double disservice of 'seeing African literary works [exclusively] in terms of the ethnicity of their authors' and of 'resurrect[ing] decadent ethnic myths and traditionalia, [trying] to project these onto the screen of contemporary literary works' (Amuta 1989: 23). Amuta leaves us in little doubt as to his feelings about anthropology, which he, like several of his peers, considers to be irredeemably tainted by its associations with the colonial enterprise in Africa.[5] His anger here, however, is more specifically directed against those literary critics of 'the cultural anthropology school', who tend to see culture in static terms as coherent units or discrete entities, and cultural artifacts as little more than 'museum pieces, chipped porcelain and survivals of animistic social existence to be recovered in long-abandoned caves and the ruins of great walls and moats' (Amuta 1989: 22). For Amuta, this type of 'ethnocriticism' subscribes to a hypostatized 'traditionalist aesthetics', usually driven by romantic-idealist notions of 'traditional' African cultures and often allied to an equally spurious 'pan-Africanist universalism' (Amuta 1989: 41).

This frontal, at times splenetic, attack is calmly counteracted by Christopher Miller, one of a number of talented American Africanists unfazed by *bolekaja*-style polemics.[6] For Miller, located as he is within the Western institution, 'a fair Western reading of African literatures demands engagement with, and even dependence on anthropology' (Miller 1990: 4). The initial rationale for this is disarmingly, even embarrassingly, simple: '[G]ood reading does not result from ignorance and … Westerners simply do not know enough about Africa' (Miller 1990: 4). But Miller then goes on to provide a sophisticated defence of anthropology, both as a medium of access to 'modes of understanding that emanate from other [non-Western] cultures' (Miller 1990: 21) and as a relativising methodology that allows for the exploration of the link between (local) ethnicity and (global) ethics. Drawing on recent, self-conscious approaches sometimes loosely bracketed under the rubric of the 'new' critical anthropology (including, among others, Geertz's analyses of ethnographic rhetoric, Tyler's postmodern ethnography and Clifford's adaptations of Bakhtinian dialogics), Miller advances the confident argument that '[r]elativism, retooled as contemporary critical anthropology, … becomes indispensable as a tool of intercultural critique' (Miller 1990: 66).[7] This critique, founded on a conversation between the texts of literature and those of ethnography, is tempered by the ironic awareness that 'access to non-Western systems is mediated through a discipline that has been invented and controlled by the West' (Miller 1990: 21; see also Mudimbe 1988: chap. 1). Miller still insists, however, that 'without some reliance on anthropological texts, Westerners will not be able to read African literatures in any adequate way' (Miller 1990: 21).

Is there any way of reconciling these two seemingly incompatible positions – the hardline anti-idealism of Amuta, which sees anthropological readings of African literature as wedding ethnic particularism to romantic fancy, and the soft-pedal relativism of Miller, which sees anthropology (more specifically, ethnography) as both necessary supplement and potential corrective to textual analysis, and as an instrument with which to understand African literature's important ideological function as intercultural critique? The middle ground is arguably occupied here by critics such as Simon Gikandi, who stop short of rejecting anthropology out of hand as a tool for students of African literature, but who point out the dangers of misunderstanding and/or misapplying anthropological models, which might result in the type of (pseudo-)anthropological reading that assumes literature 'to be a mere reproduction of reality, and language a *tabula rasa* that expresses a one-to-one correspondence between words and things' (Gikandi 1987: 149; see also Quayson 1994). It would be easy enough to show that the reception of African literary texts – to give the famous if by now clichéd example of Chinua Achebe's *Things Fall Apart* (1958) – is awash in such anthropological misapprehensions, which have often proved useful in the fuelling and reconfirmation of Western ethnocentric myths (Quayson 1994). The misconceived notion, for instance, that an African text offers unmediated access to an African culture, or even 'African culture', may be reinforced rather than dispelled by inaccurate views of what anthropology is, does, represents. Hence the frequent recourse to exoticising readings that begin by latching onto the cultural information putatively presented in the text, only to reincorporate that information into an available body of Western cultural myths. These types of readings also tend to succumb to the temptations of naive reflectionism (Gikandi's 'one-to-one correspondence between words and things') and, as a consequence, consistently undervalue the aesthetic complexity of African literary works – their structured interplay between modified local and imported aesthetic traditions; their cultivated ambiguities; their subtle modulations of voice and perspective in the multifaceted portrayal of the various cultural environments they represent. Thus, despite Miller's strictures, there is a risk of the dialogue between literature and anthropology labouring under a double misapprehension – both of the rhetoricity of ethnographic modes of representation and of the capacity of literary criticism to produce contending, possibly 'resisting', interpretations of the text. What is at stake here is not so much the referential validity of the text, its degree of ethnographic 'accuracy', but rather the *politics of representation* in which it is embedded and in which its writers and readers inevitably intercede. A comment made by the anthropologist Talal Asad in the course of an essay on Salman Rushdie's ill-fated novel *The Satanic Verses* (1988) helps bring this politics into focus. The key issue for anthropological practice, says Asad, is not:

> whether ethnographies are fiction or fact, or how far realist forms of cultural representation can be replaced by others. What matters more are the kinds of political project cultural inscriptions are embedded in. Not experiments in ethnographic representation for their own sake, but modalities of political intervention should be our primary object of concern.
>
> (Asad 1990: 260)

This emphasis on political purchase might allow for a productive alliance between literature, literary criticism and critical anthropology in a creative revisioning of Africa that undoes the work of centuries of racist European representation.[8] As previously suggested, the particular 'modality of political intervention' favoured by many African writers involves a critical re-engagement with Western anthropological metaphors and myths. Like other postcolonial literatures, African literature might be seen in very general terms as having both a recuperative and a deconstructive dimension: recuperative insofar as it conscripts the literary text into the service of a continually refashioned cultural identity; deconstructive insofar as it plays on and challenges Western readerly expectation, and in so doing works toward dismantling self-privileging Western modes of vision and thought.[9] An anthropological understanding of African literary texts might situate itself in this latter (deconstructive) context, not just in back-and-forth – what Edward Said might call 'contrapuntal' – readings of literature and ethnography, but also in a critical analysis of the different modes of *ethnographic counter-discourse* that circulate in contemporary African literary works.[10] The next part of the chapter analyses three of these modes, anchoring each to a well-known, if hardly 'representative', work of African literature: first, the deployment of ethnographic parody in Chinua Achebe's foundational Nigerian novel *Things Fall Apart* (1958); second, the exploration of a metaphorics of anthropological fraudulence in Yambo Ouologuem's scabrous pseudo-historical chronicle *Le devoir de violence* (1968); and third, the literary reworking of anthropological insider-outsider positions in *The Collector of Treasures* (1977), the Botswana-based short-story collection of the late South African exile, Bessie Head. Each of these literary case-studies operates to some extent as an ethnographic counter-narrative that scrutinises the questionable assumptions behind Western anthropological descriptions of, and inscriptions upon, 'non-Western' cultures. The objective of these counter-narratives, however, is not so much to provide a fictional corrective to anthropology's interpretive methods, but rather to explore some of the contradictions embedded within a certain anthropological way of *reading*. This exploration depends on the construction of a Western model reader who views African literature, Africa itself, through the distorting filter of the anthropological exotic. Yet this, it goes without saying, is not the only type of reader these works are addressing. In Achebe's case, in particular, the possibility emerges for a kind of fictionalised 'autoethnography' (Pratt 1992)[11]: one which, adeptly moving between oral and written modes of representation, appears to address itself to an African readership at least partly familiar with the particular cultural practices it describes. In other words, a kind of 'double consciousness' (Du Bois 1990)[12] is at work in Achebe's narrative: the invitation to read anthropologically might be a trap for one kind of reader while providing for another a pleasurable, if inevitably mediated, recognition of familiar cultural codes. The semiotic circuits through which the signs of Igbo culture are encoded and decoded in Achebe's novel highlight asymmetries of power inherent in the anthropological project of cultural translation (Asad 1986). An anthropological reading of the work (as will also prove to be the case, in rather different contexts, with Ouologuem's novel and Head's short stories) is therefore likely to focus on the power-politics of cross-cultural perception; and on the different culturally encoded interpretive strategies that are deployed in the writing and reading of African literature, among that large body of other 'culturally translated' postcolonial works.

A relatively recent edition of the Heinemann *Things Fall Apart*, in its 'Classics in Context' series, features a formidable battery of prefatory notes, including a glossary (also provided in some previous editions) and a short essay by Don Ohadike, professor of African history at Cornell University, on Igbo culture and history. These notes, as explained in the Preface, are intended to 'help non-Igbo readers to better understand Achebe's classic in its social, historical, and literary context' (Achebe 1996: v). In its anthropological context, too; for what Ohadike's essay offers is a concise, historically contextualised explanation of some of the Igbo customs and social structures described in fictional form in Achebe's novel. Clearly, the novel's publishers are inviting us to read it anthropologically – a smart marketing move when one considers the novel's prevalence as a high-school introduction to a 'foreign culture', particularly in the United States. But to what extent does the novel itself encourage such a reading? What is its constructed status, not just as a 'universal classic' and a 'foundation text' of African literature, but also as a work of what the anthropologist Nancy Schmidt (Schmidt 1981) has described as 'ethnographic fiction'?

One criterion that Schmidt uses to demarcate ethnographic fiction is a preponderance of cultural information contained more or less conspicuously within the body of the text. *Things Fall Apart* certainly fits this basic criterion; and it also matches, while admittedly complicating, George Marcus and Dick Cushman's longer (1982) checklist on the minimum requirements for ethnographic realism as a written anthropological form: namely, the avoidance of authorial intrusion; the contextualisation of indigenous concepts; and the emphasis on daily events that represent the reality of a particular way of life.[13] Literary critics and reviewers have also repeatedly drawn attention to the anthropological dimensions of the novel, including David Carroll ('With great skill Achebe in his novels of traditional life combines the role of novelist and anthropologist, synthesising them in a new kind of fiction' – Carroll 1990: 191) and, more recently, the biographer Adebayo Ezenwa-Ohaeto ('Chinua Achebe is surely the most interesting of those … writers who are enlarging our horizons by documenting unknown territory, spiritual as well as geographical, from the inside' – Ezenwa-Ohaeto 1997: 100). Achebe himself, meanwhile, has seemed to encourage an anthropological reading of the novel, claiming reassuringly in an interview with the sceptical Simon Gikandi that '[i]f someone is in search of information, or knowledge, or enlightenment about the total life of these people – the Igbo people – I think my novels would be a good source' (Lindfors 1991: 26).

But what *kind* of anthropological reading does a novel like *Things Fall Apart* call for? Despite Achebe's claim – bolstered by his vision of himself as a teacher of his people,[14] as well as by a tradition of didacticism in Igbo artistic practice – Gikandi is surely right to be suspicious of the view of the novel, and indeed of the African novel in general, as a source of ethnographic data (Lindfors 1991: 26). For one thing, its explanations of local events such as the New Yam Festival, or of tribal beliefs such as that in the Evil Forest, are unusually contrived in a work of such consummate, and frequently understated, rhetorical skill. For another, its description of the amateur-anthropological exploits of the District Commissioner (who, it will be recalled, wants to insert the protagonist Okonkwo's experiences into a book called *The Pacification of the Primitive Tribes of the Lower Niger*) is clearly placed within the tradition of the postcolonial parody-reversal – in this case, Kurtz's diabolical manifesto on the future of the 'primitive' races in *Heart of Darkness*. And for a third, any role the novel might play in providing an anthropological 'cultural translation' must be offset by Achebe's ironic treatment of translator-figures throughout the novel – figures who make it clear that translation is an intensely political exercise of mediation between two or more parties, often of unequal size and, almost always, of unequal power.

What we are left with then, I would suggest, is in part a deconstructive exercise in ethnographic parody, a series of pointedly exaggerated, at times caricatural, cultural (mis)readings aimed at a Western model reader confronted with the limits of his/her cultural knowledge and interpretive authority. And it is also in part a recuperative attempt at celebratory autoethnography: one which, turning the language of Western evolutionist anthropology against itself, enables an allegedly 'subordinate' culture to regain its dignity; and to reclaim its place, not within the imagined hierarchy of civilisations, but as one civilisation among others – and a sophisticated one at that. As the term 'autoethnography' implies, however, there is no access to an authentic indigenous culture uncontaminated by outside influences and safeguarded against the disruption of its traditional customs and routines. If 'things fall apart' for the Igbo, it is because the culture is in transition, not because (in what would amount to another romantic-idealist anthropological misconception) the incursion of the white man, exposing the culture's flaws, has doomed it to imminent extinction. Such ideas of 'disappearing cultures', and of an untrammelled cultural authenticity, are the stuff of a European anthropological exotic that is indirectly parodied in Achebe's text. Such ideas, nonetheless, have proven remarkably durable in the critical reception of Achebe's novel. One reason for this might be, as the cultural anthropologist James Clifford has suggested, that the Western romantic ideal of ethnographic salvage has an ideological function that carries far beyond the boundaries of the discipline.[15] Achebe's recuperative autoethnography, by definition, maintains ironic distance from such self-serving romantic mythologies while also ironising, through Yeats's poem, the notion that Western modernity carries within it the seeds of its own destruction. It is widely recognised that one of the greatest achievements of Achebe's self-consciously hybrid African novel is that it succeeds in attaching a local – largely ancestral, orally transmitted – body of cultural knowledge to an imported ironic sensibility, the sensibility of the modern European novel. But it is surely one of its most delicious and frequently unacknowledged ironies that some of the more fanciful anthropological readings it has inspired, once made to confront their own unspoken biases, have themselves begun to unravel – to 'fall apart'.

If, in *Things Fall Apart*, ethnographic parody is used to display an exaggerated regard for local events and customs that need to be explained to an uneducated Western readership, in the Malian writer Yambo Ouologuem's novel *Le devoir de violence* (1968), it is ethnographic *satire* that is deployed to show a frank disregard for the explanations and achievements of outside 'experts'. Ouologuem's novel, a sweeping satire on Africa's romanticised cultural heritage, directs one of its most vicious tirades against the German archaeologist/anthropologist Leo Frobenius. Frobenius's exploits, mercilessly lampooned through the figure of the fraudulent 'anthropologist-tourist-explorer', Fritz Shrobénius, are set in the context of a wider attack on the profiteering motives behind European anthropological expeditions to colonial Africa. Christopher Miller, who has written illuminatingly on the novel, has drawn attention to the irony that Frobenius was lavishly praised by the leading Negritude poet, Léopold Senghor (Miller 1985). As Miller suggests, Senghor's enthusiasm for Frobenius as a champion of the cause of Black Africa was at best misplaced, overlooking the fact that the German anthropologist's tendentious model of African culture, based on the schematic division between lighter-skinned (Hamitic) and darker-skinned (Ethiopian) races, had developed out of transposed European rivalries, thereby providing him with a feeble rationale for his Teutonic antipathy toward France (Miller 1985; see also Ita 1973: 322).[16] Frobenius's assimilationist views were not welcomed, at any rate, by a later generation of post-independence African writers; nor was there support for his oppositional grid, whose arbitrary distinction between the Hamitic and the Ethiopian was potentially disruptive of the many African states containing both ethnic 'groups'. Finally, Frobenius's identification of Hamitic values with Islam appeared to invite a religious conflict that 'would [eventually] benefit no-one except the ex-colonial powers' (Ita 1973: 335; see also Huggan 1994a: 115).

Ouologuem's novel feasts with cynical delight on the glaring contradictions in Frobenius's anthropology, using it as the basis for a wider meditation on fraudulent conceptions of Africa's cultural history. Frobenius's separation of African culture into positive and negative components (the Ethiopian and the Hamitic, respectively) is brutally satirised in the novel, the romanticisation of the one being derided while the vilification of the other is merely accentuated. In a typical encounter, Shrobénius's blonde, blue-eyed daughter seduces the scarcely unwilling tribesman Madoubo in what Wole Soyinka has memorably described as 'a levelling down of the Aryan Myth, the symbolic blonde beast [being] brought to rest in the degenerate earth of black Nakem ... [and all] in the context of the highest quest conceivable to German civilization – the quest for Kultur!' (Soyinka 1976: 102). The mercenary motives underlying Shrobénius's acquisitions – the relics he collects are later sold off at exorbitant prices to European museums – make a mockery of his historical counterpart's celebration of a 'pure' African aesthetic in which the Ideal Essence of African culture translates into the physical beauty of African art.[17] For Ouologuem, Shrobénius's exoticist ravings are more than just misguided sentiment; they are also an alibi for self-enrichment and a symptom of 'anthropological fraud' (Huggan 1994a). Here, the anthropological exotic matches fraudulence with cultural voyeurism – a voyeurism in which the Western reader, pornographic conspirator, becomes complicit. Shrobénius's fetishisation of African culture is ironically complemented by the sexual antics of his daughter; the European encounter with Africa is duly symbolised in the wilfully violent – mutually annihilating – erotics of interracial coupling, and Africa itself emerges as a fiercely seductive, if ultimately self-consuming, object of desire.

The satirical construction of Africa as an object of desire through which spiritual fervour masks physical appetite is further exemplified in an encounter between Shrobénius and the wily local potentate, the Saïf. Seeing through Shrobénius, the Saïf proceeds to use the German's tactics to his own ends by creating a market for acquisitive Western ethnologists eager to claim their share of the African past. A particularly successful ploy involves the fabrication of a series of 'genuine' tribal masks which, first aged to look like the originals, are then unearthed at opportune moments for the delectation of itinerant collectors – and the personal profit of the Saïf. The European invention of an ideal Africa is thus strategically reinvented by Africans themselves as a means of perpetuating a lucrative system of material exchange. The exotic myth of an unchanging, uncontaminated Africa is parodically preserved in European museum collections of fake cultural relics; in disinterring the masks, the Saïf simultaneously uncovers the hypocrisy of Western 'anthropologist-tourist-explorers' whose attempts to disguise the economic motives behind their appreciation of African art fool no one but themselves.

Through the figure of Shrobénius, Ouologuem explodes the myth of an 'original', unblemished Africa – the very Africa that Senghor, among others, had previously touted as the cradle of civilisation. Ouologuem emphasises the irony, instead, of a Western anthropological mission whose proclaimed discovery of other cultures actually reinforces the priority of its own. Indeed, the whole novel can be read as a satire on origins, textual as well as cultural, with its author taking every opportunity to violate the protective copyright of artistic originality. A tissue of intertextual references involving the 'theft' of barely modified sequences from other

European and African works, *Le devoir de violence* flaunts its plagiarism in the face of accepted conventions of literary/cultural ownership.[18] Ouologuem's refusal to respect the sanctity of textual origins reflects further on the double standards of those (diffusionist) ethnographies where the origins of a culture are inscribed within the wider framework of a redemptive narrative proclaiming its 'salvation' of Africa (Huggan 1994a: 116–17). Ouologuem's postulation of the origin as a site of duplicity and/or violent contestation thus arguably mines the contradictions inherent in anthropological projects in which the alleged retrieval of another culture's origins provides a spurious moral justification for the material success of one's own.

Ouologuem's novel, like Achebe's, indicates the absurdity of those narratives of ethnographic salvage in which it is assumed 'that the other society is weak and needs to be represented by an outsider [who then becomes] the custodian of an essence, unimpeachable witness to an authenticity' (Clifford 1986: 117). Through the composite figure of the 'anthropologist-tourist-explorer', with its confluence of imperial gazes, this fraudulent testimony is arguably transferred onto a voyeuristic model reader. *Le devoir de violence* thus suggests, not only the spuriousness of redemptive anthropological narratives, but also the violence embedded in their exoticised, ostensibly romantic-idealist way of *reading*. Not that other readings fare any better in the novel; for as Ouologuem implies, the interpretations of the indigenous griots, which might be held to effect a different kind of cultural retrieval based on traditional, orally disseminated wisdoms, are no more authentic or unimpeachable than the tendentious accounts of Western anthropologists. Not for Ouologuem, then, the recuperative autoethnography of Achebe, or the double consciousness that might allow for shared recognitions of a culture's past; instead, as Wole Soyinka concludes, one 'tradition of falsification' is substituted for another, and the novel ends up by becoming 'a fiercely partisan book on behalf of an immense historical vacuum' (Soyinka 1976: 104).

Both *Things Fall Apart* and *Le devoir de violence* implicitly address a Western model reader who is constructed as an outsider to the text and to the cultural environment(s) it represents. At the same time, both novels (especially Ouologuem's) complicate the notion of insider knowledge, suggesting that insider status, however conferred, offers no guarantee of inviolacy, and that the epistemological quandary of how knowledge is obtained about a 'culture' or a 'people' is inevitably imbricated with ideological problems – with questions of power. Anthropology (which, as a discipline, has continually reformulated this insider/outsider dialectic) thus becomes a conduit for the interrogation of power relations, both within the text itself and in its connection to different readers and interpretive communities. Such questions of power are arguably central to an understanding of African literature as a hybrid product that tends to highlight the conspicuously uneven material conditions governing its own production. Certainly, they are central to the work of the (late) South African writer Bessie Head, in which the sense of being an outsider – no doubt exacerbated by Head's own tragic life-story – comes to assume overwhelming, almost pathological, proportions. All of Head's work can be seen as an impassioned exploration of various strategies of exclusion: marginalisation on the grounds of gender, sexual preference, ethnic affiliation; sanctioned expulsion and the propitiatory identification and punishment of scapegoat-figures; the irrevocable banishment that accrues to excommunication and life imprisonment. These strategies are ostensibly deployed to keep society 'pure'; but as Head suggests, they mostly act to consolidate the position and maintain the authority of those in power. They also raise the question of the *reader's* position and degree of involvement. Is the reader, drawn almost inexorably into sympathy with Head's gallery of courageous exiles, outcasts and undesirables, himself/herself constructed as an outsider – if, in this case, an apparently privileged one – to the text? How is the reader positioned, and how much authority is he or she given? And which reader? For are there not different types of implied or model readers interpellated in Head's fictions; and different interpretive options available for these readers, both *in* and *of* the text?

Here again, the limits of an anthropological way of reading are tested, primarily through the construction of an enigmatic reader-figure within the text who slides almost imperceptibly between 'participant-observer' and 'informant' positions.[19] This subtle interplay is probably most evident in the short-story collection *The Collector of Treasures* (1977), Head's fictive exploration of the changing social habits, but continuing social injustices, of village life in post-independence Botswana. The stories, taken as a whole, represent an anthropological portrait of a society in transition – confused, susceptible to new as well as older forms of corruption. Yet, as in *Things Fall Apart*, this anthropological portrait is from the outset heavily stylised, mediated through an ingenious conflation of Zulu proverbial and Christian hagiographic storytelling traditions. What emerges (and again, the analogy with Achebe's novel proves instructive) is a series of interlinked ethnographic folktales, which pit the communal wisdom of a more or less cohesive, orally transmitted culture against the deeply suspect explanatory accounts of a series of shadowy outsider-figures: independent researchers, visiting observers, amateur fieldworkers, storyteller-historians. In *The Collector of Treasures*, however, the relationship between these two primary knowledge-sources is mutually subversive. Certainly, the first knowledge-source proves no more reliable than the second: for one thing, it is suggested that the wisdoms encapsulated within, and disseminated through, Tswana oral traditions are vulnerable to ideological manipulation; and for another, these traditions themselves are shown in several cases as being reinvented to serve individual self-interest or to legitimise already established, as well as newly emergent, hierarchies of power. But then again, it becomes apparent that it is precisely this informed neo-Marxist interpretation of Tswana society that forms the basis for an anthropological reading that is insistently ironised in the text. Take the opening, contextualising sentences of the story 'Witchcraft':

> It was one of the most potent evils in the society and people afflicted by it often suffered from a kind of death-in-life. Everything in the society was a mixture of centuries of acquired wisdom and experience, so witchcraft belonged there too; something people had carried along with them from ancestral times. Every single villager believes that at some stage in his life 'something' got hold of him; all his animals died and his life was completely smashed up. They could give long and vivid accounts of what happened to them at this time. The accounts were as solid as the reasons people give for believing in God or Jesus Christ, so that one cannot help but conclude that if a whole society creates a belief in something, that something is likely to become real. But unlike Christianity which proposed the belief in a tender and merciful God eager to comfort and care for man, there was nothing pleasant in this 'dark thing' in village life. It was entirely a force of destruction which people experienced at many levels. Since in olden times, the supreme power of sorcery or witchcraft was vested in the chiefs or rulers, it can be assumed that this force had its source in a power structure that needed an absolute control over the people.
>
> (Head 1977: 47)

It is tempting to read the story that follows, involving the 'bewitchment' of an embattled single mother, Mma-Mabele, as a fictional exemplification of the (pseudo-)anthropological principles delineated in its opening paragraph. Yet this interpretation is clearly inadequate and, as in several other stories, readers are left to draw conclusions that question, even contradict, the cultural information with which they have been provided. Whatever the case, the rhetorical overkill of the opening passage ('Everything in the society'; 'Every single villager') sits uneasily with its highly tenuous hypotheses and working assumptions ('one cannot help but conclude that'; 'it can be assumed that'). With a tone unsettlingly poised between anthropological specificity and storytelling axiomatics, and a narrator simultaneously identified as authoritative insider ('informant') and speculative outsider ('participant-observer'), the story immediately puts us on our guard about the cultural practices it claims to examine, and which its informed anthropological perspective seems in the end to mystify in its turn.

Other stories in the collection confirm these suspicions, setting confident beginnings against ironically anti-climactic endings ('Life', 'Snapshots of a Wedding'), and the sober edicts of scientific rationalism against the spirited inventions of magical thought ('The Wind and a Boy'); or, at their most extreme, emphasising the lack of understanding, the alienation even, of a modern, educated narrator who is clearly out of touch with the 'primitive' society whose rites she disapprovingly observes ('The Special One'). The narrator of 'The Special One' might herself be seen as special: a self-confessed outsider, the most obviously judgemental of Head's significantly anonymous female narrators. Yet perhaps it would be more accurate to see her at the far end of a spectrum of ironically treated observer-figures in Head's stories – figures who are neither fully involved in nor completely disengaged from the social mores they claim to witness. Although Head, unlike Achebe or, particularly, Ouologuem, makes no explicit reference in the text to anthropological (mal)practice, it is at least implied that these various observers are attempting – with no great success – to avail themselves of anthropological interpretive techniques. Yet in channelling cultural information through the alternative, constitutively unreliable medium of the communal storyteller, Head also suggests the limits of a reading based on alleged insider experience. Head's narrators might be seen in the end, then, as breaking down the conventional (if by now somewhat dated) anthropological distinction between the foreign 'participant-observer', possessor of analytical expertise, and the local 'native informant', owner-guardian of cultural knowledge. An anthropological reading of the stories thus arguably challenges the twin shibboleths of ethnographic authority – outsider expertise and insider experience – while also questioning the boundary between these two apparently divergent interpretive sources. Such a reading, ironically enough, is entirely compatible with current trends in anthropological thinking. In this sense, Head appears less interested than Achebe or Ouologuem in exposing the follies of 'cod' anthropology, and in exploring the implications that such aberrant anthropological readings might have for an uninitiated audience eager to translate what they read into more familiar codes; rather, she is concerned to show how anthropology and (oral) literature might enter into productive dialogue – by providing a series of cautionary parables on the illusoriness of absolute cultural understanding, and on the power-politics that underlies contending claims to cultural knowledge.

Things Fall Apart, *Le devoir de violence* and *The Collector of Treasures* might all be seen as varied examples of a counter-ethnographic impulse within African literature that warns of the dangers of self-privileging anthropological misreadings of literary works. What happens, though, when such anthropological misreadings are reinstated in these works' reception; and when the anthropological exotic forms an integral part of the metropolitan marketing machinery that has helped bring African literature into the limelight, and upon which it still largely depends? It is impossible within the mostly speculative context of this chapter to 'prove' a hypothesis such as this one, which would require considerable (and not always readily available) statistical support. What the remainder of the chapter does, instead, is to trace a set of narrative guidelines that suggests the retention of an 'anthropological fallacy' in African literature at the level of the *institution*. The particular institution I have in mind here is the publishing industry – more specifically, the operations of the world's largest publisher and distributor of English-language African literature: the British-based company, Heinemann Books. The Heinemann African Writers Series (AWS) has undoubtedly performed a valuable service, both in fostering the reputations of many gifted African writers and in bringing an increasing number of African literary works – the Series now runs into the hundreds – to the public eye. The emergence of English-language African writing in the 1950s and 1960s, and the wide respect in which it is held today, would be unthinkable without the momentum provided by Heinemann's promotional enterprise, worldwide distributional networks and financial support. But *how*, exactly, has Heinemann chosen to promote African literature? A cursory history of the Series suggests that Heinemann, for all its well-intentioned activities, may have contributed to the continuing exoticisation of Africa through misdirected anthropological images; and that the Africa it has promoted by way of its talented literary protégés has been subjected to a self-empowering, implicitly neocolonialist 'anthropological gaze' (Lizarríbar 1998: chap. 4).

The development of the Series, established in the early 1960s under the stewardship of its veteran impresario, Alan Hill, must first be understood in the wider context of the African publishing crisis to which I previously alluded. This crisis, as I suggested, might itself be seen as a single component in the vast neocolonial engine that drives relations between Africa and other Third World regions and their First World 'benefactors' today. The publishing industry in Africa, indeed, affords a rueful object lesson in how structural conditions of underdevelopment produce reliance on the very outside sources that reinforce cultural, as well as economic, dependency (Kotei 1981). Low literacy rates; a fragile intellectual infrastructure; the prohibitive costs involved in printing, transporting and purchasing books in such a huge, divided and desperately impoverished continent; the perceived lack of a cultural atmosphere conducive to the development of local production/consumption networks (Irele 1990) – all of these are contributing factors to a history of catastrophically low levels of book production in Africa and to the continuing, largely enforced reliance on importation and outside agencies of support. Yet these are also indicators of a neocolonial knowledge industry: of the educationally reinforced dependency-mechanisms by which many African writers and, by corollary, their local readers are persuaded to believe that cultural value, as well as economic power, is located and arbitrated elsewhere.[20] Camille Lizarríbar, to whose pioneering history of the African Writers Series I am greatly indebted here, sums up the position for many contemporary African writers as follows:

> African authors will often turn to foreign publishers because of a general mistrust in local publishing, and to be assured of a higher quality product. Therefore, both writers and books are geared primarily towards an outside audience. This vicious circle seems to be a well-established mechanism which hinders the growth of an African book industry by continuously directing its resources and products towards an external supplier and consumer.
>
> (Lizarríbar 1998: 58)

Unquestionably, this state of affairs lies behind the unparalleled success of the Heinemann African Writers Series, and goes some way toward accounting for its (along with other leading Euro-American publishers') virtual monopoly over the distribution of African literature today.

Various myths of origin surround the emergence of the Series. Several of these relate to the formative role played by Chinua Achebe: one of the Series' founding editors; the author of its inaugural and, in several respects, catalytic volume (*Things Fall Apart*); and still far and away its leading generator of revenue (it has been estimated that Achebe's novels alone are responsible for a third of the Series' total sales). Another relates to the landmark decision of Van Milne, an experienced recruit from one of Heinemann's competitors, Nelson, to launch a low-priced trade-paperback series that would effectively piggyback on the existing African educational market. The most important figure, though, and self-designated founder of the Series, was Alan Hill, the then director of Heinemann's lucrative educational branch, Heinemann Educational

Books (HEB). As Hill, now retired, relates in his self-congratulatory autobiography, *In Pursuit of Publishing* (1988), the overseas development of HEB was serendipitously connected with the demise of the British Empire. A three-day visit to Bombay in the mid 1950s was enough to persuade Hill that '[t]he India which British soldiers and administrators had lost was being regained by British educators and publishers' (Hill 1988: 93), especially Longman and Oxford University Press. Enter HEB and, shortly thereafter, the African Writers Series, which was also to profit from what Hill called 'the winds of [political] change' in Africa (Hill 1988: 192).

As Lizarríbar convincingly demonstrates, the self-important, blatantly neo-imperialist rhetoric of Hill's autobiography 'sustains contemporary theories which propose a form of neo-colonialism of Third World countries by the former colonial powers of the West, this time through economic and educational channels' (Lizarríbar 1998: 74). *In Pursuit of Publishing* is also remarkable for its redeployment of atavistic 'Dark Continent' imagery in the service of pioneering First World enterprise, as Hill's numerous formulaic allusions to Conrad's *Heart of Darkness* attest. (Here, for example, is our man in Nigeria: 'Periodically we slithered off the wet track into the darkness of the bush; but thankfully we always skidded back on again. Occasionally we would cross a clearing with a circle of primeval mud huts. It seemed like a journey back into a deep past' (Hill 1988: 122).) As Lizarríbar concludes of the abundant light-and-dark images that traverse Hill's expeditions of African 'discovery', his vision of the creation of the African Writers Series can be seen as:

> a mixture of the … missionary mentality, which proposed education as the route into the light of Christianity, and [a combination of] western values and his own business savvy, which made him aware of the potential market involved. As a modern missionary, Hill would not merely bring light into the Dark Continent; … he would provide a light that would allow the Dark Continent to reveal its own mysteries through the mediation of literature and good business sense.
>
> (Lizarríbar 1998: 83–4)

While it would be exaggerating the case to claim that the Series has moulded itself to Hill's self-image, its marketing approach has often shown symptoms of a controlling imperial gaze. This gaze is evident, not just in patterns (especially early patterns) of selection and editorial intervention, but also in the blatantly exoticist packaging of AWS titles, particularly their covers. As emerges from early assessments of titles earmarked for the Series, a certain style and tone were expected, often conforming to Euro-

American preconceptions of 'simplicity', 'primitivism' and 'authenticity' (Lizarríbar 1998: chap. 4). These preconceptions also hover round the edges of the early titles' covers, several of which feature emblematic images and designs and, in black and white on the back cover, a crudely amateurish photograph of the author for what appears to be ethnic identification purposes. These covers arguably betray a preoccupation with the iconic representation of an 'authentic Africa' for a largely foreign readership, a preoccupation also apparent in appreciative assessments of the works' putatively anthropological content. Hill's triumphal vision of the corrective role to be played by the Series shows this clearly:

> In place of the misconceptions of colonialist times [the African Writers Series] has given us a true picture of African traditional societies as they move into the modern world, depicting their humanity, their artistic achievements, as well as their cruelty and superstition – a mixture very familiar in the history of Western European civilization.
>
> (Hill 1988: 145)

This pseudo-anthropological view, in which the reconfirmation of exoticist stereotype masquerades as the newly minted expression of a previously misunderstood cultural reality, has been influential in the metropolitan reception of AWS titles – not least because of their insertion into a ready-made educational market. As an offshoot of HEB, the Series was initially intended to function within a residually colonial African educational system modelled on European standards (Lizarríbar 1998: 121). As James Currey, in charge of AWS from 1967 until 1984, remarks matter-of-factly: 'This was a series published by an educational publisher and used in Africa for educational purposes, at university as well as at school level' (Unwin and Currey 1993: 6). Yet as soon became clear, the educational function of the Series was by no means restricted to Africa; it could be geared to the education systems of Europe and America as well. And a valuable marketing strategy – particularly though by no means exclusively outside of Africa – was to play up the anthropological dimensions of literary texts often touted as virtually unmediated representations of African society, culture and history. Literature emerged as a valuable tool for the student of African customs, a notion reinforced by the provision of glossaries and other paratextual phenomena – introductory essays, photographs and illustrations, the paraphernalia of annotation.[21] Yet this well-intentioned work of sociohistorical explica-tion, still intrinsic to the ethos of the Series, did little to correct stereotypical views of a romantic Africa of 'primitive', even primordial, tribal existence. Hill again on Achebe:

The great interest of [*Things Fall Apart*] is that it genuinely succeeds in presenting tribal life from the inside. Patterns of feeling and attitudes of mind appear clothed in a distinctive African imagery ... [Achebe's] literary method is apparently simple, but a vivid imagination illuminates every page, and his style is a model of clarity.

(Hill 1988: 121)

Hill's account of the development of the Series, charted through a series of glibly classified stages or period-movements, oscillates between a diachronic, 'historical' view of African social transformation and a synchronic, 'anthropological' view of a distinctive African culture. Both views, largely essentialised, indicate alternative reflectionist readings of African literature as either a window onto the 'real' Africa or a barometer of its changing culture.

Several caveats, however, should probably be entered here. Hill's philosophy, while influential, can hardly be said to enshrine AWS policy, which, as might be expected, has undergone numerous changes in the four decades of its existence. The Series during that time has expanded far beyond its original educational mandate, and the vision of Africa it presents is far more varied and complex than Hill's suspiciously disingenuous classifications imply.[22] The AWS, while certainly marketed for a foreign and, increasingly, a global audience, has always catered for a sizeable African reading public as well, as is still very much the case today. (This can be seen, for example, in Bernth Lindfors's 1990 statistics on the prevalent use of AWS texts as school/university set texts – Lindfors 1990, 1993.) What is more, African writers have chosen by and large to send their works to Heinemann, in the hope not just of financial reward and a large overseas, as well as African, audience, but also in the legitimate expectation of unbiased treatment and professionally conducted peer review. The view of African literature – to repeat – as an exotically cultivated export product risks falling victim to the same historical inaccuracies and cultural homogenisations of which Hill himself might stand accused. All of these might be considered as extenuating circumstances. For all that, the history of the Series, relaunched in 1987 under Vicky Unwin and still as active as ever, arguably reveals at least some of the characteristic preoccupations of the anthropological exotic: the desire for authenticity, projected onto the screen of a 'real' Africa; the insistence on the documentary value of literary and, especially, fictional sources; the attempt to co-opt African literature into a Euro-American morality play centring on the need to understand 'foreign' cultures; the further co-optation of this educative process for the purpose of lending moral credence to a self-serving romantic quest. Thus, while it remains true that the AWS has done much to provide the working conditions in which African literature continues to flourish, it has done so under circumstances that might be considered, at best, as inconsistent with many of its writers' overtly anti-colonial beliefs. And, at worst, it might even be claimed that the Series has helped – inadvertently no doubt – to project a certain image of an emergent continent, 'expressed' through its literature, that 'reinforces negative stereotypes which have defined the "Dark Continent" and its people to the Western world' (Lizarríbar 1998: 140).

As I have suggested, this negative view summons up the image-repertoire of an anthropological exotic which serves to celebrate the notion of cultural difference while at the same time assimilating it to familiar Western interpretive codes. These assimilationist tendencies are also apparent in what Achebe calls 'colonialist criticism': the type of Euro-American response that raids African writing for evidence of 'universal' (read, Western) patterns of human history and behaviour.[23] (Hill's view of the Series as providing a 'mixture [of humanity and cruelty] very familiar in the history of Western European civilization' might be taken here as symptomatic.) But at this point, what should we make of Achebe's own formative role in the development of the Series; or of the respects he pays Hill in his unequivocally appreciative foreword to *In Pursuit of Publishing*? Might there not be a danger here in subscribing to a *bifurcated* reception model – one in which African writers, through their dealings with Western 'agents of legitimation' (Bourdieu 1993), are inevitably compromised, suckered into successive reinventions of an Africa that the White Man has known all along? While there are several well-documented instances of African writers locking horns with Western publishers, reviewers and critics (within the context of the Series, two names that come immediately to mind are those of Ayi Kwei Armah and Kole Omotoso), it would be unwise to conclude from this that African literature and the Western literary/critical industry are necessarily at loggerheads; that Western publishers and critics inevitably misrepresent Africa, and that Western readers are automatically complicit in such misrepresentations; and that a guaranteed corrective can be provided for these patterns of abuse by the encouragement of homegrown epistemologies, the cultural-nationalist protection of resources, and local ownership of and control over the means of cultural production. Such 'nativist topologies', as Kwame Anthony Appiah calls them, often depend on a binary 'us/them' rhetoric which negates the transculturative potential inherent in a lengthy history of European encounters – however invasive – with Africa, as well as in more recent developments of capitalist globalisation – however uneven – that have made an irrevocable impact on the configuration and transformation of African national cultures;

which blinds itself to the crucial understanding of modern African literature as a product of the colonial encounter, rather than as 'the simple continuation of an indigenous tradition [or] a mere intrusion from the metropole' (Appiah 1992: 69–70); and which risks merely supplanting the Western-academic 'rhetoric of alterity' with a form of 'ersatz exoticism', through which Africans vainly attempt to assert their cultural autonomy by fashioning themselves 'as the image of the Other' (Appiah 1992: 72). For Appiah, it is pointless trying to forget Europe by erasing the European traces of Africa's past: 'since it is too late for us to escape each other, we might instead seek to turn to our advantage the mutual interdependencies history has thrust upon us' (Appiah 1992: 72).

I would echo Appiah's insistence that Europe is, like it or not, a part of Africa; and that African literature is best regarded as neither celebratory self-expression nor reprehensible Western imposition, but rather as a hybrid amalgam of cross-fertilised aesthetic traditions that are the historical outcome of a series of – often violent – cultural collisions. The anthropological exotic in which African literature is implicated is, in part, an attempt to convert this violence into palatable aesthetic forms. This attempt, perhaps, comprises what I would call the 'postcoloniality' of African literature: its global market-value as a reified object of intellectual tourism, or as the reassuringly educative vehicle of a cultural difference seen and appreciated in aesthetic terms (see Introduction). But the anthropological exotic is also, like other forms of the exotic, a medium of unsettlement; it contains unwanted traces of the violence it attempts to conceal. As I have suggested in this chapter, the deployment of strategically exoticist modes of representation in African literature, often ironically mediated through an anthropological discourse of 'scientific' observation, has a destabilising effect on the readers it addresses. Destabilising in several senses: first, because it reminds these readers of their interpretive limits and of the inevitable biases behind their attempts to construct Africa as an object of cultural knowledge; second, because it redeploys the anthropological technique of participant-observation as the metaphor for a self-empowering, but also potentially self-incriminating, cultural voyeurism; and third, because it illustrates the 'epistemic violence' (Spivak 1987) that underwrites the colonial encounter – an encounter of which anthropology, as well as African literature, is the historical product (Asad 1972). It has been said, uncharitably no doubt, that the current 'literary turn' in anthropology is another variant on the motif of ethnographic salvage – the discipline's attempt, through heightened powers of critical self-reflexivity, to save itself from itself and from its own exoticising tendencies. I favour the more generous view – also espoused by Miller – that anthropology remains a useful, if inevitably flawed, tool of cultural exploration and self-critique (Miller 1990: esp. chap. 1). But on the question of whether anthropology is a necessary supplement to the critical work of textual analysis, I must confess to a certain scepticism. There is an anthropology *in* African literature that is less about the establishment of techniques for information retrieval and interpretation than about a cultural politics of reading in which the desire for 'information' itself becomes deeply suspect. Miller is quite right, I think, to warn about the dangers of cultural ignorance. But African literature does more than warn about these; it also suggests the dangers of a misappropriated cultural knowledge. These dangers become apparent when we turn to the global knowledge industry and to the – often predetermined – role that an ostensibly postcolonial literature is made to play within neocolonial knowledge networks. African writers, almost by definition, are well aware of this dilemma – a dilemma that several of them have chosen to dramatise in their works. Perhaps what is needed is less an anthropological understanding of African literature, more a sociological grasp of the specific material conditions under which such understandings are constructed; and a wider historical sense of how cultural knowledge about 'foreign' cultures is effected, through which channels that knowledge is routed, and in whose interests it is deployed.

2 Consuming India

1997

On 5 October 1997, the British weekend newspaper the *Observer* carried a full-page spread devoted to the fiftieth anniversary of India's independence. The display, tastefully arranged – and no doubt handsomely paid for – by the India Tourist Office in London, features a series of marketing blurbs by British-based tour operators. The centrepiece blurb, to which the others refer, announces reasons to celebrate, not least of these being that 'the attractions of India are as diverse as the tour operators who organise holidays there' (10). The familiar Orientalist icons are then dramatically unfurled, with a 'profusion of romantic palaces, impressive forts and extraordinary temples' counting among the many 'wonders of India's fabled shores' (10). The operator blurbs are similarly gushing, with an emphasis on the exclusive, offering 'classical tours' escorted by well-heeled 'guest lecturers' (Lady Wade-Gery MA [Oxon]), or holding out to 'the discerning traveller' the chance to 'relive the opulence of the Maharajahs' (10). Here again then, skilfully marshalled, is the Orient as exhibition[1]; and here a further example of the twisted logic of the tourist industry, more than capable of turning the occasion of a half-century of independence into a fanfare for colonial nostalgia and the invented memories of imperial rule.

Marketing such as this, aimed at a generation of latter-day Questeds, helped stake out India's anniversary celebrations as a prime tourist event. This touristic sensibility was also much in evidence in a plethora of 'new' anthologies and special issues on Indian writing timed to coincide with the festivities of Golden Jubilee year. This chapter briefly analyses four of these bumper anniversary products: the special Golden Jubilee issues of *The New Yorker* (in the United States) and *Granta* (in Britain); *The Vintage Book of Indian Writing*, edited by Salman Rushdie and Elizabeth

West, and rushed out to dovetail with the anniversary celebrations; and a commemorative academic conference in Barcelona, 'India: Fifty Years After', which I had the good fortune to attend over four days in late September 1997. I shall argue that mediated events such as these are characteristic of the current appeal of India, and more specifically of Indian literature in English, as a literalised *consumer item*. 'I have been a swallower of lives', says Saleem Sinai, the narrator-protagonist of Rushdie's *Midnight's Children* (1981), 'and to know me, just the one of me, you'll have to swallow the lot as well. Consumed multitudes are jostling and shoving inside me' (Rushdie 1981: 4). The metaphor, as Rushdie recognises, is ironically applicable to his own novels, and to Indian literary works in general, as the reified objects of a seemingly inexhaustible will to consumption. Perhaps India itself has been transformed through this general process into a consumable. Whatever its status – consumer or consumed – India is currently very much in fashion; and several of its best-known writers, most of them living in the diaspora, have become minor metropolitan celebrities, late twentieth-century household names, exponents of the latest literary craze – the new 'Indochic' (Mongia 1997).[2]

The aura that surrounds these writers – their collective media image – is archly confirmed by a group photograph that acts as a centrepiece for the Golden Jubilee issue of *The New Yorker* (23/30 June 1997). The photograph features nearly all of India's familiar literary figures. In the foreground, Salman Rushdie and Arundhati Roy beam happily into the camera; but at the back, Amit Chaudhuri seems slightly bewildered, while an out-of-focus Amitav Ghosh looks merely disgruntled. Bill Buford's mischievous lead-off comments neatly capture the ironies of this transparent publicity venture. The photograph's subjects, Buford informs us,

> are India's leading novelists, and the fact that this was the first time that many of them had been in one place reveals something about what it means to be an author from the subcontinent. They had, of course, encountered each other in print ... [a]nd they had all read *about* each other, in newspapers and magazines – the hype of the Indian novel, one author called it. And yet the same author, infected by an excitement that finally touched everyone, ventured the thought that maybe the hype is true after all. Maybe there *is* such a thing as Indian literature.
>
> (Buford 1997: 6)

Buford, albeit facetiously, echoes the common view that Indian literature as a composite entity is largely a fiction of the Western press, a metropolitan media creation. This unexamined view (like the view of African literature as pure export product critically analysed in the last chapter) is itself a media chimera; it corresponds to the metropolitan myth of a fetishised body of 'Indian writers', the decontextualisation of whose work merely serves to enhance its commercial appeal. Here appears to be another example, then, of the commodity fetishism exposed by Aijaz Ahmad, who bitterly complains that the vision of India (or, more vaguely still, of an undifferentiated Orient) continues to be identified in the West through the latest patterns of metropolitan consumption (Ahmad 1992: 216–17). The reality is of course more complex; but certainly the Golden Jubilee *New Yorker* issue, for all its trademark self-amusement, seems to help subscribe to the myth of a disparate nation brought together by Western marketing moguls, and made available to a relatively informed, if not necessarily discerning, consumer public who are prepared to suspend disbelief in a cultural 'essence' that has been so artfully distilled.

Paradoxically, this 'essence' is represented in the special issue of *The New Yorker* in a clutch of essays, stories and photographs tailored to the magazine's readily identifiable house style. As in the photograph, many of the 'big names' (Salman Rushdie, Ved Mehta, the younger writers Kiran Desai and Vikram Chandra) are arbitrarily brought together, with little introduction, less interaction, and still less attempt to contextualise their work. Elsewhere in the magazine, the consumer focus is literalised in that Western exoticist staple, 'Eastern cuisine'. James Peterson, for example, setting off in elusive search of the meaning of Indian 'curry', comes up with the following, necessarily provisional definition for the delectation of his American readers: '[A] stew flavored with a subtle, customized mixture of spices and finished with any of an assortment of thickeners, enrichers, and natural colorings. Requesting a more precise answer is like asking a table of French truckers to define a cassoulet' (Peterson 1997: 138). One wonders whether a similar definition might serve *The New Yorker* for Indian literature; certainly, John Updike, in his glowing review of two recent Indian novels – Arundhati Roy's *The God of Small Things* (of which more later) and Ardashir Vakil's *Beach Boy* – merely adds to the gastronomic clichés strewn across Western writing about India, thus completely missing the obvious irony that these clichés are reproduced *for deflating purposes* in several contemporary Indian works, Roy's and Vakil's included among them. All in all, the impression conveyed in the pages of the commemorative *New Yorker* is of a largely depoliticised 'ethnic sampling' for inquisitive American readers. These readers might be ironised to some extent for their voyeuristic tendencies; but they are still given full control of what Aijaz Ahmad, citing Edward Said only to slight him, has called an 'imperial geography', a global but unevenly developed space of culture-based consumption whose contours are traced in part by the Western market in 'ethnic' goods.[3]

This impression is replicated, if in a rather different context, in the special issue of *Granta*, whose celebrations of the fiftieth anniversary of Indian independence (no. 57, Spring 1997) capitalise paradoxically on the lucrative late twentieth-century trade in Raj nostalgia.[4] *Granta*'s general marketing formula is not dissimilar from *The New Yorker*'s. Like its better-known American counterpart, *Granta* is a widely respected literary magazine with a celebrity cast of contributing writers, offering an engaging, commercially viable mixture of quality reportage, travel writing, topical photography and recent fiction. Both magazines retail a distinctively literate brand of cosmopolitan bonhomie, a kind of intellectual populism at once familiar in its gestures and occasionally challenging in its selections of current writing and debate.

Although *Granta* is generally less given than *The New Yorker* to celebrate its self-importance, the magazine arguably shows signs of a cultural complacency of its own. The most memorable broadside against it, by Charles Sugnet in the American journal *Transition*, focuses on the self-indulgence of its travel writing selections. A contradiction exists, according to Sugnet, between *Granta*'s claims to literary novelty and the conservatism of many of its choices, particularly in the travel writing field. Sugnet is especially harsh on two of *Granta*'s favourite sons, Redmond O'Hanlon and the late Bruce Chatwin, whose travelogues, belonging to the Old Boy's club of colonial adventure, hold out a series of comforting myths to their equally self-satisfied British audience. Writers like O'Hanlon and Chatwin, fully paid-up members of *Granta*'s coterie of 'young fogeys' (Sugnet 1991), indicate the core of cultural parochialism underscoring the magazine's international outlook; they also draw attention to its tacit investment in the forms of nostalgic mythmaking (Raj revivalism, Conradian atavism, and so forth) that contribute to what cultural critics, following Edward Said, have termed 'colonial discourse'.[5] Sugnet's argument is overstated in the nature of polemics, taking little account of O'Hanlon's and Chatwin's celebrated propensity for self-irony or of *Granta*'s tradition of liberal journalism, both at home and in the field. He succeeds, nonetheless, in scoring a few palpable and, for *Granta*, embarrassing hits. For there *is* something irritating about *Granta*'s literary camaraderie, as evidenced in the mutual regard – the apparent clubbability – of its favoured writers, and in the paradoxically establishment feel of its up-to-the-minute house style. (Similar things might be said of *The New Yorker*, with its long tradition of fashionable scepticism.) And there *is* more than a touch of cultural nostalgia in its selections, a sense of a changing world with Britain still somehow at the centre. Which brings me back to the special issue commemorating Indian independence, and more particularly to the issue of *what*, or *who*, is being remembered and celebrated.

The *Granta* special issue is, above all else, a festival of cross-cultural memory, with long-established Indo-Anglian writers (like Nirad Chaudhuri and Ved Mehta) looking back at their internationally fashioned literary careers, and equally well-known British figures (like Jan Morris) reminiscing about Britain's and India's shared imperial past. This exercise in international *détente* sits uneasily with a history of disruption – one in which Britain has played, and continues to play, a major part. (The Queen's bungled visit in 1997, and the diplomatic furore surrounding Foreign Secretary Robin Cook's offer of 'assistance' in Kashmir, merely afford fairly recent examples of unburied animosity, and of Britain's failure to grasp the arrogance behind its 'conciliating' role.) It is significant that, while some of the pieces in the *Granta* issue are alert to regional conflict – notably the photographic 'gallery of memories' centring on the Partition riots (23–38), or James Buchan's and William Dalrymple's reports on the troubles in Kashmir and Bihar, respectively (59–84, 173–84) – there is little sense in the volume of the continuing conflict between India and *Britain*. Instead, India is presented as a nation in transformation, to whose at times self-destructive vitality British journalists can 'objectively' attest. The format of the issue also helps declaw it by exhibiting a series of snapshots, offering only a fleeting glimpse of the historical upheavals they document, still less of the more immediate histories behind their own production. (This is particularly troubling in the interviews of low-caste workers, whose stories are presumably intended to counterbalance the more sustained life-narratives of the cultural elite – see, for example, the translated testimony of the Harijan agricultural worker Viramma (*Granta* 1997: 186–92).) The photographs themselves are mostly portraits, with the National Geographic smile much in evidence, reinforcing the classically Orientalist view of India as a pageant or historical frieze.[6] The stories by Indian writers – Amit Chaudhuri, Anita Desai and, in a publicity coup, the 'newly discovered' Arundhati Roy – are for the most part anodyne and unthreatening, focusing on domestic mishaps and comic scenes of mass confusion. A seemingly statutory homage is paid to V.S. Naipaul, described without irony as 'an [unequalled] delineator of modern India', whose work 'ranks alongside the fiction of Kipling, Forster, and Rushdie and the films of Satyajit Ray as a key influence on the way we imagine India' (194). And to cap it all (or, perhaps better, to set the tone for what follows) is editor Ian Jack's introduction, a curious amalgam of sentiment and hard statistics, which speaks with great authority on the state of post-independence India while noting with great affection that one of the attractions of India is, or at least was, its 'Anglophilia'.

Jack's introduction, which in fact neither introduces nor frames the subsequent material, leaving it deliberately decontextualised, is written in what might charitably be called the spirit of informed tourism; and it is this spirit that is captured, if not in the pieces themselves, then in the mode of their collection. The *Granta* special issue, for all its attempts to present varied perspectives on modern India, begs the question of what is being celebrated, and for which reasons, and most of all for whom. My own argument would be that, like *The New Yorker*, *Granta* presents an image of India as object of metropolitan fascination: an India which, while it cannot be fully comprehended, can certainly be consumed. There is little sense in the magazine of an independent India, one that has freed itself from Britain to pursue an always uncertain future; instead, what comes out clearly is Britain's continuing *dependence* on India, less as a material possession than as an imaginative resource. The *Granta* special issue, ostensibly celebratory of India's capacity to reinvent itself, pays as much tribute to the tenacity with which Britain has ridden India's coat-tails, and with which it using the new India, as it used the old, to rejuvenate itself.

The Vintage Book of Indian Writing, 1947–1997 appears at first to belong to another category. A well thought-out anthology, edited by Salman Rushdie and Elizabeth West, *The Vintage Book of Indian Writing* aims to bring together, in the words on its back cover, 'the finest Indian writing of the last fifty years'. Rushdie, as one might expect, proves to be an able compère, and his characteristically provocative introduction is one of the highlights of this thoroughly engaging book. In the introduction, Rushdie goes to some lengths to justify the choice of *English* writing, claiming not unreasonably (if somewhat smugly) that 'English has become an Indian language' (Rushdie and West 1997: xiii). Much more controversially, however, Rushdie goes on to assert that the writing, particularly the prose writing, produced in the last fifty years by Indian authors is not only 'a stronger and more important body of work than most of what has been produced in the 16 "official languages" of India', but represents 'the most valuable contribution India has yet made to the world of books' (Rushdie and West 1997: x; see also Rushdie 1997: 50). Unsurprisingly, this 'wild assertion', as the Indian scholar Ania Loomba indignantly calls it (Loomba 1998: 206, responding to Rushdie 1997: 50), has not gone down well in India. U.R. Ananthamurthy, for example, the distinguished Kannada novelist, has expressed shocked surprise that:

a sensitive and creative writer like Rushdie should speak with such arrogance. ... No Indian writer in any of the languages can presume to know what is happening in the other Indian languages. Rushdie does not even live in India. How can he make such an enormous assumption?

(Ananthamurthy 1997: 19, qtd in S. Narayan 1998: 264)

K. Satchidanandan, the Malayalam poet, goes further, asserting sniffily that Indian literature in English is 'but a peripheral region of Indian literature', and that 'there is an obvious disparity between the publicity it attracts and its literary quality' (Satchidanandan 1997: ix, qtd in S. Narayan 1998: 264). Nabaneeta Deb Sen, the Bengali writer and critic, is more forthright still, comparing Rushdie's comments to Lord Macaulay's infamous Minute, and conceding with dripping irony that '[w]e always bow to the supreme wisdom of one who reads no Indian language' (Deb Sen 1997: 4, qtd in S. Narayan 1998: 264). As Shyamala Narayan, from whose highly critical review of *The Vintage Book of Indian Writing* the above quotations are drawn, is moved to conclude, Rushdie is both out of touch with current academic debates surrounding the so-called 'vernacular' languages in India and apparently unconversant with most of these languages, despite the fact that he claims to speak on their practitioners' behalf.[7]

These comments are well-founded if at the same time symptomatic of the battle-lines that frequently tend to be drawn around Rushdie's work. Rushdie appears to have steeled himself, as usual, for the battle. Thus, while he freely admits that the growing Indo-Anglian canon might be seen by homegrown critics as an outside imposition, he asserts that even if Indo-Anglian writing is at least in part the product of Western market forces, it is also a sign of literary creativity and, by extension, of cultural health. Western publishers and critics, claims Rushdie,

have been growing gradually more excited by the voices emerging from India; in England, at least, British writers are often chastised by reviewers for their lack of Indian-style ambition and verve. It feels as if the East is imposing itself on the West, rather than the other way around. And, yes, English is the most powerful medium of communication in the world; should we not then rejoice at these artists' mastery of it, and at their growing influence? ... One important dimension of literature is that it is a means of holding a conversation with the world. These writers are ensuring that India, or rather, Indian voices (for they are too good to fall into the trap of writing *nationalistically*), will henceforth be confident, indispensable participants in that literary conversation.

(Rushdie and West 1997: xiv–xv, Rushdie's italics)

Rushdie's is a by now familiar defence of the literary migrant; literature, he stresses, 'has little or nothing to do with a writer's home address' (Rushdie and West 1997: xv).[8] Still, the ethnic label sticks – not English, but *Indian* writing – and all the more so in a collection 'published to coincide with the anniversary of India's independence' (back cover blurb). One is reminded here once more of Aijaz Ahmad's impassioned critique of Third World literature in English as a vehicle for commodity fetishism, and as a manufactured object of Western metropolitan desire.[9] To dismiss critiques such as Ahmad's, as Rushdie seems to do here, as parochial is to miss the force of India and, by extension, the Third World as a *global* merchandising tool. Moreover, few writers are better positioned than Rushdie himself to understand this. As Rushdie remarks with mock-disapproval, citing one of his Indian critics, Indian writing in English has been described as 'suffering from a condition that … Pankaj Mishra calls "Rushdieitis … [a] condition that has claimed Rushdie himself in his later works" ' (Rushdie and West 1997: xiii). 'Rushdieitis', as its progenitor recognises, is less a literary phenomenon than an effect of the reception of the representative writer's work (see also Introduction). Rushdie's corrective here is to point out that Indo-Anglian writing – one of several current descriptive terms, none of them particularly elegant, for Indian literature in English – is a many-headed creature; that it has evolved several different, and by no means immediately identifiable, literary styles.[10] Among the writers, for example, whose work is included in the anthology,

> the Stendhalian realism of … Rohinton Mistry, the equally naturalistic but lighter, more readily charming prose of Vikram Seth … and the elegant social observation of Upamanyu Chatterjee can be set against the more flamboyant manner of Vikram Chandra, the linguistic play of I. Allan Sealy and Shashi Tharoor and the touches of fabulism in Mukul Kesavan.
>
> (Rushdie and West 1997: xxi–xxii)

Few would dispute the claims of these writers to be represented in the anthology, or the deftness of the broad-brush strokes with which Rushdie characterises their work. The selections, too – although one might quibble about the value of excerpting novels – are largely unexceptionable, and give plenty evidence of the technical and linguistic diversity that Rushdie praises. Yet despite the neat, if unevenly distributed, biographical blurbs included at the back of the anthology, an overall sense of context is perhaps inevitably missing. The introductory appeal of literary anthologies such as this one needs to be weighed against the exoticising effect they are likely to have on at least some of their audience. This effect is enhanced, it seems, by the anthology's celebratory mandate, which is largely removed, like *Granta*'s, from the set of material circumstances under which it (like the anniversary of independence with which it has been timed to coincide) is produced.

In addition, far from presenting a showcase for the autonomy of the Indian nation, the anthology deliberately de-emphasises the national distinctiveness and/or political oppositionality of Indian writing. It does so, and here I would agree with Rushdie, for several compelling reasons: first, because Indian writing, especially in English, is to a large extent a transnational, diasporic phenomenon, the product of complex collisions (and, some might argue, collusions) between East and West; second because literary works are rarely if ever direct expressions of national identity, with characteristics that might go some way toward 'explaining' aspects of national culture; and third, because Indian writers, though not necessarily freewheeling world citizens, move in a global environment shaped by mediated social forces. The irony of the anthology, as indicated in its preliminary reception outside of India, is that it is likely to be assessed for the 'Indianness' its publisher, if not its editor-in-chief, promotes. And that 'Indianness' is conceived of largely, not as a post-independence ethos, but rather as an infinitely rechargeable, universally applicable market tool.

The 1997 Barcelona conference provides the last of my examples of the tailoring of an independent India to metropolitan market tastes. Like my other examples, the conference can be regarded in its own terms as a highly successful event. Superbly organised by the British expatriate professors Kathleen Firth and Felicity Hand and their team of Spanish student helpers, the conference brought together over the space of three days in late September some hundred or so academic specialists, many of them from the subcontinent. The conference took in papers on the Indian diaspora, on gender issues in Indian studies, and on cultural links between India and Catalonia. Sponsored in part by various Catalan cultural agencies, the conference assumed something of the aura of an international diplomatic event. (Strangely though, in the panels themselves, where diplomatic niceties were no longer necessary, an opportunity was lost for a critical comparison of the event-filled histories of Indian and Catalan independence. As with the *Granta* and *New Yorker* special issues, also the Vintage anthology, the subject of independence and its varied implications was kept at the outskirts of otherwise fruitful cultural debates.)

Social events, though, as they often are at academic conferences, were very much at the centre. These included a bus tour of Barcelona, a supper at a Hare Krishna restaurant and an Indian buffet, followed by a performance of classical Indian dancing. The conference, seen in this context, was an appropriately festive occasion, with a muted nationalism underscoring many of its cross-cultural performances and a series of liberal gestures being made to the reciprocity between 'European' and 'Asian' cultures. Such liberalism, as can also be seen in the Vintage and, especially, the *Granta* collections, has its disadvantages. For one thing, it risks collapsing cultural politics into a kind of 'ethnic' spectacle, reclaiming culture as a site not of conflict but of pleasurable diversion. And for another, it places emphasis on the mutual *consumption* of the other, literalised in the themed performance, the touristic circuit, the 'ethnic' meal.

Two further examples come to mind that bear upon this topic. The first of these (to which I shall return later) was a fine individual paper by the Indo-American scholar Padmini Mongia, in which she examined, tongue only half in cheek, what she called the 'Roy phenomenon' – the extraordinary sequence of events that had already overtaken the publication of Roy's first novel *The God of Small Things* (1997), and which would culminate shortly after the conference in the award to Roy of the self-consciously 'prestigious' Booker Prize (on the Booker Prize, see also Chapter 4 of this book). As Mongia's paper demonstrated, the publicity Roy's novel attracted, and which it continues to this day to generate, has helped place it firmly within the recent media-invented tradition of 'Indo-chic'. The journalistic label is appropriately catchy; it is also global in its implications, coinciding with the recognition of India's emergence as a world economic power (Mongia 1997). 'Indo-chic', and Roy's contribution to it, are not simply to be seen as naive Western constructs; they are products of the globalisation of Western-capitalist consumer culture, in which 'India' functions not just as a polyvalent cultural sign but as a highly mobile capital good.

The flexibility of 'India' as a commercial cultural marker is also implicit, albeit in parodic form, in my second Barcelona example. Walking one evening with a friend in the pleasant if crowded pedestrian zone of Barcelona (the *Ramblas*), I came across, among many other street entertainers, an extraordinary sight. A black man up a tree, adorned with 'New Guinean' headfeathers and 'Aboriginal' tribal markings, motioned soundlessly to passers-by, pointing at his 'African' collection gourd. After a while, the man climbed down and assumed a supplicant 'guru' posture, before putting on some 'rasta' dreadlocks and pinning a 'ghettoblaster' to his ear. One didn't know what to make of this vaudeville of glaring racial stereotypes, the impact of which, presumably intended, was more one of dis-ease than of delight. Naipaul's mimic men had nothing on this grinning 'ethnic' impostor, whose antics seemed to rehearse his – predominantly white – spectators' fantasies and fears. This staging of global otherness, in which the 'ethnic' signs were twisted, seemed to provide an ironic counterpoint to our own cross-cultural venture. To what extent, I asked myself, was the 'India' being celebrated at the conference cosmetic; to what degree was the conference spectacle of intercultural *détente* just that – a show? And, for all its goodwill, was the conference complicit in the global merchandising of Third World products – 'ethnic' performances, intellectualised exotica, a range of culturally 'othered' styles and goods? Was this travesty – this dumbed-down dumbshow – somehow related to the 'Roy phenomenon', or even to the conference itself as a highly mediated cultural event?

To suggest as much is no doubt churlish or, at best, needlessly trivial-ising, yet these were questions that interested me back then, and they continue to interest me now. For India and, by extension, the Third World is very much a central player in what I described earlier as a global 'alterity industry' catering mostly, if not exclusively, to the capitalist societies of the West (see Introduction). This industry is closely linked to what Simon During has called the 'global popular', to mediated images of cross-cultural harmony in which 'consumption warmly glows' (During 1992: 343).[11] It is also linked to the contemporary massification of exotic merchandise – to the range of often tawdry 'ethnic' goods which, filtering through global channels, eventually land in a shop or shopping mall or street market near you. But it is linked, as well, to more obviously middle- or highbrow forms of cultural production: to the marketing, for instance, of high-class tours to the cultural monuments of 'fabulous India', or the rush-packaging of literary anthologies to coincide with Golden Jubilee year. As Sara Suleri argues, the Western academy is also complicit in the fashioning of an alteritist discourse that replicates 'the familiar category of the [European] exotic' (Suleri 1992a: 12). The art historian Deborah Root, too, has drawn attention to the role of higher education in the perpetuation and reinvigoration of profitable myths of cultural difference. Ours, says Root, is a cannibal age of mass appropriation, in which otherness no longer announces inaccessibility or mute incomprehension but, on the contrary, the clatter of the cash-tills as the latest 'ethnic' product makes its way to the latest customer, its 'difference' already half-consumed. Thankfully, the symbolic power of India's independence cannot be reduced to another sales-tag or diluted into another commodi-fied (post-)anniversary event; 1997 was too important a year to be left to somebody's shopping list, or to be consigned to the next empty pickle-jar in some edible version of the Indian past (Rushdie 1981: 459–61). Nonetheless, it proved to be a year in which India was given festive competition; and in which its own 'consuming multitudes', as in a Borges story or Rushdie novel, found themselves, their country, turned into the objects of others' consumption.

1981

A banner year for Indian literature in English was 1981; for this was the year that saw the publication of Salman Rushdie's *Midnight's Children*, runaway winner of the Booker Prize and, twelve years later, unanimous recipient of the commemorative 'Booker of Bookers', and widely thought to be one of the best English-language novels of its generation. Michael Gorra's eloquent tribute to the novel in his recent study *After Empire* (1997a) testifies to the inflationary rhetoric that has frequently surrounded it. Gorra also indicates the popular metropolitan perception that Rushdie's novels, especially *Midnight's Children*, have played a formative, even foundational, role in the development of the modern Indian novel in English. Any account of the Indian novel in English, asserts Gorra,

> must recognize that Rushdie has given it a new start, a new and bolder life. No one else has done so much to make English into an Indian language; no one else has so fully used that language to probe the nature of national identity or to define a model for the postcolonial self. No other writer in English has so energetically and joyously peopled the immigrants' London or the great city of Bombay; and no one since Dickens has offered as engaging a gallery of self-dramatizing rogues and charlatans and madmen.
>
> (Gorra 1997a: 147–8)

Midnight's Children has attracted praise, and rightly so, for its verbal richness and stylistic pyrotechnics, as well as for its ebulliently satirical portrait of post-independence India. Commercially, it has ridden the wave of international magical realism (Durix 1985), while academics have energetically debated its indebtedness to the discourses of postcolonialism and postmodernism (Birch 1991; Dingwaney Needham 1988/9). Some reviewers and critics, mostly Euro-Americans, have championed the novel's distinctively 'Eastern' qualities (Swann 1986); others have taken its author to task for trivialising India's recent history and for reinforcing negative Orientalist stereotypes (Ali 1982). Its multifacetedness has served it well; but although reception patterns for the novel show no clearly delineated differences in the criteria used by its various 'valuing communities' (Frow 1995), it is probably fair to say that the accolades it has received have come on the whole from outside of India. This should not surprise us. Rushdie, after all, has lived for most of his life away from India, and continues to be seen by many Indians as a purveyor of marketable Euro-American fantasies about Indian and other 'Oriental' cultures. In addition, he has situated himself within a largely mainstream tradition of highly mobile cosmopolitan writers, a privileged group to which few resident Indians – and fewer still from non-English-speaking backgrounds (so-called NESBs) – have gained admittance. This is not to suggest a revenge motive for the negative press Rushdie has sometimes received in India; it is merely to point out that Rushdie's success, and the near-talismanic status he and his work have been accorded, are unthinkable outside of the context of an internationally minded, but largely *English*-speaking, public culture.

Within this context, as Timothy Brennan has suggested, Rushdie has played an ambivalent role as a 'cosmopolitan celebrity', combining the seemingly incompatible positions of the freewheeling oppositional intellectual and the slightly unwilling cultural spokesperson, dispensing wisdoms for the embattled mother country from the relative comfort of the diaspora.[12] This spokesperson's role – partly interpellated, partly self-conferred – is much in evidence in the metropolitan reception of *Midnight's Children*; indeed, one of the most striking features of the voluminous response to Rushdie's novel has been the apparent desire to ascribe a representative status, both to the work and to its author. Clark Blaise's enthusiastic review in *The New York Times Book Review* is symptomatic. For Blaise, himself no stranger to India,[13] Rushdie's novel triumphantly stamps a whole nation with its distinctive literary imprint: 'At last', exclaims Blaise in a phrase later picked up as a blurb for the Picador cover of *Midnight's Children*, 'the literary continent [of India] has discovered its voice!' (Blaise 1981: 23). Language like this is standard fare for blurbs and other forms of media puffery; but there is still a hint that a different kind of 'Rushdieitis' (Mishra) might have afflicted some of Rushdie's followers – an amnesiac condition, fixating on instant celebrity, that conveniently forgets several thousand years of Indian literary history (Huggan 1994b: 24).

A further, possibly related strain of 'Rushdieitis' involves the inevitably frustrated desire for historical accuracy – as if Rushdie himself were to be held to account for his narrator's self-serving historical deceptions; and as if the novel were to be recuperated, for all its extravagant mythmaking, as a reliably informative guidebook to a nation's recent cultural past. As Rushdie wryly complains in one of his critical essays on *Midnight's Children*,

> [T]he book's success – its Booker Prize, etc. – initially distorted the way in which it was read. Many readers wanted it to be history, even

the guide-book, which it was never meant to be; others resented it for
its incompleteness, pointing out, among other things, that I had
failed to mention the glories of Urdu poetry, or the plight of the
Harijans, or untouchables, or what some people think of as the new
imperialism of the Hindi language in South India. These variously
disappointed readers were judging the book not as a novel, but as
some sort of inadequate reference book or encyclopaedia.

(Rushdie 1991b: 25)

These literalist fixations, attributed here somewhat condescendingly to
the naive reader, might be seen as having arisen out of the specific
conditions in which the novel was consumed. It is significant that
Rushdie cites the Booker Prize as an index of consumption, as a symbolic
marker for the potentially deleterious effects of commercial success. For
the prize, as prizes will, not only brought a wider audience to *Midnight's
Children*, turning the novel into the site of intensely mediated conflict,
but also conferred upon it a perhaps unwanted patina of authority and an
imprimatur of the 'authenticity' its author apparently wished to
disclaim.[14]

This bogus authenticity pertains to several different 'Indias', each with
a history in accordance with its particular reader's views. One such 'India',
for example, belongs to the realm of the exotic; this 'India' is a collective
fiction that history is conjured up to reconfirm. As Hugh Eakin has
argued, the assimilation of Rushdie's novel to the Euro-American literary
mainstream has had the effect of robbing it of much of its oppositional
(anti-imperialist) power; instead, it has been co-opted as a latter-day
'exotic novel', experimental in design but still part of the familiar fabric of
the 'mysterious East'. Rushdie, according to Eakin, is well aware of 'the
risk inherent in the canonization of the exotic novel: like travel writing
and guide books, it depicts a cultural other that [metropolitan] readers
want to believe in and experience, with little regard for its factual basis'
(Eakin 1995: 5). Historical facts are disregarded, that is, other than those
that can be manipulated or reinvented to meet the ideological requirements of the mainstream consumer culture.

Eakin's reading of *Midnight's Children* confirms that the battle played
out in the novel over historical representation is inextricably bound up
with its status as a canonical work and a mainstream cultural commodity.
The magical-realist aspects of the novel also seem to lend support to this
view. For magical realism, it could be argued, has itself become a
commodified, increasingly formulaic aesthetic through which the histories
of diverse cultures are effectively levelled out; while the charge of
'trivialisation' that has occasionally been levelled at the novel suggests an

ideological aversion to the manipulation of history for the purposes of commercial gain. In both cases, the implication is that *Midnight's Children* has been successful because its author has catered, or even pandered, to the exoticist predilections of his Western metropolitan reading public.

This view of a 'target public' is inevitably reductive, falsely implying that *Midnight's Children* is primarily or even exclusively directed at a Western metropolitan audience. It should not be forgotten that the novel enjoyed, as Rushdie's other novels have enjoyed, a large readership in India, nor should it be imagined that responses to his novels are culturally and/or geographically determined in any simple way. As in the last chapter on the reception of African literature outside of Africa, it cannot be assumed that audiences are neatly separable by ethnicity, class, gender, location – still less so in an age where reading communities, as well as individual writers, are products of an increasingly diasporised world. In any case, the fear that Rushdie might be pandering to a wonder-seeking Western readership is immediately allayed by the strategically exoticist methods by which he draws attention to his novel as an object of Western consumption. Like several of his literary contemporaries, Rushdie has an ironic relation to Orientalism, emphasising the ideological shortfall of self-serving Orientalist myths. (In this sense, the classic companion text to contemporary Indian literature in English is perhaps Gita Mehta's *Karma Cola: Marketing the Mystic East* (1979), a wickedly funny debunking of the Western propensity for spiritual tourism, and an equally astute analysis of the various ways in which Indian writers/thinkers have capitalised on Western exotic myths – see also Chapters 3 and 7.) Like Mehta, Rushdie demonstrates his awareness of the commercial implications of an Orientalism specifically tailored to metropolitan mass-market tastes. Hence the figure of Saleem Sinai, the novel's narrator-protagonist, as an Orientalist *merchant*, cannily inviting the reader to sample his own, and India's, exotic wares. Snake-charmers, genies, fakirs; elegant saris and crude spittoons – most of the familiar semiotic markers of Orientalism are on display. By emphasising the status of these items as commodities, Saleem/Rushdie ironically constructs the metropolitan reader as a voyeuristic consumer. Rushdie's parody of the reader-as-consumer is reinforced by gastronomic metaphors: people, places and events – the country itself – become an edible; Indian history is 'chutnified' and preserved for future use (Rushdie 1981: 442).

The ingenious interplay between myth and history, which several critics have praised as being one of the strengths of *Midnight's Children* (Price 1994; Riemenschneider 1984), is the result of Rushdie's confrontation of the mediated representation of India's recent past. It is the awareness of this mediation, rather than the shift to a post-independence time-frame or the articulation of a 'colonized perspective' (Todd 1996), that most marks *Midnight's Children* as a work of postcolonial fiction. As well as any other, Rushdie's novel dramatises a conflict between oppositional 'postcolonialism' and recuperative 'postcoloniality' (see Introduction) – a drama played out in the pages of the work, as well as in the circumstances behind its production. This conflict signals Rushdie's interest, not just in decolonising Indian history, but in critiquing the commodification of India(s) both past and present. The intertextual aspects of *Midnight's Children*, which, as is well known, incorporates jocular references to the canonical works of Anglo-Indian writers as well as to the Hindu epics the *Mahabharata* and the *Ramayana* (Shepherd 1985; Merivale 1990), help situate the novel as a further parody of the already self-parodic literature of East-West contact. But Rushdie also draws attention to the *material* effects of such commodified contact-narratives. One of the ironies of his career to date is that it has been built on opposing, while also perpetuating, the commodified exoticisms that are endemic to East-West literary encounter.[15]

Part of *Midnight's Children*'s function as a watershed novel for metropolitan reviewers and critics has been that of a touchstone for the assessment of subsequent Indo-Anglian literary works.[16] 'Midnight's Children Come of Age' is the catchy title of Bruce Palling's 1993 newspaper article on the efflorescence of Indian literature in English (*Weekly Telegraph*, 22 September 1993); while four years later, Michael Gorra, in a review of *The God of Small Things* for *The London Review of Books* (19 June 1997), makes the legitimate complaint that 'too much new Indian fiction has carried the birthmark of *Midnight's Children*' (Gorra 1997b: 22). Certainly, it is true that few Indian novels in English to appear on the scene since the early 1980s have escaped comparison with Rushdie's or have not had their work measured, at times invidiously, against the yardstick of Rushdie's success. The much-hyped publication of Vikram Seth's gargantuan novel *A Suitable Boy* in 1993 was no exception. Here, the media hoopla, especially in Britain, exceeded even that surrounding Rushdie's novels; and, as the publicity stakes rose ever higher over the latest 'Indian masterpiece', even the inevitable comparisons to *Midnight's Children* were outdone. *A Suitable Boy* found itself instead in the glittering company of Eliot's *Middlemarch* and Tolstoy's *War and Peace* – fatuous analogies eagerly seized on, only to be dismissed, by several of the novel's subsequent reviewers (O'Shaughnessy 1993; Furbisher 1993), and summarily derided by *Publishing News*, in its fiercest media-watchdog role, as 'particularly sorry examples of blurb writers' drivel' (qtd in Grove 1993: 15). Not that the newspapers, the magazines and, to a lesser extent, the academic journals were averse to capitalising on the phenomenon of a thousand-and-a-half page novel with a half-a-million dollar sales-tag and upwards of a million in total global advances. (Nor was this phenomenon new; instead, *A Suitable Boy*, for all the staged surprise at its author's windfall, became merely the latest instance in a long British history of fetishised literary bestsellers.) The figures that catapulted Seth to instant literary-millionaire status were read by some as further, not necessarily welcome, proof of the new commercial impetus of 'serious' English-language fiction – an impetus provided by the escalating publishing wars and the irreversible move toward corporate sponsorship, and encapsulated in such rapidly institutionalised arbiters of literary taste as the Booker Prize (Todd 1996; see also Chapter 4). For others, staunchly defending the besieged citadel of traditional 'English literature', the wild success of *A Suitable Boy* appeared merely faddish, linked to a misperception that the modern English novel might have ossified into set patterns or to the fear, equally misguided, that the more traditionally minded writers might temporarily have run out of things to say. William Dalrymple, in his review-article in *Harpers & Queen* (June 1997), proves himself to be one of the more vociferous sceptics:

> Since [the publication of *A Suitable Boy*], many other moderately good Indian novels have been promoted well above their weight, with several of them … given ludicrously craven reviews in the more politically correct press. It is often interesting to compare the meas-ured and balanced response of Indian reviewers writing about these books, say in *India Today* or *The Times of India*, with the whoops of PC ecstasy that tend to greet even the most ordinary Indian novels in the modish and fad-conscious books pages of the *Guardian*.
>
> (Dalrymple 1997: 115)[17]

There is something to be said for this argument, although *A Suitable Boy*, at least, was warmly received in India, if generally regarded in its own terms rather than as a 'legitimate successor' to *Midnight's Children*. And it is difficult to dispute the quality of the writing that other diasporic Indians have produced in the last couple of decades, if once again necessary to correct the self-serving metropolitan assertion that Indian writing in English is *only* a product of the diaspora. Dalrymple is probably right, though, that the continuing hunt for 'Indian masterpieces', especially in Britain, is tied in both with an exoticist perception of India filtered through the familiar topoi of Raj nostalgia and with a metropoli-tan desire, through this reified 'India', to rejuvenate a humdrum domestic culture. This appropriative desire manifests itself in responses like Trevor Fishlock's (*Sunday Telegraph*, 21 March 1993) which, awash in Orientalist clichés ('Vikram Seth's vast novel [is] as broad and flowing as the Ganges itself'), attempt to commandeer the novel as the inclusive portrait of a continent – 'all India is here'. This metonymic fallacy, already identified by Edward Said (Said 1978) as a classic Orientalist strategy, has been parodied by many an Indian writer, of whom Rushdie and Seth are merely among the best-known examples. But this strategy has re-emerged with a vengeance in the packaging of several recent Indo-Anglian novels, as well as in the type of uncritical response to them that highlights their provenance, symbolic if not material, from an 'exotic culture'. (Self-irony forms part of the pattern: hence Manik Mehta's wryly informative article in *India Abroad* (23 August 1996) on the reception of Indian writing in Germany, where as he says, tongue firmly in cheek, 'there has been a surge in demand for translations of works by writers from exotic cultures, particularly from the Indian subcontinent' (M. Mehta 1996: 47).)

A further problem emerges when looking for more *critical* responses to Seth's novel. There is relatively little academic criticism on *A Suitable Boy* (or, for that matter, on Seth's other works to date, notably the engaging travelogue *From Heaven Lake* (1983), the critically acclaimed novel in verse *The Golden Gate* (1986), and several volumes of poetry), and fewer signs still of the bustling critical-theoretical industry that has sprung up around Rushdie's work. This partly has to do, as previously mentioned, with the self-perpetuating patronage systems that lead to writers (especially those perceived as coming from 'marginal' or 'exotic' places) becoming representative figures, and with the more specific legitimising processes that underwrite the consecration of particular authors and their works.[18] But it also has to do with more obviously practical considerations: after all, *A Suitable Boy*, despite its undoubted popularity, is hardly the likeliest of candidates for inclusion in school and university curricula; nor does Seth's novel have the aura of self-conscious intellectual sophistication that might encourage, as it has certainly done for Rushdie's work, the type of theoretically informed research that is a current requirement of the academic profession. This is a pity, since the novel is worthy of closer critical consideration as a late twentieth-century historical novel that gestures affectionately, if also mischievously, back to both its Indian and European nineteenth-century literary antecedents. It is also a subtle example of the generic code-switching – historical novel, political allegory, domestic melodrama, exotic romance, and so forth – for which more obviously ludic metafictional writers like Rushdie have earned their reputation. Seth's novel is a more self-conscious work than has generally been supposed, wryly aware of the popularity of its melodramatic romantic sequences and of the false inclusiveness conferred upon it by its panoramic vision and encyclopaedic scope. To a lesser extent than *Midnight's Children*, to be sure, *A Suitable Boy* anticipates its own reception as a technically proficient blockbuster novel that seeks (and inevitably fails) to encapsulate a deliberately exoticised India. It is aware, that is, of the metropolitan formulae within which it is likely to be read and evaluated, and to some extent it plays up to these, challenging its readers by pretending to humour them, to confirm their expectations. And it is aware, not least, of the commercial viability of these formulae, which depend upon marketable European clichés about a 'distinctively Indian' sensibility – clichés neatly turned on their heads here in an Indian's 'distinctively European' novel.[19]

Like *A Suitable Boy*, Arundhati Roy's novel *The God of Small Things* (1997) is most remarkable for the publicity it generated, both as the arrestingly good first novel of a young, little-known and unusually attractive writer and as an example of the star-making industry, the media-driven process by which a writer can be catapulted to a quasi-mythical celebrity status. As had been the case before with Seth, this process was greeted with considerable scepticism, with grumbling in the press about excessively generous advances (around a million dollars in total) and the equally inflationary praise given to a writer of as yet unproven talents. For some, the marketing of the novel was an object lesson in commodity fetishism, with a carefully managed excitement at the latest literary 'discovery', and some salacious details about the private life of the writer – described by one reviewer, in another example of the touchstone effect, as an 'unsuitable girl' (Maya Jaggi, *Guardian Weekend*, 24 May 1997) – thrown into the mix. Such was the media hype surrounding the novel and its author that it became almost predictable that it would win that most media-conscious of awards, the Booker Prize. Riding the crest of a wave of heady journalistic clichés, *The God of Small Things* duly emerged as the latest (post-)Orientalist blockbuster – the latest Westernised novel of the East. Since then, some critical attention has been paid to its status as a so-called 'tourist novel', recycling intoxicating myths of a fabulous but dangerous Orient to an eager Western readership already attuned to the exotic formulae of Indian fiction (Dalrymple 1997; Mongia 1997). Meanwhile, other reviewers and critics, snobbishly suggesting that the novel might be too reader-friendly, have paid Roy the backhanded compliment of calling her novel an accomplished 'popular' work (Chisholm 1997).

Roy's *is* an accomplished novel, and more sophisticated than it has been given credit; what interests me in this particular context, though, is how the novel (and here the analogy with Seth and, before him, Rushdie seems appropriate) both anticipated and participated in the global processes of its own commercial promotion. *The God of Small Things*, as Padmini Mongia has suggested, is a partly self-referential title: it intimates a magical discovery also hinted at in its cover, where the tiny but brilliant lotus-flower appears miraculously among the choking weeds (Mongia 1997). The novel announces itself, that is, as a talismanic presence, drawing its reader inexorably to the mysteries it uncovers. The same might be said of its author; for Roy, incorrigibly photogenic, has clearly worked hard on her image, her marketably exotic looks. In the weeks following publication, and then again later after the award of the Booker, the face of Roy could be seen almost everywhere: as one interviewer put it, the 'goddess of small things' (McGirk 1997: 18). This myth was fed by Roy's alleged bohemianism (Jaggi 1997) and, almost inevitably, her diminutive stature; and Roy herself proved good interview-value, with a life-story containing almost as many carefully leaked secrets as her book.

All of this indicates that Roy, like Rushdie (and, to a lesser extent, Seth), is highly skilled at self-promotion, and at the media-friendly manufacturing of exotic ('Oriental') romance.[20] But while Roy is undoubtedly talented at cultivating her own self-image, there is a not-so-hidden irony behind her mediatised success. For *The God of Small Things*, like *Midnight's Children* – to which it is indebted in several ways – is a novel partly *about* (media) promotion. It both displays and implicitly ironises its own lushly romantic images, its metaphor-laden language, its transferred Conradian primitivist myths. It is aware of the recent history of Indo-Anglian fiction, and of the parallel history of imperialist nostalgia in the West: the films of Lean and of Merchant and Ivory; the profitable *Heart of Darkness* industry; the travel writing business with its recuperative parodies of imperial heroism and derring-do. In bringing these histories together, Roy's novel shows the continuing presence of an imperial imaginary lurking behind Indian literature in English, among other putatively postcolonial products. But this imaginary is turned precisely to *commerce*, to a currency of nostalgic images; and these images are held up derisively to the very readers they attract. Roy's, like Rushdie's, might be seen then as a *strategic* exoticism, designed to trap the unwary reader into complicity with the Orientalisms of which the novel so hauntingly relates. It is also to some extent, also like Rushdie's, a *meta*-exoticism. In laying bare the grounds of its own material production – in examining the procedures that might lead to its own commercial success – Roy's novel helps reveal the link between the perceptual mechanism of the exotic and the metropolitan marketing of Indian literature in English in the West.

2000

The future of Indian literature in English at the millennium seems indisputable, the reputations of its best-known writers intact, its commercial success virtually ensured. Yet it remains a cause for concern that nearly all the recognised writers, with a few notable exceptions, are located in the diaspora; what is the future, then, for English-language writing *in India*? John Updike, at the end of his review-article on *The God of Small Things* and Ardashir Vakil's *Beach Boy* (1997) in the Golden Jubilee issue of *The New Yorker*, frames the question as follows, pondering the gastronomic longings of Vakil's protagonist, Cyrus Readymoney, in his own characteristically pithy prose:

> Is India trying to fill with delicacies the void in our young hero [Cyrus Readymoney], whom a confusingly hybrid culture has left unconsoled and bewildered, or is the author, as he envisions tropical fruit in gray London, trying to fill himself? Arundhati Roy lives in New Delhi, as far from Cochin [the setting for *Beach Boy*] as Boston is from Miami. Is there a place, these novels make us wonder, for an English-language literature within India, where a bristling nationalism staves off Asian neighbors and a Hindu fundamentalism arises to compete with the Islamic variety? A writer is a spy in childhood and a self-interrogator as an adult. Who will read the debriefing report? These two writers certainly have a past – vivid, problematical, precious – but where is their future?
>
> (Updike 1997: 161)

Updike's fashionable concern arguably masks a greater sense of cultural arrogance; certainly, his question overlooks a number of English-language writers who, living and publishing in India, appear to have escaped his (and, presumably, many other Westerners') attention. Such oversights are clearly linked to power differentials in the global knowledge industry – differentials maintained in part by the hegemony of the multinational publishing companies. As previously noted (see Chapter 1), there are clear asymmetries of power in the exchange of knowledge between the First and Third Worlds; publishing is an integral part of this complex neocolonial network. To put it simply, even crudely, many Third World writers/thinkers are rewarded, or imagine that they will be, for setting their sights abroad; but the gaze is far less likely to travel in the other direction.

This dilemma is likely to manifest itself differently, however, in different Third World countries. In India, by and large, publishers play a less directly neocolonialist role than in most of Africa, where 'virtually all books are published in the metropolitan language … and the 80 to 95 percent of the population who do not know English or French are effectively barred from the higher levels of education' (Altbach 1975:

229; see also previous chapter). Most Indian publishers, according to Philip Altbach, 'do not follow a consciously neocolonialist policy of trying to maintain foreign influence on the subcontinent. Rather, they perceive that the largest market for books is in English and that, in fact, the only national market is for such material' (Altbach 1975: 229). For these among other reasons, publication in English continues to thrive in India, recently estimated to be the world's third largest publisher of English-language books (Ezenwa-Ohaeto 1995: 9; see also Kachru 1986). But this does not mean of course that these books will be read by a large percentage of Indians – in Altbach's estimation, less than 5 per cent of the population is literate in English (Altbach 1975: 229). Nor does it mean that these books will be widely read outside of India; for most Indian publishers, like their Third World counterparts, find it hard to compete in the global marketplace. All of these factors contribute to the common – and of course thoroughly mediated – perception that Indo-Anglian writing is the product of a roving band of privileged diasporics; that it has become the happy hunting ground of a fairly small group of clubbable cosmopolitans, who are producing a self-consciously globalised literature 'written by élites, and defined and canonized by élites' (Boehmer 1995: 239–40).[21]

The rumour of a diasporic club, though fairly widespread, is largely unfounded, although it remains true that the metropolitan market in Indian literature in English has helped sustain the fiction of a close-knit family dominated by a few immediately recognisable names (witness the *New Yorker* picture). Part of the problem here is the blatant bias, the raft of cultural presuppositions, that often surrounds contemporary definitions of Indian literature in English. Some recent publications, notably the 1997 Vintage anthology, have attempted to 'solve' this problem by simply ignoring the implication that English, while globally disseminated, remains a minority language in India. Aijaz Ahmad, in contrast, has put the case for a properly historicised, pluriform definition of Indian literature which, drawing on all of India's languages, might better engage with the unparalleled linguistic and cultural heterogeneity of the Indian subcontinent:

> [M]ultilinguality and polyglot fluidity seem to have been the chief characteristics – possibly *the* characteristics – which gave 'Indian literature' its high degree of unification in the pre-modern phase. ... Multiplicity of languages is the fundamental characteristic of this civilization, this nation, this literature, and the structure of its unity is positivistically far less quantifiable than in Europe or in Europe's offshoots in North America.
>
> (Ahmad 1992: 248, 256, Ahmad's italics)

Ahmad recognises that 'direct knowledge of an "Indian" literature presumes the knowledge of so many languages that only rare specialists could command them all' (Ahmad 1992: 250). Still, he campaigns vigorously for a more heteroglot understanding of Indian literature that might combat the current trend for English to become 'the [dominant] language in which the knowledge of "Indian" literature is produced' (Ahmad 1992: 250). As Ahmad notes, English has become the language in which 'the largest archive of translations [from other Indian languages] has been assembled so far' (Ahmad 1992: 250); it has served as a lingua franca for the nation's highly disparate literary intelligentsia. But the artificial dominance of English, reinforced by a neocolonial education system in which excessive weight is still given to traditional 'English literature' (Trivedi 1993; Viswanathan 1989), overlooks the obvious fact that 'the vast bulk of the literary intelligentsia in India is not and has not been very proficient in English, even as a reading public, regardless of what the upper layers of half a dozen cosmopolitan cities may believe' (Ahmad 1992: 250).

Ahmad's concern is that translation in India usually means translation into English. A different kind of concern is the one Rushdie points out in his introduction to the Vintage anthology – the current shortage of good-quality translations into English of literary works written in other Indian languages. This shortage, needless to say, may have one effect in India but quite another in the metropolitan centres of Europe and North America. In the latter case, it could be argued, Indian literature in English has itself become a kind of translation, a culturally mediated view of India made accessible to the wider English-speaking world. But what is clear is that writers like Rushdie himself ironise this process of translation – poking fun, for example, at the types of readers who might see his novels as an opportunity for cultural voyeurism; or who, themselves contaminated by the Sinai family's metonymic affliction, might obsessively inspect narrative fragments for the signs, allegorical intimations, of national wholes (Rushdie 1981). Writers like Seth and Roy, too, have proven adept at playing on readerly expectation, rehearsing but also transforming those literary formulae of an imagined India which capitalise on the illicit adventures and extravagant clichés of exotic romance. It is worth pondering, though, whether ironic self-consciousness and a strategically deployed exoticism are not very much part of the commercial formulae these and other contemporary Indo-Anglian writers claim to uncover. Part of the fashionable appeal, that is, of contemporary Indian literature in English is its capacity for an ironic recycling of the clichés that have historically dominated Orientalist representation (Said 1978). Hence the coming together in several of these works of a form of historically located oppositionality – postcolonial 'resistance' – and a form of free-floating intellectual scepticism – postmodern 'belatedness' – that seems at times incompatible with it. For Timothy Brennan, a mark of this commodified strand of cosmopolitan Third World literature is the conversion of politics itself into a source of aesthetic play (Brennan 1997: chap. 1; see also Introduction). As a description of at least some of the writing this is accurate; as a blanket judgement of the writers it is too harsh. The aestheticisation of political issues is arguably intrinsic to the genre of the political novel, while philosophical scepticism and political commitment need not be seen as mutually exclusive. In any case, some of the writers (Vikram Seth, for instance) would probably not see their work as being political; and even if it is, it still seems likely that Indian, among other Third World, literary works will be political *in different ways*. Brennan's assertion that Third World literature has become the object of a homogenising metropolitan gaze might itself be seen as unduly homogenising; all the same, he is surely right that current definitions of Third World, more specifically Indian, literature in English are often subject to (global) media-filtration processes that compromise the cultural specificity of the writing and thus risk robbing it of its political force. And he is right, as well, that many of the writers, especially the celebrity writers, *know* this. The success of writers like Rushdie and, more recently, Arundhati Roy owes to the skill with which they manipulate commercially viable metropolitan codes. They are conscious that their writing, ostensibly oppositional, is vulnerable to recuperation; in ironically rehearsing a continuing history of imperialist perceptions of an 'othered' India (India as available spectacle; as alternating object of horror and fascination; as world of magic, mysteries and wonders; as site of colonial nostalgia; as forbidden space of cross-cultural desire; as romantic tourist goal; and so on), they know that their work might still be used as a means of reconfirming an exoticising imperial gaze. They are aware of all this, and they draw their readers into that awareness in their writing. If postcolonial literary works often dramatise the material circumstances of their production, this would be equally true of writers like Rushdie and Roy *at the level of consumption*. Part of the reason, surely, that Indian literature in English has become so fashionable is that it has been made to stand in metonymically for India itself as an object of conspicuous consumption. Rushdie and Roy, among others, have contributed to this contemporary mode of consumption while also critiquing it; and as I have implied here, their critique might itself be seen as part of the general consumption process. Nor was there any let-up on this process at the millennium. For 1999–2000 was a further cause for celebration: 'Visit

India Year'. The India Tourist Office, in a near-replica of its 1997 advertisement, put it this way:

> This millennium, India offers a mouthwatering menu of attractions. Try these for starters. ... To commemorate the forthcoming millennium, we'll be staging some very special festivals, fairs and events throughout the country. As if our traditional selection of monumental forts and palaces, dramatic wildlife and dazzling beaches wasn't enough already.
>
> (*Observer*, 8 November 1998: 24)

So India, it seems, is more available than ever for consumption; and more prevalent than ever are the gastronomic images through which the nation is to be consumed.

3 Staged marginalities
Rushdie, Naipaul, Kureishi

It has become commonplace for intellectuals to claim the margins as a site of resistance. For the African-American feminist critic bell hooks, '[u]nderstanding marginality as position and place of resistance is crucial for [all] oppressed, exploited, [and] colonized people' (hooks 1990: 342); while for the US/Palestinian cultural critic Edward Said, marginality is at once the blessing and the curse of a global intellectual cadre, whose (self-) exclusion from the cultural mainstream is the condition of using 'a language that tries to speak the truth to power' (Said 1994: xvi). To think at, and from, the margins is to challenge the authority of the mainstream, a mainstream usually defined in some combination of white, male, heterosexual, middle class. Counterhegemonic thought arguably con-stitutes the new academic orthodoxy, as different interest groups fight it out for the right to make the margins their own. The spectacle of – mostly privileged – academics claiming marginal status can at times be unedifying, particularly when their infighting seems so often to be far removed from the realities of social struggle. Marginality is no mere abstraction of course, nor is it to be found only outside the academy. But the cachet that the category brings indicates something other than a social burden – it suggests that 'resistance' itself has become a valuable intellectual commodity.

A similar point might be made for so-called 'marginal' or 'minority' writing. It is usually assumed that minority literatures are written at least in part out of the experience of social marginality, as undergone at some combination of individual, collective and institutional levels. As David Lloyd and Abdul JanMohamed argue in their introduction to the collection of essays *The Nature and Context of Minority Discourse* (1990), '[c]ultures designated as minorities have certain shared experience by virtue of their similar antagonistic relationship to the dominant culture, which seeks to marginalize them all' (Lloyd and JanMohamed 1990: 4). Lloyd complicates the issue when, in a later essay in the collection, he makes the useful distinction (via Deleuze and Guattari) between a literature of minorities, which is written in a minority language, and a 'minor' literature, which is written by minorities but in the major language of a dominant culture. 'Minor' literature, says Lloyd,

> is so termed in relation to the major canon, and its characteristics are defined in opposition to those which define canonical writing. To enumerate them briefly … [these] characteristics would involve the questioning or destruction of the concepts of identity and identification, the rejection of representations of developing autonomy and authenticity, if not the very concept of development itself, and accordingly a profound suspicion of narratives of reconciliation and unification.
>
> (Lloyd 1990: 381; see also Deleuze and Guattari 1990)[1]

'Minor' literature, as Lloyd understands it, is necessarily oppositional to its 'major' counterpart, but its resistance takes the form of an anti-essentialist undercutting of the narratives of development and coherence that are used to bolster the self-identity of the dominant culture – and to keep minorities in their place. There are numerous problems, as Lloyd himself recognises, with this formulation. First, the insistence on the counter-hegemonic function of 'minor' literature risks setting up a series of potentially essentialised straw categories – 'major literature', 'the dominant culture', and so on – against which it allegedly reacts and on which it continues to some extent to depend. Second, the idea of a 'minor' literature which attacks, or even 'destroys', hegemonic concepts of identity and identification leaves little room, if any, for the numerous literary texts written by minorities in major languages which apparently support and draw their strength from some form or other of identitary affiliation (Lionnet 1995; see also Chapters 5 and 6). And third, the notion that a 'minor' literature automatically opposes canonical status is apparently challenged, if not contradicted, by the consecration of several writers whose work might otherwise be seen as legitimately 'minor' – Sandra Cisneros, Maxine Hong Kingston and Alice Walker in the United States; Kazuo Ishiguro, Caryl Phillips and Salman Rushdie in the United Kingdom. No doubt, as Lloyd admits, the capacity of 'minor' writing to combat a dominant culture is at times outmatched by that culture's ability to recuperate 'minor' writing for its own aesthetic and political purposes.[2] Previous chapters have already drawn attention to the recuperability of putatively marginal literary/cultural products and to the diverse, often contradictory effects of that recuperative process: from the hyperbolic touting of a blatantly exoticised 'Third World literature' in the global marketplace to the neglect or exclusion of writers who work with less familiar formulae or who publish in languages other than English (see Chapters 1 and 2). As Lloyd and JanMohamed succinctly put it, '[a]ttending to minority cultural forms requires … a double vigilance, both with respect to their availability for cultural recuperation and to their strategies of resistance' (Lloyd and JanMohamed 1990: 5; see also Ferguson *et al.* 1990). Much depends, as ever, on who defines these vexatious labels – 'minority' culture, 'minor' literature, 'marginal' writer, and so on. The politics of definition conjures up a series of openly contradictory questions: are so-called marginal writers self-designated combatants with a clearly defined political agenda, or are they called upon to revitalise a listless mainstream culture? Is marginal writing adversarial or paradoxically assimilative? Does it work toward social change, or does it tacitly preserve the *status quo* while claiming to celebrate cultural difference? And who qualifies, exactly, as that most apparently self-divided of creatures – a marginal writer?

Consider the case of Britain and two of its most accomplished living writers: Salman Rushdie and V.S. Naipaul. Both were born outside Britain but have spent most of their working lives there. Both are mainstream figures who are nonetheless affiliated to diasporic (South Asian/Caribbean) minority cultures. Both have been subjected to a vigorous, at times vindictive, politics of labelling, where conspicuously indefinite terms such as 'cosmopolitan', 'migrant', 'postcolonial' and 'Third World writer' have been appropriated, deployed and renegotiated in the continuing effort to stake out territory in wide-ranging cultural debates – over the future of the Third World; over the relationship between 'developed' and 'developing' societies; over the role played by creative writers in upholding the principles of Western rationality and democracy; and so forth. Significantly, it is rare for either to be designated as a *British* writer. Even some of the most culturally sensitive of critics have been known to persist in the view that Naipaul and Rushdie originally come from 'other' places – to suggest that in some deep-rooted, almost atavistic sense, they are immigrant writers who 'really belong' somewhere else.[3] Are these two obviously well-known writers still marginal on account of their ethnicity? Or because they choose in their work to fictionalise their own experiences of displacement? Or because they are seen, in spite of themselves, as First World informants for their native Third World cultures?

Such terms are clearly worrisome, not least because they seem to allow for conflation. Rushdie and Naipaul, it need hardly be said, have very different ideological outlooks, different sets of values that emerge in works that are themselves dispersed, uneven. The critical reception of their work has been frequently polarised, notoriously so in the case of Naipaul, much loved by conservatives who plumb his work for universal (read, Western) causes, much reviled by radicals who see him as a traitorous imperial ally.[4] Rushdie, meanwhile, is appreciated in the West for his staunchly democratic principles, although rather less so, as previously suggested, by those with a closer knowledge of South Asian cultures (see Chapter 2). Let me make things clear from the beginning: I have no great wish to rehabilitate Naipaul, who seems to me to invite much of the criticism he receives; nor do I wish to vilify Rushdie, who surely needs no further enemies at present. I would raise an eyebrow, nonetheless, at suggestions that they are on opposite sides of the barricades. Naipaul, for all his truculence and his Olympian pronouncements on 'second-hand' cultures, remains in much of his work a fiercely anti-imperial critic; while Rushdie, for his part, shares Naipaul's Oxbridge education and (pre-*fatwa*, at least) his cosmopolitan privilege, even if – also like Naipaul – he has suffered for the colour of his skin, as well as for his unwelcome political opinions.

In this chapter I want to focus on a further point of contact between Naipaul and Rushdie: the role both writers play as ironic commentators on British culture. Rushdie is best known, of course, as a tongue-in-cheek chronicler of modern India, or as a dangerously facetious gadfly to Islamic religious orthodoxies; while Naipaul, as Rob Nixon has dubbed him, is the First World's Third World expert, a relentless diagnostician of corruption in Africa and on the Asian subcontinent, as well as a formidable moral accountant of his native Caribbean.[5] Both writers, though, have written extensively about their adopted country, Britain, from a perspective that shows awareness of a marginal position. In the rest of this section, accordingly, I shall compare two works, published within a year of one another, which focus sharply on Britain: Naipaul's subtly elegiac semi-autobiographical novel, *The Enigma of Arrival* (1987), and Rushdie's stylistically exuberant, if ultimately ill-fated, intercultural blockbuster, *The Satanic Verses* (1988).

The two novels, an obvious pairing, have inspired several comparative critical essays (see, for example, Gurnah 1995; van der Veer 1997). These essays, as might be expected, are at pains to distinguish between *The Enigma of Arrival* and *The Satanic Verses*; and it is certainly true that the two novels present plenty of opportunities for contrastive analysis. One fruitful area of comparison is the fictionalised treatment of patterns of social adaptation; for both novels are perhaps best seen as meditations on impermanence, as reminders of the need to keep pace with rapid, and at times bewildering, social change. Here, *The Enigma of Arrival*, set in rural Wiltshire, strikes a note of wistful nostalgia, as the narrator struggles to reconcile his idea of ancestral England with a reality that consistently outmanoeuvres it; *The Satanic Verses*, on the other hand, moving between present-day London and a mythicised Orient, seeks terms that are flexible enough to express the migrant's 'double vision', and to describe an urban society in a constant state of transformation. Both novels set up a dialectic between inheritance and invention; but whereas Naipaul's seems almost paralysed by the weight of England's cultural heritage, Rushdie's mobilises the forces of Ovidian/Lucretian metamorphosis and projects these onto a country whose past (like its present and, eventually, its future) must be reinvented.

Yet there is more in common between Naipaul's and Rushdie's novels than might at first sight be supposed. Like Rushdie, Naipaul advocates the cause of flexibility: the need to adapt to changing circumstances, to reinvent oneself if necessary. And like Naipaul, Rushdie finds a place in his novel for the rituals of mourning – his characters reconcile themselves to a past that they can change but never abandon. My initial focus here, however, will be on the novels' *theatricality* and on their staging, more particularly, of disparate experiences of social and cultural marginalisation. My term 'staged marginality' comes initially by way of the sociologist Dean MacCannell, who in his influential 1976 study of modern tourism analyses the trope of 'staged authenticity'. For MacCannell, staged authenticity refers to the ways in which tourists are given access to 'real-life' settings or, alternatively, to touristic objects that are made to display their 'authenticity'. As MacCannell wryly notes, tourist settings are designed so as to 'promise real and convincing shows of local life and culture. Even the infamously clean Istanbul Hilton has not excluded all aspects of Turkish culture (the cocktail waitresses wear harem pants, or did in 1968)' (MacCannell 1989 [1976]: 106). The 'reality-effect' (to adapt Barthes' term) that is produced by such obviously manufactured settings is carefully orchestrated so as to cater to tourists' expectations of exotic peoples and/or cultures (see also Chapter 7). Staged marginality refers to a similar phenomenon, but in a domestic setting: it denotes the process by which marginalised individuals or social groups are moved to dramatise their 'subordinate' status for the benefit of a majority or mainstream audience. Staged marginality is not necessarily an exercise in self-abasement; it may, and often does, have a critical or even a subversive function. As James C. Scott remarks in his wide-ranging study of hidden codes of oppositional practice, *Domination and the Arts of Resistance* (1990), it is possible to see subordinates' apparently willing participation 'in a piece of theater that serves their superior's view of the situation [as being] maintained in their own interests. In fact, the stereotypes of the dominant are, from this perspective, a resource as well as an oppression to the subordinate' (Scott 1990: 34). The possibility for what Scott calls the 'tactical manipulation of appearances' (44) by socially subordinated individuals or groups has been underlined more recently by Homi Bhabha in his seminal work on colonial mimicry. In mimicry, says Bhabha (via the psychoanalytic theories of Lacan), 'the representation of identity and meaning is rearticulated along the axis of metonymy … [M]imicry is like camouflage, not a harmonization or repression of difference, but a form of resemblance that differs/defends presence by displaying it in part, metonymically' (Bhabha 1994b: 131). For Bhabha, this self-conscious display or ritualised enactment of 'partial resemblances' may be disruptive; for if the outward show – the simulated *performance* – of obedience is seen as containing the traces of its own resistance, it then becomes possible to envision colonial subjects as tacitly resisting subordination by appearing to embrace it (Bhabha 1994b: 131–2).[6]

As Scott points out, however, the practical results of this covert resistance are usually limited; more likely than not, stagings of this kind merely act to reconfirm the disempowerment of 'subordinate' groups *vis-à-vis* the dominant culture (Scott 1990: 32–3). However, they may still be useful in revealing structures of power – as proves to be the case in Naipaul's and Rushdie's fictionalised treatment of ethnic minorities in mid 1980s Britain. Both *The Enigma of Arrival*, on a more personal level, and *The Satanic Verses* can be seen as explorations of the apparent paradoxes inherent in ethnicised performances of staged subordination or marginality. While the local conditions for the two novels are obviously very different, the performative paradigm they deploy is essentially the same: by simulating the conditions in which the dominant (in this case, white Anglo-Saxon) culture perceives them, marginalised people or groups may reveal the underlying structures of their oppression; they may also demonstrate the dominant culture's need for subaltern others, who function as foils or counterweights to its own fragile self-identity.

In *The Enigma of Arrival*, staged marginality plays its part in a multi-layered drama of dislocation. Like so much of Naipaul's work, the novel explores myths of displacement and their relation to the historical forces – especially colonialism – that (re)produce global inequality.[7] The players on this particular stage act out seemingly fixed roles. First, there is Jack, 'the gardener'; then there are 'the overseers', the Phillipses. At the centre of the estate is 'the lord of the manor', a barely visible but still apparently powerful presence. And watching them all from the wings is the figure of 'the itinerant writer' – the narrator of the novel, who, we are given to understand, both is and is not Naipaul, and whose rented cottage lies significantly at the *edge* of the landlord's estate. What are we to make in the novel of the narrator's staged marginality? Is it, as some critics have concluded, little more than an act of contrived allegiance to his own idea of England: one in which the feudal manor segues into the (post-)imperial estate, and where the latter-day colonial, manipulated by an unseen hand, continues against the historical grain to rehearse his own subjection?

Here, I would side with Helen Tiffin in her assessment of the novel and of Naipaul's work in general. Tiffin counters those – mostly conservative – critics who have seen Naipaul's writing as 'an obedient response to colonial interpellation'; instead, she argues, it should be read 'for the subversive strategies it contains' (Tiffin 1989: 45). And that subversion, in *The Enigma of Arrival*, consists in a kind of textual self-implosion – in the cumulatively disintegrative process through which the novel is made to enact, and ironically fulfil, its inbuilt obsolescence. The manor, it transpires, 'had been created at the zenith of imperial power, a period of high, even extravagant, middle-class domestic architecture … [I]t had been built like a steamship. But like a steamship, it was liable to breakdown and obsolescence' (Naipaul 1987: 261). The manor, like an ageing stage-set, has outlived its original usefulness, while its owner, himself well past his prime, acts out a role for which he is clearly no longer fit. Continuing well into his dotage to indulge his childhood fantasies, he clings to a vision of Empire whose history is now replayed as farce. And he is surrounded by figures apparently no less anachronistic than himself – including the narrator. As the narrator tells us,

> I was [the landlord's] opposite in every way, social, artistic, sexual. …
> An empire lay between us [but] this empire at the same time linked
> us. This empire explained my birth in the New World, the language I
> used, the vocation and ambition I had; this empire in the end ex-
> plained my presence there in the valley, in the cottage, in the
> grounds of the manor. But we were – or had started – at opposite ends
> of wealth, privilege, and in the hearts of different cultures.
>
> (Naipaul 1987: 191)

The modifier 'or had started' is crucial, for the narrator is no longer the landlord's lackey. He does not work on the estate, as his ancestors had been obliged to do on the plantations; he is financially independent with a future more secure than the landlord's own. What draws him to the landlord, it seems, is a psychic – apparently neurotic – need to reenact the past, and to cast himself as an interested witness to the decline of a shared idea of Empire. The narrator's marginal position is not involuntary but *strategic*, allowing him both to play his minor role in a post-imperial drama and to recognise that drama as impossibly belated. One of the many paradoxes of *The Enigma of Arrival* is that it contrives to regenerate itself through the enactment of exhaustion. If in the end Naipaul's novel, Naipaul himself, are unable to liberate themselves from their potentially paralysing subject – British imperial history – they are still able to play that history back in different voices, in different locations, at different speeds. And if the narrator remains haunted by the spectre of his own death, as well as burdened by reminders of the mortality of those around him, he still survives to record the fluctuating rhythms of creation and decay in his environment; and to register the continuing fear of his insignificance in a repetitive, but also subtly displaced, theatrical idiom that uses the instability of the present to mock the permanence of the British imperial past. In its mock-pastoral setting, in which ancient monuments (the megaliths of Stonehenge) share space with fake 'historical' buildings (the false fronts of the manor), Naipaul's self-consciously anachronistic novel stands in ironic relation to its own historical contrivances. *The Enigma of Arrival* effectively upstages the history to which it claims to pay rich tribute; far from delivering an elegy to naturalised colonial hierarchies, Naipaul's novel effectively stages a worn-out pyschodrama of imperial imposture.

In *The Satanic Verses*, in contrast, staged marginality is brought right up to date, played out for the age of video, virtual reality, and instant entertainment. The theatricality of Rushdie's novel need hardly be stressed: its interlinked protagonists, Gibreel Farishta and Saladin Chamcha, are both extravagant performers, the former hamming it up in the type of Bombay religious movies known in the trade as 'theologicals', the latter in British radio shows where his gift for mimicry earns him the title of the 'Man of a Thousand Voices and a Voice' (Rushdie 1988: 60). Chamcha's particular claim to fame, however, is as the co-star of a grotesque TV sitcom, *The Aliens Show*. Here he plays the part of the extraterrestrial wannabe, Maxim Alien, who will change his hairstyle, his clothes, and even shed or grow a limb or two, in his unrelenting efforts to achieve his ambition of becoming a TV personality. Rushdie's description of the show emphasises the commodified hybridity which is characteristic of a novel that exhibits the metamorphic processes of intercultural fusion in a series of self-parodic commercial products:

> *The Aliens Show*, by *The Munsters* out of *Star Wars* by way of *Sesame Street* … was a situation comedy about a group of extraterrestrials ranging from cute to psycho, from animal to vegetable, and also mineral. … The stars of the show, its Kermit and Miss Piggy, were the very fashionable, slinkily attired, stunningly hairstyled duo, Maxim and Mamma Alien, who yearned to be – what else? – television personalities. They were played by Saladin Chamcha and Mimi

Mamoulian, and they changed their voices along with their clothes, to say nothing of their hair, which could go from purple to vermilion between shots, which could stand diagonally three feet up from their heads or vanish altogether; or their features and limbs, because they were capable of changing all of them, switching legs, arms, noses, ears, eyes, and every switch conjured up a different accent from their legendary, protean gullets.

(Rushdie 1988: 62)

The show, as might be suspected, attracts a good deal of criticism. It is seen at best as weird and at worst as politically reactionary, reinforcing in a society – Britain's – not known for its tolerance toward immigrants the idea of 'aliens' as freaks and as hopeless aspirants to mainstream culture. Saladin *aka* Maxim Alien is dubbed a 'brown Uncle Tom', brainwashed if not lobotomised by media images of white culture, and driven by a self-destructive need to assimilate into a society that despises him. (Ironically, Chamcha is later fired from the show on the grounds of his ethnicity. The 'deracialised' show is remodelled for export to the United States, where it promptly flops.) Chamcha, however, as his various transmutations indicate, is resistant to labels: he outruns his pursuers from both Right and Left, exchanging identities with the same facility as his television viewers switch channels. For Chamcha is aware from the outset of the provision-ality of self-construction; he knows that identities can be staged at different times for different audiences – and different goals. The aspiring immigrant, marginal to society's concerns, later metamorphoses into the racial villain. Chamcha mirrors the fears and prejudices of his mostly mainstream viewing public; at the same time, his shape-shifting shows the malleability of racial and cultural myths. Above all, he succeeds, to some extent at least, in outmanoeuvring polarising social constructions (white/black, mainstream/margin, inside/outside, and so on); he ends up needing his puritanically minded detractors much less than they need him.

Rushdie's deconstructive allegory of British cultural identity was always likely to win him enemies, if not necessarily in the way he had foreseen. For Saladin Chamcha, like the figure of the writer in *The Enigma of Arrival*, provides a catalyst for the dominant culture's self-disintegration. In Naipaul's novel, the dominant figure – the landlord – turns out in the end to be curiously marginal; while in Rushdie's, Gibreel-Saladin defy the logic of segregation, demonstrating at once the irremediably hybrid make-up of contemporary British society and the central role played in it by those who are usually seen as being on its margins.[8]

This reading of the novels is appealingly coherent; on closer inspec-tion, however, its celebratory rhetoric turns out to be suspiciously utopian.

In Rushdie's novel, as well as in Naipaul's, there is an impetus toward (physical) return and (psychic or spiritual) reconciliation that suggests, in Simon Gikandi's words, that it is 'condemned … to reinscribe the very normativities – nation and empire – that it seeks to negate' (Gikandi 1996: 208). Critical commentary on the novel has by and large concurred with Rushdie's own rationalisation of it as a celebration of 'hybridity, impurity, intermingling, the transformation that comes of new and unexpected combinations of human beings, cultures, ideas, politics, movies, songs' (Rushdie 1991b: 394). Homi Bhabha's essay 'How Newness Enters the World' (1994a) is characteristic in the mapping of this promiscuous hybrid aesthetic onto the transgressively liminal figure of the shape-shifting postcolonial migrant. Thus Chamcha, in Bhabha's reading, becomes:

> the discriminatory sign of a performative, projective sign of a British culture of race and racism – 'illegal immigrant, outlaw king, foul criminal or race hero' [Rushdie 1988: 288]. From somewhere between Ovid and Lucretius, or between gastronomic and demographic pluralisms, he confounds nativist and supremacist ascriptions of nation(alist) identities. This migrant movement of social identifications leads to the most devastating parody of Maggie Torture's Britain.
>
> (Bhabha 1994b: 228)[9]

Yet the deconstructive potential of the marginalised migrant figure to undermine the national(ist) ethos is itself arguably recuperated in a novel which self-consciously traffics in commodified images drawn from an identifiably postcolonial repertoire of intercultural hybridisation. Gikandi says it well again:

> Rushdie's work is self-consciously performative in its engagement with the cultural politics of postcoloniality, spaciously deploying many [postcolonial] tropes but also undermining [their] authority in its many self-referential moments. … *Migrancy, exile,* and *hybridity* have become stock terms in postcolonial literature. The originality of *The Satanic Verses* … lies in its jettisoning of [such] alternative terms. … The novel [thus] insists on being read as a set of irresolvable oxymorons.
>
> (Gikandi 1996: 208, 213)

Gikandi's reading of the novel as a 'metacommentary on the postcolonial condition' (Gikandi 1996: 213) permits another rephrasing of the by now familiar dialectic between 'postcolonialism' and 'postcoloniality' I have already sketched out in previous chapters (see, particularly, Introduction).

For it is not just that Chamcha's various postcolonial identities are ironically negotiated within the terms of metropolitan commodity-exchange (as in the various, often hilarious, instances in the novel of a conflation of commercialised images of intercultural fusion (e.g. Rushdie 1988: 405–6)), but that the discourse of *postcolonialism itself* is found to circulate as a commodity. This puts a rather different perspective on the staging of marginality in Rushdie's novel. On the one hand, as already argued, Chamcha's stereotypical ethnic performances might be seen as uncovering the racial fears and fantasies of his mainstream audience, and as opening up a space of postcolonial cross-cultural encounter within which the racial polarities that underscore the process of colonial subjectification might be outmanoeuvred and undermined. But on the other, the novel's numerous, self-consciously theatricalised parody-reversals of imperialist image-making are themselves contained and prescripted – they are bound, that is, by the commercial contract that governs late twentieth-century metropolitan consumer society. To put it rather less obliquely, Chamcha's allegedly disruptive transformations are still largely *programmed* – quite literally in the case of *The Aliens Show*. Within this context, Chamcha's gift for mimicry appears to function rather less as a sign of his capacity for subversive personal/cultural recodings, and rather more as a symptom of his subjection to a vast, metropolitan-based image-making industry – an industry that continues to manipulate his multiple cultural self-fashionings for its own financial ends.

It is tempting to read Chamcha's plight as a *mise en abyme* for Rushdie's irresolvably self-conflicted postcolonial novel. Certainly, Rushdie sets up a link in the novel between the overcoded language of mainstream metropolitan advertising and the 'neocolonial traffic in [marginal] cultural identity' (Spivak 1996: 239) in which postcolonial literatures are engaged and through which many of its texts have come, often in spite of themselves, to be appreciated and legitimised, commercially packaged, institutionally 'known'. Neither Rushdie nor, in a different context, Naipaul could be accused of not being alert, hypersensitive even, to the possibly compromising implications of their success in reaching out to a wider consumer public. (*The Enigma of Arrival*, after all, was a national bestseller, while *The Satanic Verses* went one better, becoming an international *cause célèbre*.) Elsewhere in their work, both writers had already shown themselves to be skilful negotiators, adept at manipulating the master codes of metropolitan economic dominance (see also Introduction). The exhibitionistic deployment of exoticist clichés in *Midnight's Children* is a case in point (see Chapter 2), as is the deliberately scandalising vocabulary of Naipaul's African stories, journalistic essays and novels. Are Rushdie's early works, in particular, cashing in on the durable exchange-value of a deliberately exoticised Orient? Is Naipaul's protracted sequence of catastrophist Third World parables telling reactionary First World audiences what he thinks they want to hear? Both charges have repeatedly been levelled and argued for with some conviction; but as I suggested in the last chapter, it perhaps makes more sense to speak of Rushdie's readers being mockingly exposed for their own exoticist predilections. And I would advance a similar argument for Naipaul's dangerously, at times derisively, primitivist representations of Black Africa and the Caribbean – this in spite of the fact that precisely the opposite case has more frequently, and by no means unconvincingly, been made.[10] Moreover, both writers use similarly double-edged tactics in their later, British-based novels. Marginality, it goes without saying, is a primary strategy of commodity culture, which thrives on the retailing of cultural products regarded as emanating from outside the mainstream. In *The Enigma of Arrival* and *The Satanic Verses*, Naipaul and Rushdie go some way toward upsetting this distinction – in part by showing their own ironically disruptive relation to British national culture, and in part by simulating the apparently collaborative but tacitly adversarial conditions under which marginal identities, as well as marginal products, are (self-) constructed, represented to others and collectively consumed.

It is at this stage of the argument that I wish to introduce a third player into the arena – Hanif Kureishi. Kureishi (whose allegedly voracious, but also ambiguous, sexuality had already been alluded to with typical indelicacy in *The Satanic Verses*, where he emerges as a cross between the priapic lawyer Hanif Johnson and the mysterious Ms Qureishi (Huggan and Wachinger 2001)) is best known for his provocative forays into the sexual and ethnic politics of 1970s/1980s 'multicultural' Britain. These forays, which have resulted in the novels *The Buddha of Suburbia* (1990), *The Black Album* (1995) and, more recently, the autobiographical *Intimacy* (1998), as well as the better-known screenplays for *My Beautiful Laundrette* (1986), *Sammy and Rosie Get Laid* (1988) and *London Kills Me* (1991), have helped earn Kureishi a carefully cultivated reputation as one of the *enfants terribles* of the contemporary British pop-art scene.

Certainly, Kureishi's work to date has capitalised on its capacity for fashionable provocation. And admittedly there is something of a staged quality to the – at times explosive – anger that circulates throughout Kureishi's screenplays and fictions; as if the controversial issues they discuss (institutionalised racism, sexual intolerance, class and generation conflict, the tyranny of authoritarian systems) were in the end to be seconded to a highly stylised, ultimately self-ingratiating narrative of mildly anti-social capers and sexual high jinks. Yet this view of Kureishi's work fails to account for the political dimensions of its own theatricality –

a politics that (like Rushdie's in *The Satanic Verses*) centres on the *performances* of Britain's embattled ethnic minorities and otherwise marginalised social groups. In all of Kureishi's work to date, minority cultures appear to exist in an antagonistic relationship with a white, mostly middle-class mainstream even as they are invited to provide it with a steady supply of self-indulgent 'ethnic' entertainment. Minorities are encouraged, in some cases obliged, to stage their racial/ethnic identities in keeping with white stereotypical perceptions of an exotic cultural other. Yet as Kureishi makes clear, such stagings can be seen on one level as parodies of white expectations and, on another, as demonstrations of the performative basis of all identity formation. One is immediately reminded here of Judith Butler's important work on the performativity of the gendered body, which 'has no ontological status apart from the various acts which constitute its reality' (Butler 1990: 136). For Butler, these acts 'are performative in the sense that the essence or identity that they otherwise purport to express are fabrications manufactured and sustained through corporeal signs and other discursive means' (136). Gender is thus 'always a doing, though not a doing by a subject who might be said to preexist the deed' (Butler 1990: 25). The gendered performances of Kureishi's homosexual, bisexual or sexually ambiguous characters – Karim Amir and Charlie Kay in *The Buddha of Suburbia*; Johnny and Omar in *My Beautiful Laundrette*; the lesbian lovers Rani and Vivia and the puckish cross-dresser Danny-Victoria in *Sammy and Rosie Get Laid* – all emphasise that identities are fashioned, rather than merely expressed, by corporeal activities, signs and functions; and that the queering of sexual identity is at once a reminder that 'the substantive effect[s] of gender [are] performatively produced and compelled by the regulatory practice of gender coherence' (Butler 1990: 24) and an indication that such 'regulatory practices', and the normative model of 'gender coherence' they serve to uphold, may yet be exposed and undermined.

Yet queer performativity, in Kureishi's work, is by no means restricted to the self-fashioning of sexual identity. Rather, Kureishi explores the possibilities inherent in various forms of staged marginality in which the displacement of identity onto the performative operates on the level of ethnicity, class and nationality, as well as that of gender.[11] Let me elaborate this argument here by briefly analysing a few examples, taken first from Kureishi's playfully satirical novel of sexually/culturally permissive Britain, *The Buddha of Suburbia*, then from his two more ostensibly political screenplays for Stephen Frears' movies, *My Beautiful Laundrette* and *Sammy and Rosie Get Laid*.

The Buddha of Suburbia, set mostly in London and its dreary southeastern suburbs, is suffused with the decadent atmosphere of post-emancipated 1970s Britain. Kureishi captures very well the contradictions of the decade: its often caustic combinations of conservative prudery and newfound sexual permissiveness; of inbred racism and self-congratulatory multicultural openness; of residual belief in the nurturing role of the traditional family and increased awareness of the anarchically hedonistic pleasures of individual experimentation. These contradictions are themselves embodied in Kureishi's colourful cast of characters: from the narcissistic, image-conscious adolescents on the make, Karim Amir and Charlie Kay (*aka* Charlie Hero), to Charlie's fashionably permissive New Age mother Eva, to Karim's cheerfully cynical Indian-born father (also Eva's lover), the eponymous buddha of suburbia. It is the latter whose guru-like antics dominate the first half of the novel, much to the delight of his credulous suburban audiences and the half-amused bewilderment of his son. As Karim reflects on one of these performances,

> He was certainly exotic, probably the only man in southern England at that moment (apart, possibly, from George Harrison) wearing a red and gold waistcoat and Indian pyjamas. He was also graceful, a front-room Nureyev beside the other pasty-faced Arbuckles with their tight drip-dry shirts glued to their guts and John Collier grey trousers with the crotch all sagging and creased. Perhaps Daddio really was a magician, having transformed himself by the bootlaces (as he put it) from being an Indian in the Civil Service who was always cleaning his teeth with Monkey Brand black toothpowder manufactured by Nogi & Co. of Bombay, into the wise adviser he now appeared to be. Sexy Sadie! Now he was the centre of the room. If they could see him in Whitehall!
>
> (Kureishi 1990: 31)

Haroon Amir (Karim's father) has arguably succeeded only in exchanging one form of mimicry for another; for as Karim muses, '[h]e'd spent years trying to be more of an Englishman, to be less risibly conspicuous, and now he was putting it back in spadeloads' (Kureishi 1990: 21). But as Karim comes to recognise, Haroon's act is a means of exposing, not so much his own insecurities, but rather the self-serving enthusiasms of his captive audience, for whom Eastern philosophising is little more than the latest temporary panacea to their own middle-class suburban boredom. Haroon's charlatanism can be seen to some extent as a retroactive New Age parody of the post-1960s commodification of Eastern spirituality, so devastatingly analysed elsewhere in Gita Mehta's wicked satire on Western bourgeois myths of a mystical India, *Karma Cola: Marketing the Mystic East* (1979) (see also Chapter 2). In *Karma Cola*, Mehta casts a withering gaze on all those latter-day 'casualties of spiritual tourism [who have confused] the profound with the banal in their attempts to levitate above reality' (G. Mehta 1979: x). 'The trick to becoming a successful guru', says Mehta archly, 'is to be an Indian, but to surround yourself with increasing numbers of non-Indians' (G. Mehta 1979: 37–8). Which is of course what Haroon does, with the added twist that he is a naturalised *Englishman*, whose rediscovery of his 'ethnic roots' is part of an ultimately self-defeating effort to show others the hollowness of their provincial lives – a life he himself leads, and whose self-centred materialist values he shares. Haroon's 'transformations', like Saladin Chamcha's in *The Satanic Verses*, are thus something of a double-edged weapon, exposing the fraudulence of his middlebrow suburban public, whose feeble efforts to appear sophisticated merely accentuate their own provincialism, but at the same time advertising his own complicity with the larger consumer society (and its niche-marketed cottage-industries in ethnic fashion, international decor, world music, and so on) that sparks their competitive material curiosities while also profiting from their ephemeral spiritual needs.

Karim himself is later drawn into a similar vicious circle when he is offered the opportunity, this time in suburban north London, to play the elephant-riding Indian boy-hero Mowgli in a putatively avant-garde stage-adaptation of Kipling's juvenile classic *The Jungle Book*. The opening exchange between Karim and the play's self-professed anti-racist director, Jeremy Shadwell, is instructive, not to mention hilarious, in revealing stereotypical metropolitan expectations of an unsullied 'native authenticity'. Karim grudgingly accepts the part, only to discover to his horror that his costume for Shadwell's supposedly revisionist version of the play is a loin-cloth and brown make-up. But there is worse to come. After the first few stuttering rehearsals, Shadwell takes his inexperienced lead-actor aside:

'A word about the accent, Karim. I think it should be an authentic accent.'

'What d'you mean authentic?'

'Where was our Mowgli born?'

'India.'

'Yes. Not Orpington [Karim's birthplace]. What accent do they have in India?'

'Indian accents.'

'Ten out of ten.'

'No, Jeremy. Please, no.'

'Karim, you have been cast for authenticity and not for experience.'

(Kureishi 1990: 147)

Equipped with requisite singsong accent and primitive wild-boy costume, Karim is coerced into performing an 'authentic' racial/ethnic identity that was never his in the first place.[12] But as his subsequent stage-performances show, the semiotic markers of staged ethnicity (accent, gesture, dress, etc.) can be twisted to reveal the prejudices of those who require them. Hence his deliberately provocative impersonation of his eccentric uncle Anwar; or, more pointed still, his self-indulgently caricatural portrayal of the put-upon Indian immigrant, which effectively sabotages the would-be radicalism of a socialist 'firebrand' drama designed to highlight racial injustice, and to launch a series of 'flame-throwing attacks on [the] pusillanimous Labour governments' (Kureishi 1990: 220) that have failed to address, still less to cure, the country's ills. While Karim's antics are dismissed by some – including some of his own closest friends and family members – as a pernicious study in abjection, their more usual effect is to mirror the desires and fears of those who seek to control his volatile self-image. One of these fears is that 'Englishness', like 'Indianness', might be an inherently unstable entity; that national identities might be reinvented, and identity itself continually reper-formed.[13] As Karim's long-suffering English mother reminds him after one performance,

'[Y]ou're not an Indian. You've never been to India. You'd get diar-rhoea the moment you stepped off that plane, I know you would.'

'Why don't you say it a bit louder,' I said. 'Aren't I part Indian?'

'What about me?' Mum said. 'Who gave birth to you? You're an Englishman, I'm glad to say.'

'I don't care,' I said. 'I'm an actor. It's a job.'

'Don't say that,' she said. 'Be what you are.'

(Kureishi 1990: 232)

But what Karim 'is' is what he makes of himself or, rather, of the roles that are foisted upon him – roles that are less demeaning to the actor who performs them than upsetting to those who see their own identities as given, their origins as binding, their politics as correct. The queering of identity in Kureishi's novel thus punctures the illusions and undercuts the false assertiveness of those who see their positions in society as easily distinguishable and their worldviews as more or less fixed. But it also draws attention to the commodity-function of apparently oppositional – what the urban theorist Dick Hebdige might call 'subcultural' – identitary categories, in which style and image become inseparable from the social identity of their consumers, and fashionable possessions become a paradoxical marker of enlightened (meaning mostly in the novel anti-establishment) political views.[14] A further irony is that the novel's protagonists never really escape from their condition of continually restaged marginality. Touring in New York, Karim and his trendy London-based colleagues play the role of English provincials all over again, 'resentfully afraid of capitalist contamination' (Kureishi 1990: 243) even as they envy the bright lights and boundless hedonism of a city that makes 'decadent' London seem merely staid. In this sense, Kureishi's novel, like Rushdie's, fails to clear a space for its nominally transgressive energies, arguably falling back instead on a reinscription of the manufac-tured cultural hierarchies, dictated largely by the fashions of the moment, that its ebullient performances of queer identity – sexual, ethnic, sociopolitical, national – had done their best to demystify, expose to ridicule and undo. Perhaps it is appropriate, then, that Karim's last role is in a shoddy, if financially viable, British soap opera; for in his acting career to date, he has been nothing if not a prisoner to repetition. But then again, as his brother, who is the first to congratulate him, tells him in what might well pass for the novel's ambivalent motto, 'We can't pretend we're some kind of shitted-on oppressed people. Let's just make the best of ourselves' (Kureishi 1990: 268). And maybe Karim, always the performer, will.

In *The Buddha of Suburbia*, the space of performance, shifting from one margin to another, repeatedly destabilises the controlling narratives that define ideas of 'centre'. This destabilising process is also apparent in Kureishi's screenplays for Stephen Frears' films, *My Beautiful Laundrette* and *Sammy and Rosie Get Laid*, both of which have been read as transparent attacks on the imperialist ethos of Thatcher's Britain and as more obliquely self-ironic exposures of the various fictions of solidarity that underlie the formation of that fiction of fictions – a uniform national subject.[15] Unsurprisingly, most commentators have tended to see Kureishi's sympathies as lying with the underdog (and not just the *racial* underdog, for several of the oppressed urban poor in *My Beautiful Laundrette*, like the evicted squatters in *Sammy and Rosie*, are white). But such is the indeterminate subjectivity of both films – the contradictoriness of their characters, their unresolved ethical dilemmas, their wryly tragicomic representation of conflicted histories and divided allegiances – that they end up striking an ironic attitude to their own (imagined?) radicalism.[16] Radhika Mohanram, among others, still insists on reading the films, particularly *My Beautiful Laundrette*, as subversively queer national allegories in which 'the foreclosure of homosexuality … causes it to function as nationalism's Other, thereby providing the nation with its identity through opposition' (Mohanram 1995: 126). Yet both films (especially *Sammy and Rosie*) appear to question, even mock, the assumption that homosexuality is inevitably subversive, or that its association with 'illicit' interracial desire provides the catalyst for a coalition of marginalised social groups. Much as in his novels, Kureishi's complex, at times debunking, treatment of identity politics seems to compromise the very forms of oppositional behaviour (gay/lesbian defiance, ethnic-minority solidarity, crusading anti-imperialism) it persistently invokes. Also as in the novels, the films display a rampant, sexually rapacious individualism that tends to cut across group alliances: contradicting the unifying rhetoric of supposedly collective causes (Salim and Nasser's pledged support for 'their [Pakistani] people'); turning revolutionary credos into alibis for autocracy (Rafi's decolonised Pakistan); using social unrest and the apparent breakdown of moral order as ideological justifications for a promiscuous lifestyle based on little more than the search for physical self-gratification (Sammy and Rosie's riot-torn London).

What space is left in the films, then, for a productive staging of marginality that might not only unmask dominant structures of power but also pose a social alternative to them? Two heavily stylised sites – less utopian than heterotopian (Foucault 1986)[17] – immediately come to mind here: the laundrette (in *My Beautiful Laundrette*) and the derelict patch of ground briefly occupied by the New Age travellers (in *Sammy and Rosie*). Both of these are presented, significantly, as spaces of surreal performance in which marginal communities temporarily assemble, only to be crudely dispersed. The laundrette scenes in *My Beautiful Laundrette* might be read on one level as an allegorical variant on Bakhtinian carnivalisation – as an extravagantly comic overturning of the anti-immigrant 'whitification' policies of the Thatcher decades.[18] (As usual, Kureishi takes the idea and plays it to its preposterous limits: Omar, the Pakistani-British caretaker of the laundrette, is nicknamed 'Omo' – a playful reference not just to his sexual orientation but also to the well-known brand of soap-powder.) In such a reading, the renovated laundrette becomes a classless space of intercultural celebration, in defiance of the racial battles fought almost daily outside its windows. But it is also, equally, a space of surrealistic excess: in one nocturnal scene, a black couple dance dreamily, 'holding each other … as they are waiting for their washing' (Kureishi 1986: 52); in another, a white man sings along to an aria from (naturally) *Madama Butterfly* blaring from the laundrette's stereo system; in still another, a man reaches inside a washing-machine and pulls out a supply of freshly washed prawns. It is only a matter of time, of course, before this urban idyll is shattered – literally, when after a vicious fight involving Omar's white lover Johnny, his crooked cousin Salim and a gang of neo-Nazi loafers, one of these latter throws a bin (in the original screenplay, a lump of wood) through the laundrette window, showering its customers with broken glass. As so often in Kureishi's work, conflicting realities in the 'outside world' break in on, and effectively destroy, a space of communitarian illusion (even if, in this case, the laundrette arguably retains its capacity to offer private pleasure and, as in the final sequence, to harbour the 'forbidden' homosexual/interracial desire that is fore-grounded elsewhere in the film).

In *Sammy and Rosie*, similarly, the waste-ground where the New Age travellers have taken up temporary residence is eventually claimed by greedy property developers, and in one of the film's culminating scenes, the bulldozers move in as the travellers, anarchic to the last, make their triumphantly chaotic exit. The travellers, seen intermittently in a variety of guises and locations (e.g. as buskers in the London underground), represent a kind of floating signifier within the structural economy of Frears'/Kureishi's film. Their marginality to society's concerns is reiterated in a number of exaggeratedly theatricalised contexts; and yet in their way they are central to the film, providing the forum for some of its most dramatic sequences (the tryst between Danny and Rosie, the unmasking of Rafi, the final eviction), as well as an intimation of an alternative social order based on loosely communitarian principles, sexual freedom, and an open contempt for fixed standards of conduct, bourgeois property values and government rules. In a sequence that enlarges on the earlier, madcap laundrette scenes in *My Beautiful Laundrette*, Danny, *de facto* leader of the travellers, guides Rafi through the strange labyrinthine world – more Fellini than Virgil – of the London Underground. Kureishi's stage directions read as follows:

> In the tunnel [a] straggly band of musicians are playing. … They play the theme song of the movie – there are trumpeters, saxophonists, a hurdy-gurdy player, bassoon groovers, etc. Rappers. … As DANNY and RAFI walk past, everyone in the band says simultaneously, 'Wotcha, Danny boy.' DANNY nods regally. Also, a couple of girls and boys are dancing to the music. If we could film them from the

front for a moment, we could easily see for a second, the whole tube
tunnel dancing, like in a Cliff Richard film.

(Kureishi 1986: 19)

This scene is later counterpointed when Danny and Rosie are serenaded
by a 'straggly band outside [Danny's] caravan dancing in celebration of
joyful love-making all over London' (Kureishi 1986: 44). The carnival
atmosphere (replete with a high-camp parody of straight fancy dress)
holds the routinised race/class warfare of the city momentarily at bay,
allowing for a riotous union reinforced by the split-screen image of three
energetically fornicating interracial couples – Rafi and Alice, Sammy and
Anna, with Danny and Rosie given pride of place in the central frame.
Danny, the 'marginal' figure, is thus once again placed at the centre in a
performance that highlights the film's mockery of the sanctioned
demarcation of social roles.

Yet perhaps not too much should be made of Danny's attractively
indeterminate qualities, of his trickster-like capacity to subvert fixed
identitary categories by playing seemingly contradictory roles: amiable
stud and would-be drag-queen; clueless drifter and underclass rebel;
politicised black subject and innocent object of white desire; or, in short,
in Gayatri Spivak's memorably tongue-in-cheek phrase, 'the nicest all-
around hybrid you could wish for' (Spivak 1993c: 253). Nor, it appears,
should too much be made of the film's apparently transgressive spatial
dynamics, of the systematic way in which it brings the cordoned-off spaces
that protect bourgeois values, or that separate one imagined community
from another, into jarring contact. For the question remains moot as to
the extent to which a film whose characters talk obsessively about
politics can itself be construed as political. Certainly, Frears' film (in
tension, perhaps, with Kureishi's screenplay) *tries* to be political. Frears
himself is in little doubt, declaring in an interview that the film is 'overt
in its attempt to rally the troops' (Friedman and Stewart 1992: 226). But
which troops? And for which cause? While the film's anti-Thatcherite
rhetoric may be glaringly obvious, even counterdemagogic in its intensity,
its playful intermingling of documentary and surrealistic cross-cutting
techniques arguably has a distancing, derealising effect. As Leonard Quart
argues in an astute review, *Sammy and Rosie* seems more than slightly
disabused of its own radicalising tendencies. No-one is left unscathed;
instead, a ubiquitous 'politics of irony' entraps the movie's characters,
revealing their hypocrisies, their designs on power, and their self-serving
'radical chic' (Quart 1992). Meanwhile, even the race-riots with which
the movie opens are ironic displacements of *cinéma vérité*, with '[t]he
rioters themselves enact[ing] Keystone Cop routines with the London

police and pos[ing] for photographs while burning cars blaze around them' (Quart 1992: 226). As Quart concludes provocatively, '[n]one of the rioting seems to be truly serious – a great deal of posturing and performing with little political design or effect' (Quart 1992: 226).

A similar conclusion might be reached about much of Kureishi's work to date, arousing the suspicion that sexual narcissism might be the ultimately self-defeating outlet for an intense frustration with the *lack* of social change in late twentieth-century, 'multicultural' Britain.[19] As in *The Satanic Verses*, there is a sense of limited options: political struggles, however viable, are susceptible to recuperation; alternative spaces for social interaction are opened up, only in the end to be foreclosed; the creative possibilities offered by different forms of intercultural fusion are found to operate, to some extent at least, as decoys for the maintenance of a socially divisive *status quo*. It is interesting in this context to reflect again on the doubleness of staged marginality, and on the ambivalences inscribed within what we might call a postcolonial politics of performance. On the one hand, performative models of identity formation and reconstruction allow for a creative reconceptualisation of national culture based on syncretic fusion, interethnic mixture and a continual shifting of personal and sociocultural alliances. To see the different aspects of identity – sexual, ethnic/racial, national, sociopolitical – as elements of a wider cultural performance permits an understanding of marginality in terms other than those of social disadvantage and exclusion. Marginality becomes, instead, a self-empowering strategy within minority discourse, which Homi Bhabha (with characteristic optimism) has seen as setting:

> the act of emergence in the antagonistic *in-between* of image and sign, the accumulative and the adjunct, presence and proxy. It [minority discourse] contests genealogies of 'origin' that lead to claims for cultural supremacy and historical priority. Minority discourse acknowledges the status of national culture – and the people – as a contentious, performative space of the perplexity of the living in the midst of the pedagogical representations of the fullness of life.
>
> (Bhabha 1994a: 157, Bhabha's italics)

Then again, it seems unlikely that the developers who ordered in the demolition crew in *Sammy and Rosie* would care to appreciate the theoretical niceties and rhetorical intricacies of Bhabha's rarefied academic prose. The New Age travellers in Frears'/Kureishi's movie play a performative role that is in many ways quite similar to the syncretic model set up here by Bhabha: they dramatise their marginal status, that is, in ways that not only unveil oppressive power-structures but also subtly displace the identitary categories, and the underlying ideological rationale, that serve to justify such structures, allowing those in power to implement their goals. On another level, though, the issue of the travellers' social marginality – however self-conferred – remains unresolved. As the bulldozers surge in, the disembodied voice of Thatcher booms out over a patriotic musical backdrop; there is an ironic sense in which, as in *The Satanic Verses*, 'Maggie Torture's' Britain wins. The staging of marginality in such a context may become little more than a reconfirmation of relative powerlessness – a sober note on which to end, but one which challenges increasingly conventionalised readings of Kureishi's and, especially, Rushdie's work as positing joyously hybrid alternatives to a bleakly neo-imperialist *realpolitik*. I persist, somewhat glumly no doubt, in the view of both as deeply pessimistic writers, for all their verbal brio, their comic disruption of authority, and the passionately anti-imperialist rhetoric of their critical essays (for good examples, see Kureishi's 'The Rainbow Sign' (1986) and Rushdie's 'The New Empire within Britain' (1991f)). For perhaps, in the end, it is in the frenzied self-indulgence of a novel like *The Satanic Verses* or a film like *Sammy and Rosie*, rather than in the muted self-irony of a novel like *The Enigma of Arrival*, that a postcolonial politics of performance might best be placed to confront its own ideological contradictions; and that a postcolonial theory of cultural hybridity might best be able to consider its own practical limits.

4 Prizing otherness
A short history of the Booker

> The [Booker] Prize has become a British institution, rather like Derby Day.
> (*The Economist*)

> We had the cash; we came home; what were we to do?
> (Sir Michael Caine, former Chairman of Booker plc)

Introduction

Literary prizes have existed in one form or another for many centuries. In former times, literary prizes were frequently bestowed by rulers, monarchs and other powerful individual patrons who cannily deployed them for the double purpose of proving their munificence while reconfirming the loyalty of their subjects (Winegarten 1994). Such reciprocal ties of patronage, while by no means unknown today, have become increasingly uncommon. Literary prizes as we know them now are best seen as a phenomenon of the late nineteenth and twentieth centuries: as reflections of shifting patterns of patronage, with an increasing emphasis on public sponsorship, and, above all, as signs of the dominant role played by international industry as a legitimising agent for literature and the other arts. In a global cultural economy controlled by huge multinational companies, the corporate sponsorship of the arts has become an indisputable fact. The corporate prize, like the endowed Chair, is a 'gift' that brings publicity to the company while functioning as a symbolic marker of its authorising power. As state subsidies of the arts have dwindled, alarmingly in many countries, corporate sponsors have emerged to dominate the literary/artistic scene. Corporate sponsorship has largely overtaken the earlier, predominantly hierarchical systems of private and public patronage through which ideas of literature and literary value were upheld (Bourdieu 1993). The evaluative criteria for corporate sponsorship vary widely; it would clearly be misguided to see it as a uniform 'regime'

(Appadurai 1986; see also Introduction). A structural analysis of types of sponsorship patterns – types of award, funding requirements, social and ideological factors, and so on – risks underestimating the historical trajectory that each particular sponsoring agency takes. This is no less the case with agencies operating across geopolitical boundaries: for example, international literary awards bestowed by globally active companies. Such awards, it could be argued, have emerged, many of them in the later twentieth century, as a response to the globalisation of – especially English-language – literature (Todd 1996). This view overlooks, however, the continuing asymmetries of power that are attendant on the production and consumption of world literature in English. Hence Bernth Lindfors' provocative suggestion that the most famous of all international literary awards, the Nobel, established in 1901, has had a distinctly Eurocentric bias since its inception (Lindfors 1988: 222).[1] The same might be said for more recent, and more obviously corporate, awards like the Booker. As Hugh Eakin has suggested, the Booker, despite its 'multicultural consciousness', has arguably done less to further the development of 'non-Western' and/or postcolonial literatures than it has to 'encourage the commerce of an "exotic" commodity catered to the Western literary market' (Eakin 1995: 1). In this chapter, I shall examine Eakin's proposition further by inquiring into the history of, and histories *behind*, the Booker Prize.

Two cheers for Booker: the emergence of a literary patron

> Wuk, nuttin bu wuk
> Maan noon an night nuttin bu wuk
> Booker own me patacake
> Booker own me pickni.
> Pain, nuttin bu pain
> Waan million tous'ne acre cane
> (David Dabydeen, 'Song of the Creole Gang Women')

In David Dabydeen's poem 'Song of the Creole Gang Women' (1994), Booker features as a cruel plantation-owner, ruthlessly preying upon his disempowered female workforce. A footnote to the poem reads, simply enough: '*Booker*: British sugar company that owned Guyana'. Booker, it would appear, has a history in contradiction with its current reputation as a postcolonial literary patron. Not surprisingly, Booker plc, formerly the Booker McConnell company – a leading multinational agribusiness conglomerate employing over 20,000 people and generating annual revenue in excess of $5 billion (Todd 1996: 63) – has been eager to downplay its nineteenth-century colonial past. But as Hugh Eakin notes with requisite irony, the Booker judges' 'recognition of postcolonial authors carries the dubious tincture of the company's history' (Eakin 1995: 2). The company, initially formed in 1834 to provide distributional services on the sugar-estates of Demerara (now Guyana), achieved rapid prosperity under a harsh colonial regime. At the onset of independence the company was relocated to London, which remains its headquarters today. It was in London in the early 1960s that it established its book division, primarily designed to buy up copyrights of famous popular-fiction writers (Agatha Christie, Ian Fleming, etc.). This proved a lucrative enterprise, prompting the company a few years later to found the Booker Prize for literature in English. Sponsored by Booker plc but administered since 1971 by the charitable concern the Book Trust (formerly the National Book League), the Prize, first awarded to P.H. Newby (*Something to Answer For*) in 1969, soon grew into one of Britain's most recognisable cultural institutions.

The history of the Prize itself is no less conflicted than its donor's past. As Tom Maschler has suggested, the Prize took its inspiration from the then better-known French Prix Goncourt – a hierarchy since arguably reversed, with *Le Figaro* describing the Goncourt as the 'French Booker' (Maschler 1998). Originally established as a £5,000 award to the best full-length English-language novel of the year, the Prize grew both monetarily and, exponentially, in prestige. Widely regarded today as one of the world's top literary prizes, the Booker has acquired and cultivated a mythology of its own. Much of this has to do, of course, with careful media management. Newspaper coverage was solicited, and granted, from the beginning; but probably the crucial step was taken in 1981, when the Prize's final award-ceremony was first televised on BBC. Currently broadcast on Britain's culturally oriented Channel Four, the ceremony and the lavish gala dinner that accompanies it have become the subject of endless anecdotes; television, as Hermione Lee wearily suggests, has 'ensured that Booker [will] forever be identified by the word "razzmattaz"', playing up to its vulgar Miss World aspect and fixing in the British eye a peculiar view of writers as dinner-jacketed gormandisers' (*The Times*, 21 September 1993: VII). Sir Michael Caine, former Chairman of Booker plc as well as of the Prize Management Committee, is equally wry in noting the costs involved in attracting such high-level publicity:

At first, the Management Committee organised both the award procedures and the ceremony. Gradually, the ceremony and its form became a wholly Booker matter. The costs bear this out. In the beginning, the selection process and the prize were 70% of the costs and the ceremony 30%. Over the years, these proportions have been reversed.

(Caine 1998: 9; see also Appendix for details on the management of the Prize)

The Booker, now more than ever, is a meticulously staged media event; it succeeds seemingly effortlessly in drawing attention to its bombastic televised finale and, no less, to the inevitable wrangling that accompanies its 'controversial' run-up debate. The timelag between the announcement of the shortlist and the declaration of the winner successfully generates suspense while maximising commercial appeal (Todd 1996).[2] Even the betting shops do good business (although ironically the only odds-on candidate, Salman Rushdie at 4/5 on for *The Moor's Last Sigh* (1995), failed to win (Todd 1996: 74)). Prizewinners and, often, finalists are guaranteed commercial success: sales of Booker prizewinning novels have historically increased by three- or fourfold; large advances are distinctly possible for the successful authors' subsequent books; TV and film rights beckon, as for, most recently, Michael Ondaatje, the film-version of whose novel *The English Patient*, a co-winner in 1992, has collected several prizes of its own. Such is the Booker's impact on the economies of the book trade that authors, in league with publishers, carefully time the appearance of their books.[3] All in all, there can be little doubt that the Booker, more than any other literary prize in recent history, has blazed a trail in the commercialisation of English-language literature (Todd 1996). As the stakes get ever higher, the Prize exerts a major influence over the cultural perceptions, as well as the reading habits, of its consumer public (Eakin 1995). As Merritt Moseley says, surveying the scene from the other side of the Atlantic with mock-astonishment, 'The Booker Prize exercises an influence on the publishing world – and more surprisingly, on the minds and enthusiasms of people well outside that world – which is by American standards impossible' (Moseley 1993: 613). Controversy, manufactured or not, continues to stalk the Booker. The commercial puffery and media hoopla have reached, for some, unacceptable levels; and while the Prize has been acknowledged as a 'wonderful marketing idea' (Moseley 1993: 613), it has also been seen more sourly as 'writing and commerce … blatantly put together' (*The Economist*, 20–6 October 1990: 114). Some critics of the Prize have claimed that its 'media-circus aspect interferes with the exercise of sound critical judgment' (*The Economist*, 21–7 October 1989: 101); others have accused the judges of nepotism, chauvinism, or petty squabbling; still others have seen the authors as angling for a prize or pandering to a commercial public. Individual selections have been singled out by the media as 'catastrophic' (Keri Hulme's Maori novel *The Bone People*, a controversial winner in 1985, appears to be the favourite here, despite its critical acclaim and its relative commercial success, especially in Australasia); while individual authors have been lambasted for 'obscurity' (Hulme again) or 'obscenity' (particularly the Scottish writer James Kelman, whose expletive-filled 1994 winner, *How Late It Was, How Late*, attracted reviews that spluttered with sanctimonious wrath). The gala dinner, meanwhile, has been tainted by incendiary speeches and spoilt-boy tantrums. In the former category we might place John Berger, who, upon being awarded the Prize in 1972 for his 'scandalous' experimental novel G, proceeded to cause further scandal by donating half his prize-money to the militant Black Panther movement: on the grounds, as he said in his acceptance speech – swiftly covered up as an 'embarrassment' (Goff 1989) – that 'they resist, both as black people and workers, the further exploitation of the oppressed; and because they have links with the struggle in Guyana, the seat of Booker McConnell's wealth – the struggle whose aim is to appropriate all such enterprises' (*The Times*, 21 September 1993: VII). The latter category might include Salman Rushdie, worthy winner in 1981 for *Midnight's Children*, but not-so-gracious runner-up two years later for the heavily favoured *Shame*. (The story goes that Rushdie thumped the table in rage at losing, declaring to anyone within earshot that J.M. Coetzee's *Life & Times of Michael K*, which had beaten him to the line, was a 'shitty winner' (Goff 1989).) Such criticisms might be seen as having a primarily anecdotal value, merely adding to the commercial overkill of a media-inflated event. A more serious criticism, however, concerns the highly ambivalent status of the Prize and its donor company as legitimising agents for global English-language fiction. A word is needed here, then, on criteria for eligibility, and on the implications of a perceived shift from 'English literature' to English-language literature 'published in Britain' (Todd 1996).

In his book *Consuming Fictions* (1996), Richard Todd suggests that the Booker Prize, particularly in the last two decades, has played a vital role in raising consciousness of the global dimensions of English-language fiction:

> [The] unprecedented exposure of fiction from English-speaking countries other than the United Kingdom or the United States led to an increasingly global picture of fiction in Britain during the course of the 1980s. It is now the case that the line-up of half or more of a typical late 1980s or 1990s Booker shortlist is not centred on Britain. This reflects a new public awareness of Britain as a pluralist society,

and has transformed the view that prevailed in the 1960s, that English-language fiction from 'abroad' meant fiction from the United
States.

(Todd 1996: 83)

For Todd, this global picture is postcolonial in perspective, replacing
earlier, now clearly anachronistic views of a Commonwealth of literary
nations.[4] Pico Iyer, in a high-profile 1993 article in *Time*, underscores the
postcolonial consciousness that is apparently endorsed by internationally
minded prizes like the Booker. Like Todd, Iyer sees Salman Rushdie's
Midnight's Children (1981) as a watershed novel, a major catalysing force
behind the emergence of a postcolonial literary era (see also Chapter 2).
The Prize, since Rushdie won it, has gone to:

> two Australians, a part Maori, a South African, a woman of Polish
> descent, and an exile from Japan. Runners-up have featured such
> redoubtably English names as Mo and Mistry and Achebe; when a
> traditional English name takes the prize – A.S. Byatt, say, or Kingsley
> Amis – it seems almost anomalous.
>
> (Iyer 1993: 46)

Tongue only partly in cheek, Iyer sees this international cast of characters
as 'writing back' to a literary Empire whose centre can obviously no longer
hold. A new 'frontierless' writing has emerged to challenge Britain's
insularity, and to interrogate the glib nostalgia with which it clings to its
imperial past. 'Postcolonial', for Iyer, is the codeword for these transnational operations: it describes both the impetus toward anti-imperial
struggle and the celebration of a cultural pluralism that cannot be
contained within national boundaries (Huggan 1994b: 24). This usage of
'postcolonial' is strategically malleable, conflating patterns of commodified eclecticism and multicultural cachet. What Iyer fails to account for is
the possibility that prizes like the Booker might work to *contain* cultural
(self-)critique by endorsing the commodification of a glamorised cultural
difference. Even Todd's more sophisticated treatment, while noting
assimilationist tendencies, does not acknowledge the ironies behind his
own phrase 'fiction published in Britain' (Todd 1996: 83). The postcolonial dynamic, for Todd, involves a process of pluralist rejuvenation
whereby the English language and, by extension, English-language fiction
are recognised as a 'shared cultural fund' (Todd 1996: 83). This view,
ostensibly liberal, avoids confronting structural differences in conditions
of literary production and consumption across the English-speaking
world.[5] In Africa, for example, English-language publishing is severely

hindered, not only by a lack of funding and a weak commercial infrastructure but by a foreign-held monopoly over English-language books. The English language might be 'shared', but access to English-language literature is channelled through foreign markets, not least through the agency of the British-based Heinemann African Writers Series (see Chapter 1, section three).

Booker plc's supportive role can thus be seen within the wider context of a symbolic legitimation of 'multicultural' and/or exotically 'foreign' goods. The discursive link is provided here by exoticist objectification, as English-language literature splinters into a variety of commercially viable 'othered' forms. This fetishisation of cultural otherness risks merely reduplicating the authority of the assimilationist paradigms (e.g. Commonwealth Literature) that such multicultural writing apparently seeks to replace.[6] The Booker might be seen, in any case, despite Todd's charitable disclaimers, as remaining bound to an Anglocentric discourse of benevolent paternalism. Eligibility for the Prize has historically been organised around Commonwealth literary principles, with Commonwealth nationals, plus Pakistani, Irish and (now readmitted to the Commonwealth) South African writers entitled to win the spoils. Most of the judges, however, and crucially, the *seat* of judgement remain British, thereby reinforcing the earlier, now largely discredited view that far-flung Commonwealth fictions should be referred for validation back to the 'parent [British] stock' (Walsh 1970). In this light, Todd's view of the Booker Prize as endorsing *British* cultural pluralism seems ironically appropriate. All the more so when individual authors and their prizewinning novels are considered; for while the judges have certainly striven to maintain a healthy critical balance, prompting sceptics such as Hugh Eakin to wonder whether the Prize might not be 'some form or other of affirmative action for marginal literatures' (Eakin 1995: 6), there is still a residual conservatism playing about the Booker's edges – a conservatism brought out in approaches to the prizewinning novels' themes. One such theme, sometimes considered to be a gauge of the Booker's postcolonial leanings, is *revisionist history*. More than half of the prizewinning novels to date investigate aspects of, primarily colonial, history or present a counter-memory to the official historical record.[7] In the next section of this chapter I shall explore some of the implications of these historical representations, focusing on four prizewinning novels whose subject is, at least in part, colonial India. These novels, in chronological order, are J.G. Farrell's *The Siege of Krishnapur* (1973); Ruth Prawer Jhabvala's *Heat and Dust* (1975); Paul Scott's *Staying On* (1977); and, more recently, Michael Ondaatje's *The English Patient* (1992).[8] Having traced the ambivalent history of the Booker Prize and its wealthy corporate sponsor, it is now time to inquire into the role of history in the works its judges favour.

Revision and revival: Booker versions of the Raj (and after)

> Anyone who has switched on the television set, been to the cinema or entered a bookshop in the last few months will be aware that that the British Raj, after three and a half decades in retirement, has been making a sort of comeback.
>
> (Salman Rushdie, 'Outside the Whale')

In his polemical essay 'Outside the Whale' (originally published in 1984), Salman Rushdie locates a 'revisionist enterprise' at the heart of Thatcher's Britain, the aim of which is the 'refurbishment of the Empire's tarnished image' (Rushdie 1991e: 91). Included in this enterprise are various commodified vehicles of Raj nostalgia, from literary bestsellers like Paul Scott's *Raj Quartet* to popular TV serials like *The Far Pavilions* to blockbuster films like Richard Attenborough's *Gandhi* and David Lean's adaptation of *A Passage to India*. Rushdie gives short shrift to products like these, obviously designed for their wide appeal on the commercial market, accusing them of being little more than 'artistic counterparts to the rise of conservative ideologies in modern Britain' (Rushdie 1991e: 92). Rushdie's argument, in the nature of polemics, is boisterously hyperbolic, tarring works of varying quality with the same broadsweeping brush. Nonetheless, his essay serves a useful purpose in drawing attention to the reactionary implications of some contemporary revisionist narratives seeking to rework imperial themes. Historical fictions such as Scott's, while ostensibly debunking imperial glories, might still be seen as peddling commercially profitable imperial myths. And one of those myths, as Rushdie points out, is that the history of the end of the Raj can be reduced to a summation of 'the doings of the officer class and its wife' (Rushdie 1991e: 90):

> Indians [in *The Raj Quartet*] get walk-ons, but remain, for the most part, bit-players in their own history. Once this form has been set, it scarcely matters that individual fictional Brits get unsympathetic treatment from their author. The form insists that *they are the ones whose stories matter*, and that is so much less than the whole truth that it must be called a falsehood.
>
> (Rushdie 1991e: 90, Rushdie's italics)

For Rushdie, Scott's *revisionist* critique of the late history of imperial India masks a *revivalist* ideology – one which tacitly rehearses imperialist myth-making even as it transforms the Empire into a helpless witness of its own decline.[9] This view, while debatable, certainly helps cast a critical perspective on three Booker prizewinning novels that deal with a British view of (post)colonial India. One of these is Scott's *Staying On* (1977), often seen as a coda to *The Raj Quartet* – an ironic swansong both to the Empire, memorialised by its ageing servants, and to Scott's own literary career (while writing the novel he was ill with cancer, and he died not long after receiving the Prize). The others are by J.G. Farrell, whose tragicomic Mutiny narrative, *The Siege of Krishnapur*, turned out a winner in 1973; and by the Polish-born Ruth Prawer Jhabvala, whose multi-layered novel *Heat and Dust*, awarded the Prize in 1975, reconstructs the story of a colonial misalliance, only to find itself condemned to repeat it. In each of these novels, the interplay between revision and revival is given subtly ironic treatment, both on the level of historical representation (Rushdie's 'Raj revivalism') and on the level of literary reinterpretation (Brontë, Kipling and, especially, Forster).

These two levels – the historical and the literary – are inextricably interconnected. As Judie Newman shows in her book *The Ballistic Bard* (1995), Farrell's novel wittily dramatises the postcolonial axiom that English literature is highly effective as an instrument of imperial power (see also Trivedi 1993 and Viswanathan 1989). Newman picks a comic example from Farrell's heavily fictionalised representation of the siege at Krishnapur (1857), where the electroplated heads of British poets, converted into makeshift weapons, are fired from cannon onto a suitably bewildered foe:

> [T]he most effective [head] of all had been Shakespeare's; it had scythed its way through a whole astonished platoon of sepoys advancing in single file through the jungle. The Collector suspected that the Bard's success in this respect might have a great deal to do with the ballistic advantages stemming from his baldness. The head of Keats, for example, wildly festooned with metal locks … had flown very erratically indeed, killing only a fat money-lender and a camel standing at some distance from the field of action.
>
> (Farrell 1973: 335, qtd in Newman 1995: 1)

Heat and Dust effects rather more subtle, if no less lethal, intertextual manoeuvres. The novel's cross-hatched historical narratives are interwoven around the descendants – more specifically, the female descendants – of the Rivers family. (Their literary precursor St John, it might be recalled, had gone to India a century earlier to convert the heathen, only to succumb there to disease – his foretold death concludes *Jane Eyre*.) Jhabvala re-envisions Brontë's allegory of the White (Wo)man's Burden by displacing its sacrificial rhetoric onto the embodied colonialist trope of *sati*.[10] Scott's *Staying On*, published two years later, then shifts the Burden to the present, evoking comic pathos for the failed Civilising Mission and a post-Forsterian awareness that the British in India were always already too late.

All three novels are connected, albeit with a measure of ironic distance, to a literary genealogy of Orientalist representation (Said 1978). What is apparent in each case, though, is that a history of literary representations of British India is being conscripted into the service of recurring myths of self-defeat. Rushdie is surely right to draw a connection between Raj nostalgia and the ideological requirements of Thatcher's post-imperial Britain. Yet this connection may involve, not so much the will to revive former successes as a seemingly pathological fascination with current *failures*. Hence the figure of nostalgia as an index of self-mockery in novels which, like *The Siege of Krishnapur* and *Staying On*, are suffused with the historical past. In the former novel, nostalgia coheres around memories of the Exhibition – a showcase for British inventiveness and imperial achievement.[11] Yet as the novel proceeds, the siege lays waste to such delusions of cultural grandeur; Anglo-Indian culture – a veneer over power (Newman 1995) – succumbs derisively to the law of entropy, as its accoutrements are either destroyed or hurled as weapons into the fray. In the latter novel, Tusker Smalley and his wife, the ageing couple who have 'stayed on' in post-independence India, weave a skein of comforting memories to protect themselves from a troubled past. But such protection proves illusory; nostalgia emerges as a correlate to physical deterioration, as a thinly disguised rationale for the characters' admission of self-defeat (Scott 1977: 81–3). Susan Stewart, in her discussion of nostalgia in *On Longing* (1984), provides a useful supplement to these readings. Nostalgia, according to Stewart, engenders a process that is always ideological; the past it seeks:

> has never existed except as narrative, and hence, always absent, that past continually threatens to reproduce itself as a felt lack. Hostile to history and its invisible origins, and yet longing for an impossibly pure context of lived experience at a place of origin, nostalgia wears a distinctly utopian face, a face that turns toward a future past, a past which has only ideological reality.
>
> (Stewart 1984: 136)[12]

This is the past of the Raj, itself an ideological construct, with little historical basis other than in European imperial fantasy.[13] Such recourse to historical fantasy might be seen as an indication of the atrophying of historical consciousness in postmodern Western society (Jameson 1991). But it might also be seen as an instance of a neocolonial 'othering' process – of the process by which history, transformed into an exotic cultural spectacle, becomes a packageable commodity for metropolitan consumption (see also Chapter 2). This exoticisation of (colonial) history is most obviously achieved in epic film (*Gandhi*, *A Passage to India*, and so on); but literature participates as well in the spectacularisation of a cultural otherness that is projected out in mythicised space and back in imagined time. Novels such as Scott's, Farrell's and Jhabvala's are arguably complicit in this process, even if they show an ironic awareness of their own belated status.[14] While it might be going too far to suggest that the Booker Prize *drives* such potentially retrograde cultural products, it certainly helps *legitimise* them, promoting them for a wider public. A preliminary analysis of patterns of reception among the Booker's historical novels also suggests that history is being marketed and read in particular ways. Contradictions abound here: history, on the one hand, is retooled for mass consumption as a recognised series of easily packageable exotic myths; while on the other, it is upheld, despite the authors' fabrications, as a more or less transparent window onto verifiable past events.

The Booker prizewinning novel that best exemplifies these contradictions is, of course, Rushdie's aforementioned *Midnight's Children* (1981). Ostensibly, *Midnight's Children* is a radically revisionist novel, a work of 'historiographic metafiction' (Hutcheon 1984/5) that shows the inescapably ideological character of historical facts. Yet, as previously suggested (see Chapter 2), this has not prevented the novel being read – and judged accordingly – as a surrogate guidebook, or as a medley of incomplete historical narratives that engage with India's (post-)imperial historical past. While deconstructive of historical accuracy, *Midnight's Children* has still been accused of being inaccurate; while critical of the commodification of an Orientalised India, it has profited precisely by circulating such commercially viable Orientalist myths. The Booker Prize has not only advertised, but has also arguably helped produce, these contradictions. Hence the irony that the novel has been exploited, directly or indirectly, for the Raj nostalgia it despises; and that its author has been rewarded, not so much for writing against the Empire, but for having done it so *amenably*, with such obviously marketable panache.[15]

A similar argument might be made for Michael Ondaatje's *The English Patient* (1992), a less obviously commercial novel than Rushdie's but still one with considerable exotic cachet. Like Rushdie, Ondaatje has occasionally been criticised for pandering to a wonder-seeking Western readership (Mukherjee 1985); but his is better seen, like Rushdie's, as a strategically self-conscious exoticism and, also like Rushdie's, as a stylishly hybridised literary/cultural text. Both writers share a postcolonial concern with historical revisionism – a concern born of the need to complicate all forms of historical representation, but also to critique the narrowly ethnocentric view 'that project[s] the *West* as history' (Prakash 1994: 1475 n.1; see also Chakrabarty 1992). Finally, Ondaatje, like Rushdie, has made the jump to literary celebrity on the back of symbolic capital acquired largely from the Booker Prize. Thus, while the film was certainly responsible for reactivating sales of Ondaatje's novels, particularly in America, it was the Prize that was instrumental, as Rushdie's had been a decade earlier, in pushing a talented writer into the international limelight.

Clearly, the film, with its emphasis on torrid melodrama in a series of spectacularly exotic locations, was always likely to affect perceptions, as well as sales, of Ondaatje's book. Yet exotic appeal seemed to contribute as well to the earlier success of *The English Patient* (in terms of sales-figures, largely Booker-driven), as did the ephemeral quality – 'Englishness' – that the novel sought to suppress. The dismantling of a unifying 'Englishness' in an age of 'multicultural consciousness' (Eakin) has itself become something of an industry – consider, for example, the recent fetishisation of Scottish literature and film in Britain and elsewhere.[16] Enter Ondaatje's novel, with its (Hungarian) 'English' patient – the absent centre around which the (hi)stories of the other, conspicuously displaced, characters revolve. The interweaving of private and public spaces, of micro- and macro-historical narratives; the persistent undercutting of national identitary labels; the disruption of the normative relationship between the colonial 'margins' and the imperial 'centre'; the emphasis on displacement and the diasporisation of cultural knowledge – all of these indicate a postcolonial sensibility at work in Ondaatje's novel that insists on the right to reclaim its stories from the moribund 'English' (cultural) body.

Nowhere is this clearer than in the transition from *Kim* to Kip – from Kipling's Orientalist novel, allaying emergent British anxieties, to Ondaatje's canny Indian sapper, defusing left-over German bombs. Kip is in the service of the British – not 'English' – army; but as soon transpires, he has a will and a history all of his own. The 'English' patient self-destructs; Kip rescues others from destruction. Yet this postcolonial lesson in the politics of dependence has arguably been overshadowed by the book's recently revitalised commercial success. *The English Patient*, like *Midnight's Children*, risks being brought to attention as the latest in a series of publicly endorsed 'multicultural' products. One of the effects of this sponsored multiculturalism is a levelling out of different histories, and an aestheticised celebration of diversity that disguises the lack of sociohistorical change.[17] Another is the tendency to assimilate 'marginal' cultural products, rejuvenating, but also protecting, the beleaguered mainstream culture (see Introduction; also previous chapter). The Booker Prize, as a popular retailer of the postcolonial exotic, exemplifies the double standards in promoting 'multicultural' goods. On the one hand, it has certainly played a role in broadening definitions of 'Englishness' and 'English literature'; as Jonathan Wilson says in an admiring 1995 article on the Booker for *The New Yorker*, the Prize reflects an increasing cultural, as well as commercial, recognition that 'the better books have been coming not out of England per se but out of the old colonies of England' (Wilson 1995: 99). On the other hand, the Prize, in assuming a common ('English') cultural heritage, might be accused of availing itself of a patron's proprietary rights. Eakin puts it succinctly:

> [F]or the prize to have a coherent center in London while calling itself a Commonwealth-wide award, it must reinforce to some extent the shared colonial heritage of included nationalities. In this sense, a British cultural-linguistic hegemony has begun to replace the old one.
> (Eakin 1995: 3–4)

Booker plc's inability to shake off the ghosts of its own colonial history might be seen here as symptomatic of a much wider cultural malaise. This malaise, and the forms of 'imperialist nostalgia' (Rosaldo 1993) it tends to engender, engage the contradictions of a postcolonial (literary) era. In this era, Britain, no longer a player in the world's economic sweepstakes, still accumulates symbolic capital as a legitimising cultural force. Eakin again: 'It is ironic that just as the old British imperial government used its colonies for the interests of capital enterprise at home, it is again London that is – through the Booker Prize – using its Commonwealth in the interests of literary consumerism in Britain' (Eakin 1995: 6). This reversion to the 'centre' haunts multicultural celebrations; it also acts as a secret sharer in the postcolonial cause. What emerges from these scattered speculations on the intertwined histories of (and in) the Booker is the need for a much more detailed sociological study of the literature it promotes. Much of this literature, I have argued here, might be loosely defined as 'postcolonial'. In other chapters of this book, I go some way toward suggesting what might be at stake in a sociology of postcolonial literatures, and what might underlie the emergence of these literatures, both as targets of commercial enterprise and as celebrated objects of academic study. This chapter is a contribution, however provisional, to such investigations; in its concluding section I shall offer some general thoughts, extrapolating from the case of the Booker, on the seemingly conflicted relationship between the oppositional politics of postcolonialism and the assimilative machinery of the 'global' literary prize.

Conclusion

Literary prizes, according to Bourdieu, function as legitimising mechanisms that foreground the symbolic, as well as material, effects of the process of literary evaluation (see also Introduction). As Bourdieu suggests, prizes reflect as much upon their donors as their recipients; part of a wider struggle over the authority to consecrate particular works or writers, they are powerful indicators of the social forces underlying what we might call the politics of literary recognition. Far from offering tributes to an untrammelled literary excellence, prizes bring the ideological character of evaluation to the fore. So much is clear, for example, from recent arguments that have broken out over the Nobel Prize for Literature, which, as several commentators have pointed out, has shown more evidence of the parochialism than of the much-vaunted impartiality of its selection committee.[18] Renee Winegarten's complaints, in her helpful overview article, are symptomatic: the Nobel Prize, if not openly biased, is nonetheless guilty of sins of omission, having overlooked 'some of the greatest writers of the century, including Joseph Conrad, Henry James, Leo Tolstoy, Marcel Proust, James Joyce, Federico García Lorca, to name a few that spring to mind' (Winegarten 1994: 65); it tends to look to Europe as a locus of cultural activity and development; it considers writers and/or their work to be representative of their respective countries, inspiring an 'intense patriotic gratification' that makes the Prize 'akin to a victory in international sport' (Winegarten 1994: 74); it has a history of rewarding writers who are already internationally recognised and thus resembles, in George Bernard Shaw's memorable phrase, 'a life belt thrown out to a swimmer who has already reached the shore' (qtd in Winegarten 1994: 65). But behind these complaints, in themselves legitimate, lies a conservative fear that 'too many political and geographical motives come into play [in the adjudication process], too many extraneous considerations that have little or nothing to do with the act of writing or the art of literature as such' (Winegarten 1994: 65). Laments such as these may serve to replicate the Swedish Academy's naive insistence that the evaluative process, like the work itself, be freed from ideological constraint. The opposite is more often the case, and not only with the Nobel; for as I have suggested, the history of the Booker also demonstrates that the attempt to reward literary excellence, however generous or well intentioned, may well contain an unannounced ideological agenda – a hidden politics – of its own.

While the same might also be said to some extent for other, more 'postcolonially' oriented prizes – the Commonwealth Writers Prize, for example, or the Neustadt, specifically designed as a more globally conscious alternative to the Nobel – it is the Booker's unusual history, as well as the commercialism that sustains it, that has helped turn it into the most significant index of conflicting public, as well as more narrowly academic, perceptions of the globalisation of English-language literature in the post-independence era. What effects has the Booker had on the postcolonial field of production, other than that of drawing attention to the ambivalent role of its ostensibly benevolent commercial sponsor? Two effects, already mentioned, might be briefly reiterated here. The first of these is that the Booker Prize, even as it has expanded public awareness of the global dimensions of English-language literature, has paradoxically narrowed this awareness to a handful of internationally recognised postcolonial writers. While the Booker judges can hardly be accused, as has sometimes been said of their Nobel counterparts, of falling back on the safest options – the 'courage' of some prizewinning selections has almost inevitably gone on to become part of Booker Prize lore – it would still be true to say that several, though by no means all, of the Booker prizewinners belong to a recognised postcolonial canon; and that these writers comprise by and large a list of international figures whose names circulate freely within the media and on school/university curricula and examination lists. This self-perpetuating process of recognition, much enhanced of course by the global media, is reflected in the regular appearance of the 'big names' (Achebe, Atwood, Naipaul, Rushdie, etc.) on many of the Prize's heavily publicised shortlists. Thus, while the South African J.M. Coetzee is the only writer to have won the Prize twice (for *Life & Times of Michael K* in 1983 and *Disgrace* in 1999), Rushdie has won once and finished three times on the runners-up list, while Naipaul, Atwood, Rohinton Mistry, Anita Desai, Kazuo Ishiguro and Timothy Mo have all won and/or made it onto the shortlist more than once. This is not to question these writers' undoubted literary abilities; nor is it to accuse the judges of outright favouritism, which would be unfair in the extreme. Rather, it is to suggest that the Prize has participated in a process of canonisation which, as such processes will, tends to reproduce the value-systems of 'culturally and otherwise dominant members of a community' (Herrnstein Smith 1984: 34). Obviously, the various ideological apparatuses and 'reading formations' (T. Bennett 1990) underlying the canonising process are much more complex than I am giving the impression here. However, the point still holds that while canons usually function to support establishment values, even those works with apparently '*anti*-establishment interests participate in the cultural re-production of canonical texts' (Herrnstein Smith 1984: 34, my italics).[19] Within this context, prizes like the Booker, while apparently opening the door for a more politicised view of 'Englishness' and 'English literature', might also be seen to operate to some extent at least as what Fredric Jameson calls 'strategies of containment' (Jameson 1981). They function, that is, as mechanisms for the management of subversive political tendencies, and for the redirecting of oppositional energies into the mainstream of Western metropolitan cultural thought.[20] It remains moot, in any event, as to how 'subversive' or 'anti-establishment' the Booker's selections were, and are, in the first place; as Timothy Brennan has argued convincingly, the privileging of a certain kind of highly aestheticised 'political writing' under the sign of the postcolonial has had the ironic effect of shutting down, or at least deflecting public attention away from, more radically unorthodox alternatives.[21] Whatever the case, the obvious horror with which the Booker Committee greeted John Berger's anti-imperialist tirade in 1972 (and then succeeded in brushing off J.G. Farrell's repeat criticisms of economic hegemony the following year – see *The Times*, 21 September 1993: VIII) seems to provide a fair indication, both of the company's and of the Prize's institutional boundaries and ideological limits.

Such self-defensive gestures also help set up a context for those wider institutional processes through which postcolonialism's anti-imperialist imperatives may be partly defused by being rerouted into the commodified aesthetics of 'multiculturalism' and 'the global village'. Here, it seems worth turning again for a moment to Pico Iyer's aforementioned article in *Time* – itself of course a highly commodified piece of image-conscious journalism (Brydon 1994). In the article, Iyer, who tellingly uses the terms 'postcolonial', 'multicultural', 'transcultural' and 'global' almost interchangeably, defines the 'new transcultural' writers as:

> the products not so much of colonial divisions as of the international culture that has grown up since the war, and they are addressing an audience as mixed up and eclectic and uprooted as themselves. They are creators, and creations, of a new postimperial order in which English is the lingua franca, just about everywhere is a suburb of the same international youth culture, and all countries are a part of a unified CNN and MTV circuit, with a common frame of reference in McDonald's, Madonna, and Magic Johnson.
>
> (Iyer 1993: 48)

For Iyer, the Booker Prize, 'London's way of formally commemorating and coronating literary tradition', has helped to register a general shift in public awareness toward the new global 'polycultural order' (Iyer 1993: 46). While the writers the Prize has celebrated are more striking for their differences than their similarities, many of them, of non-Anglo-Saxon background,

> born more or less after the war, and choosing to write in English … are situated at a crossroads from which they can reflect, and reflect on, the new forms and Mississippi masalas of our increasingly small, increasingly mongrel, increasingly mobile global village.
>
> (Iyer 1993: 48)

Iyer's article, as previously suggested, joins postcolonial literary/cultural production to a naively celebratory global cosmopolitan sensibility in which conspicuous inequalities of technological resources and international divisions of labour are elided, and where the continuing anti-imperialist concerns of contemporary postcolonial writing are emptied out.[22] This is postcoloniality with a vengeance, and it is associated, significantly, with a prize apparently designed to 'illustrate how the [literary] Empire has struck back' (Iyer 1993: 46). Iyer's article, in advertising its own complicity with the late-capitalist global commodity culture it celebrates, might well appear to be a paradigmatic example of the literary/cultural phenomenon I have been describing in this book as the postcolonial exotic. Yet the postcolonial exotic is by no means restricted to consumer-oriented writing like Iyer's, or to such blatantly commercialised literary extravaganzas as the annual Booker Prize. As should be clear by now, the postcolonial exotic is integral, rather than peripheral, to the postcolonial field of cultural production – a field in which 'commercial' and 'academic' products intermingle; and in which a constant vigilance is required to the ideologies that underlie evaluative procedures, and to the institutional frameworks within which such procedures have evolved.

Appendix: Booker Prize management and adjudication procedures

At present, the management of the Prize is entrusted to a committee comprising an author, three publishers, an agent, a bookseller, a librarian, the Prize administrator and Public Relations consultant (for the most part of its thirty-odd year history, Martyn Goff), with the chairman being appointed by the sponsoring company, Booker plc (Goff 2000; see also

Goff 1989: 12). The administration of the Prize, from the first moment of calling in entries – which in recent years have tended to hover around the hundred mark – to the eventual announcement of the winner, was handed over after the first few years to the independent charitable trust, the National Book League (still in charge, though since 1986 under the new, radically simple name of Book Trust). The Booker Prize, as its administrator claims, thus has some reason to take pride in a relatively flexible system of management that involves its sponsoring company while still managing to keep them at a respectable arm's length (Goff 2000; see also Goff 1989: 12).

For all this flexibility, the composition of the Management Committee itself has been slow to change. Similarly, the five judges selected by the committee to adjudicate the entries – while changing each year – have arguably shown a certain establishment bias, with several recurring names (Professor Gillian Beer of Cambridge University, for instance, has judged the Prize twice inside the last decade). The judges, according to Goff, are picked to maintain a healthy balance between the Chairman (who is picked first, and has a casting vote) and the other contributors, usually 'an academic, a critic or two, a writer or two and the [wo]man in the street' (Goff 1989: 18). Not surprisingly, this last category (now freely acknowl- edged as comprising a celebrity or 'major figure' – Goff 2000) has caused the occasional upset, such as in 1985, when the actress Joanna Lumley, pronouncing judgement *in absentia*, objected in the strongest possible terms ('over my dead body') to the winner. Adjudicatory committees of the past have also been vulnerable to the criticism of white (upper) middle-class British bias – a bias also seemingly reflected in the demo- graphic make-up of the Booker Management Committee. The make-up of both committees thus arguably gives historical support to those who have attacked the Booker Prize as arrogating a different form of colonial authority, and lends a certain strength to the argument that there continues to be a mismatch between 'postcolonial culture' and 'postimpe- rial criticism' – between sites of literary production and seats of cultural legitimation and control (Eakin 1995; W.J.T. Mitchell 1992).

Adjudication procedures for the Prize, while somewhat modified in their finer details, have retained throughout a simple structure. Submis- sions are made by publishers in conjunction with the authors themselves and their agents, with a closing date of 30 June (sometimes extended, under mitigating circumstances, until the end of July – Goff 1989).[23] Publishers are currently limited to two submissions, although a third may be added if the title is by an author who has won or has been shortlisted for the Prize over the last ten years. (Each publisher may also submit up to five additional titles, with the judges eventually calling in between eight and twelve of these titles for further consideration (Goff 2000).) In the second half of August, the Prize Administrator asks each judge for his or her six frontrunners; a provisional shortlist is thus established, whittled down after subsequent meetings to a shortlist of first twenty to thirty, and then the final six. The all-important meeting at which the winner is decided does not take place until the afternoon of the gala dinner at which the Prize is presented. (In recent years, however, media leaks have abounded, rumours have proliferated, and it has become increasingly difficult to keep even the final stages of the adjudication process secret.) The process, already drawn out, is then brought to its suspense-filled conclusion with the ceremonial dinner. It is at the dinner, with the cameras trained, that the announcement of the winner is finally issued – whereupon the debate re-opens in the media, and the wrangling already begins over who might win, perhaps, *next* year.

5   Exoticism, ethnicity and the multicultural fallacy

Introduction

In a provocative essay for the journal *Critical Inquiry* (1997), the American academic Stanley Fish attempts to distinguish between two versions of multiculturalism. The first of these, says Fish, is so-called 'boutique multiculturalism', and is typified by such celebratory but largely cosmetic fare as 'ethnic restaurants [and] weekend festivals, and [by] high profile flirtations with the other in the manner satirized by Tom Wolfe under the rubric of "radical chic" ' (Fish 1997: 378). The other is 'strong multiculturalism', of the sort that does not wear its tolerance lightly, and which is 'strong because it values difference in and for itself rather than as a manifestation of something basically more constitutive' (Fish 1997: 382). Whereas 'the boutique multiculturalist', according to Fish,

> will accord a superficial respect to cultures other than his own, a respect he will withdraw when he finds the practices of a culture irrational or inhumane, a strong multiculturalist will want to accord a *deep* respect to all cultures at their core, for he believes that each has the right to form its own identity and nourish its own sense of what is rational and humane.
>
> (Fish 1997: 382)

But with his customary rhetorical skill, Fish then goes on to dismantle the opposition he has just created, suggesting in effect that neither 'boutique' nor 'strong' multiculturalists are able to come to terms with the cultural differences they affect to foster. Fish sketches out the dilemma as follows:

> The boutique multiculturalist does not take difference seriously because its marks (quaint clothing, atonal music, curious table man-

ners) are for him matters of lifestyle, and as such they should not be allowed to overwhelm the substratum of rationality that makes us all brothers under the skin. The strong multiculturalist takes difference so seriously as a general principle that he cannot take any *particular* difference seriously, cannot allow its imperatives their full realization in a political program, for their full realization would inevitably involve the suppression of difference. The only way out for the would-be strong multiculturalist is to speak not for difference in general but for *a* difference, that is for the imperatives of a distinctive culture even when they impinge on the freedom of some other distinctive culture.

(Fish 1997: 384)

Fish's aim, obviously enough, is to cut the ground from beneath the feet of those whose liberal views on difference run up against 'illiberal' forms of cultural behaviour, or even 'illiberal' cultures, they can neither countenance nor condone. Fish concludes that multiculturalism, on one level, represents an incoherent theoretical concept that articulates the contradictions within certain strands of Western (Euro-American) liberal-pluralist thought – the irreconcilable pull, for instance, between particularist aims and universal precepts; or the irresolvable conflict between individual rights and collective goals.[1] This does not mean, however, that multiculturalism does not exist; on the contrary, it is a 'demographic fact' of contemporary American society (Fish 1997: 385). And not just American society; for as Fish suggests, quoting approvingly from a seminal essay by the Anglo-Canadian philosopher Charles Taylor, all societies are becoming increasingly multicultural in a rapidly evolving global process – a process that is more likely, in both the short and the long term, to present urgent practical problems to be tackled than complicated philosophical/theoretical issues to be 'solved' (Taylor 1994: 63, qtd in Fish 1997: 385).

Fish's pragmaticist views, despite their global implications, are primarily designed as an intervention in the so-called multiculturalism debates that have been taking place over the last decade or so in the United States.[2] This chapter aims to extend the range of debate to two other former settler colonies – Canada and Australia – where multiculturalism has been institutionalised (without, for all that, becoming conceptually clearer) to a greater extent than has so far been the case in the United States. Some of the questions the chapter seeks to address might be briefly outlined here as follows: to what extent have local conditions and changing historical problems dictated multicultural policy in these two countries? What effects have multicultural polices had on these countries' respective literary output; for if multiculturalism is notoriously difficult to define, is it any easier to categorise a nation's multicultural writers? Might multiculturalism and/or multicultural writing be taken as a measure of putatively postcolonial societies, or are such terms better seen as indicators of those societies' inability to resolve their own internal contradictions? Are Canadian and Australian multiculturalisms viable mechanisms for adjustments of power within historically white-dominated societies; or are such multiculturalisms essentially cosmetic – 'boutique' even when they are attempting to be 'strong'? My argument, in brief, will be that multiculturalism, for all its conceptual limitations, may yet serve as a workable model for civic tolerance in societies still struggling to free themselves from the burden of their white-supremacist past (Hutcheon and Richmond 1990); but I shall also suggest that multiculturalism continues to operate as a form of wilfully aestheticising exoticist discourse – a discourse which inadvertently serves to disguise persistent racial tensions within the nation; and one which, in affecting a respect for the other as a reified object of cultural difference, deflects attention away from social issues – discrimination, unequal access, hierarchies of ethnic privilege – that are very far from being resolved.

Comparing histories: Canadian and Australian multiculturalisms

It is sometimes assumed that Canadian and Australian multiculturalisms have pursued a more or less parallel history – an affinity, however, which proves on closer inspection to be somewhat misleading (Hawkins 1982). A few historical notes on the development of multiculturalism in these two settler societies might therefore be in order here. While in Canada, multiculturalism was not officially enshrined as state policy until 1971, and was later reinforced through the passage of such humanitarian bills as the Canadian Human Rights Act (1977), the Charter of Rights and Freedoms (1982), and the Canadian Multiculturalism Act (1988), it is possible to argue that the country's conception of itself as multicultural had first been institutionalised almost a century earlier, with the establishment in 1867 of Quebec as a semi-autonomous province (Will 1990: 82). The jury is still out on whether multiculturalism developed as a 'natural' extension of this bicultural framework or whether it was primarily designed to deflect attention away from Quebecers' insistent demands for a distinct society.[3] Whatever the case, it seems fairly certain that the Official Languages Act of 1969, which made French an official language throughout Canada, opened the floodgates for Canada's many other ethnocultural groups to press for similar, if not necessarily language-based, forms of recognition

(Will 1990: 85; David 1997: 5). These demands were partly met with a series of policies introduced in 1971 by the Trudeau government, which presided over the establishment of new government agencies like the research-based Multiculturalism Directorate and the ethnic advisory body the Canadian Consultative Council on Multiculturalism, and which pledged itself on a more abstract level to 'overcome cultural barriers to full participation in Canadian society', and to 'promote creative encounters and interchange among all Canadian cultural groups in the interest of national unity' (Trudeau, qtd in Breton 1986: 51). As this last excerpt from Pierre Trudeau's landmark speech to the House of Commons suggests, early attempts to institutionalise cultural pluralism in Canada were not without their integrationist undertones. As Daryn David remarks,

> [C]ultural pluralism could be asserted through multicultural policies as long as [it] was seen as the new road to an overarching Canadian identity. The key question here [was] how much Canadian identity was to be based on the bicultural framework of the past, with ethnics merely spicing up the established structure, or how much Canadian identity itself was to be fundamentally changed.
>
> (David 1997: 5–6; see also Ubale 1992: 12–13)

This question still remains moot, despite significant increases in government aid to ethnic minority groups and projects in the 1980s and 1990s, and despite concerted attempts on both federal and provincial levels to counteract what some critics have seen as the systemic racial discrimination built into Canadian society.[4] Indeed, the ambiguity of state-sanctioned multiculturalism, as evidenced in the remarkable opacity of the rhetoric that surrounds it, has led some sceptics to see it as little more then a device for the maintenance of the white Anglophone *status quo*. Thus, while the term 'multiculturalism' might be designed to 'neutralize the hierarchical connotations contained by [its largely discredited sister-term] "ethnic" ', it is still associated primarily 'with groups distinct from the monolith … of the dominant social order' (Golfman 1996: 179). Bhausaheb Ubale, reflecting sadly on his mixed experiences as Ontario's first Race Relations Commissioner, puts it this way:

> [M]ainstream, white English Canadians define themselves as 'Canadian' and all others as 'immigrants' or 'non-Canadians'. … Thus, ethnocultural and, in particular, racial minorities are seen as different, as 'non-Canadian' and therefore as less acceptable and less worthy of holding the same positions as 'true Canadians'.
>
> (Ubale 1992: 6)

If multiculturalism is identified – and Ubale's experiences have persuaded him it usually is – with racial minorities and other putative 'non-Canadians', its compensatory policies might well be seen as further marginalising the very communities they set out to assist. Similarly, the allocation of funds and resources to disadvantaged communities might be considered, less as necessary adjustments to an unbalanced power-structure than as attempts to consolidate the political control of ethnic minority groups 'through the skillful puppetry of pulling financial strings via a plethora of granting agencies' (Mazurek 1992: 24).

I shall return to these criticisms later; but for the moment it seems worth summarising the central tenets of multiculturalism in Canada as these have developed in the last three decades since Trudeau's historic 1971 announcements. Leon Litvack, in a couple of useful overview articles, identifies three principal strands – the sociopolitical, the ideological, and the demographic. Multiculturalism may thus refer, either to 'the social policy of encouraging retention of group heritages and full participation in Canadian society', or to the articulation of a 'philosophy or ideology of cultural pluralism', or to 'a measure of ethnic diversity within a society', or, most commonly, to some combination of these three elements (Litvack 1996a: 126; see also Litvack 1996b). In Australia, as in Canada, these three interrelated components of multiculturalism can all be witnessed, even though they have developed along different historical lines and the interaction between them has produced rather different results. A crucial difference in the development of multiculturalism in Australia has arguably been the 'bottom-line' economistic thinking underlying the nation's increasing acceptance of cultural diversity within its ranks. (Even this difference, however, should probably be seen less as one in kind than one of degree; for the proto-multiculturalist rhetoric that began to find voice in Canada in the 1950s and, especially, the 1960s proved wholly commensurate with the need to expand the post-war economic boom by bringing in a supplementary immigrant workforce (Will 1990: 84; David 1997: 3).)

Now as is well known, Australian history, from the late nineteenth century until the mid-part of the twentieth century, had been marked, some might say marred, by a state-enforced ideology – the White Australia Policy. The White Australia Policy was founded on the view that immigration, while not in itself harmful to the nation, should be restricted to those white Europeans, ideally British, who could most easily be assimilated to the dominant 'Anglo-Celtic' culture.[5] By the 1950s, however, this policy had become much more difficult to justify, still harder to enforce. For one thing, it was becoming clear that British immigration was insufficient to meet the demands of an expanding economy; for another, an important trade-bloc had been established in south-east Asia, particularly Japan; and for a third, a newly prosperous Europe had become a magnet for Australians, several of whom were beginning to emigrate in the opposite direction (Castles *et al.* 1988). All of this necessitated an abrupt about-turn on the veto on 'non-white' immigration, particularly though not exclusively from Asia, if not a significant departure from the assimilationist ideology that had formerly underpinned the White Australia Policy. Thus, Australia's newfound willingness to open its doors to highly skilled non-Europeans, or to encourage those already there to transfer their status from temporary to permanent, did not diminish the expectation that these immigrants (or New Australians, as they were called) would wish to integrate or, better still, assimilate directly into the self-perpetuating behavioural codes and value-systems of a traditionally white-dominated society (Castles *et al.* 1988: 52; Martin 1978: 30).

During the 1970s, Australia experienced severe stagflation and the recruitment of non-European labour was no longer considered a pressing issue. Instead, the Labor government under Whitlam turned its attention to improving services to those ethnic minority communities already resident in Australia, in part as a means of stealing a march on the opposition by securing the sizeable Vietnamese Asian and Eastern European vote (Grant 1983: 246). It was in 1973 that the first mention was made of multiculturalism in a speech by Minister of Immigration Al Grassby, who argued eloquently that 'the increasing diversity of Australian society [had] rendered untenable any prospect there might have been twenty years ago of fully assimilating newcomers to the Australian way of life' (Grassby, qtd in Castles *et al.* 1988: 59). Grassby's speech proved to be a turning point, and multiculturalism was soon fully integrated into the daily currency of Australian political discourse. Notwithstanding, it came as no surprise that the subsequent Liberal government under Fraser, while trumpeting the virtues of cultural pluralism in Australia, was rather more circumspect when it came to attributing the problems of Australia's ethnic minority communities to inbuilt inequalities in the ruling capitalist system (Castles *et al.* 1988: 67). Instead, a series of often picturesque metaphors (e.g. 'salad-bowl' multiculturalism) were deployed to mystify unequal relations of power; to disguise continuing, economically motivated manifestations of xenophobia and racial prejudice; and to distract attention away from the numerous, frequently conspicuous social disadvantages being experienced by Australia's latest minority workforce in an increasingly competitive urban-industrial society.[6] Much as in Canada during a similar period, government attempts to reach out to ethnic minority communities drew criticism as a surreptitious form of economic and ideological self-protection. As Andrew Jakubowicz among others has argued, the Fraser government's was a multiculturalism that aspired to the 'ideological domination of ethnic communities', both through the strategic management of state/federal resources and via the media-generated myth of limited social discontent (Jakubowicz 1984a: 39; see also Jakubowicz 1984b and David 1997: 8).

Subsequent governments, both Liberal and Labor, have proved vulnerable to the criticism (which also holds valid to some extent for Canada) that state-sponsored multiculturalism has provided a means for the incorporation of ethnic minorities into mainstream society without necessarily changing the way the mainstream views itself (Ang 1996: 40; see also Chapter 3). Other criticisms of multiculturalism, equally applied in either country, have by now become familiar: that its emphasis on heritage programmes and modes of cultural preservation lock minority groups into ethnic compartments while promoting a nostalgic view of the past that hinders, or simply fails to recognise, sociocultural transformation; that it patronises the socially disadvantaged groups it claims to help and whose marginality it continues to determine; that it pits ethnic minority communities against one another in the competition for government funding; that it effectively excludes or ghettoises the cultures it singles out as distinctive or unique; that by putting, as Trinh Minh-ha says, 'an aura around the exotic other' (Minh-ha 1991, qtd in Ang 1996: 44), it acts as a brake on the process of intercultural understanding it claims to set in motion; that it serves to occlude the very discriminatory practices it proposes to redress; that it substitutes a culturalist, more specifically a *symbolic* appreciation of the trappings of ethnic diversity for an understanding of the wider economic forces that have contributed to the deprivation of ethnic minorities, among other historically disadvantaged groups. While many of these criticisms have come, broadly speaking, from the Left, the range of attacks coming from the Right has been equally noticeable in both countries. Among these might be mentioned the anti-immigration platform of the Canadian Reform Party and the crudely nationalistic jingoism of the New Right in Australia, from Geoffrey Blainey to Stephen Rimmer to Pauline Hanson's 'One Nation'. Rimmer might be briefly quoted here from his book *Fiscal Anarchy: The Public Funding of Multiculturalism* (1988), if only to show how multiculturalism has succeeded in drawing to itself very different ideological opponents. Multiculturalism, says Rimmer,

> appears to share many important aspects of the ideology of liberalism. Both claim that individual freedom, and expression of that freedom, are valuable to society ... [L]iberalism and multiculturalism each

stress the need for state intervention to protect the freedom of individuals, especially those in disadvantaged groups ... [b]ut multiculturalism has also adopted central tenets of the ideology of socialism.
Multiculturalism and socialism both tend to emphasise the need for
equality between groups, as distinct [from] equality for individuals. ...
By claiming that non-English-speaking (NES) migrants are disadvantaged and therefore require state assistance to facilitate equality of
outcome through various policies, ... multiculturalism can ... be
described as a socialist ideology.

(Rimmer 1988: 3)

Needless to say, such an ideology does not meet with Rimmer's approval;
nor is he any less shocked by the continuing prospect of multiculturalism
as a transparently 'anti-nationalist vehicle', and as a form of 'fiscal
anarchy' that is dependent on ethnically determined welfare handouts
'more in tune with corporatist ideology than the values of a liberal
democracy' (Rimmer 1988: 5, 15, 48).

Then again, Rimmer's views are perhaps no wilder than, say, the
diatribes of African-Canadian poet-activist Marlene Nourbese Philip,
who defines multiculturalism reductively as 'a configuration of power at
the centre of which are the two cultures recognized by the constitution of
Canada – the French and the English – and around which circumnavigate
the lesser satellite [ethnic minority] cultures' (Nourbese Philip 1992: 181);
who appears to see multiculturalism's overriding intent as being 'to diffuse
potential racial and ethnic problems' (185); and who, after making the
legitimate criticism that 'multiculturalism has no answers for the problem
of [institutional] racism' (185), proceeds to dismiss it out of hand as 'at
best ... a mechanism whereby immigrants indulge their nostalgic love of
their mother countries' (186). But while a self-righteous victim rhetoric
occasionally vitiates some of the more radical critiques of multiculturalism
in both Canada and Australia, this by no means invalidates the very real
discrimination that continues to be experienced on many different levels
by ethnic minority communities in both countries.

A special case should probably be made here for First Nations/Aboriginal
communities, which have traditionally been wary of seeing themselves as
just another ethnic minority (Castles *et al.* 1988: 65), and which have
distanced themselves accordingly from multiculturalism as a 'reward system'
for historically marginalised groups.[7] As Suvendrini Perera has argued,
multicultural policies in Australia (and a similar case might again be made
for Canada) have perpetuated the marginalisation of Aboriginal communities by attempting to assimilate their experiences to a master-narrative of

the immigrant nation. In the process, the more dangerous 'Aboriginal' has been supplanted by the safer term 'ethnic':

> In settler societies, 'the ethnic' has emerged as a sign that is less forbidding than that of the indigene; [the Aboriginal writer] Mudrooroo (1990) has referred to the political implications of constructing indigenous populations as the first in a long line of diverse ethnicities, a naturalizing of the process of nation-making that subsumes the earliest inhabitants within 'a country of immigrants.'
>
> (Perera 1996: 401)

The anthropologist Elizabeth A. Povinelli, in a 1998 article in *Critical Inquiry*, pursues a similar argument by showing, through a detailed analysis of the complex discourses surrounding Native title, how 'state multicultural discourses, apparatuses and imaginaries defuse struggles for liberation waged against the modern liberal state and recuperate these struggles as moments in which the future of the nation and its core institutions and values are ensured rather than shaken' (Povinelli 1998: 579). Multiculturalism, for Povinelli, has been conscripted to a grand narrative of reparation, in which the nation shamefacedly confesses to its past misdemeanours and promises in the future to make good:

> Australian state officials represent themselves and the nation as subjects shamed by past imperial, colonial, and racist attitudes that are now understood as having, in their words, constituted 'the darkest aspect' of the nation's history and impaired its social and economic future. Multiculturalism is represented as the externalized political testament both to the nation's aversion to its past misdeeds, and to its recovered good intentions.
>
> (Povinelli 1998: 581)

This critique of multiculturalism, while in itself extremely convincing, runs the risk of seeing multicultural policy as little other than the sop to a white settler society's collective historical guilt. Similarly, the dismissive view of multiculturalism as no more than an underhand vehicle of white supremacy needs to be weighed against evidence that multicultural policies in both Canada and Australia have worked to improve the socioeconomic conditions, as well as to increase the symbolic capital, of disadvantaged ethnic minority groups. Such evidence, however, has historically been difficult to gauge. As Cornelia Will has argued in the case of Canada, multiculturalism may be viewed in a more positive light as enhancing a more equitable society, but only … if the allocation of symbolic resources is followed by prac-tical steps, e.g. steps to improve socioeconomic status, steps decreasing racism and discrimination, steps increasing equality. If the policy was only introduced to preserve the interests of the dominant Anglo-Celtic group, it is not clear what steps should have been taken at all to protect minorities or to improve their status in Canadian society.

(Will 1990: 97)

But as Will is forced to admit, it has been much safer for recent Canadian governments to support a variety of symbolic actions (e.g. the encourage-ment of 'cultural pride' through the state sponsorship of ethnic minority festivals and art exhibitions) than it has been to provide genuine incentives for the economic advancement and social mobility of ethnic minority individuals and groups (see also Mazurek 1992: 23; David 1997: 10–11). As Linda Hutcheon among others has concluded, a considerable gap still exists between the *ideal* of multiculturalism and an *ideology* of cultural pluralism that often ends up reinforcing the stereotypes and marginalising tendencies it is apparently designed to counteract.[8] To what extent would this also be true of so-called multicultural literature in Canada and Australia? This is the question that the next section of this chapter seeks to address.

Comparing literatures: Canadian and Australian multicultural writing

The 1980s and 1990s saw an explosion of multicultural writing in both Canada and Australia, as represented in a plethora of anthologies, among the best known of which are those edited by Linda Hutcheon and Smaro Kamboureli (in Canada) and Sneja Gunew and Kateryna Longley (in Australia). It seems worth noting, though, that the majority of these anthologies have been put out by smaller presses, and are often heavily dependent on state subsidies, whereas more mainstream publishers – Penguin and HarperCollins, for example – have sometimes appeared to favour multicultural writers who *distance* themselves from their ethnic origins.[9] The commercial success of some of these latter, it has been suggested, comes at a price. Hence the no-holds-barred attack by Arun Mukherjee on Michael Ondaatje for 'sacrific[ing] his experience of … otherness in Canada' (Mukherjee 1985: 50) – a curious if by no means isolated example of the Left-critical backlash against privileged writers from mixed cultural backgrounds, who are accused of having bypassed their ethnic ancestry or as having neglected to discuss their experiences of social marginalisation and displacement.[10] Mukherjee's argument, in several respects, appears to be profoundly counter-intuitive; after all, it might well be asked, who or what should oblige a writer like Ondaatje to explore his tangled cultural affiliations; to articulate a marginality he may not have experienced; to embrace an ethnic identity of which he is evidently suspicious, and which he perceives – like all such constructed identitary categories – as both unreliable and unstable? (Huggan 1995).

Mukherjee's criticism is valuable, still, in drawing attention to some of the criteria that might be used to distinguish the work of multicultural writers from that of their mainstream literary counterparts. The first and arguably most important of these criteria is the testimonial impulse, as evidenced in writers whose semi-autobiographical works attest to the trials, but also sometimes the pleasures, of the so-called 'migrant experience'.[11] A second apparent criterion is the sociological import of literary works – usually though not always fiction – which trace patterns linking intimate group dynamics to wider social relations and which, in so doing, explore the workings of power at both micro- and macrolevels of society.[12] A third, more fundamental criterion is the writer's minoritarian ethnic background: a background which is frequently though not necessarily convoluted or conflicted, but one which is invariably to be distinguished from that of writers who belong to or affiliate themselves with the dominant culture – in the case of Canada and Australia, the problematically conflated 'Anglo-Celtic' strand.[13] And a fourth criterion for the work is its designated oppositionality – its perceived status as a 'minor' literary form that stands in critical, possibly antagonistic, relationship to the legitimising narratives of the cultural mainstream.[14]

These criteria might create the impression of a kind of ethnic formula-fiction – an impression that would be as inaccurate as it is demeaning to those writers whose work is thus described. To their credit, anthologisers in Canada and Australia, many of whom are themselves from ethnic minority backgrounds, have consistently shown their awareness of the dangers of condescension implicit in a politics of minor/ity literary labelling. Smaro Kamboureli, for instance, in her introduction to *Making a Difference: An Anthology of Canadian Multicultural Literature* (1996), makes it clear that:

> I did not want this anthology to be an instance of tokenism. … By holding on to the 'otherness' of writers … in relation to the dominant culture's self-image, tokenism assigns a single meaning of cultural differences [that] masks the many nuances of difference. … I have attempted to avoid such pitfalls by considering the contributors to this anthology as Canadian writers, and not as representatives of cultural groups. … My selection process has also been informed by my

desire to represent Canadian multicultural literature by bridging the gap between established and emerging authors.

(Kamboureli 1996: 3)

Similarly, Sneja Gunew, in her introduction to *Framing Marginality: Multicultural Literary Studies* (1994), makes a point of saying that her earlier collection *Beyond the Echo: Multicultural Women's Writing* (1988), is 'emphatically *not* an anthology of migrant writing. ... It signalled a desire ... to be considered as part of literature rather than sociology' (Gunew and Mahyuddin 1988: 9; Gunew's italics).

The defensiveness of Kamboureli's and Gunew's statements indicates an anxiety over literary categories and identitary labels that is perhaps intrinsic to the representational battles played out over the anthology as a selective form (Golding 1995; see also Chapter 8). This anxiety is more acute, however, in the case of minor/ity writing: as Patricia Eliades wryly remarks of the boom in collections of so-called migrant women's writing in late 1980s and early 1990s Australia, such 'anthologomania' served to create 'a literary orthodoxy with practices no less restrictive than those of the orthodoxy it set out to deconstruct' (Eliades 1995: 74). The question here is clearly not just of which label to use – although Gunew, for one, defends the use of 'multicultural' over and against the narrower 'ethnic' or 'migrant', on the grounds that the former is hierarchically exclusive while the latter implies a transitory relationship to the country that amounts to rootlessness (Gunew 1994: 22–3).[15] The question is rather whether individuals or groups considered as operating outside the mainstream of literary/cultural activity might not end up being marginalised further by being accorded special status. The Greek-Australian writer George Papaellinas has been particularly vehement in his criticisms of 'the categorisation of particular writers ... according to their cultural or chromosomal origins', and of an ethnic compartmentalisation of their writings that is often pursued 'regardless of subject matter, aesthetic[s], politic[s] or most importantly, language' (Papaellinas 1991: xi). While Papaellinas sees this categorising fervour as part of an attempt to redress marginalisation, he thinks 'it only encourages marginality. I agree [says Papaellinas] with [fellow Greek-Australian writer] Dimitris Tsaloumas who said that "it reflects only the official sanctioning of a cultural ghetto for non-Anglo writers which is to be patronised but only as a margin of Australian literature" ' (Papaellinas 1991: xi; also qtd in Gunew and Longley 1992: 166).

While we should be wary of construing such polemical comments as representative, they might be taken as indicating that there has been a higher degree of antagonism toward the patronising implications of multicultural literary/artistic projects in Australia than has so far proved to be the case in Canada. Why the apparent distinction? Part of the reason might be, as Gunew suggests in her introduction to *Framing Marginality*, that 'Canada is not as unrelentingly English as Australia. ... The very fact that Canada has two founding languages and cultures has made quite a difference to the level of tolerance for non-English cultures and languages' (Gunew 1994: 4). Added to this, says Gunew, is the greater critical mass of research on multicultural issues in Canada:

> [M]ore people are working on these issues in Canada, and the Canadians have achieved much more detailed work on the histories and writings of specific cultural groups. Comparable work in Australia has been much more sporadic and *ad hoc*, and bedevilled by a slightly different battery of obstacles and prejudices.
>
> (Gunew 1994: 4)

Some of these differences were already mentioned in an earlier section of this chapter. If the following speculation can be risked, an inbuilt distrust of ethnic minorities, particularly non-European minorities, runs deeper in Australia than in Canada – which might go some way toward accounting for the slowness of reception in Australia to ethnic minority writing ('Ethnic minority writers will at this stage have made little or no impact on most Australian readers' – Lumb and Hazell 1983: xiii), or toward explaining the paternalistic attitude that has prevailed there, particularly in early anthologies and collections ('This is not to say that ethnic writers can provide the qualitative stimulus of the great authors of their own national literature. They can, however, introduce a much broader and richer spectrum to Australian writing' – Jurgensen 1981: v).

A related problem here is the perceived political content of such collections. Anthologies such as Gunew's and Kamboureli's make it clear that multicultural writing is by definition politicised, even if the writers do not share the same ideological agenda or necessarily work toward the same social goals. Gunew, for example, sees multicultural writing, along with the critical discourse that seeks to validate it, as an exercise in positive discrimination designed to confront universalist assumptions 'in social areas as broad as education and employment, the law and welfare' (Gunew and Mahyuddin 1988: xix). Kamboureli goes still further, seeing her anthology *Making a Difference* (1996) as 'represent[ing] Canadian writing while calling into question representation itself' (Kamboureli 1996: 2):

> *Making a Difference* attempts to question representation in a number of ways, perhaps most significantly by challenging the concept of

minority … [I]t becomes apparent that 'marginalization,' from an individual as well as a collective perspective, is impossible to define in any stable way. These authors' experiences with Canadian publishers, the reception of their work, their personal histories in Canada, how they position themselves with regard to their cultural differences, the diverse treatment of their racial and ethnic groups by the Canadian dominant society, how (if at all) these experiences are translated into literature – all these and other related issues argue persuasively … that the concept of marginality has no inherent meaning in itself.

(Kamboureli 1996: 2)

Like several other such anthologies, Kamboureli's emphasises the material conditions under which multicultural writing is produced, consumed and disseminated – conditions of which the writers cannot help but be aware, and which several of them choose to highlight as an integral aspect of their work.[16] In a characteristic move, Kamboureli narrows the gap between the literary work and the critical discourse in which it participates, thereby playing up the self-appointed role taken on by anthologiser-critics in bringing the wider sociocultural issues raised by multicultural writing to the public eye.

Two interrelated caveats should probably be entered at this point. The first of these concerns the discrepancy between academic and popular perceptions of multiculturalism, the second the continuing debate over multicultural writing's aesthetic merits. As Francesco Loriggio has suggested in an article on multiculturalism and literary criticism in the Canadian interdisciplinary journal *Mosaic* (1996), 'the multiculturalist moment is that phase of criticism which best presents academic criticism in its ambivalence, forever caught between the desire to escape itself, to be relevant, to participate in the discussion of value to society at large, and the constraints it must impose on itself' (Loriggio 1996: 190). Anthologies such as Kamboureli's (or Gunew and Longley's in Australia) might best be seen in this context as part of a salutary, if somewhat contradictory, effort to make sophisticated academic theorising accountable to the society of which it speaks. But as Loriggio rightly contends,

There is no doubt that if one … thinks in terms of academic versus non-academic criticism, one has to score the controversy over multiculturalism – like the equally loud brouhaha over PC or over the curriculum – in favor of the editorial-page writers, the newspaper or magazine reviewers. In North America it is this group – the individuals whom university specialists usually do not even bother to malign –

who have been able to make themselves heard and with whom it has counted the most, i.e., in the public sphere and with the public at large.

(Loriggio 1996: 187)

This discrepancy needs to be borne in mind when considering two self-consciously controversial books that have served as conversational catalysts for the ongoing multiculturalism debates in Canada and Australia, respectively. These books, Neil Bissoondath's polemical treatise *Selling Illusions: The Cult of Multiculturalism in Canada* (1994) and Helen Darville-Demidenko's scandal-mongering novel *The Hand that Signed the Paper* (1994), are not only notable for their unprecedented success in mobilising public opinion, but also, especially the latter, for refocusing critical debate on the legitimisation of contemporary multicultural writing. Both books, and the controversies that surround them, deal head on with the perceived *exoticism* of multicultural writings. Such writings might be considered on the one hand as capitalising – mendaciously in some cases – from the portrayal of a cultural otherness set in apparent opposition to the Anglo-Celtic mainstream but, on the other, as falling victim to the self-serving establishment desire to assign and manipulate categories of cultural difference by attributing value to literary works primarily rewarded for representing a fetishised 'ethnic voice' (see also Introduction and Chapter 6). What is at stake here, in other words, is not just the cultural authenticity – or lack of it – supposedly embodied in these writers and their writings, but the degree of agency they are able to exercise over the production and, no less important, the subsequent reception of their work. As I have suggested in previous chapters of this book, the location of agency – or, more accurately, multiple agencies – is crucial to the unravelling of a postcolonial literary/cultural evaluative process in which 'aesthetic' and 'political' considerations are mutually imbricated and entwined. Such agencies, however, are by definition unstable, unreliable, shifting. The controversies generated by Bissoondath's and Darville-Demidenko's work serve in this context as a further illustration of the complex politics of value that surrounds the production, distribution and reception of culturally 'othered' literary/cultural works; while these debates may be used more specifically to identify the intersecting regimes of value that come into play in the continuing critical assessment of multicultural writing in Canada and Australia today.

Bissoondath and Demidenko

Few recent interventions in Canada's multiculturalism debates have proved more contentious – more ideologically divisive – than Penguin

Books' publication in 1994 of Neil Bissoondath's *Selling Illusions: The Cult of Multiculturalism in Canada*. It is tempting to see the book, an impassioned attack on the failures of government-sanctioned multiculturalism in Canada, as a strategic attempt to consolidate Bissoondath's already firmly established reputation as a controversial literary figure. Certainly, Bissoondath had already attracted a certain amount of critical, if not necessarily wider public, attention with the publication of embattled fictions (*Digging Up the Mountains*, 1985; *A Casual Brutality*, 1988; *The Innocence of Age*, 1992) that were clearly inspired by, if not directly modelled on, the combination of limpid prose and incendiary rhetoric that had long since made his uncle, V.S. Naipaul, famous.

Yet if *Selling Illusions* is undoubtedly marked by the desire to reflect on and further incite public controversy on 'the multiculturalism question', it is equally characterised by an ironically deflating tone that avoids, or at least seeks critical distance from, the more sensationalist aspects of the debate. Hence Bissoondath's frequently deployed tactic of homing in on, and then proceeding to ironise, other people's overdrawn opinions, thereby positioning his own argument – often similarly hyperbolical in its effect – as something approaching 'common sense'. Irony becomes the default mode of the self-styled anti-ideological critic, fending off the politically motivated views of his opponents in order to reassert the inalienable commonalities of human experience (Bissoondath 1994: 169, 178).

These commonalities, according to Bissoondath, have been overlooked by 'the psychology and politics of multiculturalism, ... [which] have made divisiveness in the name of racial and ethnic rights socially acceptable' (Bissoondath 1994: 185). Dependent on stereotype and a radical simplification of cultural differences, multiculturalism has ensured 'that ethnic groups will preserve their distinctiveness in a gentle and insidious form of cultural apartheid' (Bissoondath 1994: 89). The very term 'ethnic', for Bissoondath, is synonymous with a racialised perception of the other – one which hypostatises cultural difference, turning ethnic minority communities into 'museums of exoticism' (Bissoondath 1994: 111). Thus, while on the face of it multiculturalism:

> insists on [cultural] diversity, ... a case can be made that it is a diversity that depends on a vigorous conformity. Trading in the exotic, it views the individual not as a member of society at large but as a unit of a smaller group ethnically, racially or culturally defined – a group comforted by the knowledge that it has access to familiar foods, music, etc. But this is multiculturalism at its most simplistic, and in some ways most insidious, level. It is the trade-off

of the marketplace, an assurance of creature comforts in exchange for playing the ethnic game.

(Bissoondath 1994: 214)

Multiculturalism, in other words, turns ethnicity into a commodity, encouraging a view of ethnic cultures, or even culture itself, as 'a thing that can be displayed, performed, admired, bought, sold or forgotten' (Bissoondath 1994: 83). Multiculturalism thus both embodies and legitimises the spectacularising process of the exotic, a process that converts people into alternating objects of attraction and resentment (Bissoondath 1994: 122). It is possible, Bissoondath admits, to embrace this theatricalised sense of cultural otherness,

> [b]ut for those who would rather be accepted for their individuality, who resent being distinguished only by their differences, it can prove a matter of some irritation, even discomfort. The game of exoticism can cut two ways: it can prevent an individual from being ordinary, and it can prevent that individual from being accepted.

(Bissoondath 1994: 116)

By bringing multiculturalism into alignment with exoticism, Bissoondath stresses the former's capacity for the decontextualisation of sociocultural experience. But *Selling Illusions* itself arguably partakes of the theatricality it calls in question; reliant on a series of highly publicised, journalistically rendered 'incidents' to support its broad-based opinions, Bissoondath's text appears to advertise the very exoticising processes it sets out to critique. The theatricality of the text is nowhere more apparent than in the casting of its various players as semi-caricatural performers subject to Bissoondath's quasi-Prosperan control. Nor is Bissoondath necessarily averse to theatricalising himself as a performer, or rather as an aggregate of the different performers who inhabit his fictional texts:

> I have written not only from the viewpoint of young, brown-skinned men of East Indian descent born in the Caribbean and living in Canada but also from the perspective of a young Japanese woman, young black men and young black women, a young Central American girl, a middle-aged Spanish man and an elderly Jewish man, a young white woman and a young white man, a Marxist revolutionary and a CIA agent. I have written about the left and the right and their victims. I have written about political oppressors and the politically oppressed.

(Bissoondath 1994: 168–9)

This list, ostensibly a rejoinder to those critics who have accused him of Eurocentric racial stereotyping,[17] is then used to justify the view that, however he and his work may continue to be defined by others, he himself has no political axe to grind, 'no ideology to sell' (Bissoondath 1994: 169). Such self-exonerating statements, reminiscent once more of Naipaul, cannot help but seem disingenuous; as if Bissoondath wishes somehow to dissociate himself from the controversy he knows he is creating. After all, there is nothing more ideological than the 'fair-mindedness' Bissoondath believes himself to be propagating; nor is it unreasonable to suspect that he is fully aware of the complicity of his 'common-sense' views with the bogus universalism of the Canadian New Right.[18] The creation of polemic, as Bissoondath well knows, is aided and abetted by the *faux-naïf* disclaimer; the generation of controversy is only enhanced by the unassailable evidence of self-contradiction. Hence a text that deplores the 'simplification of culture', only to simplify – often mightily – in its turn; that abhors media slogans and clichés yet reproduces them in abundance; that attacks the processes of commodification without acknowledging its own status as a commodity; that critiques superficiality while itself remaining, for the most part, on a surface level. Hence a text, as well, that courts the same demagogic populism from which it claims ironic distance – a text designed to attract widespread attention to itself while self-consciously alienating 'out-of-touch' academic experts (Bissoondath 1994: 7). Here, Francesco Loriggio's nettled response seems right on cue:

> [*Selling Illusions*] is sorrowfully lacking [in] the leaps of imagination, the insights one might expect from a writer of creative literature who has turned to social criticism: the book never strays too far from the surface, and could as easily have been written by the average MP from the back benches or by the average neighborhood columnist. ... Out of the approximately one hundred and ninety quotations, over one hundred come from four Toronto and Montreal newspapers, the rest mostly from magazines or from novels. Not surprisingly, the press did not wait long to consecrate Bissoondath's book ... spurring it on to the mild bestsellerdom it achieved.
>
> (Loriggio 1996: 189)

Loriggio's annoyance derives to some extent from his previous acknowledgement that 'serious' academic scholarship has been outflanked by 'sensationalist' journalism as the primary catalysing agent for the Canadian multiculturalism debates (see quotation above).[19] Such a state of affairs is in itself hardly unusual; what is surprising is that Loriggio, along with several other academically oriented critics and reviewers, has failed to recognise that Bissoondath's book both invites and *anticipates* the critical backlash it produced. For there is a sense in which the book, media-conscious as it is, conditions its own critical responses, drawing its readers into a public debate where largely predictable ideological positions need to be restated, defended and staked out. As Noreen Golfman anecdotally puts it,

> Upon meeting people who have read *Selling Illusions* ... I have discovered that we quickly establish our positions like tourists from the same country meeting in a foreign pub. It seems socially important to declare where one is on multiculturalism these days.
>
> (Golfman 1996: 176)

As my next example will demonstrate, the so-called 'Demidenko affair', also largely media-driven, has had similar ramifications in Australia: dividing a nation on issues such as anti-Semitism and cultural appropriation; sparking a public outcry against intellectual impoverishment and the abuses of government arts funding; and stimulating heated discussion in both the academy and the mass media of the adjudicative mechanisms currently being used to determine the status, and regulate the value, of Australian multicultural writing.

Like *Selling Illusions*, *The Hand that Signed the Paper* is a manipulative work that also questions manipulation – a work that appears ironically to prefigure its own reception, and to raise doubts about the evaluative criteria that are likely to be used in its own assessment. Demidenko's multiple award-winning novel, offering a series of highly tendentious 'historical' perspectives on the collaboration of Ukrainian conscripts in the Nazi death-squads, was accused from the outset of anti-Semitism and of wilfully misconstruing the historical record (see, for example, Manne 1996). The flames were fanned when it was revealed that Demidenko – née Helen Darville, a white Anglo-Australian with no discernible Ukrainian connections – had not just reinvented history for her own imaginative purposes, but had also effectively made herself up by falsely assuming a Ukrainian name. This later revelation sparked a flurry of enraged media responses; some of these were modified, however, by positioning Demidenko in a long line of Australian literary hoaxers, all too easily duping a 'politically correct' literary establishment seemingly fixated on commandeering writers for the nation's multicultural cause. The following excerpts from the review section of the conservative daily *The Australian* make the explicit connection between multiculturalism and exoticism, revealing the underlying racism behind sanctioned celebrations of cultural difference while taking the opportunity to offer a few distinctly patronising, and suspiciously racist, comments of their own:

> Some Australian artists have long suspected that in the fiercely competitive business of securing grants and subsidies a touch of exoticism goes a long way. ... Perhaps the pen name Demidenko was a superb marketing ploy and a savvy pitch for prize money in a society which often appears to treat Anglo Celts as poor cousins to those of richer ethnic stock?
>
> (Kate Legge, 21 August 1995)

> Demidenko's false identity has clearly been designed to exploit our culture's overweening need to be seen to be promoting its obscure or exotic minorities by fashioning art out of right-on social policies.
>
> (Rosemary Neill, 24 August 1995)

> The early players in the Demidenko affair were easily duped because, for various reasons, they wanted to be seduced by the siren voices of multiculturalism. And, in a dramatic sense, they were.
>
> (Luke Slattery, 13 September 95; all of the above qtd in Jost *et al.* 1996)

These responses, and others like them, helped propel the novel into a fiercely contested – and of course highly mediated – morality play in which liberals wavered between the acceptance of a certain artistic licence and the condemnation of unethical cultural appropriation, while conservatives felt themselves bound to analyse the moral symptoms of a nation's inexorable cultural decline.[20]

What interests me here, though, is less the various accusations, serious though these are, that have been heaped on Darville-Demidenko and her novel than the implications of her work being seen as an implied commentary on the politics of multicultural literary recognition in Australia. Vijay Mishra cuts to the quick in an excellent 1996 article in the literary/cultural journal *Meanjin*:

> [I]f, as it seems, the name [Demidenko] was taken to position the author as a native informant of Ukrainian culture and thereby make postcolonial claims about the text's allegorical status, then we need to know the conditions under which the 'exotic' is incorporated into mainstream Australian culture. As for Demidenko herself, we need to ask whether she consciously parodied the seeming valorization of

multiculturalism in Australia. Was she, in effect, a functionary of a new form of [postmodern] racism?

(Mishra 1996: 350)

Mishra concludes in the affirmative; and I, for one, find it difficult to disagree with his assertion that 'Darville knew exactly what she was doing' (Mishra 1996: 350):

> She knew that an otiose settler tradition needed the multicultural writer. And she knew that naivety (the unmediated, raw style of the author) would be seen as the characteristic of a multicultural writer not quite in control of her intertexts. This is the judgement not only of the official judges (Vogel, Franklin and ASAL) [for the prizes the novel won] but of the common reader as well. Whatever the origin of the name, the effect is of confirming that the 'ethnic' enters Australian culture as an already read text. This is the essence of postmodern racism.
>
> (Mishra 1996: 350–1)

Setting aside the thorny issue of intentionality for a moment, it seems worth asking what Darville-Demidenko might have had to gain by playing a self-incriminating trick on her reading public and, more pointedly, on the Australian literary establishment. Yet this question, while staple to the debate, is perhaps irresolvable other than on the level of psychopathology. Here, it might be surmised, Darville-Demidenko must surely have guessed that the accuser would eventually turn victim; that in attempting, however indirectly, to pronounce judgement on others' evaluative prejudices, she herself would be the one to be judged, to be found guilty of fraud, to be ceremonially unmasked and punished? Ruminations like these, while purely speculative, might provide the context for a reading of the novel, less as a deconstructive allegory of the barbarities meted out on, and/or ascribed to, civilisation's designated others than as a twisted self-dramatisation of the desire to become and, eventually, *suffer as* someone else. I shall not pursue this reading here, though; instead, I shall offer some related thoughts on the novel's startlingly resonant title, and on the implications this might have for the controversy surrounding the perceived exoticism of multicultural literature and the appropriation of a commodified 'ethnic voice'.

The Hand that Signed the Paper owes its title at first sight to one of its two opening epigraphs, drawn from Dylan Thomas's eponymous poem. I shall reproduce the two quoted stanzas from Thomas's poem in their entirety here, juxtaposing them with an abridged quotation from the novel – the turning point where the protagonist Vitaly Kovalenko, acting out of what appears to be a revenge motive for Russian-Jewish atrocities previously perpetrated against his own and other Ukrainian communities, volunteers his services and is officially signed up for the Nazi death squad, the SS. Here is the first quotation:

> The hand that signed the paper felled a city;
> Five sovereign fingers taxed the breath,
> Doubled the globe of dead and halved the country;
> These five kings did a king to death.
>
> The hand that signed a treaty bred a fever,
> And famine grew, and locusts came;
> Great is the hand that holds dominion over
> Man by a scribbled name.

And here is the second:

> Vitaly leans over the desk. He notices the two Germans admiring his hair and eyes. They shove the form towards him … Vitaly stares at the paper blankly. The two Germans start to titter. The form is upside down.
>
> 'You can't fill in the form?'
>
> Vitaly shakes his head, burning with shame.
>
> 'I wouldn't worry. You're not alone.' The more senior of the two Germans takes it, gripping his fountain pen with the assurance of regular use. 'Get a move on up there, you lot,' Vitaly hears from some distance in the queue behind him.
>
> 'Name?'
>
> 'Vitaly Fyodorovich Kovalenko.'
>
> 'Age?'
>
> 'Nineteen.'
>
> 'Date of birth.'
>
> 'October 17th, 1921.'
>
> 'Any family?'
>
> 'No, sir.'
>
> The German looks up. 'You related to the last fellow?'

'Yes. He's my brother.'

'Put your mark here,' he indicates. Vitaly's callused index finger smudges the ink.

'Good. Proceed.'

(Demidenko 1994: 56–7)

Allowing, along with Mishra, for the possibility that Darville-Demidenko might have misunderstood (or deliberately misread) Thomas's poem, both of these quotations hint at the ambivalences of agency that are explored throughout the text. The hand that signs the paper is not the one that pulls the trigger (Wark 1997); the signatory of the text (Demidenko) is not the author of the novel (Darville). Such disjunctions might be read on one level as an implied plea for diminished responsibility; or as oblique testimony to the novel's relativisation of absolute evil; or as one example among several others of the narrative's morally dangerous sliding between literal and metaphorical versions of Holocaust events.[21] On another level, though, the excerpts cited here seem to gesture toward something like the opposite – to issue graphic reminders of the moral accountability of the writer as historical agent and of the formidable, potentially destructive power of writing as an instrument of authoritarian control. In this latter sense, the much-interrogated radical perspectivism of the novel might be seen to raise, not lower, the moral stakes in writing creatively about the Holocaust. As in a number of other contemporary, postcolonially inflected Holocaust narratives – Anne Michaels's *Fugitive Pieces* (1996) and Caryl Phillips's *The Nature of Blood* (1997) are two that come to mind – the writer's dialogue with the past, filtered through a tracery of other people's texts and voices, pushes the very boundaries of imaginative representation. Darville-Demidenko's own particular form of ventriloquism draws interesting connections between questions of historical agency and the 'ethics of [literary] passing' (Mishra 1996); all the same, it seems worth questioning the strategy of joining a tortured post-Holocaust mnemonics to the naively celebratory politics of multiculturalism in contemporary Australia. The conjunction amounts, at best, to a curiously self-destructive literary conceit; at worst, it appears little better than a barefaced (meta)racist prank. Notwithstanding, the novel and the debate it spurred have been useful in demonstrating the contradictions opened up within conceptions of multiculturalism that are reliant, however inadvertently, on stereotypical views of the ethnic other. If multiculturalism, as Bissoondath argues, is one of the primary conceptual mechanisms through which ethnicity is turned into a commodity, then Darville-Demidenko, successful 'multicultural writer', certainly availed herself of that mechanism – not least to expose the assumptions of some of those who helped most to promote and legitimise her work. But the same mechanism also arguably contributed to her demise; for one of the ironies of the Demidenko affair is that she herself fell victim to the process examined in and around her novel – the double-edged process by which the exotic other metamorphoses, at times almost imperceptibly, from a shimmering talisman of collective desire into a concentrated object of resentment.

Elliott and Egoyan

A similar process might also be brought to bear on two critically acclaimed 'multicultural' films of the 1990s – the Canadian writer-director Atom Egoyan's multiple award-winning psychological thriller *Exotica* and the Australian filmmaker Stephan Elliott's rambunctiously camp musical extravaganza *The Adventures of Priscilla, Queen of the Desert* (both 1994). Both films mischievously exhibit their awareness of their own commodity status, playing with considerable (if perhaps not entirely convincing) irony on the marketability of Western exotic myths. Elliott's *Priscilla* is a colourful road movie set in the Australian interior and featuring three crossdressing 'showgirls' – more accurately, two gay male drag queens and a transsexual – in search of recognition in a hostile, homophobic country; while Egoyan's *Exotica* is a darkly offbeat, Canadian-based psychosexual drama, alternating between ironically mirrored 'exotic' locations at a pet shop and a strip club, and manipulating the exoticist tropes of voyeurism, nostalgic transference and untouchability. Both films are self-consciously exoticist in their spectacularisation of sexual/racial difference and in their ironic portrayal of the gendered body as a 'forbidden' fetish object; but both also comment on the surveillance and containment of nominally transgressive desire in societies which, for all their claims to multicultural diversification, are still beset by fears and fantasies surrounding the figure of the ethnic other.

Priscilla, a big box-office success in both Australia and North America, impressed audiences and reviewers alike with its extravagant theatricality; with its flamboyant costumes and dance routines; and above all, perhaps, with the virtuoso performance of matinée idol Terence Stamp in the unaccustomed role of the soul-searching 'tart-with-a-heart' transsexual, Bernadette. The film, described by one reviewer as a 'post-Queer, post-"Supermodel" *La Cage aux Folles*' (Francke 1994: 384), can be seen on one level as a triumph of camp performance, with memorable moments in the desert, where our three outrageous hero(in)es strut their stuff, resplendent in their spangled outfits, to the initial bafflement but eventual delight of their impromptu Aboriginal audience; and at the end of their journey in Alice Springs, when they climb – as Bernadette self-mockingly calls them, 'three cocks in frocks on a rock' – to the top of the King's Canyon, from where they proceed, out-camping even Julie Andrews, to serenade the setting sun.

For all its comic extravagance, the film exhibits dubious sexual and racial politics. The problem centres here on the film's – admittedly ironic – manipulation of exoticist tropologies as a means of attempting to defuse the sexual/racial threat of the other by rerouting it back to the ideology of the same.[22] The figure of the drag queen, for instance, can itself be construed as paradigmatically exotic – cosmetically transgressive and yet in the end largely unchallenging; neither unimaginably other nor yet reassuringly the same.[23] As Ann Seaton, in one of the few negative reviews of *Priscilla*, remarks acerbically,

> Drag queens appear to threaten the notion of heterosexual masculinity, yet they may … serve as a potent reminder in the face of the threat of castration that the penis does actually exist. Exotically different and yet as familiar as masculinity, drag queens are figures that may be appropriated in order to stage a drama about loss, castration, and ultimate intactness.
>
> (Seaton 1996: n.p.)

Priscilla, for Seaton, is best understood as such a drama, 'in which the potentially … threatening spectacle of the [exotic] drag queen diffuses much of its potential for subversion by constantly being associated with racist, nationalist, and misogynist points of view' (n.p.). Perhaps the best example here is in what Seaton describes as *Priscilla*'s defining 'multicultural moment' – the appearance in the film of another, more obviously threatening kind of 'exotic dancer'. This latter figure is Cynthia, belligerent wife of kindly Bob the car-mechanic, who repairs the drag queens' ailing tour-bus (the eponymous Priscilla), and who appears during the course of the movie to develop an attraction to the transsexual, Bernadette. Cynthia – inarticulate, overbearing, and of indeterminate Asian origin – clearly sees herself as a rival to the Anglo-Australian drag queens, outdoing them with a little ping pong ball-spitting *chinoiserie* of her own. The scene is a disturbing one, not only from the perspective of gender (with the demonised Asian woman's *vagina dentata* symbolically castrating her husband, as well as exposing the drag queens' obvious genital 'deficiencies'), but also because it substitutes for boorish homophobic insult the no less offensive discourse of patriotic racial slur.

As might be expected, the drag queens win out in the end, disarming the 'Oriental menace'. As Seaton puts it, 'the strange exchange of homophobia for racism is a lesson in the politics of exoticism: a serious threat, Asia, is deferred by the admittance of a less serious [one], white male Australian crossdressers' (n.p.).

Elliott's film might be defended here on the grounds that its racist slurs are 'ocker' Australian parodies, and that its journey into the desert – itself a stock Australian motif – provides an opportunity to spoof some of the nation's most durable white male-supremacist mythic figures: the matey good bloke, the anti-establishment outlaw-drifter, the Asian *femme fatale*, the credulous Aborigine, the maverick explorer negotiating a spectacular but hazardous indigenous landscape, and so on. These myths, however, run the risk of being recuperated by the movie; reconfigured rather than seriously challenged, they are merely estranged by being dressed in gaudy drag performer's clothes. For in fact, despite its transgressive veneer, *Priscilla* is profoundly mainstream, celebrating romantic love and the nostalgic virtues of family and friendship; articulating, if also parodying, the clichéd view of a fun-loving, culturally diverse Australia, in which the threat of the racial other can be effectively contained, or at least temporarily dissolved, in endearing high jinks and palatable high-camp entertainment; and recycling the commodified vision of a rough-and-ready English-speaking country, inhabited by affable beer-swilling 'blokes' – even if some of those 'blokes' might happen to wear skirts. The teasing performativity of *Priscilla* provides the perfect alibi, allowing the serious issues the movie poses – male chauvinism, xenophobia, racial violence – to be temporarily disarmed by being converted into self-consciously trivialising exotic spectacle; and turning its various gestures toward otherness – its apparent upsetting, for example, of conventional gender categories – into mechanisms for the occlusion of white male ideologies (mateship) and racially divisive myths (the Asian threat). No doubt, the film is more finely nuanced – and less reactionary – than my brief commentary on it might have given the impression here; easy on the eye, eager to please, it is no surprise that it was generally well received in Australia and elsewhere by gay and straight audiences alike. Less subversive than accommodating, *Priscilla* demonstrates the relative conventionality – and hence commodity appeal – of drag performance; and in the end, as in drag performance, it reasserts male camaraderie, protecting phallic values which, behind the simulation of castration and loss, remain intact.

Egoyan's *Exotica*, similarly, is less transgressive than it initially appears or pretends to be. The tangled storyline concerns the misdeeds of a Toronto pet shop owner, who is smuggling exotic birds' eggs across the

US/Canadian border, and the tax inspector who comes to audit him, and soon discovers his illegal business, but who turns out to be covering up a few misdemeanours of his own. Both are traders in exotica, the bumbling pet shop owner and the taciturn tax inspector who, understandably distressed at the loss of his wife (killed in a car accident) and his daughter (brutally murdered), retreats to a strip club in search of solace and the illusion of sexual release. As the plot thickens, the film transforms into a catalogue of obsessions, with lovers crossed, 'daughters' lost and found, and sexual fantasies for every taste. What rescues the film from farce, though, making it eerily effective, is its relentless surveillance of the nominally transgressive desires of its protagonists. Thus, in the opening sequence, the pet shop owner is watched from behind a one-way mirror by customs officials who seem preternaturally alert to his illegal trade; while in a parallel scene at the club, the DJ moodily scans the customers, who are licensed to look, not touch, and are watched in turn from behind the scenes. Then the DJ mounts his platform, less eyrie than panopticon, from where he croons intros to the dancers while marshalling their clients' 'illicit' desires. And capturing it all from above is the camera, invigilating the public arena but also intruding into the private lives of those who are gathered there; beguiling the line between the routinised revelations of exotic/erotic performance and the arbitrary unmasking of far more disturbing, even potentially dangerous, ambitions and secrets.

Exotica, in short, is a highly voyeuristic movie which shows that voyeurism itself can be a profitable, if also mostly a sterile, business. Egoyan's point seems in part to be an ethical one about the policing of sexual fantasy and the commodification of longing in an organised society. 'Exoticism' becomes the codeword for this process of containment, a process which however (much as in *Priscilla*) is never quite complete. Egoyan himself suggests as much in a 1995 interview with the film critic Geoff Pevere, attributing the financial transactions that govern the relationships between his characters in *Exotica* to a complex of commodity-exchanges designed to regulate, and to some extent normalise, pathological experience:

> [T]he contracts and financial exchanges [in *Exotica*] are a way of making tangible that which is too terrifyingly abstract otherwise. They're able to crystallize and articulate the parameters of a relationship by a means which is easy to understand with the exchange of a bill. You've given me a service, and by the amount of money that I'm paying you, we've understood what that service is worth. And the moment we understand what it's worth, we're able to commodify it. Now why do we do that? Because otherwise it's frightening to under-

stand what's brought me to the point where I have to even talk to a stranger or have a stranger dance for me at a table, or to have to pick up someone at an opera, or have to drive home my niece who's pretending to babysit a child who's not home [all of the above are incidents from the film]. All these ideas are otherwise so grotesque and pathological that by putting a price to them, you're saying they work within the everyday understanding of how we define a marketplace.

(Pevere 1995: 57)

As Egoyan implies, the exoticism/eroticism nexus operates both as overt control-mechanism and as covert alibi. Under the sign of the exotic, the club provides a forum for the channelling, through carefully monitored procedures of commodity exchange, of erotic fears, desires and fantasies which, given no other outlet, might well prove to be destructive.[24] But such domesticated procedures, Egoyan suggests, may also act as a cover for more genuinely subversive forms of behaviour. The multiple, often contradictory signifiers that cluster around the term 'exotic' in *Exotica* open up a crisis of moral agency that Egoyan's movie seems unable to resolve. The self-enclosed exotic worlds of the club and the pet shop seem no more artificial, and no more ethically ambivalent, than the outside world of everyday social responsibilities from which they offer the illusion of protection and release. These different worlds do not so much collide as merge; reinforced by artful camerawork that makes good use of blurring (soft-focus shots, dissolves) and perspectival multiplication (flashbacks, inserts, mirrors), the film continually collapses ontological levels between 'real' and 'represented' worlds, public and private spaces, the past and the present. Exoticism re-emerges here as a mode of consumption (the exotic other as commodity); as a superficially attractive decoy for power; and as a performatively oriented and, above all, *embodied* technology of disguise and mystification. Less a 'moral time-out' (Rousseau and Porter 1990: 17) than a testing mechanism for what is ethically permissible, the exoticist register of Egoyan's film oscillates between the alternative poles of surreptitious social control and profoundly anti-social concealment.

In bringing these two modes together, Egoyan's film probes exoticism's gendered dialectic of attraction and repulsion (Todorov 1993). But this dialectic is also *racialised* – a dimension nowhere more apparent than in the film's oblique treatment of multiculturalism as a conceptual control-device/alibi for erotic desires projected onto the ethnic other. Not that the dancers at the club are identifiably 'ethnic'; while the owner, cannily playing up to her exotic ('Oriental') self-image, seems only too happy to front a club that makes her living, as it had made her mother's before her.

The owner's office, and the owner herself, are decked out in the stereotypically exoticist regalia of the Eastern harem, with costume and decor forming the twin iconographic components of what appears at first to be little more than a playfully commercialised parody of Orientalist image-making. But this parody is by no means as gratuitous, nor indeed as gentle, as it seems. It is helpful to posit the link here between Egoyan's presentation of 'Exotica' as a female-run strip club/simulated harem and Ella Shohat's postcolonial-feminist reading of the imaginary of the harem in Western Orientalist film. Cinematic representations of the harem, says Shohat (via Mulvey), have historically been structured around 'the scopic privilege of the (Western) master'; while many have used 'panopticonlike camera[work .. to link] visual pleasure with a kind of surveillance of manipulated female movement' (Shohat 1997: 52).

Egoyan's film ironically 'signifies' on this cinematic history while providing a transition between the imaginaries of the colonial past and the postcolonial, multicultural present. This transition is best effected in the movie's own particular multicultural moment – the surprising revelation, in a home video shot by the tax inspector, that his (now-deceased) wife and daughter are of colour. But why should this be so surprising? Is Egoyan throwing down the gauntlet here to an implied white-mainstream audience, confronting them with the surprise they feel on seeing the wife and daughter as a marker of their own exoticist attitudes to race? The possibility cannot be discounted; while the film also appears to suggest that the multiculturalism of urban societies like Toronto's (and, by extension, Canada's) provides a patina of integration that overlays a gulf of continuing ignorance and hate. Not that the film tells us much about the tax inspector's relationship with his wife (other than that she was having an affair with his brother). Nor does it tell us if his daughter fell victim to racially motivated abuse; for Egoyan, typically, makes his audience work by deliberately keeping his characters' motives uncertain (Pevere 1995). However, the film does demonstrate clearly that the discourse of exoticism is far from harmless; and that beneath the alluring spectacle of exotic/erotic entertainment, there is a play of desires that is no less violent for being monitored and controlled (Todorov 1993: 323).

If *Priscilla* and *Exotica* are to be seen, in any sense, as 'multicultural' movies, then the multiculturalism that they portray belongs to the order of performance, more specifically spectacle. The spectacularisation of ethnic difference in either film, especially Elliott's, has distinctly racist overtones – ones in which both filmmaker and audience are apparently complicit. Clearly, however, neither Elliott nor Egoyan is unaware of these implications, and their self-consciously exoticist approach to (multi)cultural spectacle performs a demythifying function appropriate to their purpose of social critique. *Priscilla* and *Exotica*, in their different ways, explore how the current debates surrounding multiculturalism, ethnicity and sexual difference are frequently mediated through, as well as mystified by, the aestheticising discourse of exoticism. It might of course be argued that both films partake of the exoticism(s) they set out to critique; but in so doing, they also hint at the discrepancy between official multicultural policy and the commodified multiculturalisms of the arts and entertainment industries. In this sense, *Priscilla* and *Exotica*, for all their superficial glamour, present a serious warning that multiculturalism's celebratory 'rainbow' visions can easily be appropriated – as a means of recycling profitable exotic myths about the threatening sexual/racial other as an object of dangerous erotic desire; and about the availability of society's others as a source of commercial spectacle.

Conclusion

This chapter has attempted to show up faultlines within contemporary multicultural discourse by concentrating on the moments when it intersects with, and becomes scarcely distinguishable from, exoticist modes of representation and symbolic exchange. Such moments might be seen as instances of a 'boutique multiculturalism' in which the emphasis on spectacle and a commodified appreciation for the cultural other occlude the underlying political mechanisms through which more 'traditional' racial/ethnic hierarchies are preserved. After all, it is the singular ambiguity of the term 'multiculturalism' that has allowed its proponents to implement it – often seemingly simultaneously – as a corrective liberal-pluralist programme of minority recognition/social integration and as a closet-conservative ideology of separate development that patronises even as it promotes respect, ghettoises even as it fosters inclusion. Similarly, debates over the possible 'meanings' of multiculturalism (political, ideological, demographic, etc.) have sometimes tended to cloud specific issues of application and agency – when and where multiculturalism has been deployed; by and for whom it has been instrumentalised and effected. If the exoticist parameters of multicultural discourse – the construction and commodification of the cultural other; mystified processes of reification and museumification; the decontextual-ised appreciation of non-mainstream cultures and cultural forms; the fetishisation of a cultural difference centred on and mediated by the gendered/ethnicised body – make anything clear, it is how *unclearly* multiculturalism continues to operate, both as institutional practice (the day-to-day effects of government policy) and as idealised perception (the future-oriented vision of how different cultural entities might peacefully co-exist and productively interact with one another within a larger, usually national, framework).

This is not to say that multiculturalism should be dismissed as chimerical or unworkable, or that it should primarily be seen as the brainchild of a white government-élite looking to protect its own hegemonic cultural interests. It is merely to point out that multiculturalism is, almost by definition, conceptually conflicted and ideologically riven – conflicts and rifts papered over, but also paradoxically articulated, by its own exoticising manoeuvres. This chapter, in focusing on the debates surrounding multicultural writing and, to a lesser extent, film in present-day Canada and Australia, has sought to bring some of those conflicts and constitutive contradictions to light. Such debates help reveal the mechanisms – (self-) packaging of multicultural products, (self-)staging of their producers, etc. – through which multiculturalism functions in mainstream society as a powerful *discourse of desire*. And as I have shown, this desire – that other voices be heard, that non-mainstream views be included and celebrated – can easily lend itself to various forms of exploitation and manipulation. For example, one of several lessons learnt from the Demidenko affair is that the theatricalised perception of cultural otherness implicit in the term 'multicultural literature' might allow for exploitative stagings of ethnic identity that profit from, while also critiquing, the cultural assumptions and evaluative prejudices of their assessors. Such multiply mediated processes of cultural self-fashioning shed further light on the commodity fetishism that attaches itself to 'ethnic' products usually regarded as, and sometimes rewarded for, emanating from outside the cultural mainstream. If multiculturalism, to repeat, describes while also mystifying the process through which ethnicity is turned into a commodity, then that commodity passes through the hands of, is both consumed and endorsed by, many different people. Thus, to gauge the extent to which multicultural writing might be considered 'exotic' is to confront a complex evaluative machinery in which several competing interests, not least commercial ones, are at stake. Rival interests and agendas, some of which may be deeply troubling; for if 'boutique multiculturalism' is increasingly acknowledged as being mediated through the self-privileging discourse of exoticism, might it not be time to recognise exoticism itself as 'a boutique form of xenophobia'? (Papaellinas, in Gunew and Longley 1992: 166).

6 Ethnic autobiography and the cult of authenticity

Introduction: the demand for autobiography

Ethnic autobiography, like ethnicity itself, flourishes under the watchful eye of the dominant culture; both are caught in the dual processes of commodification and surveillance (see previous chapter).[1] This might help explain why the work of writers who come from, or are perceived as coming from, ethnic minority backgrounds continues to be marketed so resolutely for a mainstream reading public as 'autobiographical'. Granted, many of these writers have experimented with one form or other of autobiography – a literary genre which, while less flexible than some, undoubtedly provides a range of useful models for the recuperative articulation of lived experience. Still, as Susan Hawthorne among others has argued, even when such writers – particularly women writers – have produced other literary forms, especially novels, 'their attempts to universalise their experience [have tended all too often to be] reduced to the particularities of a lived life' (Hawthorne 1989: 262). Why should this be so? One reason, Hawthorne suggests, is that there is a mainstream *demand* for ethnic (minority) autobiography that is 'precipitated [in part] by voyeurism on the part of the dominant culture' (Hawthorne 1989: 263). Ethnic autobiographies, in this context, signal the possibility of indirect access to 'exotic' cultures whose differences are acknowledged and celebrated even as they are rendered amenable to a mainstream reading public. As Hawthorne suggests, ethnic autobiographies might be construed as less imaginatively rich than other, more canonical works of Western literature; for while '[t]he particularities of the dominant culture are [often] taken to be universal by those who transmit the canon to lay readers ... the particularities of the non-dominant culture are [usually] taken to be simply that: particularities' (Hawthorne 1989: 263). Notwithstanding, there are compensations: for one, the 'ethnographic' translation of personal experience into a composite metonymy for a range of cultural practices invested with an authenticity that the dominant culture either professes to lack or that it claims to have lost, and for which it feels a mute nostalgia. Under these conditions, ethnic autobiography provides the basis for a redemptive exploration of a putatively threatened cultural authenticity – an authenticity, however, not so much recuperated as retranslated to meet the dominant culture's needs.[2]

Now, this market-oriented view of ethnic autobiography is nothing if not simplistic, and unsurprisingly it has been challenged in recent years by an increasing number of literary/cultural critics who have tended to emphasise the hybrid construction of the minority or postcolonial cultural subject. Françoise Lionnet, for instance, in her 1995 study of postcolonial women's autobiography, *Postcolonial Representations*, suggests how postcolonial women writers 'are searching for new cultural forms and hybrid languages that better represent the particularisms of the communities about which they write' (Lionnet 1995: 19). These new forms and languages imply a critique, even a dismissal, of essentialist forms of cultural authenticity that are no longer commensurate – if they ever were – with the experience of multiply affiliated cultural subjects in today's postcolonial world. In such a world, says Lionnet via the anthropologist Renato Rosaldo,

> the view of an authentic culture as an autonomous internally coherent universe no longer seems tenable. ... Neither 'we' nor 'they' are as self-contained and homogeneous as we/they once appeared. All of us inhabit an interdependent late 20th century world, which is at once marked by borrowing and lending across porous cultural boundaries, and saturated with inequality, power, and domination.
>
> (Rosaldo 1988: 87, qtd in Lionnet 1995: 15)

Ethnic autobiography is a privileged mode for the exploration of fractured postcolonial subjectivity, since, as Caren Kaplan suggests, 'the burden of ethnic autobiographical writing is to participate in at least two different registers at all times, even two separate temporalities' (Kaplan 1988: 148). However, there seems to be an obvious danger here in collapsing the distinction between 'ethnic' and 'postcolonial' autobiographical writing – a conflation most often found in the United States, where inter- or transnational postcolonial paradigms tend to be conscripted, at times uncritically, for national minority concerns (see Conclusion). A further danger exists in conflating the themes, issues and forms of *ethnic* autobiographical writing with those of the – usually oral-based – life-narratives of *indigenous* peoples. As I argued in the last chapter, the terms 'indigenous' and 'ethnic' are not only ontologically dissimilar but are also likely to raise rather different, possibly incompatible, social, cultural and ideological concerns. In this chapter I shall suggest, against the grain perhaps, that 'ethnic' and 'indigenous' autobiographies may both be seen in a wider postcolonial context. However, I shall also test the limits of the applicability of the term 'postcolonial' to a particular literary form, and in a specific cultural context, where it has most often been rejected: Aboriginal life-writing.[3] Finally, I shall consider, as I have done in previous chapters, the obvious tensions created between oppositional forms of 'marginal' writing and the multiple constraints placed upon them by the mainstream demands they are invited – or even expected – to meet. These tensions centre on rival conceptions of, and competing demands for, *cultural authenticity*; and they are played out, as I shall demonstrate, in the market-oriented 'paratextual apparatuses' (Genette 1987) that characteristically surround contemporary Aboriginal women's life-narratives. But first, a word is needed here on the implications of the term 'authenticity'; on its relevance to the autobiographical writings of historically marginalised individuals/peoples; and on the distinction between a *culture* of authenticity (Taylor 1991) based on the ethically driven, historically situated quest for self-fulfilment and a *cult* of authenticity (see also Brydon 1990: 195) in which 'the authentic' becomes simultaneously anxiety-ridden sign of loss and redemptive fetish.

Autobiography, gender and the paradoxes of Native authenticity

How can 'authenticity' be defined? For the Canadian philosopher Charles Taylor, it is best defined in terms of the moral ideals behind self-fulfilment. Authenticity, in other words, constitutes first and foremost an ethical imperative – an imperative, put in the simplest possible terms, to be true to oneself (Taylor 1991: 15). For Taylor, the ethic of authenticity can be traced back to the end of the eighteenth century, when the individually oriented philosophies of Locke, Rousseau and Descartes provided a platform for today's pervasive culture of self-fulfilment. However, as Taylor acknowledges, the dividing-line is by no means clear between the endorsement of self-fulfilment and the licence for self-indulgence; as a result, authenticity always runs the risk of sliding into narcissism or solipsism, with an 'authentic' way of life being valued for little more than its own, or its owner's, sake.

A further problem is that if authenticity conveys the idea of self-discovery through experience, the desire to get in touch with one's 'true feelings', this desire may often betray its opposite – the fear of loss or alienation, of being or having become somehow inauthentic. Hence, on a more collective level, the interpellation of the authentic *other* as a compensatory or redemptive strategy – the invocation of Native spirituality, for example, as a necessary antidote to a Western culture rendered inauthentic by its attachment to material excess. Here, as Deborah Root among others has shown, the paradoxes begin to multiply. For one, Native authenticity (and other non-Western authenticities) have undeniably become valuable *commodities*; as Root puts it wryly, 'authenticity is [now] the currency at play in the marketplace of cultural difference' (Root 1996: 78).[4] As Root points out, the commodification of, say, a Native American tribal artifact does not necessarily rob it of its authenticity; rather, it fulfils a separate function according to whether it is seen and assessed in terms of use-value or exchange-value (Root 1996: 80). Still, the paradox remains that authenticity is valued for its attachment to the material contexts of lived experience even as it is so palpably the *decontextualisation* of the commodified artifact that enables it to become marketably authentic. Another form this paradox takes is in what the anthropologist James Clifford has called 'ethnographic salvage': the attempt, through state-managed projects of conservation – galleries, museums, etc. – to rescue 'authentic' cultures from the threat of dissipation, contingency and loss. As Clifford remarks pointedly, 'authenticity is something produced, not salvaged'; and it is produced primarily 'by removing objects and cultures from their current historical situation' (Clifford 1988: 250, 228).[5] One paradox generates another; for if authenticity as marketing tool depends on a perception of cultural distinctiveness, the market itself often assumes the virtual interchangeability of authentic cultures and cultural goods.[6] And still another; for while the authenticity of the commodified ethnic/tribal artifact depends to some extent on what we might call an illusion of transparency – that it is externally recognisable as authentic, that it is what it appears to be – its authenticity also remains to be discovered, a mysterious essence hidden beneath the veil of surface appearances.

These paradoxes may also be brought to bear on ethnic and, especially, indigenous writing, both of which forms can be co-opted to bolster the authenticity of the cultures from which they are perceived to spring. Nor is it just a question of certain features of the writing being identified as 'authentic' semiotic markers;[7] it is rather the case that *authenticity itself* can be made to circulate as a commodity, in such a way that often clichéd 'representations, images, and stereotypes of the [authentic] Native become the abstract figures of a late-capitalist currency' (Emberley 1993: 125). As Julia Emberley argues in her materialist study of Native women's writing in Canada, *Thresholds of Difference* (1993), the documented discovery of an indigenous literature in Canada over the last three decades might be seen as suppressing Native agency even as it pretends to acknowledge and celebrate it:

> The emergence of a new literary object – Native literature – ... has drawn attention to the overwhelming 'silencing' of Native cultures, the degree to which their writings have either been denied or been made invisible, and their virtual absence from the Canadian main-stream publishing industry.
>
> (Emberley 1993: 126)

The search for authenticity arguably forms part of that neocolonial silencing process, leading critics such as Margery Fee to suggest forcefully that

> [t]he demand for 'authenticity' denies Fourth World writers a living, changing culture. Their culture is deemed to be Other and must avoid crossing those fictional but ideologically essential boundaries between Them and Us, the Exotic and the Familiar, the Past and the Future, the 'Dying' and the Living.
>
> (Fee 1989: 17)

Sonia Kurtzer, in a 1998 essay on Aboriginal literature in the Australian journal *Southerly*, also sees authenticity as part of a wider exoticist representational mechanism through which images of the indigenous other are created, manipulated and controlled by the dominant culture. The aim, as in most other forms of exoticist representation, is to create and transmit a familiar, domesticated difference (see Introduction). In this context, says Kurtzer, the increasing attention being paid to Aboriginal literature in Australia is not necessarily the sign of a new multicultural openness; rather, it registers 'the [conventional] desires of the hegemonic culture to hear "authentic" tales of the "other" ', preferably in accordance with those tales and images of otherness already possessed (Kurtzer 1998: 20). The liberal 'politics of recognition' (Taylor 1994), in Australia and elsewhere, is by no means immune from similar criticisms; in fact, as Gareth Griffiths goes so far as to suggest, the 'writing of the Australian Aboriginal under the sign of "authenticity" [might even be seen] as an act of "liberal" discursive violence, parallel in many ways to the inscription of the "native" (indigene) under the sign of the savage' (Griffiths 1994: 71).

We should be wary, of course, of perpetuating patterns such as these by creating the fiction of a homogeneous body of 'Fourth World' writing, or by insisting that white inscriptions on 'Fourth World' cultures, however well intentioned, are necessarily – structurally – oppressive. It still seems safe to suggest that escalating demands for Native authenticity on the part of mostly white middle-class consumers belong to a machinery of representation that constrains Native writers even as it provides an outlet, and an audience, for their work. This, in brief, is the argument put forward by Stephen Muecke in 'Aboriginal Literature and the Repressive Hypothesis' (1988), an influential essay first published more than ten years ago but still relevant to today's debates.[8] For Muecke, taking issue implicitly with Emberley's cultural-imperialist thesis, '[t]he story of Aboriginal relations to the publishing industry is not [as is often believed] one of persecution and struggle' (Muecke 1988: 412). On the contrary, says Muecke, the more recent history of these relations indicates a 'readiness, even eagerness, to publish work by Aboriginal writers' (Muecke 1988: 413). But, as Muecke adds later,

> this general situation of acceptance tends to hide a more complex series of apparatuses of exclusion and co-option. As different stories are demanded by different groups, Aboriginality tends to be defined in advance. It is defined differently in the legal, anthropological, medical and just about every other social sphere. While these (white) constructions of Aboriginality are necessarily artificial, it is also a problem for Aborigines to 'express' a true Aboriginality independently of them.
> (Muecke 1988: 417)

As Muecke acknowledges, the idea that there might be a 'true Aboriginality' that can be 'expressed' is part of the problem, a problem whose origin lies less in the hands of Aboriginal writers themselves than in the horizon of expectations set up by the mainstream culture industries they – sometimes involuntarily – serve. One set of expectations revolves around issues of endangered authenticity; another around the 'ethnographic realism' that accrues to texts perceived as coming 'from the other side' (Muecke 1988: 409). And a third strand has to do with forms of autobiographical self-representation in which the historical contingencies of cultural production are set aside to make way for a dissenting version of 'the Romantic legacy of the expressive self' (Muecke 1988: 416). The idea of Aboriginal autobiography as a recuperative paradigm for personal/cultural self-expression is coterminous with a view of 'Aboriginal literature [as] the psychological outcome of social oppression' (Muecke 1988: 416). This view, as Muecke demonstrates, is not only inherently oversimplified, but also lends support to a politics of guilt and reparation that risks co-opting Aboriginal writing to the white-liberal Australian cause. Authenticity functions here, we might say, less as a validating mechanism for collective Aboriginal consciousness than as a kind of cultural fetish reminding white Australians of the discrepancy between past material gains and present spiritual losses.[9] Meanwhile, the autobiographical trope of triumph-over-adversity, filtered through the evergreen legend of the 'Aussie battler', can be appropriated for a white reading public eager to learn about 'Aboriginal experience', more eager still to assimilate that experience to their own formative cultural myths. Lastly, there is 'the addition of a feminist response which has in recent years endorsed and revalued feminine subjectivity according to the repressive hypothesis: out of silence or absence comes the reconstruction of selfhood, and this effect is redoubled with the female Aboriginal subject' (Muecke 1988: 409).

It seems worth pausing here to consider the implications of this apparent 'double colonisation', through which a recovery of female agency is rendered coextensive with the authenticity of the marginalised autobiographical subject. As Sidonie Smith and Julia Watson argue in their introduction to the collection *De/Colonizing the Subject: The Politics of Gender in Women's Autobiography* (1992), both the word and the practice *autobiography* 'invoke a particular genealogy, resonant ideology, and discursive imperative' (Smith and Watson 1992: xvii). Autobiography, for Smith and Watson, is tied in with Enlightenment notions of a coherently modelled self, 'ontologically identical to other "I"s, [that] sees its destiny in a teleological narrative enshrining the "individual" and "his" uniqueness' (Smith and Watson 1992: xvii). 'Traditional' conceptions of autobiographical selfhood are bound up, that is, with Enlightenment ideals of authenticity, but also with privileges of race, class and, especially, gender that are elided in the figure of the 'universal human subject' (Smith and Watson 1992: xvii).[10] Smith and Watson, among others, see women's autobiographical writing as tacitly or explicitly resisting these universalist models. However, the idea (or ideal) of authenticity is not necessarily abandoned; rather, it is modified in accordance with the specificities of female experience. Hence the dual agenda implicit in, say, Rita Felski's conceptualisation of 'feminist confession', a literary mode that 'exemplifies the intersection between the autobiographical imperative to communicate the truth of unique individuality and the feminist concern with the representative and intersubjective elements of women's experience' (Felski 1989: 93). In the work of Françoise Lionnet, feminist and postcolonial agendas are brought together in a paradigm of female ethnic autobiography in which 'autobiographical mythologies of empowerment are usually mediated by a desire to revise and rewrite official, recorded history' (Lionnet 1995: 22). Lionnet's emphasis is on the communitarian, rather than individualistic, modes of self-expression that colonised or marginalised peoples have historically adopted, both as a means of coming to terms with their own subject positions and of 'helping to transform the mentality of the oppressed' (Lionnet 1995: 22). A kind of *counter-authenticity* emerges here that is empowering to those who posit it, but is also deconstructive of the conventional (masculinist) autobiographical authority of the universal human subject. There are problems of course associated with Lionnet's theoretical model, not least in the easy assumption that postcolonial/ethnic autobiographies automatically resist imperial authority, and that women's autobiographies, insofar as these are agreed to have 'subversive' tendencies, are likely to do so more than men's. The lure of counter-authenticity – communitarian, feminist, anti-colonial – seems to risk substituting one form of identitary essentialism for another; Lionnet's model appears, moreover, to risk falling prey to the same expressivist fallacy that Muecke and others have seen as indirectly limiting the agency of historically marginalised peoples.

Further problems emerge when we begin to consider the particularities of *indigenous* autobiographical narratives. For one thing, these narratives offer frequent reminders of the oral sources from which they are drawn; for another, they are collaborative attempts to transmit, not just one but a whole heritage of life-stories.[11] It is certainly possible to assimilate indigenous autobiographies, like other forms of indigenous writing, to a grand narrative of anti-imperialist resistance. But a lingering sense remains in which such writing evades the categories into which it is drawn – the categories of genre and history, certainly, but possibly even the commodified category of 'resistance' itself (Longley 1992: 382–3). Indeed, such are the specificities of indigenous autobiographical narratives – and this includes the particular material circumstances under which they are produced, as well as the alternative ontologies and (life-)histories many of them deploy – that the more specialised term of 'life-story' or 'life-narrative' is now generally preferred, not least by indigenous writers themselves. As Mudrooroo, for example, argues in his critical study of Aboriginal writing, *Milli Milli Wangka* (1997), the term 'life-story' has the advantage of escaping

> the genre of biography or autobiography which often does not fit this kind of writing. 'Auto' in this sense often means 'self' and biography too is concentrated on self, often to the exclusion of community. When [for example] we come to [an autobiographical narrative such as] *Auntie Rita* (1994), we enter the realm of collaboration; not the collaboration between an Indigenous woman and a European person, but that between a Queensland Murri woman and her daughter [the co-authors of the work, Rita and Jackie Huggins].
>
> (Mudrooroo 1997: 187–8; for a further discussion of *Auntie Rita*, see below)

Mudrooroo's distinction between two forms of collaboration, with the latter clearly being favoured, raises the complex issue of the editorial role played by – usually white – transcribers and intermediaries in the production of Aboriginal texts.[12] Mudrooroo's vision of an authentic Aboriginal life-story seems to be one produced by Aborigines for Aborigines, rather than 'a heavily edited literature written and revised in conjunction with a European', and whose aim is in large part to 'explain Indigenous individuals [and, one presumes, societies] to a predominantly white readership' (Mudrooroo 1997: 16). Mudrooroo acknowledges that this latter type of literature, among which he includes the best-known life-narratives of the late 1980s, Sally Morgan's *My Place* (1987), Glenyse Ward's *Wandering Girl* (1988) and Ruby Langford Ginibi's *Don't Take Your Love to Town* (1988), has helped contribute to what he calls – with more than a hint of sarcasm – Australia's Period of Reconciliation; but he also sees it as having promoted a normative view of Aboriginal authenticity that is simultaneously tailored to the mass market and adapted to the needs of a politically concerned white-liberal elite. In the process, says Mudrooroo, 'activist literature' has been largely replaced by a 'literature of understanding' – one that seeks to translate Aboriginal experience into a language that white readers can grasp and appreciate (Mudrooroo 1997: 16). One wonders whether this accommodation of the white reader is as complete as Mudrooroo supposes, or whether the contestatory authenticities surrounding Aboriginal writing – particularly autobiographical writing – are as unequivocally opposed as he claims. The overdrawn distinction between an 'activist literature' and a 'literature of understanding' reveals anxieties over Native authenticity that arguably stem from Mudrooroo's own intermediary position between the white academy for which he works and publishes and the Aboriginal communities on whose behalf he wishes to speak.[13] His argument indicates, nonetheless, that the continuing battles played out over authenticity in Aboriginal literature extend beyond fundamental issues of cultural proprietorship and historical origins to address changing material conditions of production and market concerns. Such conditions and concerns place pressure on Aboriginal writers to produce work that attracts a wider audience while remaining acceptable to members of their own communities. Authenticity, in this context, becomes a bargaining chip in the ongoing negotiation of rival interests. Sonia Kurtzer describes the dilemma well:

When [an Aboriginal] author speaks to a 'white' audience he/she is constrained to speak in terms that the audience recognises as 'authentic' and must also construct a story that will not threaten. A non-threatening story may then, however, raise issues of 'authenticity' for the indigenous community. … Indigenous authors are having difficulties within their own communities in having their life experiences recognised as authentic and this in part is due to the demand for particular kinds of stories from 'white' audiences. As the less threatening, contained stories of the 'other' are embraced by 'white' Australians, frustration is expressed by those who do not wish to or cannot construct such stories. This frustration would be better directed at the hegemonic culture which seeks to control the manufacture and public circulation of images of Aboriginality, so ensuring that 'white' understandings of Aboriginality are not threatened.

(Kurtzer 1998: 27–8)

Kurtzer's analysis, though admirably succinct, raises the question of how audiences themselves are constructed or, in John Frow's and Tony Bennett's terms, how 'valuing communities' and 'reading formations' are produced that are not simply representative of, or isomorphic with, distinct social groups (see Introduction). It would be as reductive to speak of 'white' and/or 'mainstream' versus 'Aboriginal' and/or 'local' audiences for Aboriginal writing as it would to posit a coherent vision of authenticity that attaches itself to each of these designated interpretive communities. A less risky generalisation might be that the changing politics of Aboriginal literary/cultural production in Australia over the last three decades has brought alternative, culturally constructed notions of authenticity into discursive conflict. The next section of the chapter explores this conflict further by looking at the packaging of contemporary Aboriginal life-stories, especially those written by women, and at the different sets of cultural expectations those stories and, above all, their *paratextual* elements bring into play.

Aboriginal women's life-narratives and the construction of the 'market reader'

In an important, if overlooked, article for the *Canadian Review of Comparative Literature*, Wendy Waring discusses the 'paratextual traces' in a series of recent postcolonial texts that 'render the process of cultural production visible' (Waring 1995: 455). These traces – cover design, front- and back-cover blurbs, glossary notes, epigraphs, italicised quotations, and so on – indicate a tension between what the text says and what its various promoters, its 'legitimizing agents' (Bourdieu 1993), would have it do. Now, it could be argued simply that the primary objective of such paratextual devices is to sell books; but as Waring demonstrates, a further function is the interpellation of a globalised 'market reader', who is constructed as a kind of 'anthropological tourist' of the unfamiliar world(s) represented in the text (Waring 1995: 462). The homogenised figure of the 'market reader', Waring stresses, is not the same as the reader – or, better, the different reader-positions – inscribed throughout the narrative; on the contrary, the text itself may demonstrate awareness of the implications of its own commercial packaging, playing on the expectations of the 'market reader' by providing a series of internal paratextual commentaries or translations of its own (Waring 1995: 461).

One of the examples Waring cites is Ruby Langford Ginibi's autobiographical narrative *Don't Take Your Love to Town* (1988), one of the most popular and commercially successful of the spate of Aboriginal life-stories to be published in the last decade or so.[14] Waring focuses initially on the back cover blurb, which reproduces a paragraph from the original text but edits it in such a way as to elide or attenuate the text's otherwise conspicuous race and class markers (Waring 1995: 461). Such strategic elisions, when considered together with the pared-down front-cover tribute ('the ultimate battler's tale'), help frame the book within 'a genre of individualistic success narratives which relate racism as a thing of the past to a popular reading culture' (Waring 1995: 461).

Waring does not mention, however, other features of the front and back cover that frame the text in rather different – and frequently ambiguous – ways. For example, the cover painting for the Penguin edition depicts a series of vaguely threatening Mimi (Dreaming) spirits. Animated figures painted on bark, they yield little to the uninitiated reader; their primary function, on the cover at least, might be taken to be that of an unspecified marker for the (spiritual) authenticity of an Aboriginal text. We see into the figures without being able to intuit their 'meaning', announcing a play between surface and depth that marks the text as multiply coded, simultaneously accessible and hidden. Further clues are given two pages in, when we learn that the spirits 'will sometimes lure an unwary person to their cave. If he or she succumbs to their temptations, the visitor becomes a Mimi and can never return to human life'. The reader is thus invited to make an early comparison between the book's seemingly ironic admonitory title and the warning offered by the figures. This warning, however, appears to have several targets. It might apply, for instance, to the uninitiated reader, reminding him/her of the penalties of untutored curiosity; or alternatively, as Waring suggests, it might function 'as an injunction which plays on the difficulty of urban life for Aboriginal people, and [thus] positions Ruby Langford, as both narrator and author, to give advice to her community through storytelling' (Waring 1995: 462). (The title, we learn later, is taken from a popular American folksong, providing a further layer of autobiographical irony as the singer [Kenny Rogers] warns his subject [the eponymous Ruby] not 'to take her love to town'.)

This ironic play is a feature of a text that consistently belies its surface simplicity, and that challenges its own description on the back cover as the unmediated narrative of 'a life … as close to the eyes and ears as print on the page makes it'. The myth of authenticity, posited here as a function of direct access to life-experience, is dispelled elsewhere in the layering of a text that clearly operates on several different discursive levels. Not least on the paratextual level, a good example being the three epigraphs that precede the opening, prefatory section. The epigraphs are taken, first, from Kenny Rogers's aforementioned country-and-western song; second, from a feminist poem by the Aboriginal writer and activist Bobbi Sykes; and third, from Walt Whitman's epic poem of personal/national apotheosis, *Song of Myself*. The epigraphs work together to show the various strands of Langford's narrative: the cautionary parable of urban experience (Rogers); the coming-to-political-consciousness of an Aboriginal woman (Sykes); the uplifting conjunction of narratives of personal ambition and national destiny (Whitman). This eclectic range of reference gestures toward a mixed (white/Aboriginal) readership while gently ironising those readers who might be tempted to favour a 'popular', 'political', or universally 'transcendent' reading of the text. The ironies of Langford's text, in other words, do not merely develop out of the relationship between narrative and frame, textual and paratextual elements; they also evolve from an interplay between alternative paratexts and paratextual combinations, and between those paratexts, their implied commentary and, in some cases, their 'internal translation' (Waring 1995). (Examples of the latter are the translations of glossary footnotes in the text. As Waring notes, these translations provide a series of British and, especially, North American cultural referents ('echidna', for example, is glossed as 'porcupine') that help set up the fiction of an identifiable 'market reader' who is 'homogenised and white, a mid-Atlantic anthropological tourist' (Waring 1995: 462).)

It is difficult to assess the degree to which Langford herself is complicit in this construction of the 'market reader'. Waring argues, convincingly enough, that the text addresses a mixed readership while demonstrating awareness that its primary market is white (462). A more intriguing possibility, however, is that the paratextual apparatuses surrounding Langford's narrative gesture toward a 'heterogeneity of reception' (Waring 1995: 462) while also providing an ironic commentary – 'signifying', as it were – on the processes by which the book's multiple readerships are constructed. An interesting example here is the Acknowledgements page, which begins with the announcement that the book is 'a true life story of an Aboriginal woman's struggle to raise a family of nine children in a society divided between black and white culture in Australia', and which then continues with a dedication to the members of her family, both living and deceased. A further, shorter dedication follows: 'Dedicated also to every black woman who's battled to raise a family and kept her sense of humour'. These statements belie the back-cover implication that the book is 'relat[ing] racism as a thing of the past to a popular reading culture' (Waring 1995: 461); instead, they perform what might best be described as a form of reverse assimilation, by means of which a popular individualist paradigm, 'the battler's tale', is reappropriated for the purposes of collective racial/ethnic empowerment and critique. Langford's insistence that the text be read as a 'true life story' also posits a claim of authenticity that both supplements and subtly undercuts the commodified authenticities alluded to elsewhere (the legitimacy of personal struggle, the illusion of mimetic transparency, and so on). Finally, Langford's self-congratulatory tribute to her own, as well as other black women's, enduring humour indicates a mischief-making quality in the text that is by no means assimilable to commercialised 'triumph-over-adversity' myths. A comparison with the first sentence of the back-cover blurb is instructive here: 'Ruby Langford is a remarkable woman whose sense of humour has endured through all the hardships she has experienced. Her autobiography is a book which cannot fail to move you.' Here again one notes the strategic elision of racism as a primary source of hardship. By removing racial markers, the back-cover blurb creates a domesticated fiction of common experience that produces the necessarily unthreatening conditions under which the white 'market reader' can identify, and thus empathise, with an autobiographical text.[15] Humour is co-opted for this reassuring purpose – a purpose it by no means fulfils in Langford's profoundly unsettling book (Rowse 1993). This deliberate misreading of the function of humour allows for a strategy of containment through repetition – as if the trope of humour-against-all-odds could ultimately be absorbed in, and thus rendered indistinguishable from, a universal cathartic process. This is presumably what Mudrooroo means when he says that autobiographical narratives like Langford's have been rendered ideologically compatible with a national project of reconciliation – one in which the prevailing message of intercultural tolerance 'may be a good thing in regard to an Indigenous place in a multicultural Australia', but one which is not overly concerned 'with the future aims and aspirations of the Indigenous people' (Mudrooroo 1997: 16). Mudrooroo is surely right to be concerned about the assimilative repackaging processes by which Aboriginal writing, Langford's included, continues to be inserted into an Australian national narrative of collective self-improvement (Brewster

1995; see also Povinelli 1998 in the last chapter). On the other hand, as previously suggested, works like *Don't Take Your Love to Town* are implicitly critical of such processes. These critical tendencies emerge on the paratextual level in rival authorising narratives in which the function of humour (more specifically, irony) is to draw attention to the ideological differences between alternative 'battler's tales'. They also emerge in a plethora of non-identical explanatory devices (blurb summaries, prefatory epigraphs, glossary footnotes, etc.) that run counter to the attempt to read the narrative in comfortingly unifying terms. And last, they emerge in the layering – intertextual as well as paratextual – of a narrative that effectively refuses to be read on one level, and that adopts a canny, even combative attitude toward the different readerships it addresses. As Waring argues, '[t]he paratexts of *Don't Take Your Love to Town* demonstrate a heterogeneity of reception to which professional readers – particularly those whose interests lie in the realm of challenging ideologies – should pay heed' (Waring 1995: 462). And what better way to challenge those ideologies than by revealing the conflicting authorising mechanisms through which writers draw attention to, and intervene in, the material circumstances surrounding the reception of their work?

As Amanda Nettlebeck has shown, the reception of Aboriginal women's life-narratives is bound to be affected by their presentation, even though that presentation is often ambiguous, interpretable through a variety of 'reading cues' (Nettlebeck 1997: 45). One of the most important of these cues is the cover design, which can be seen as telling its own primary story (Nettlebeck 1997: 45), and as setting up – to adapt Iser's and Jauss's terms – an initial horizon of readerly expectations that is subsequently confirmed or, more likely, modified in the narrative that follows.[16] As Nettlebeck suggests, the cover designs for Aboriginal women's life-stories are exercises in indeterminacy, offering a series of cues (and clues) for interpretation by different readerships rather than a set of readily identifiable guidelines for a single target group. Nettlebeck's examples are taken from the covers of two collaborative life-narratives published in the early 1990s, Evelyn Crawford's *Over My Tracks: A Remarkable Life* (1993, as told to Chris Walsh) and Alice Nannup's *When the Pelican Laughed* (1992, with Lauren Marsh and Stephen Kinnane). Nettlebeck's readings of both covers suggest very well the ideological implications of interpretive uncertainty. The cover of *Over My Tracks*, for example, features images of red earth and Aboriginal painting – standard icons for the marketing of an 'authentic' Australia to a white (inter)national audience. But as Nettlebeck points out, these images remain 'silent about their particularity to Evelyn Crawford's life [and may thus] also become cues for some readers to what Stephen Muecke calls the "romantic apparatus" which white Australia often brings to its readings of Aboriginality' (Nettlebeck 1997: 46). The cover design for *When the Pelican Laughed* turns out to be similarly ambiguous, featuring two superimposed images of Nannup framed against an 'empty' Western Australian outback landscape. The different media used (photography and painting), allied to variations in perspective, scale and image resolution, create a layering effect, poised between revelation and mystery, not dissimilar to the one presented in Langford's *Don't Take Your Love to Town*. In the photograph, the solitary figure stands sentinel against the backdrop of a featureless desert landscape; in the painting, Nannup's facial profile, enlarged and grainy, seems almost to have been hewn from the landscape itself. As Nettlebeck suggests, such images cannot help but conjure up 'the romanticised visions [that] are often implicit in publicly circulated impressions of Aboriginal "authenticity" ', and that have been satirised by Langford, among others, when she writes: '[White people think that] the only real Aborigines are the tribal ones out in the desert sitting on a rock' (*Weekend Australian*, 1993, qtd in Nettlebeck 1997: 50). Optimistically perhaps, Nettlebeck also sees the possibility for satirical intent in Michael Fracas's cover painting, musing that 'the juxtaposition of the red landscape with Alice's mainstream respectability is [possibly] intended to expose that "romantic apparatus" … which white Australians tend to bring to a notion of Aboriginal "authenticity" ' (Nettlebeck 1997: 51). Whatever the case, Nettlebeck concludes, 'these are potentially conflicting cues to the reading process which can only be resolved [if resolved at all] by the more powerful authority of the narrative itself' (Nettlebeck 1997: 51).

Nettlebeck's focus on the reception of Aboriginal literature by white Australians leads her to overlook the international market appeal of Aboriginal works such as, most notably, Sally Morgan's *My Place* (1987). *My Place*, by any accounts a massively successful international bestseller with close to half a million copies sold in the decade since its publication, has taken on the status of a foundation text with a 'touchstone effect' for Aboriginal literature not dissimilar from that exercised for Indian writing in English by Rushdie's *Midnight's Children* (see Chapter 2). Thus, it comes as no surprise to find an authorising comment from Morgan on the back cover of *When the Pelican Laughed*, which helps situate Nannup's narrative within a tradition of embattled Aboriginal women's life-stories: 'Alice Nannup courageously tells us exactly what it was like to grow up as a black woman in Australia, and through her book she has passed on a precious heritage. There are many unsung heroines in Black Australia and Alice is one of them.' The blurb is interesting for its insistence on the unimpeachable authenticity of oral testimony ('Alice Nannup … tells us *exactly* what it was like to grow up as a black woman in Australia'), offering an unambiguous reading cue that appears at odds with other paratextual indicators – and with the main body of the text itself. As in *Don't Take Your Love to Town*, the most striking aspect of the paratextual material is its superabundance: Morgan's eulogy is also reproduced on the inside leaf, along with an endorsement by another 'foundational' Aboriginal writer, the playwright Jack Davis; the narrative is framed by an explanatory introduction, which provides the editors' rationale for transcribing Nannup's story, and a brief postscript, which rationalises it further by inserting it into a memorial testimony of 'collective loss' (Nannup 1992: 225); and Nannup's biography is repeated twice, both on the inside cover outline and on the next page, where it stands alongside brief biographical blurbs for her two editors, Lauren Marsh and Stephen Kinnane (himself Aboriginal). (These latter also flank her in a group, 'happy-family' photograph at the top of the page, for which the blurbs serve as complementary captions.) The effect of paratextual excess is not just, as Waring claims, to reconfirm the heterogeneity of the book's reception by sending out a series of cues for interpretation by readers of different cultural backgrounds and competencies; it also works to relativise the truth-claims made on behalf of the main narrative, which emerges nonetheless as the central, though by no means overriding or unequivocal, authorising source.

If Morgan's endorsement is a significant feature in the multiple authorisation of Nannup's narrative, her own life-story is legitimised in its turn by a front-cover tribute from the African American writer Alice Walker. The choice of Walker, a writer best known for her marketable combination of ethereal mysticism and political activism, indicates an attempt both to reach out to politically conscious 'mid-Atlantic' readers (Waring 1995) and to assimilate Morgan's narrative to a transnational New Age parable of personal healing and spiritual awakening. The half-amazed tone and dreamy diction of Walker's blurb certainly suggest this, as she praises a book that is 'sad and wise, and funny'; a book that is 'unbelievably and unexpectedly [*sic*] moving'; a book, above all, 'with heart'. (It is interesting to reflect here on a phenomenon we might uncharitably call 'interethnic endorsement' – African Americans being called upon to legitimise works written by Australian Aboriginals, a minority group with an entirely different culture located on the other side of the world. Interethnic endorsement emerges as the paratextual by-product of a market-model of authenticity, one of whose effects – as already mentioned – is to posit the interchangeability of 'exotic' cultures and cultural goods.)[17] Not that other contributors are to be outdone; for a whole range of hyperbolic tributes are accumulated on the book's inside pages, drawing on as many American as Australian sources, and including such luminary publications as the *Staten Island Advance* and the *Rocky Mountain News*. This bestseller format, clearly designed to appeal to 'ordinary', mass-market readers ('a book for everyone', *New York Times Book Review*) as well as more sophisticated, academically minded ones ('[Morgan] writes well, with the art which conceals art, so that a series of narratives becomes a complex exploration of the meaning of the past', *Westerly*), complements a text which persists in being read in comfortable, unchallenging terms (Muecke 1988: 409). Yet even here, where the ideological mismatch between text and paratext seems so conspicuous, the possibility remains to read the paratextual material in different, potentially conflicting, ways. Thus, adjoined to a text whose simple title belies its often painful charting of successive displacements is a body of explanatory/descriptive citation that is itself highly mobile, fractured, assembled in a series of disparate fragments. This paratextual machinery operates according to what we might call, loosely following Derrida, the logic of the supplement.[18] On the inner-leaf page, for example, we find the following sequence of non-identical declarative statements: 'What started out as a tentative search for information about her family turned into an overwhelming emotional and spiritual pilgrimage'/'[A] fascinating story unfolds – a mystery of identity, complete with clues and suggested solutions'/'Sally Morgan's *My Place* is a deeply moving account of a search for the truth, into which a whole family is gradually drawn'/'*My Place* is a powerful autobiography of three generations, by a writer with the gift for language of a born story-teller.' Once again, as with Langford's narrative, a sense of interpretive indeterminacy prevails over the attempt to pin down a text that refuses to respect generic rules. And once again, the various paratextual cues and clues offered up to Morgan's prospective readers carefully elide issues of race and racism – as if the universal language of affect ('overwhelming emotion', 'deeply moving account', etc.) were sufficient to confirm a *shared* narrative of human(ist) concern. The illusion of identification with the embattled cultural other confirms the authenticity of the reading experience for the liberally minded 'market reader'; and yet this same gesture paradoxically robs the text of the authenticating markers of ineradicable difference on which its validity, and potential commercial success, as an 'Aboriginal text' would otherwise be most likely to depend. In this context, ironically enough, *My Place* raises the unanswered, possibly unanswerable question of where authenticity is *located*. Is authenticity situated in the specificities of individual experience, or is it rather to be found in the potential for shared humanity and collective knowledge? Is authenticity located in a deep-seated understanding of the material conditions of cultural existence, or is it limited instead to a superficial appreciation for cultural phenomena purposefully dislodged from their everyday material context? Does authenticity convey the illusion of unmediated access to other people's life-experiences, or is it better seen as the symbolic representation of what is felt to be missing from one's own – the simulacrum of loss, the manufactured nostalgic moment?

These alternatives suggest that the discourse of (cultural) authenticity is deeply riven, and that the identitary concerns and anxieties it displays are inextricably linked to differential relations of power. Hence the use of authenticity as an empowering political strategy for disadvantaged minority communities, even as its use by dominating cultures acts as a constraint on those communities' political power. Hence the fear, as well, on the part of several Aboriginal writers that the expansionist imperatives of multinational publishing, allied to the no less powerfully appropriative impulses of national projects of revisionist self-reckoning, might have the effect of assimilating their work into some vast collective enterprise – one in which the appearance of co-operation masks continuing tensions and imbalances in the social structure, and the fluid myth of Native authenticity continues to be deployed as a resource for other people's needs and ends (Nettlebeck 1997; see also Goldie 1989).

This fear, historically well grounded, has resurfaced recently in auto-biographical texts such as Rita and Jackie Huggins's *Auntie Rita* (1994), which has been seen, somewhat splenetically, as gesturing toward cultural autonomy by closing ranks on white producers (Mudrooroo 1997) and, more realistically, as offering a trenchant commentary on the uneven development of white/Aboriginal literary collaboration (Brewster 1995; Nettlebeck 1997). *Auntie Rita* raises the self-reflexivity already apparent in earlier life-narratives like *Don't Take Your Love to Town* to a new level, offering steely comments on the contemporary politics of Aboriginal publishing – 'We still face the fact that most publishing in this country is controlled by white people who have little knowledge of our culture' (Huggins and Huggins 1994: 4); throwing down the gauntlet to the white literary establishment to 'develop more co-operative relations with Black writers [and to find] ways of involving Black people more closely with production decisions' (Huggins and Huggins 1994: 4); and placing Aboriginal literary production within a wider colonialist framework in which the problems that continue to face aspiring Aboriginal writers – condescending publishers, interfering editors, and so forth – are indirectly linked to a history of violence 'that [has] attempted to alienate (with varying degrees of success) Black people's access to knowledge of their own culture and history' (Huggins and Huggins 1994: 3).

For all that, the Hugginses stop some way short of disdaining white editorial assistance, forging what Jackie Huggins calls a 'productive collaboration' with a white Australian editor, Alison Ravenscroft. Pride of place is given, however, in the foreword to another family member, Lillian Holt. Holt's foreword, like several of the other framing devices for Aboriginal life-stories examined so far in this section, sends out ambivalent signals. On the one hand, Holt insists that the story is in part a response to racist calumny, 'which has been the lot of fellow visible Aboriginal people in Australia' (Huggins and Huggins 1994: ix); on the other, she repeats her view of Rita Huggins as a battling 'universal spirit' (Huggins and Huggins 1994: ix, x), thus leaving room for an accommodationist reading that seems out of keeping with an otherwise combative, even confrontational work. The text, however, is surrounded by not one but multiple narrative framings; in this sense, the paratextual material for the book (as for other such books) is better seen in combination, with a productive tension emerging between the personal eulogy of Holt, the affirmative memory-work of Rita Huggins, and the overtly politicised, at times antagonistic commentary of her daughter Jackie.[19] The packaging of the text, less obviously commercial than is the case with, say, *My Place* or *Don't Take Your Love to Town*, therefore aims at creating the conditions for an open dialogue – conditions maintained throughout the narrative, which remains strategically incomplete (Nettlebeck 1997). The authenticity of the text is thus vouchsafed, less in the assertion of ethnic belonging, traditional ties, or collective unity than in the intimate conversation between two highly articulate but not always like-minded Aboriginal women, and in the wider dialogue opened up with a readership sensitive to their historical cause.

Works such as *Auntie Rita* are clearly not designed or packaged for the 'market reader', and arguably the problems of assimilation that come with mass-market publications are less acute. Brought out by Aboriginal Studies Press in Canberra and financed with the help of the Aboriginal Arts Unit of the Australia Council, *Auntie Rita* is the type of small-scale, government-sponsored publication that largely escapes commodity circuits, and that is able, through its exploration of the shared history behind a mother–daughter relationship, to 'give a degree of authenticity not often found, especially in those lifestories or histories written by [what Mudrooroo slightingly calls] "born-again" Aborigines' (Mudrooroo 1997: 188). Yet the implication of a hierarchy of authenticity, as previously suggested, is problematic, not least when based on personal perceptions of other people's degree of, or even right to, cultural affiliation. Perhaps the highly personal nature of much Aboriginal writing, which reaches its apogee in the life-story, cannot help but bring invidious questions of 'eligibility' to the fore. Hence the continuing debate in Australia over what we might call the ethics of artistic passing – a debate that, as several commentators have pointed out, has come to assume almost pathological proportions (Mishra

1996: see previous chapter). It is not the place of this chapter to enter into detail on the various cases currently being discussed – 'Eddie Burrup', 'Wanda Koolmatrie' and, more recently, Mudrooroo himself – cases that need to be carefully sifted within the larger context of debates about social responsibility, cultural proprietorship and aesthetic freedom. Instead, I shall close with some thoughts on another case that has recently been re-evaluated – that of B. Wongar (Sreten Bozic) – in the light of continuing arguments over the instrumentalisation of Aboriginal authenticity.

Conclusion: competing authenticities, or, some passing thoughts on passing

In a 1998 article in *Antipodes*, the Australian critic Maggie Nolan traces a brief reception history of the work of B. Wongar, whose 'Aboriginal stories' were popular in the 1960s, and whose identity has since been revealed as that of the Serbian migrant, Sreten Bozic. As Nolan shows, the reception of Wongar's work – oscillating between exaggerated praise, sceptical inquiry and moral condemnation – reveals profound anxieties about (in)authenticity that can be related to continuing attempts to control the meaning of Aboriginality in postcolonial Australia. For Nolan, the desire for authenticity so marked in early reviews of Wongar's stories indicates a 'longing for an impossibly pure context of lived experience at a place of origin' (Nolan 1998: 8). '[T]he presence that these reviews desired', says Nolan, 'was, like all myths of origin, haunted by absence' (Nolan 1998: 8). Nolan's is a familiar argument about the place of the 'absent Aborigine' in the Australian psyche – an argument explored more fully in the work of Bob Hodge and Vijay Mishra (*Dark Side of the Dream*, 1990) and, more recently, in the work of Ken Gelder and Jane Jacobs (*Uncanny Australia*, 1998). Equally familiar is the conclusion Nolan reaches, that 'the reductive demand for an authentic Aboriginality [on the part of white reviewers and critics] functions as cultural imperialism' (Nolan 1998: 12). Nolan thus neatly turns the tables on those who have accused Bozic himself of cultural imperialism, not just for his wilful appropriation of a Native voice but for daring to masquerade as Native (see also the discussion of Helen Darville-Demidenko in the previous chapter). Susan Hosking's response is characteristic:

> At a time when Aboriginal writers are finding their own voices, there is a justifiably strong resistance against a European writer who not only speaks as if he were an Aborigine, but who originally pretended to be an Aborigine. This is cultural imperialism.
>
> (Hosking 1992: 14, qtd in Nolan 1998: 12)

Attacking Hosking in her turn, Nolan suggests that one of the reasons Bozic has been vilified is 'for not inhabiting, in any stable manner, the pre-constituted subject position assigned to him by discourses of the authentic' (Nolan 1998: 12). Far from being peremptorily labelled as a cultural imperialist, says Nolan, Bozic is to be congratulated for having subtly manipulated *expectations* of authenticity in his work. By posing as Wongar, Bozic implicitly 'questions the systematic closure of Aboriginality as an imperial construct, and its pretensions to authenticity, autonomy, and purity' (Nolan 1998: 9). If these are rather large, possibly dubious claims, Nolan still makes a good case for a more inflected critical discourse on authenticity that goes beyond categorical assertions of the type that either rush to praise Wongar's work as 'genuine' or to condemn its author as 'fake'.[20]

Nolan's essay is deliberately provocative; I want to use it to offer some provocative conclusions of my own. Nolan's argument might be seen, in a sense, as rephrasing Terry Goldie's important thesis that one aesthetic effect of the anxiety over ownership and origins in postcolonial settler societies such as Australia has been a rash of attempts to represent 'the impossible necessity of becoming indigenous' (Goldie 1989: 13). For Nolan, a similar anxiety leads to a different phenomenon – the impossible necessity that the indigene be wholly himself/herself. And still a further anxiety emerges here; for if the desire to construct an authentic Aboriginal voice, as Nolan implies, runs the risk of eliding 'properly aesthetic' questions of textuality – point of view, subject position, and so on – then does the (white) demand that Aboriginals be allowed to speak or write for themselves require that such aesthetic and epistemological questions be put on hold? Interestingly enough, these very questions are often foregrounded in so-called 'migrant' or 'multicultural' writing (see previous chapter). Why the critical hesitation to see *indigenous* writing in terms of a multiplicity of speakers, a complex tracery of shifting personae, identities and subject positions? If indigenous life-writing needs to be distinguished, as I believe it does, from a Western autobiographical tradition, does this necessarily entail the dismissal of (Western) theoretical questions about the construction of the autobiographical subject? If indigenous literatures need to be differentiated, as I believe they do, from the literatures of relatively privileged white-settler societies, does this exclude them from the purview of a postcolonial critical theory that, in comparing the two, might itself be seen as practising a form of cultural imperialism?[21] My short answer to the last two questions would be a blunt 'of course not', although the proviso would need to be added that indigenous writing be seen in a continuum with local cultural practices, and interpreted within the wider context of belief- and value-systems that are by no means readily understood. A longer answer might bring us back to the competing authenticities that underwrite Aboriginal – and other indigenous – representations, and that demand a closer attention than has sometimes been paid both to the political contexts behind literary (self-)labelling and to the material circumstances behind the production and circulation of Aboriginal images and cultural goods. It is nonsense, of course, to suggest that authenticity is purely a market phenomenon, misguided to imagine that the commodification of Aboriginality has robbed Aboriginal writers of all their representational rights. Yet there is still a sense in which, as Mudrooroo remarked at the beginning of the 1990s,

> the Aboriginal writer exists in a state of ambiguity. White people assume that he or she is writing for the white world, the world of the invader. It is a curious fate – to write for a people not one's own, and stranger still to write for the conquerors of one's people.
>
> (Mudrooroo 1990: 148)

The search for authenticity in such an obviously compromised context involves the reaching out to alternative readerships, including the people one regards as being one's own. As I have suggested, it also involves a reflexive approach to authenticity – one that plays on the expectations of the international 'market reader', as well as on a readership more likely to be acquainted with the text's (inter)cultural nuances and representational codes. Perhaps, in this sense, the most fitting paradox of Native authenticity is that it can be used for self-empowering purposes, even as its potential is recognised as a mechanism for the representation of otherness and as an objectifying market tool. And if Aboriginal writers remain constrained to some extent by a commodified discourse of authenticity that serves majority interests, several of them have proved singularly adept in 'playing the market' to their own ideological ends. The struggle that ensues is a function of global economic demands as well as local cultural interests; thus it is that Aboriginal writers, like many of their 'Fourth World' indigenous counterparts, have succeeded in articulating their own highly distinctive life-narratives and histories while continuing to engage energetically with the global condition of postcoloniality in which their works, and lives, are enmeshed.

7 Transformations of the tourist gaze

Asia in recent Canadian and Australian fiction

Exoticism and the tourist gaze

This chapter is about the links between exoticism and tourism, and the part both discourses play in the production, representation and exploitation of the cultural other. The exoticist discourse of cultural otherness, and the expansionist imperatives that discourse sanctions, have been crucial to the development of the modern tourist industry. Tourism, in the early twenty-first century, is the world's largest and fastest growing industry, generating revenue in excess of 10 per cent of the global economy (MacCannell 1989). The expansion of the tourist industry has brought with it numerous socioeconomic problems; as Dean MacCannell points out in his seminal study *The Tourist* (1976, rev. edn 1989),

> Tourism has developed at a rate faster than have its support institutions. For the last several years, in the month of August, there are several days during which every resort in the temperate climates in Europe, Africa, Asia, and the Americas is filled in advance – the whole world is booked solid.
>
> (MacCannell 1989: 166)

Overcrowding, along with the conspicuously uneven distribution of resources, combine to make tourism a primary cause of structural underdevelopment. As John Frow says, 'the logic of tourism is that of a relentless extension of commodity relations, and the consequent inequalities of power, between centre and periphery, First and Third World, developed and underdeveloped regions, metropolis and country-side' (Frow 1991: 151). For all its appeals to world peace and the need for intercultural understanding, tourism continues to feed off social, political and economic differences. The jury is out on tourism, but even its fiercest critics admit that the industry can only continue to prosper; several have turned their attention instead to 'humane' concerns and the sustainability of resources (Cohen 1973; Krippendorf 1987; MacCannell 1989).[1]

The appeal of exotic peoples and places constitutes tourism's staple diet: 'the product the industry sells is a commodified relation to the [cultural] other' (Frow 1991: 150). But as Malcolm Crick wryly observes, the majority of tourists cannot tolerate too much otherness:

> They need to travel in an environment 'bubble' [Cohen], which gives them a vicarious encounter with the Other, yet at a safe distance, with all the security of the familiar around them. So, it is the task of the industry image-makers to create a place which is exotic but not alien, exciting yet not frightening, different but where they speak your language, so that fun and relaxation, untroubled by the concerns of the real world, are possible. Such a space, of course, requires sweeping most of social reality under the carpet.
>
> (Crick 1991: 12)

Exoticism's utopian rhetoric serves as tourism's protective smokescreen, allowing the industry to promote and market the myth of innocuous pleasure. Exoticist aesthetics, and the exoticist mythologies from which the tourist industry derives its profits, disguise the real differences they help to cause by appealing to ones of their own imagining. Exoticism and tourism might be seen here as parting company. The former, after all, promotes and perpetuates a mystique of inaccessibility; the latter presents a counter-myth of limited cultural contact. But this myth depends, in turn, on a perceptible need for cultural *distance* – the tourist world maintains itself by pushing onwards 'beyond the frontiers of existing society' (MacCannell 1989: 183).

Tourism, it is often said, cannot help but defeat its own objectives. As a global enterprise dependent on international capital and worldwide communications systems, tourism contributes to the sameness of a world whose differences it needs to make its profits. Tourism thus requires the other that it repeatedly destroys. This contradiction is produced, in part, by the demands of capitalist expansion. A standard claim of the tourist industry – the availability of the exotic – proceeds according to an inexorably capitalist logic: once tourism has made the other accessible, other others must emerge to take its place.

This spiralling search for exotic alternatives is not restricted to tourist destinations; it also reflects an increasing range of choices *within* the spectrum of touristic recreation. Erik Cohen's useful typology distinguishes between four touristic roles. Two of these are institutionalised, organised and individual 'mass tourists'; the other two are not, the 'explorer' and the 'drifter'. 'Explorers' and 'drifters', according to Cohen, are more likely to make their own arrangements, to need less money, and to take more risks; 'mass tourists', on the other hand, are largely content to remain within a protective infrastructure (Cohen 1973). While models such as Cohen's emphasise that tourists are not homogeneous, they miss the point that tourists often *need* to preserve such – frequently tenuous – differences. One of the central ironies of tourism, in fact, is that it is motivated in part by its own attempted negation – by tourists' plaintive need to dissociate themselves from other tourists (Frow 1991; MacCannell 1989). The primary distinction here is that between the figures of the *tourist* and the *traveller*. Travellers – so the familiar argument runs – pride themselves on engagement with the cultures they encounter. They look down on 'superficial' tourists, whom they see as having little or no interest in the countries they visit; as contributing irresponsibly to the despoliation of their environment; and as seeking maximum enjoyment with a minimum of effort. This clichéd, but still serviceable, distinction constitutes a highly profitable myth. Other, less 'vulgar' options are open to adventure-minded travellers: the tourist industry takes full advantage of travellers' misdirected snobbery, using it to lure them down an alternative beaten track (Buzard 1993). As Jonathan Culler among others has argued, the 'ferocious denigration of tourists is in part an attempt to convince oneself that one is not a tourist. … The desire to distinguish between tourists and travelers is a part of tourism – integral to it rather than outside it or beyond it' (Culler 1988: 156).[2]

In promoting a more responsible tourism in a less exploitative environment, the industry capitalises on one of exoticism's most powerful myths – nostalgia. The exoticist 'elsewhere' conjures up a vision of a Golden Age which has long since vanished – if it ever existed. Exoticism seeks, in Chris Bongie's words, to salvage the space of an other that is beyond the bounds of modern civilisation (Bongie 1991: 4–5). Like exoticism, tourism tends to nourish itself on the invented reminiscences of pastoral. One form this nourishment takes is through the idealised nostalgia of the heritage industry; another is through appeals to the 'timeless essences' of indigenous cultures. However it is experienced, nostalgia enacts a complex dialectic of desire – it seeks a past of its own invention it knows in advance to be impossible.[3] Offering a spurious panacea for disaffection with a 'degraded' present, nostalgia's constitutive figure is Lévi-Strauss's traveller, hastening in search of a vanished reality (Lévi-Strauss 1984 [1955]: 44). But paradoxically, it is the very *falseness* of nostalgia that makes it all the more appealing. 'The "inauthenticity" of nostalgia is its own motivating force; tourism … turns this afflictive desire to [its] own material advantage, exploiting to commercial ends nostalgia's self-perpetuating anxiety' (Holland and Huggan 1998: 220). Tourism shares with exoticism the impossible search for 'uncontaminated' experience. The exoticist/tourist gaze looks beyond the world toward an ungraspable ideal entity. John Frow describes the compulsion well and the inevitable frustration it induces:

> To the tourist gaze, things are read as signs of themselves. A place, a gesture, a use of language are understood not as given bits of the real but as suffused with ideality, giving on to the type of the beautiful, the extraordinary, or the culturally authentic. Their reality is figural rather than literal. Hence the structural role of *disappointment* in the tourist experience, since access to a type can always be frustrated.
>
> (Frow 1991:125, my emphasis)

Frow is borrowing here from the sociologist John Urry's work on the semiotics of the tourist gaze. Tourist gazes, according to Urry, do not just refer to the cognitive processes by which tourists encode and decode their touristic experiences; they also relate to a socially organised system – an apparatus of preconstituted knowledges and beliefs – that underpins, and to some extent undermines, the nature of those experiences. Tourist gazes are filters of touristic perception – they provide a medium for what tourists see, but also a guideline as to how they *ought* to see. So while tourist gazes are instruments of vision, they may also function as screening devices that restrict or impair vision. Tourist gazes, in short, constitute imperfect barometric records of the diverse ways in which tourists adjust their personal experiences to the requirements of social expectation (Urry 1990).

The rest of this chapter explores the ideology of the tourist gaze in recent Canadian and Australian fiction set in Asia. It argues that the tourist gaze is principally mediated through the discourse of exoticism, more particularly through exoticist drives toward anxiety, frustration and nostalgia. Four examples are selected here to show the variability – and transformability – of the tourist gaze. The first two of these are linked to the self-deceiving fantasies of the Western spiritual tourist, the second two to the self-destructive antics of the 'anti-tourist tourist'.

Spiritual tourists

Tourism is sometimes considered to be a surrogate form of pilgrimage: 'If a pilgrim is half a tourist … a tourist is half a pilgrim' (Turner and Ash 1975: 20). There are serious problems, of course, with seeing tourism in terms of a sacred journey, not least the occlusion of the economic advantages that make that journey possible. Taxonomies of tourism are frequently misleading; in their attempt to formulate distinctions between different kinds of touristic activity, they underemphasise the fact that most tourists are driven by a multiplicity of – often conflicting – motives. One such distinction is that between holiday tourism, which is motivated primarily by the drive for intellectual and physical pleasure, and religious tourism, which has its stake in the reconfirmation of spiritual faith. As Surinder Bhardwaj, Gisbert Rinschede and Angelika Sievers note, however, recreational and religious motives for journeys are increasingly combined (Bhardwaj *et al.* 1994: 9). Contemporary pilgrimages, for instance, offer more than spiritual sustenance: free time is planned for day-trips and other sightseeing activities, while modern 'pilgrimage sites' have sprung up, fully equipped with gift shops, snack bars, restaurants and hotels (Bhardwaj *et al.* 1994: 187). This overlap is clear, not just in the mixed experiences of the modern pilgrim, but also in the ambivalent figure of the *spiritual tourist* – the holidaymaker with a spiritual, rather than a material, goal in mind.[4]

India has been, still is, a favourite destination for spiritual tourists. The mystique of India's religions, and the enigmatic beauty of its sacred sites, hold exotic appeal for Westerners disenchanted with their own materially rich but spiritually impoverished cultures (see also Chapter 2). The opportunities for self-delusion here are only too apparent, as demonstrated in the halcyon 1960s: a time when India, cutprice haven for a variety of anti-establishment 'seekers', was to reveal truths other than those its starry-eyed disciples imagined themselves to be pursuing. As Gita Mehta observes acerbically, looking back on this 'Age of Innocence',

> Global escapism masquerading as spiritual hunger resulted at worst in individual madness, at best in a hard-won awareness that the benediction of jet-stream gurus was seldom more than skywriting, and that the mystic East, given half a chance, could teach the West a thing or two about materialism.
>
> (G. Mehta 1979: x; see also Chapters 2 and 3)

Canadians in India have undergone similar rites of passage, yet the mystique lingers on, and it continues to be enhanced in the nation's writing. It has become intellectually fashionable to deride Orientalist navel-gazing – satire is never far beneath the surface of contemporary Canadian writing about India. But the familiar myths and stereotypes are still quite likely to re-emerge, as, for example, in a 1985 special issue of the Montreal-based review *Liberté*, several of whose contributing essays draw unashamed inspiration from Valéry's poetic discourse on the 'fabulous Orient'. These essays range from the rhapsodic to the portentous, with

Orientalist clichés in abundance – soaring flights of fancy brought rudely to earth, however, in a devastating piece by François Ricard. The abiding attraction of Western writers to the Orient, says Ricard, is a mark less of curiosity than of intellectual pusillanimity, of the kind that grasps at straws in the desperate search for a broader vision (Ricard 1985: 41). Ricard shows little but disdain for an Orientalism characterised by the half-truths and pseudo-mystical visions of its feeble-minded disciples, although he acknowledges the palliative effect of an anti-Occidentalism that inspires often unsubtle attacks on European privilege or the self-serving mythologies of the American Dream. The former type of attack, claims Ricard, has been prevalent in the intellectual tradition of Quebec, whose separation from the Western (European) cultural mainstream makes it more favourably disposed to an understanding of the East. Wisely, Ricard goes on to qualify this last – highly debatable – point. Perhaps, he concludes, the apparent predisposition of Quebecois writers toward the Orient is best explained in terms of a combination of cultural insecurity, particularly toward France; a romantic attachment to poverty; and a confusion of critical intelligence with the blandishments of religious discourse (Ricard 1985: 49).

Ricard's argument suggests, above all else, the profoundly *ambivalent* attitude toward Europe one so often finds in the history of both Quebecois and Anglo-Canadian literatures/cultures (see also next chapter). This attitude can also be found in two Canadian/Quebecois novels published in the early to mid 1980s, both of them set in a mythicised 'India' that is largely tailored to, but also critical of, European cultural needs. The two novels in question – Janette Turner Hospital's *The Ivory Swing* (1982) and Yvon Rivard's *Les silences du corbeau* (1986) – are dissimilar in design, but alike in being written both within and against the tradition of the Oriental quest novel. The formula is a familiar one. Restless Western dreamer takes temporary refuge in the East, hoping to find either physical stimulation or spiritual enrichment or, preferably, both; instead, said dreamer finds only the limitations of his/her own culture, a culture to which s/he nonetheless returns, suitably 'enlightened' by the experience. In their own, self-conscious adaptations of the formula, Hospital and Rivard employ similar motifs to underscore their central theme of cultural relativity. In Hospital's novel, the eponymous swing dramatises the impossibility of choosing between two apparently exclusive but actually interrelated systems (the 'East' and the 'West'). In Rivard's, the ominous crow periodically intervenes, disrupting the fluency of the protagonist Alexandre's thoughts, reminding him of the inefficacy of his philosophical quest, and implicitly ridiculing his attempt to understand and apply to his own life the concepts of a non-dualistic world view through the procedures of a dualist analysis. Both swing and crow operate at several different levels of discourse. In one sense, they represent the dilemma posed by aspiring to come to terms with the East without being able to renounce the values of the West; in another, they embody the social and political conscience of a complacent bourgeois West exploiting an impoverished – if in its way equally class-conscious – East for the purposes of its own enrichment; in still another, they accentuate the interpersonal conflict of the two protagonists, torn between alternative lifestyles and rival lovers, unable to choose which direction to take next.

More interesting, perhaps, than this tongue-in-cheek reprise of the standard fare of East-West encounter is the attempt in both novels to interrogate the assumptions underlying Western European literary *exoticism*.[5] Hospital's references to Maugham and Kipling, like Rivard's to Baudelaire and Valéry, belong to the ironic confession of a protagonist who is attracted toward India as an exotic cultural other, but who is aware at the same time of the irresponsibilities of that attraction. In Hospital's novel, the protagonist Juliet is well aware of her susceptibility to exoticist fantasy. Ostensibly in India as an unemployed 'faculty wife' – her husband David is on sabbatical, conducting ethnological research – Juliet has ample time to indulge in the pleasures of romantic reverie. She is less a spiritual tourist in the sense of a devotee or pilgrim, more a middle-aged, middle-class seeker after truths beyond the physical. These truths, however, are soon stripped bare, their hollowness revealed; instead of offering spiritual solace, the comforts of a 'transcendental tranquillity' (Hospital 1982: 46), India induces weary resignation and a realisation of personal weakness. Juliet wavers between alternative, self-defeating tourist gazes – the one envisions India as a 'place of risk and dazzle' (Hospital 1982: 67), the other as a source of boredom and unproductive self-inquiry. The two occasionally converge in clichéd Hollywood scenarios. Exhausted by the exertions of housework in the oppressive heat of southern India, Juliet drifts off into exotic reverie, conjuring up a vision in which her former lover Jeremy 'came riding out of the West to cut his way through jungle walls and rescue her with a kiss from the drowsy tropics' (Hospital 1982: 104). Juliet mocks her own propensity to such ludicrous stereotypes of the 'fabulous Orient', but she finds it difficult to distinguish between these egregious childish fantasies and an India that often seems as unreal to her as the fictive Orients of popular romance. Her grandiose vision of Jeremy riding out of the West is ironically deflated by the humbler sight that follows it, of

> the mailman on his bicycle which bucked its way along the path
> between the coconut palms. He was a bizarre figure in his widely

flared Bombay bloomers. He also wore a khaki shirt, and knee-length khaki socks and a pith helmet, and seemed to have stepped out of a Somerset Maugham story or an old movie of the British Raj.

(Hospital 1982: 105)

One form of exoticism is supplanted by another. Juliet falls back once more on the stereotypes that preclude her from seeing India in terms other than those provided by her hyperactive romantic imagination. Nurtured on nostalgia and the anachronistic images of colonial fiction, Juliet's imagination recycles the romantic fantasies of tourism.[6] Her tourist gaze reassembles India from the bric-à-brac – the false memorabilia – of European exotic myth. In her search for stimulation, she turns to well-worn formulae: Maugham stories, old movies of the Raj, and 'travelers' brocaded tales … of tigers, elephants, sandalwood and ivory' (Hospital 1982: 17). But this search only helps accelerate the process of her self-estrangement. She is caught in a double-bind: she wishes to witness India, to experience it for herself; but she is reliant in spite of herself on the fabricated testimony of others.

Unable to accept her privilege as a long-term Western tourist, exasperated by her inability to reconcile herself to India, Juliet is quick to project her frustrations and failings onto others. Her husband David is blamed for paralysing aesthetic contemplation, her sister Annie for the self-indulgence of the Western 'affluent drifter' (Hospital 1982: 135). The various one-dimensional Indian characters in Hospital's novel, meanwhile, become the objects of a tourist gaze that falls back on trivialising what it fails to understand. Pseudo-mythical or comic-strip inventions, these characters fulfil the purpose of satisfying Juliet's self-serving desire for cross-cultural understanding; or they act as expedient targets for her sanctimonious wrath. They are allowed little or no development within the context of Juliet's alternative views of India as tyrannical post-feudal autocracy or paradisal spiritual retreat.

These opposing views are perhaps best seen as obverse sides of the same exotic myth. As Tzvetan Todorov remarks in distinguishing between 'exotic' and 'colonial' fiction,

> The exotic novel glorifies foreigners while the colonial novel denigrates them. But the contradiction is only apparent. Once the author has declared that he himself is the only subject … and that the others have been reduced to objects, it is … of secondary concern whether those objects are loved or despised. The essential point is that they are not full-fledged human beings.

(Todorov 1993: 323; see also Introduction)

Juliet's objectification of India and Indians owes much to her reading habits; but true to form, she projects these limitations onto her bookish husband David, in fact a much more discerning reader of India than she is. Juliet's dogmatic Western opinions are likewise projected onto others, so that cardboard characters like the antique dealer Mr Motilal find themselves 'correctly designating' Westerners as 'tourists, diplomats, hippies and university people' (Hospital 1982: 21) – ironically in the context of the novel he is not far wrong – while the villainous landlord Shivaraman Nair frequently proffers such educated opinions as 'in the west … marriages are very bad because young people are choosing for themselves, isn't it?' (Hospital 1982: 123). Far from being the broad-minded woman of the world she believes herself to be, Juliet is in fact a thoroughgoing Orientalist – a self-involved tourist, convinced of the superiority of her liberated Western views, whose fictive version of the Orient is only temporarily demystified by the recognition that her persistent mythologisation of others has contributed to the tragic deaths of her two imagined soulmates, the put-upon servant Prabhakaran and the shackled widow Yashoda.

Hospital's ironic treatment of her liberated protagonist in *The Ivory Swing* is matched by Rivard's wry exposure of the fallibilities of his soul-searching narrator in *Les silences du corbeau*. As in Hospital's novel, India presents a hallowed site for pontifications on the timeless; or an outlet for euphoria, exploding Western rationalist categories. After a row, in *The Ivory Swing*, between Juliet and her sister Annie, the latter threatens to go back from whence she came. ' "Do that", snaps Juliet. "Go live it up with a bunch of affluent drifters getting high on meditation and self-indulgence and sex" ' (Hospital 1982: 135). Enter, as if on cue, Rivard's narrator-protagonist Alexandre, both active participant in and detached observer of the excruciatingly self-indulgent activities at the Aurobindo ashram. (One senses from his descriptions that Hospital's Annie would be well placed.) Alexandre permits himself the further indulgence of writing a journal about his experiences. Laced with sententious aphorisms and 'deep' meditations into the meaning of Life (or, more often, Death), Alexandre's journal represents a flagrant exercise in self-mythologisation. As in *The Ivory Swing*, this self-mythologisation is reinforced through the delineation of secondary characters whose main function is to shed light on the strengths and weaknesses of the protagonist. The Indian characters in Rivard's novel are of strictly minor importance, with the possible exception of the 'healer' Mère, whose tender ministrations, in any case, do little more than cater to the insecurities of her Western disciples. These latter, meanwhile, are superficial to the point of caricature, each a victim to his/her misty conception of the Orient as the panacea for a unanimous disaffection with Life. But the adoption in Alexandre's journal of an attitude of ironic detachment toward the antics of his Western colleagues does not prevent him from being one of them. Alexandre is aware of the thin line separating the (apparent) desire for self-annihilation from the (actual) licence for self-indulgence. The tourist gaze of *Les silences du corbeau* is ironically self-reflexive – it recognises the material basis for its allegedly spiritual quest. The ashram devotees pay handsomely for the right to inspect their souls. They belong, like Hospital's Annie, to the 'alternative' category of the 'drifter tourist' (Cohen 1973). The counter-cultural aspirations of drifter tourists merely reinforce their bourgeois privilege: 'Institutionalized [drifting is] on a level ... segregated from but parallel to ordinary mass tourism' (Cohen 1973: 90). Alexandre is acutely conscious of his contribution to the absurd posturing of a group of spiritual tourists, whose encounter with the Orient, like their experiments with drugs and alcohol and their feeble attempts to 'discover' themselves through the dubious media of astrology and visionary art, amounts to a reprehensible escape from their social responsibilities rather than a meaningful confrontation with their 'inner selves'.

Rivard's awareness that this particular instance of East-West encounter may be doing little more than recycling the stereotypes of earlier literary Orientalisms is demonstrated in the interpolation into Alexandre's journal of a series of references to the exoticist poetry of Valéry, Nerval and, especially, Baudelaire.[7] As in Valéry's poetry, the Orient provides a complex web of indeterminate dream-sensations. Its exotic effect depends on a theatricalised perception of distance and/or absence. The ashram devotees play the part of enlightenment-seeking spiritual tourists. In a safely insulated setting, they stage elaborate fantasies of withdrawal: they tilt at spiritual windmills and practice pseudo-yogic contortions; they make a virtue of their anxieties and their fear of contact with the outside world. With India at their doorstep, they choose to praise it – then ignore it. Exoticists, says Todorov,

> cherish the remote because of its remoteness. ... The best candidates for the exotic ideal are the peoples and cultures that are the most remote from us. ... Knowledge is incompatible with exoticism, but lack of knowledge is in turn irreconcilable with praise of others; yet praise without knowledge is precisely what exoticism aspires to be. This is its constitutive paradox.
>
> (Todorov 1993: 265; see also Introduction)

This praise is at its warmest when it is delivered out of the happy fug of intoxication. Alexandre's derision of the misguided attempts of his ashram colleagues to create their own artificial paradises recalls Baudelaire's eponymous collection, in which alcohol and drugs are described as having mystically transcendental effects. But Alexandre's mockery rebounds back on himself – his meditations are no more uplifting than the 'degraded' antics of his colleagues. Nor less commodified; for as would-be spiritual tourists, they compete with one another to prove their anti-materialist sentiments. All the while, the ashram management looks on, clips lawns, and accumulates the profits of guilty conscience. And over them all hovers the derisive presence of the crow, whose interjections stress both the futility and the inherent falseness of each of their imagined paths to beatitude. The novel, in fact, is full of false or dubious mediators, none more so than the 'divine healer' Mère who, as the wary reader has suspected all along, turns out to be an unsophisticated recruit manipulated by the ashram manager (Chitkara) for his own gratification.

Probably the most telling incident in Rivard's demystification of Baudelaire's Orient is Alexandre's traumatic encounter with the decomposed corpse of a dog, washed up by the tide as if to provide the mocking illustration for a typically vapid meditation on the Eternal Return. Shocked, Alexandre retreats to the safety of the ashram and the more familiar sights and smells of a Western breakfast of toast and coffee. The incident provides another ironic reminder of the delicacy of Alexandre's Western sensibilities; it also recalls Baudelaire's notorious poem 'Une charogne', in which the speaker uses the decomposed body of a dog as the subject for a perverse comparison between the eternal purity of love and the shortlived but consuming passion of physical desire.[8] Baudelaire's deliberately shocking contrast between the vileness of the symbol and the nobility of the idea it expresses is heavily ironic in the context of Rivard's novel, indicating the glibness of Alexandre's gaze on India – degeneration of outer forms, preservation of inner sanctity – and giving evidence, through that gaze, of his continued reliance on the polarising rhetoric of European Orientalism. The unsolicited appearance of the dog alerts Alexandre's attention to the Orientalist tendencies of his own writing, reminding him of the lingering cultural biases that contradict his pretensions to detachment, and that vitiate his self-conscious play with the clichés and conventions of East–West encounter. These biases are all the more unfortunate in that they are brought to bear upon a Quebecois writer – a writer supposedly attuned to the self-privileging practices of French colonialism and sensitive to a European literary heritage in which his own country, like India, has often been designated in stereotypically demeaning terms.

This last point seems worth pursuing, for it demonstrates the ambivalent position of Rivard and Hospital as *postcolonial* Canadian writers.

Ostensibly, the two writers adapt exoticist tropes for political purposes. By exploring the largely imaginary space of a 'non-Western' cultural other, Rivard and Hospital not only question the principles upon which such implicitly colonial representations might be based, but also challenge the ways in which those representations have historically been used to determine and maintain Canada's status at the margins of a European cultural mainstream. The debate is taken up more directly in Rivard's novel. An example is the argument between Alexandre and his English colleague Peter on the topic of the 'sad demise' of the British Empire. Using the poetic licence of exoticist nostalgia, Peter wistfully recalls the glory-days of the Raj, musing that, had the British stayed, they might have achieved 'the impossible fusion of East and West' (Rivard 1986: 96, my translations throughout). Alexandre scoffs at such starry-eyed idealism. Singling Forster out as a literary target ('Like you, he thought that it was for the good of India that England keep it', Rivard 1986: 97), he concludes, with equal snideness, that 'it is easier for a camel to go through the eye of a needle than for Britain to withdraw from the kingdom it once ruled' (Rivard 1986: 97). Alexandre's display of self-righteous indignation is reinforced by the parallel between Forster's paradoxically self-serving dream of cross-cultural synthesis and Hugh MacLennan's attempts to reconcile the 'two solitudes' of Canada and Quebec. But while Alexandre leaves us in little doubt as to his separatist leanings, he is less candid when it comes to assessing his indebtedness to France. In fact, like Juliet in *The Ivory Swing*, Alexandre seems to be much happier when railing against the prejudices of others. The elderly Frenchwoman he meets in Pondicherry, who has taken it upon herself to educate her admiring Indian lodger, is typically dismissed with the wry observation that 'colonies will exist as long as the illusions they exploit' (Rivard 1986: 64). But Alexandre himself can hardly be considered exempt: a connection duly emerges between the 'colonial' Frenchwoman, nurtured on comforting myths of cultural superiority, shuttling between her home in Paris and her holiday house in Pondicherry, and the 'postcolonial' Quebecois, whose perceptions of the Orient are filtered through French colonial stereotypes, and who returns abruptly to his own country once he has realised that India can no longer sustain his dreams.

Like Alexandre, Juliet is shocked to find herself adopting the same attitude of cultural arrogance she so deplores in others. Juliet eventually comes to understand the damaging effects of her engagement with a culture of which she knows so little but in which she is ready, at the least given opportunity, to interfere. But it is less clear if she comes to understand her ambivalent status as a Canadian; indeed, there is the disturbing implication that she looks upon her nationality as a mark of ideological neutrality. Juliet's naivety is surpassed, however, by that of her freewheeling sister Annie. In a contrived debate between Annie and the typecast Marxist student Prem, Prem accuses Annie of being one of those 'rich imperialists [who] take pleasure trips to India' (Hospital 1982: 195). Annie's response is trite, to say the least: 'Prem, I care about these things. You should not hate me because I am a Canadian' (Hospital 1982: 195). One wonders whether it would be permissible for Prem to hate her were she, say, British or American, but whatever the case, Annie's nationality neither grants her immunity nor disguises her status as a tourist – one who, by her own admission, has dropped out of law school to 'bum around Asia' (Hospital 1982: 36).

Annie flaunts her freedom in the face of her inexperienced Indian boyfriend; her introduction of Prem to the liberated (sexual) ways of Western women results in a frivolous encounter in which, while a full-scale riot is going on around them in Kerala, the two new lovers, 'oblivious to the tempo of history, moved to rhythms of their own until daybreak' (Hospital 1982: 204). As Matthew Zachariah points out,

> Hospital is so taken up by the promise inherent in sexual liberation that she has completely missed seeing in Kerala the serious attempt of previously powerless groups of people actually achieving both political and economic power. Instead, she has arranged for Prem, the student Marxist, to be cured of his radicalism with sex.
>
> (Zacariah 1985: 60)

Hospital is not as unaware of the contradiction as Zachariah implies, but there remains in the incident a specious transcendence of material conflict that lends support to the view that Hospital has allowed an excessively narrow feminist agenda to cloud her political judgement. The most worrying aspect here is not Hospital's critique of the absolutist tendencies inherent in Marxist doctrine – however clumsily her point is made – but the implication that the liberation of women is an issue that can somehow be removed from the day-to-day operations of political and economic power. That different modes of cultural production, operating in specific political and/or economic interests, have served to justify and reinforce patriarchal ascendancy is surely not a point that Hospital would wish to dispute; why is it, then, that she chooses through her protagonist Juliet to address the question of women's liberation, not in terms of the uneven relations of power that maintain social and cultural hierarchies in both India and North America, but in the suspiciously ethnocentric terms of 'basic [human] freedom'? (Hospital 1982: 146).

Like Hospital, Rivard addresses in his novel the problematic relation between sexual and political liberation. But his position, like hers, appears ambivalent. On the one hand, the exposure in Alexandre's third and last notebook of the complicit activities of Mère and her guardian Chitkara reveals a connection between the fraudulent marketing of spiritual guidance and the commercial exploitation of women. Spiritual tourism, like other forms of tourism, thrives on the availability and affordability of commodities. The aura surrounding Mère might be mysterious, but it has a price-tag; her otherness functions as a spectacle, a tantalising (commodity) fetish. Alexandre senses that Mère's elusiveness is little more than a clever market strategy; that she is being set up and 'sold' as a fetishised object of contemplation. If the ashram is a tourist site, Mère constitutes its main attraction. It is her very unattainability that makes her all the more attractive – her spiritual force emanates from her control of others' sexual frustrations. And she in turn is controlled, subjected to a tourist gaze that seeks to sublimate its longing. The revelation of Mère's indiscretions, and her eventual downfall, are pathetic; yet Alexandre's sympathies fall some way short of total comprehension. In the final scene of the novel, Alexandre escorts the abandoned Mère back to her village before himself returning to Montreal, presumably to comfort there his estranged wife Françoise. He appears to have awakened at last to his responsibilities, and to have cured himself of the destructive desire for instant sexual gratification. But how complete is the cure, how much has Alexandre really understood? His view of women, for a start, appears to be largely unchanged. The final image of Mère is as clichéd as the image that preceded it – the myth of the 'divine mother' is supplanted by that of the 'simple country girl'. Mère seems to have been released from one form of servitude only to be delivered into another, with her pledge of obedience to Chitkara being exchanged for the dubious promise of a scarcely less subservient lifestyle in her own village. Alexandre demonstrates once more his misunderstanding – or wilful ignorance – of the material conditions governing personal and social relations in contemporary India. He has not managed to disabuse himself of his romantic notions of the Orient, notions that allow him to gloss over the material context of social struggle, and that culminate in the foolish justification of his indifference toward the cripples and beggars he frequently encounters in the streets of Pondicherry: 'I have the strange impression that no-one here desires anything at all …' (Rivard 1986: 91). Alexandre's acceptance of, even admiration for, this 'undesiring' state, which he assumes to emanate from a fatalistic Hindu outlook on life, no doubt makes it easier for him to return to his own country with a clear conscience. The hypocrisy is remarkable: surely Alexandre is not so blinded by his own self-importance that he cannot see that

> the overwhelming majority of Indians are poor because their ruling elites – Indians and their erstwhile as well as extant non-Indian associates – have perpetuated on them an enslaving economic relationship accompanied by a mythology which has rationalized that enslavement with concepts such as 'dharma' and 'karma'.
>
> (Zachariah 1976: 138)

Using India as a temporary refuge from responsibilities 'back home' is bad enough; marvelling at the 'indifference' of the Indian poor is still worse. Having spent much of his time at the ashram scorning the bourgeois attitudes of his colleagues, Alexandre turns out to be just as complacent as, if not more complacent than, the rest.

Rivard and Hospital use varying degrees of irony to distance themselves from their respective protagonists. For both writers, the stereotypes of previous fictions of East-West encounter are recycled as a means of exposing continuing Western biases, and of revealing not only the pusillanimity, but also the irresponsibility, of a recourse to the Orient in which India becomes a panacea for Western disaffection or a collective symbol for the contradictory aspirations of a divided Western subject. This recourse, in both cases, centres on the figure of the spiritual tourist. The gaze of the spiritual tourist is ironically narcissistic: introspection justifies inertia and a morbid self-involvement. The spiritual tourist's needs are catered to by what Gita Mehta calls 'the trance-inducing industry' (G. Mehta 1979: 103) – by the drugs and books that facilitate the process of escape. India is bitterly blamed for agonies of indecision, and for the failure to distinguish between internal and external worlds. This mythicised 'India' is

> the lotus land, the land of *sanyasin* and meditation, where old men lay on beds of nails; and ropes, so people said, uncoiled themselves upwards into air; where no one could keep track of what was temporal and what was eternal; where things which existed in the mind had more substance than the blurred image of the external world.
>
> (Hospital 1982: 140)

It is, in short, the privileged 'other' realm of the European exotic. In both novels, exoticism accommodates the discourse of the other, of the unattainable, to an embarrassment of choices born out of evident bourgeois privilege. Juliet, in *The Ivory Swing*, and Alexandre, in *Les silences du corbeau*, spend much of their time and energy agonising about their options, confronted all the while by the more obvious suffering of those around them. Their anxieties, of course, have much to do with their advantages as tourists, not least the escape clause in their contract that grants them the option of returning home. The gaze of the spiritual tourist in either novel is self-defeating: at times, it induces blindness as to one's power and cultural arrogance; at others, it reveals complicities and the force of touristic shame (MacCannell 1989). Spiritual tourism markets the desire for profound and lasting understanding, for an experience out of time or, at the very least, out of the ordinary. Yet it seems condemned, in spite of itself, to an endless recycling of banalities. It enters here into the constitutive dilemma of the exotic – the impossibility of achieving reinvigoration through the medium of cliché (see also Introduction). East–West encounters are likewise tainted with the tawdry glitter of commercialism. The tourist industry acts as a purveyor of (pseudo-)spiritual commodities. Instant solutions belonging to this debased currency are offered up to those who are needy, or gullible, enough to take them:

> It would appear that when East meets West all you get is the neo-Sanyasi, the instant Nirvana. Coming at the problem from separate directions, both parties have chanced upon the same conclusion, namely, that the most effective weapon against irony is to reduce everything to the banal. You have the Karma, we'll take the Coca-Cola, a metaphysical soft drink for a physical one.
>
> (G. Mehta 1979: 103; see also Chapter 3)

In their self-conscious recording of an inventory of Orientalist clichés, Rivard and Hospital deploy irony, in turn, as a weapon against the banal. Yet the ironic treatment of Juliet, in *The Ivory Swing*, and of Alexandre, in *Les silences du corbeau*, can by no means be considered as a guarantee of authorial immunity. The inconsistency of Hospital's irony, and the lack of a clearly defined context against which her protagonist's fantasies might be offset, ultimately does little to dissuade her readers from viewing the novel's one-dimensional 'Indians', in their pseudo-Indian context, as merely latter-day variations on Conrad's 'Africans' – projections of European stereotypes, but also perpetuations of them. In Rivard's novel, a similar recycling of stereotypes implicates Alexandre without necessarily exculpating Rivard. The ambivalent, rather than unreservedly ironic, treatment of Alexandre in the novel cannot help but suggest that Rivard has some sympathy for the plight of his narrator-protagonist – a sympathy that Alexandre's objectionable views on poverty and women, and his self-righteous belief in the inviolability of Quebec, certainly make difficult to share. It is true, as Edward Said has pointed out, that the dilemma of abiding Western prejudices and misconceptions about the Orient is not resolved by issuing partisan decrees such as 'only Orientals can write about the Orient'; 'only literature that treats Orientals well is good literature'; or 'only anti-Orientalists can write about Orientalism' (Said 1986: 229). It is also true that neither Rivard nor Hospital is unaware of the difficulties involved in writing about the Orient as both 'outsiders' to that culture and 'insiders' to the prejudices bound up in its European literary representation. One of the risks they run is that, like their respective protagonists, they might end up reinforcing the prejudices they set out to attack. This risk assumes the proportions of a self-fulfilling prophecy. The writers' self-consciously exoticist deployment of India as spiritual/cultural other – as an index of the anxieties of modern Western material culture – eventually turns into an exercise in frustrated self-entrapment. And an exercise in obfuscation – for the otherness of exoticism, mediated through the gaze of the spiritual tourist, provides an obstacle to knowledge, a means of blocking out deeper insight. India becomes a site for the reproduction of self-deception; its (Hindu) myths are co-opted for the rehearsal of Western existential crises. ('Everything was so unreal', muses Hospital's Juliet, attributing her ignorance to Maya; 'people appeared and disappeared as swiftly and insubstantially as illusions' (Hospital 1982: 35).) India is filtered through an obfuscatory discourse of the exotic, which ensures that the culture at large remains inaccessible or opaque. India becomes instead a blur, a sign of sensory debilitation.[9] And a confirmation of the touristic impulse to reduce or trivialise culture(s), to see the surface while looking for depths, and to be offered continual reminders of that perceptual inadequacy. *The Ivory Swing* and *Les silences du corbeau* are perhaps best described as melodramas of self-estrangement, prisoners of their own escapism and their compulsion to romantic flight. And prisoners, too, of their clichéd attempts at Orientalist criticism; for the combined effect of Rivard's and Hospital's overt or hidden agendas – however viable – and of their self-conscious delight in the depiction of Oriental stereotypes – however ironic – is to blur the intended operation of cultural critique, to the extent that what emerges is not the advocation of cross-cultural understanding but something much more like its opposite, the reconfirmation of cultural bias.[10]

Anti-tourist tourists

In *The Ivory Swing* and *Les silences du corbeau*, spiritual tourism provides a vehicle for the dramatisation of cultural anxieties. These anxieties are related in part to Western existential crises – to the failure of the West to offer 'authentic' metaphysical experience (see also previous chapter). They are also related to the fear of being trapped in a vicious circle, of being sentenced to the imprisonment of seeing only oneself in the (cultural) other. More specifically, they are related to the liminal state of Canadian/Quebecois culture – to the ambivalent position of a 'peripheral' but still neo-European postcolonial nation (Lawson 1995). Finally, they are related to a broader mechanism of denial – to the process by which the tourist disclaims his or her touristic status. Spiritual tourists, in this last sense, are exemplars of anti-touristic bias. This bias remains a driving force behind the modern tourist industry; as MacCannell argues,

> The touristic critique of tourism is based on a desire to go beyond the other 'mere' tourists to a more profound appreciation of society and culture, and it is by no means limited to intellectual statements. All tourists desire this deeper involvement with society and culture to some degree; it is a basic component of their motivation to travel.
>
> (MacCannell 1989: 10)

For spiritual tourists, this deeper involvement includes a quasi-religious dimension. Society and culture are collapsed into a search for 'inner meaning', or – as in Rivard's and Hospital's India – they are reduced to the standard formulae of Orientalist mysticism (India as a source of ineffable wisdom; India as the collective embodiment of an unchanging Hindu mind; and so on). Spiritual tourism thus becomes illustrative of another paradox inherent in touristic discourse, namely that the need for deeper involvement may actually *preclude* close cultural contact. Hence, for the tourist industry, the transferability of the terms 'spiritual' and 'exotic'; for if the exotic locations advertised by the industry are often invested with a spiritual quality, spirituality itself may be conceived of as exotic, as a mystique made accessible by travel. (Not too accessible, however, for the appeal of the exotic 'elsewhere' is, precisely, that it always be out of reach – a neat marketing manoeuvre that ensures that the traveller always stays in motion.) This compulsion to move ever onwards is typical of 'anti-tourist tourists' – and of tourists in general. As one destination after another in the world is swamped by the tide of tourism, the self-appointed vanguard packs its bags again and impatiently moves on. The urge to avoid 'mere' tourists is the life-blood of modern tourism; and the guarantee, ironically, that tourism remains a mass phenomenon. It is perfectly legitimate, argue Louis Turner and John Ash in their 1975 study *The Golden Hordes*, to 'compare tourists with barbarian tribes. Both involve the mass migration of people who collide with cultures far removed from their own' (Turner and Ash 1975: 11). There is one major difference, however:

> The old Golden Horde ... was a nomadic, non-monetary people which threatened the settled urban civilisations of Europe. Today the pattern is reversed. Tourists come from the industrialist centres but, this time, it is they who are fanning out through the world, swamping apparently less dynamic societies, including the few pre-industrial ones which still remain. In the past, it was the great commercial centres of the world like Constantinople and Vienna which were threatened. Today, it is the Nomads of Affluence, coming from the new Constantinoples – cities like New York, London, Hamburg or Tokyo – who are creating a newly dependent social and geographic realm: the Pleasure Periphery.
>
> (Turner and Ash 1975: 11)

The Pleasure Periphery, as Turner and Ash define it, is a 'tourist belt surrounding the great industrialised zones of the world' (Turner and Ash 1975: 11). Relative accessibility is a feature of the Pleasure Periphery: a North American periphery might therefore include the islands of Hawaii and the Caribbean; a European periphery the coastal resort towns of the Mediterranean; a Japanese periphery the cities of Thailand, the Philippines and Indonesia; and so on. Turner and Ash are quick to recognise, however, that although these Pleasure Peripheries are promoted and to some extent safeguarded by the leisure industry, they remain fundamentally unstable. The tourist industry thrives on the expansion of its geographical and perceptual frontiers; as each individual periphery spreads, the various peripheries begin to merge, coalescing into 'one giant, global Pleasure Periphery, where the rich of the world relax and intermingle' (Turner and Ash 1975: 12). Turner and Ash's vision of the future has turned out, in this respect at least, to be remarkably prophetic. In the early twenty-first century, we live in an era of global tourism. Otherness is emerging everywhere; simulated worlds replace real ones; tourist destinations begin to look alike. What are the implications for tourism of this process of homogenisation? Does it spell an end to tourism's courtship of the exotic? And what are the effects of global tourism on national self-perception; in an age of unparalleled movement, can fictions of national identity be maintained?

These questions are addressed in two 1990s Australian 'tourist novels' set in Bali: Gerard Lee's *Troppo Man* (1990) and Inez Baranay's *The Edge of Bali* (1992). Lee's and Baranay's novels belong to a well-established tradition of Australian tourist fiction. The gaze both writers direct is disabused, second-hand, belated.[11] Bali provides an ideal site for their satirical touristic forays. Recent figures show that the island receives around a million tourists a year, about a fifth of whom are Australians (online source: *Bali Travel News*, 1999). Since the 1960s, when Bali underwent the transformation from an idyllic refuge for occasional drifter tourists, or a privileged site for a handful of Western artists and scholars, into an institutional mass-tourist attraction, the island has been a favourite destination for Australian travellers. Marketed back then as an 'island paradise', Bali continues to be sold as one today. But the times, needless to say, have changed; so much so that Turner and Ash's pronouncement on Bali now resonates, as does much of their pioneering study, with an unintended irony. 'Many aspects of Balinese culture and art are so bewilderingly complex and alien to Western models', assert Turner and Ash, 'that they do not lend themselves readily to the process of over-simplification and mass-production that converts indigenous art forms into touristic kitsch' (Turner and Ash 1975: 159). Try telling that to the store-owners at Kuta or Sanur: Bali, like other imagined outposts in the global Pleasure Periphery (certain Caribbean and South Pacific islands come readily to mind) has been remarkably efficient in marketing itself for a burgeoning tourist industry. As John Urry puts it – and this time the irony *is* intended – the more traditional-minded inhabitants of islands such as Bali have been adept at 'dramatiz[ing] their backwardness as a way of fitting themselves in the total design of modern society as attractions' (Urry 1990: 178). Fitting themselves in the design, but also profiting from it; for the Balinese have been resourceful, insofar as their limited capital permits, in reaping the benefits of a system that blatantly exploits them – a system that allows some leeway, though, for *reciprocal* exploitation.

Enter, on this far from romantic scene, Gerard Lee's vulnerable pro-tagonist, Matt Walker. Through Walker, Lee caricatures the familiar figure of the anti-tourist tourist – the man who, at other times and in other places, might describe himself as a traveller, not a tourist; as a researcher, not a holidaymaker; as a long-term appreciator of indigenous culture, not a short-term visitor to a foreign country. To describe the anti-tourist tourist in this way is of course to perpetuate the moral rectitude of those who criticise tourism. As MacCannell argues, the discourse of tourism generates a rhetoric of moral superiority; it creates and reinforces the competitive sentiment of touristic shame (MacCannell 1989). Tourism is by definition a pleasure-seeking activity; yet it provides ample opportunity for the expression, not to mention the projection, of liberal angst. Lee's angst-ridden Australian protagonist is a walking advertise-ment for touristic shame. A latter-day reincarnation of the 'innocent Australian abroad', Matt is not so innocent as to be unaware of his complicity in the tourist system. Matt despises the system; but in a classic strategy of the anti-tourist tourist (a situation not so dissimilar from the one facing Hospital's Juliet or Rivard's Alexandre) he proves adept at transferring his own indefinite guilt feelings onto others. Matt targets tourists in general; more particularly, he offloads on his unwanted travel companion Pete, a fellow Australian (this in itself to be despised), or on the cliché-spouting American couple with whom he is 'forced' to share mealtimes and, still worse, conversation at his otherwise quiet hotel in rural Ubud. Matt blames others, then, but most of the time he blames himself. And how! Like his part-time guide, the half-demented German hippie Schmetzer – a comic embodiment of Conrad's already parodic harlequin in *Heart of Darkness* – Matt risks turning his touristic anxiety into a perverse desire for self-destruction.

The opening pages of *Troppo Man* set the tone for what follows. Arriving at Kuta Beach, the first thing that Matt sees, with disappointment and disgust, is 'white bodies covering the sand. In every direction. Tourists' (G. Lee 1990: 1). Surrounded by 'vulgar' tourists, assailed within minutes by aggressive hawkers whose hard-sell tactics betray their hostility toward their wealthy but undiscerning customers, Matt quickly moves down the beach in search of somewhere less crowded. 'He was desperate to be alone. He needed time to think through what was happening here, to the Balinese. It was terrible. One of the world's most refined and spiritual cultures had been corrupted totally' (G. Lee 1990: 3). Matt has scant knowledge of Balinese culture – he has seen two documentaries on Australian TV. But this does not prevent him from becoming a spokesperson on their behalf. 'It says a lot for Balinese culture', he says in a characteristically earnest exchange with the American academic Burditt, 'that it can survive a million tourists a year. That's virtual rape' (8). Matt himself, of course, is different. 'I'm here just visiting', he says of 'picturesque' Ubud – the 'real' Bali where the shops sell 'authentic carvings, paintings and Batik'; where the people are 'happy and alive'; and where a communitarian aesthetic is 'developed and deployed in the making of ordinary objects, much like the Greek civilization' (G. Lee 1990: 31). 'It's a privilege to be in the presence of these people' (28), concludes Matt, and proves the point by smiling approvingly at Ubud's shopowners as he passes, wishing like the teacher he is to give them positive feedback: ' "Good, very good", he said to a few as they glanced up at him. "Very good work" ' (G. Lee 1990: 31). Matt's championing of the cause of 'authentic' indigenous art, and his attempt to find in Ubud the 'real', uncorrupted Balinese culture, betray his 'touristic desire to share in the real life of the places visited' (MacCannell 1989: 96). As MacCannell argues, 'the variety of understanding held out before tourists as an ideal is an authentic and demystified experience of an aspect of some society or other person' (MacCannell 1989: 94). This authenticity, perceived to be lacking at home, is to be sought for and recovered elsewhere (see also previous chapter). Implicit in this process is the exercise of nostalgia – the exoticist desire to reverse the modern 'atrophy of experience' (Benjamin 1969a: 159, qtd in Bongie 1991: 9). Authenticity resides at other times, in other places and other cultures; its 'discovery' redeems the tourist while gratifying his/her desire for cultural contact. The appeal to authenticity serves a paradoxical purpose: it grants the tourist the illusion of meaningful contact with the culture while maintaining a careful distance between observer and observed. While the conventional tourist gaze confronts only inauthentic simulacra, its anti-touristic variant seeks privileged access to the real. But what it finds instead is a counter-commodified version of reality (Pratt 1992: 221; see also Holland and Huggan 1998: 4). The anti-touristic gaze is thus fundamentally self-negating – it searches for an authenticity it prevents itself from finding, and for another time and place produced by its own self-justifying myths (Bongie 1991).

Like Lee in *Troppo Man*, Baranay in *The Edge of Bali* satirises the flagrant hypocrisies of the anti-tourist tourist: that sensitive, sometimes tortured soul whose felt contempt for the vulgarities of package tourism and romantic belief in the myth of an unsullied Native culture – a culture that s/he feels duty-bound to protect from the ravages of consumer society – merely reinforce his/her own conspicuously privileged touristic status. Baranay provides several variations on the theme of anti-tourist tourism in *The Edge of Bali*; her most convincing anti-tourist tourist, however, is the ethnographic filmwriter Marla Cavas. Sensitive to her own investment in the documentation of other cultures, alert to the stereotypes of exotic romance, Marla is quick to anticipate the criticisms of others. She has, she tells anyone who will listen, no intention of writing 'another Aussie yobbos wreck island paradise story'; instead, she is in Bali collecting background material for an 'impressionistic essay on the effects of tourism in the developing world' (Baranay 1992: 33). Like other anti-tourist tourists, Marla has nothing but scorn for the type of the vulgar tourist. 'I can't believe the mentality', she complains to her lover Carlo, who understands as she does that Bali is not for the prosaic; it is rather 'a place for art and creativity … for magic … for dreams and strange states of mind' (Baranay 1992: 92). The slovenly tourist uniform of shorts and singlet is 'so hostile really, so ugly … [T]hese people would smarten up a bit if they were going to see the great monuments of Europe' (Baranay 1992: 115). Carlo cannot agree; they wouldn't, he demurs, because 'it's everywhere, they dress like this everywhere' (Baranay 1992: 115). Marla is one-up on

Carlo, however, insofar as her research on the duplicities of modern tourism has allowed her to see through the self-authenticating clichés of the anti-tourist tourist. Carlo himself becomes a case-study. Returning after several years to live in a house in the ricefields, Carlo clearly harbours residual exoticist longings:

> A house in the ricefields was one badge of authenticity for a white native. Marla was 'only' in a bungalow at the Katak Inn. Carlo was clearly just that little bit more the white native than she. He kept insisting that he was not a tourist. That's either the first sign, or the ultimate delusion, Marla thought.
>
> (Baranay 1992: 90)

Marla, for her part, knows better than to be suckered into false notions of authenticity. She knows, for example, that Bali is a manufactured paradise, a construct imposed upon the island to reinforce the 'interrelated ideologies of colonialism, orientalism and tourism' (Baranay 1992: 1). She knows, too, that 'pseudo places define the tourist world, [that] they finally eliminate places entirely [and that] then the true like the real begins to be reproduced in the image of the pseudo, which begins to become the true' (Baranay 1992: 121). She knows, finally, that 'in the age of tourism [she] can practice only a version of tourism. Tourism with its roots in colonialism – quest and conquest – whether it's holiday tourism school of life tourism business tourism development tourism' (Baranay 1992: 201). (Later in the novel, Baranay also satirises ecotourism, poking fun at the consciousness-raising activities of the Bali-based Rainbow Group, who are 'upset about tourism [but] not upset enough not to be tourists' (Baranay 1992: 265).) Marla knows all these things, then, but she finds to her dismay that her research has seduced her into recycling the same romantic platitudes and overdetermined Golden Age myths she wishes to expose in others. Thus, like her more illustrious predecessors – Walter Spies, Margaret Mead, Miguel Covarrubias – Marla is both an investor in Bali and a reinventor of it. By a law of double negatives, the anti-tourist tourist is reinstated as a tourist *avant la lettre* – one for whom the experience of tourism, conscripted into the service of invoking an exoticist lost past, both legitimises and perpetuates its own 'semiotics of nostalgia' (Frow 1991).

As self-aware tourist novels, *Troppo Man* and *The Edge of Bali* recognise and celebrate their own artifice. If tourism, as MacCannell claims, can be seen as a barometer of the anxieties of modernity, then the playfulness of Lee's and Baranay's novels – their tendency to transmute touristic conflict into the stuff of pastiche and self-conscious aestheticism – mark both works as being at once postmodern and, in a sense, 'post-touristic'. The term 'post-tourist' is derived here from the work of Maxine Feifer, who in her 1985 book *Going Places* defines post-tourism in terms of the awareness of touristic activity as a *game*: a game whose rules can be manipulated and reinvented at will, and whose enjoyment comes from the multiplicity of experiences it offers rather than from the distinct experience of an 'authentic' culture. Post-tourists, according to Feifer, are distanced from the tourist world yet open to the many delights it offers; theirs is a democracy of taste, as likely to take pleasure in a cheap piece of mass-produced kitsch as in an expensive item of local handicrafts, aware that the one is no more genuine than the other, and that both are products of a leisure industry designed to convert the trappings of indigenous culture into a profitable supply of consumer goods (Feifer 1985). Post-tourists come close to adopting what Susan Sontag calls a camp sensibility: they are aware, that is, of the iniquities of tourism, yet prefer to make light of them, transforming the sustained moral indignation of the anti-tourist tourist into moments of melodramatic anguish.[12] Offbeat comedy befits the post-touristic experience. As in *The Edge of Bali*, where the ecotourist Dennis discusses his plans for a gigantic Bali World, which 'would contain everything ninety percent of tourists wanted from Bali [so that] no-one would come [to Bali] and the [Balinese] people could get on with their lives and prepare for the twenty-first century in peace' (Baranay 1992: 284), post-tourism deflates the high moral seriousness of the responsible world citizen. This should not be seen as giving post-tourists licence for irresponsibility; what it does is demonstrate to them the effective limits of their intervention. After all, says Feifer, whatever their politics, whatever the nature and function of their touristic experience, post-tourists 'cannot evade [their] condition of outsiders' (Feifer 1985: 271).

Lee's and Baranay's novels – like their most obvious precursor, Murray Bail's exemplary tourist novel *Homesickness* (1980) – might better be seen as post- rather than simply anti-touristic: they are arguably less concerned with the critical analysis of tourist culture than with the tentative establishment of a distinctive tourist aesthetic. ('The Tourist Style', says Bail's art-buff Borelli, consists in a parodic conflation of the different modernisms: 'Impressionism, Cubism, Futurism, Abstract Expressionism and Tourism are all related. I doubt ... whether one can do without the other' (Bail 1980: 63).) The simulated randomness and ironically discontinuous structure of *Homesickness* enact Burditt's postmodern cliché that 'there are no places on Earth now we could call *the* place ... there's no centre any more' (G. Lee 1990: 126); they also recall Marla's observation that 'these days [people] travel back and forth easily; moving to Bali isn't the end of the earth, the earth has no more ends' (Baranay 1992: 203).

Lee's and Baranay's novels, like Bail's, play on the levelling effect of tourism on an increasingly globalised culture.[13] The island of Bali, in both novels, becomes a cultural crossroads, a parody of McLuhan's global village in which local dancers imitate Michael Jackson videos (G. Lee 1990: 94) and South American tourists dress like Indian shamans (Baranay 1992: 90). In the nightclub strip at Kuta Beach, Baranay's Nelson Brodie discovers that 'everything is the same as everything else' (Baranay 1992: 15); and when Marla Cavas joins a tour-group visiting a local palace, the standard patter of the tour-guide elicits an equally standard response:

> The Head Prince posed with some of his wives and children. Flash-click-whirr. 'Five wives and twenty-nine children!' the tourist group was told. It probably got a reaction every time. 'One wife is enough!' sniggered one of the men in the tourist group. Someone said that every Puri Night. Joke.
>
> (Baranay 1992: 174)

Lee's and Baranay's tourists are galled by the fact that their hosts know as much about them as they know about Bali – a knowledge which, like theirs, is less likely to be mediated through books than through the popular channels of TV and music. The stereotypes, as they discover, can also work both ways: 'You from America?' a child vendor asks African American Tyler Evers in *The Edge of Bali*: ' "You know Michael Jackson?" She was delighted. "Number one! I'm bad I'm bad I'm bad," she sang. "Look!" She took out a patterned cloth. "Number one batik! How much you want pay?" ' And when Tyler hesitates: ' "For you wife?" asked the captivating little girl, shaking out another cloth, something different, something more like he wanted. "You know Mike Tyson?" ' (Baranay 1992: 242–3).

The demand for authenticity is not restricted, then, to the Western tourist in a foreign country; it extends to those, like Tyler's child-vendor, who seek reassurance in the confirmation of Western media images. Tourism, according to MacCannell, sets up an orchestrated sequence of acts of recognition (MacCannell 1989). In 'recognising' Tyler, the girl illustrates the transferability of the tourist gaze – the process by which the tourist himself/herself becomes an exotic object. She also demonstrates the touristic paradox that foreign peoples/cultures may be exotic, not because they are incommensurably different but, on the contrary, because they are already *familiar*.[14] Tourism, in this context, represents a premeditated activity based on the pleasurable confirmation of exotic expectation. Armed with the latest edition of, say, the Lonely Planet guidebook – that countercultural Baedeker for the modern budget traveller – 'informed' tourists in Bali may persuade themselves that they already know what they are going to see before they actually get there. Tourism, by this process, works to assimilate cultural difference, to convert it into terms which can be readily understood. Hence the prevalence in touristic discourse of the social/cultural *stereotype*. According to Stephen Foster,

> The generalizing meaning of stereotypes easily allows them to domi-nate the particularistic diversity of meaning associated with the exotic, thereby keeping it in 'control'. … Like the photograph, the stereotype freezes movement, variability, evolution, and growth, reduces the spatial dimensions from three to two, banishing depth and aspect, and misrepresents volume as shadowed surface. Selection of what is significant is given over to the observer, so that the result-ing representations express mainly the observational style and social placement of the photographer, interlocutor, or outsider.
>
> (Foster 1982/3: 29; for a more conflicted view of the stereotype, see also Bhabha 1994e)

Despite its aggressive marketing of the unusual and the extraordinary, tourism in fact sets out to create a curiously predictable world. Tourism's palatable alternatives become ironic expressions of the need to conform. Difference is incorporated into and filed within the archive, allowing the exotic to be domesticated – and priced – for private consumption. Hence, in Lee's and Baranay's novels, the reduction of Balinese customs and rituals to routine spectacle; the assimilation of Balinese music to the 'global' (read, Western) World Music scene; and the incorporation of Balinese art into the designer decor of chic Western hotels whose 'style troppo deluxe international [is] emphasized by carefully chosen artifacts' (Baranay 1992: 217). And for the more 'independent' tourist, there are always the comforting tenets of a New Age philosophy – the lingua franca of the affluent drifter – which legitimises its unconsidered conflation of different cultures by passing off half-digested ideas and politically correct platitudes as evidence of cosmopolitan sophistication. ('These people here', Carlo tells Marla, 'are like the Aborigines. They have a very Aboriginal habit. Spirits and magic and community and ancestors and so on. They can tell at once if you're racist. They understand body languages as well. They're like the people in India too' (Baranay 1992: 201).)

There is a sense, then, in which touristic discourse works to promote difference while simultaneously erasing it. One of the most significant effects of this erasure in both Lee's and Baranay's novels is the collapsing of a potentially destabilising cultural hybridity into the comfortingly vague, and falsely unifying, category of 'the transnational'. At Lyn and Ktut's home, a fashionable meeting-place for the internationally minded, Nelson Brodie meets Robbie, who is 'of mixed parentage: there was Dutch, Timorese, Chinese. He came from Timor and had lived in Timor and did some business in Timor. Or something' (Baranay 1992: 18). Later in Baranay's novel, Tyler strikes up a conversation at the Bar Zapata with 'a guy with a deep tan, dreadlocks and an indeterminate accent. Transatlantic, transpacific, transglobal, trans certain places certain people know' (Baranay 1992: 211). Baranay's emphasis on both occasions is characteristically sardonic; she realises, as does Lee, that the complacent rhetoric of global citizenship disguises the unequal power relations between First and Third Worlds upon which the practice of tourism effectively depends (Frow 1991). Both writers also recognise that the 'security' offered by tourism is illusory – and dangerous. Baranay's novel, as its title suggests, has a distinct edge to it – the impact of tourism on societies such as Bali's has led, among other things, to a marked increase in violence. The threat of violence is also everpresent in Lee's novel; its most dramatic embodiment is in the grotesque self-incineration of Schmetzer. What tourism makes apparent here is exoticism's narcissistic impulse: the frustrated desire for the other turns to self-loathing, even self-destruction. Tourism caters 'to the needs and desires of the foreigner, who then has the illusion of being able to find anything he wants in the exotic milieu' (Foster 1983/4: 25). Yet Bali will not concede to such impassioned wish-fulfilment. Its fantasies are available, but only for those who can afford them; and even then, only for those who can afford to fight off others, to compete. Tourism creates the illusion of converting suffering into spectacle – even death can be aestheticised, treated as a spectator sport. Yet tourism, far from protecting its paying customers, makes them vulnerable; it creates an environment of misunderstanding that can easily transform into conflict. The 'exotic' world of Bali is thus a world on guard, on *edge*. 'We're all just visitors in other people's countries', says Baranay's Anne Pavlou (Baranay 1992: 133): a convenient touristic dictum, but one that cannot hide the economic discrepancies, social imbalances, and physical and psychological dangers that tourists' sometimes unrestrained drive for pleasure helps create.

It seems clear from *Troppo Man* and *The Edge of Bali*, in any case, that the indeterminate status of the freewheeling transnational traveller is another of tourism's self-justifying myths; and that the myth is likely to be debunked since tourism is so thoroughly invested in the cause of the *nation*. Tourists' sense of affiliation to their own country is frequently ambivalent. While they may desire escape, they also want it to be temporary; and they are often impelled to compare the countries they are visiting, and whose attractions they are consuming, to their own homeland. As the title of Bail's novel suggests, homesickness is not just an effect of tourism; it may also be a prerequisite for it. Tourism, paradoxically, fuels the ardour of the wandering patriot: it helps instil solidarity and a collective sense of belonging. As Lee's and Baranay's novels show, however, the Australian abroad is as likely to avoid other Australians as to team up with or rally around them. What tourist novels such as Lee's, Baranay's and Bail's emphasise, above all, is the fragility of cultural origins. Constructed around an opposition between the 'homeland' and the 'foreign country', tourism is based on marketable myths of exoticism and authenticity. Yet these myths are contradicted by the lived experience of tourism. For the world opened up by tourism is transnational in its dimensions – cultural differences are levelled out by the reciprocal operations of a tourist economy in which the 'foreign' and the 'local' are manipulated by corporate owners to satisfy the demands of an international consumer public. Levelled out, but not cancelled out; for while modern tourism depends to a large extent on the global economy and on the international flow of capital that economy provides, it cannot substantiate the capitalist chimera of an undifferentiated 'global culture'. What it does instead is to commodify exoticism's cult of difference.[15] Exotic artifacts circulate as commodities in the global touristic marketplace; it is precisely their availability that renders them exotic (see also Introduction). Distance is maintained, however, through a careful decontextualisation, and through a hybridised conflation of various 'equally treated' cultures. By aestheticising difference and domesticating it for mass consumption, tourism helps to bridge the gap between cultural ignorance and cultural synthesis. As in New Age philosophy and World Music – themselves touristic forms – tourism commodifies a wide variety of decontextualised items, then claims evidence from their conjunction of a coherent International Style. Not surprisingly, a number of Lee's and Baranay's tourists are 'into' World Music and/or New Age philosophy. In one of the funniest scenes in *The Edge of Bali*, the young Australian holidaymaker Nelson Brodie is persuaded to enrol in a workshop run by the fraudulent Candi Dasa Gladiators, an international group of self-styled Hermann Hesse freaks who understand, as their mentor does, that the psyche is 'like a [giant] satellite communications dish', and that the time has now come, in the Electronic Age of the late twentieth century, 'for all the spiritual cultures to sort of feed into the world community'

(Baranay 1992: 66). (Needless to say, the Great Guru himself, eagerly awaited by his devotees, never shows up.) Baranay is playing here as elsewhere on the cliché of touristic gullibility – on tourists' willingness to ease their disaffection with the Western world by subscribing unthinkingly to alternative causes or systems of belief. Baranay's more serious (if also obvious) point has to do with touristic affluence: for if it is tourists' ability to pay that becomes a paradoxical marker of their conformity, it is that same economic privilege that differentiates them from the vast majority of people in the places they are visiting. Tourism satisfies the demand for provisional entertainment; it also caters to those, like Lee's Matt Walker or Baranay's Marla Cavas, who seek temporary disguises for their privilege. The attempt to downplay touristic advantage, however, almost inevitably backfires; it ends up most often by reinforcing economic discrepancies between tourists' country of residence and the country or countries through which they travel. Tourism, in this last sense, substitutes memory for nostalgia; it produces, not homesickness, but an unwanted reminder of home.

The status of home is frequently uncertain for the Australian tourist: home is a place to be escaped from, but also a place to which to return. What are the implications of this uncertainty for Australian national identity and, more specifically, for the ongoing construction of a national Australian literature? Australia's sense of itself – Australians' perception of their homeland and of their place within it – has arguably been mediated through the formation of an 'imagined community' (Anderson 1983). Literature, as Graeme Turner and Richard White among others have shown, contributes to the establishment of that community; Australian texts have played, and continue to play, a defining role in the dialectical process of creating national narrative (Turner 1986; White 1981). Australian literature, like any national literature, is not a homogeneous entity: its narratives and counternarratives cut across one another, creating a series of contradictory readings that continually redefine the meaning of home. Australian writers, says Leonie Kramer in her introduction to an anthology of occasional pieces, *Australians Abroad* (1967), are forever 'seeking to establish the exact relationship between [themselves] and the world outside [their] own country' (Kramer 1967: xi). But the pursuit, as Kramer recognises, is at once necessary and illusory; the 'Australian's ruling passion', she concludes, is never 'simple nationalism [or] provincial pride [but rather an] incorrigible scepticism about himself/herself and his/her position in the world' (Kramer 1967: xiv). A similar scepticism might be detected, perhaps, behind Australian writers' attempts to formulate a cultural cartography – to locate themselves within Australia, or Australia within the world, while recognising the precariousness of their own (provisional) coordinates. Exile, expatriation, migration, travel – a rhetoric of restlessness has underpinned Australia's ambivalent search for national selfhood. Torn between the need for definition and the desire to elude it, generations of Australians have sensed that they might better understand their country, or themselves, by leaving it. (And leave it they have, in their droves. Figures for the 1990s show that two to three million Australians – upwards of 10 per cent of the total population – left the country each year, for New Zealand, the Americas and the United Kingdom/Europe, mostly, but also in large numbers for Indonesia and other parts of southeast Asia. Of these annual two or three million, the vast majority were short-term tourists (online source: Australian Bureau of Statistics 2000).)

Australians live, and have lived for some time now, in an era of mass tourism. The emergence and efflorescence of the Australian tourist novel represents an ongoing attempt to account for this phenomenon.[16] Australian tourist novels act as barometers of perception – they chart the changing national self-image, as well as indexing insecurities embedded within the national psyche. As Bruce Bennett remarks in a chapter in *The Penguin New Literary History of Australia* (1988), 'The new technologies of travel and communications, together with relatively higher levels of affluence, [have] led to a reorientation of relations with the wider world, and hence of Australians' conceptions of themselves' (B. Bennett 1988: 434). Tourism, however, sets up a particular kind of reorientation of relations between the nation and the wider world – one in which the manufactured categories of 'national' and 'world' themselves come into question. 'We live', says the anthropologist Roger Rouse,

> in a confusing world, a world of crisscross economies, intersecting systems of meaning, and fragmented identities. Suddenly, the comforting modern imagery of nation-states and national languages, of coherent communities and consistent subjectivities, of dominant centers and distinct margins, no longer seems adequate.
>
> (Rouse 1991: 8)

In the postmodern era of 'transnational dissemination' (Bhabha 1990: 320), the space of the nation is being contested by minority groups who reject its claims to unity or homogeneity; by diasporic communities whose dispersal across the globe transcends the artificial boundaries of the nation-state; by multinational companies whose expansionist imperatives and drive for corporate ownership emphasise the increasing deterritorialisation of production in a global economy.[17] And, not least, by the hordes of tourists who leave their countries then return to them, and whose experiences in between may leave them unsure of their whereabouts – and of their origins. In an age of mass tourism, locating origins becomes more perilous than ever. As Aritha Van Herk argues in an essay on Bail, we inhabit a perplexing world in which, like Bail's Australian travellers, 'who discover in the railway's lost property office another railway station within which is presumably another railway station with a lost property office … we cannot be sure if we are homesick for homesickness or simply homesick for home' (Van Herk 1991: 229).

Differences remain within this world, however – differences that cannot be accounted for by the unifying rhetoric of national and/or regional community, nor yet assimilated within the fashionable catch-all discourse of 'global culture'. The Australian tourist novel provides conflicting evidence of these unassimilable differences. In dispelling the alternative myths of a homogeneous nation and of an undifferentiated global culture, it counters idealist conceptions of a national postcolonial literature – a literature that sets itself against its European forebears – by emphasising Australia's relatively favourable position within the global economy. But it also stresses that the internal fragmentation of Australia's national culture needs to be seen alongside a series of transnational movements, not only by Australia's various emigrant or diasporic communities, but also by the increasing number of Australians who can afford to pay for, and profit from, their own temporary displacement.

The Australian tourist novel operates within a tradition of displacement which emphasises the cultural relativity of the exotic. 'Nation' and 'wider world'; 'local' and 'foreign' cultures – these are terms subject to historical change, ideological leverage, reconstruction. The discourse of exoticism enacts a process of estrangement, a process that upsets the 'stable' relationship between self and other (see Introduction). The Australian tourist novel provides a record of this destabilising process. It reveals the 'political unconscious' (Jameson 1981) beneath exoticist aestheticism, countering the allegedly levelling effect of global-cultural hybridity by stressing that exoticism and tourism are inextricably interlinked. Tourism, like exoticism, betrays a privilege of movement. Yet this movement, real or imaginary, turns out to be at best restricted; and the vision that it brings with it tends to be second-hand, impaired, obscured. Disappointment, as John Frow reminds us, is integral to touristic experience (Frow 1991; see also above); it is represented best in the double-bind of the anti-tourist tourist. The anti-tourist tourist hates tourists, but cannot be other than a tourist. The anti-touristic gaze recognises its own frustrated longings; ironically self-directed, it watches over its own deceptions. And repeats them; as if the anti-tourist tourist, in moving on, realises that s/he has no place to go. The anti-touristic gaze, in mocking others, mocks only itself. Its vision, directed outwards, cancels out its own disclaimers; directed inwards, it cannot countenance an escape from the need to escape.

In *Troppo Man* and *The Edge of Bali*, Lee and Baranay mediate between the self-irony of the anti-touristic gaze, which records the inevitable failure of its attempt to locate 'authentic' cultural experience, and the self-parody of its post-touristic counterpart, which debunks the myth of authenticity only to substitute in its place a counter-myth of cool detachment. In both instances, (as is the case with Rivard's and Hospital's spiritual tourists), the tourist gaze seeks an alternative, only to fall back on itself. Exoticism becomes the medium through which this process is enacted; for exoticism's idealised others are mirror-projections of a troubled self (Bongie 1991: chap. 1). Tourism takes advantage of its clients' latent insecurities by appealing to fantasy worlds beyond the normal range of their experience. Tourists are fed the illusion that these worlds can be acceded to – and controlled. They are fantasists with power, an 'expeditionary force without guns' (MacCannell 1989: xviii). Yet their powers are strictly limited; their imperialistic zeal for exploration and appropriation may be temporarily rewarded but is likely, in time, to be frustrated. Tourists are controlled by others even as they act out their fantasies of independence; they are vulnerable to exploitation even as they flaunt their purchasing power. Not least, they are self-involved even as they seek out the cultural other. And this other remains opaque because its opacity is *needed* – required, perhaps, for tourists' unstated purpose of hiding themselves from themselves.

Margaret Atwood, Inc., or,
    some thoughts on literary
    celebrity

Preface: soundings from the Atwood industry

This chapter is about a rather different form of the exotic – celebrity glamour. But celebrity glamour, as I shall argue, shares several features with other, better-known variants of exoticist discourse, among them the creation of a commodified mystique that veils the material conditions that produce it. While less ostensibly glamorous a figure than literary compatriots like (probably most notably) Michael Ondaatje, Margaret Atwood has achieved a certain aura and a guaranteed celebrity status as far and away Canada's best-known living writer. At first sight, there is not much mystery attached to Atwood's remarkable success as a novelist, poet and literary/cultural critic. Phenomenally hardworking, Atwood has achieved a prodigious output – to date she has produced ten novels, ten books of poetry, and five works of shorter fiction, along with books of literary criticism, books for children, scripts for TV and radio, and numerous essays and reviews. The unusually wide-ranging appeal of her work, moreover, allied to a malleable and skilfully marketed self-image, has helped push Atwood into the front ranks of the world's literary superstars, where she rubs shoulders with other, perhaps more obviously attention-seeking postcolonial celebrities like V.S. Naipaul and Salman Rushdie (on Naipaul and Rushdie as celebrity figures, see also Chapter 3).[1] Atwood's factfile is impressive. Her books, translated into more than twenty languages, have been published in twenty-five countries (Howells 1995). In 1997, translations of her penultimate novel, *Alias Grace* (1996), appeared in Italian and Finnish. The previous novel, *The Robber Bride* (1993), also appeared in Latvian and Korean. Atwood's work has won the Booker Prize (for her most recent novel *The Blind Assassin*), the Canadian Governor General's Award for both poetry and fiction, the National Arts Club Medal of Honor, the Trillium Award (three times), and several other literary prizes. In 1996, *Alias Grace* won the Giller Prize and was a runner-up for the Orange Prize and the Booker. She has been rated, perhaps disappointingly, as only the fifth most influential Canadian in history, duly taking her place behind Charles Saunders, Brian Mulroney [*sic*], William Lyon Mackenzie King, and the Canadian serviceman. She also rated, in a 1997 survey of 659 British MPs, as – along with Umberto Eco and Doris Lessing – the 'world's best living author'. To cap this, she was voted *Ms* magazine's 1997 Woman of the Year. In the *Oxford Dictionary of Literary Quotations* (1997 edn), she is mentioned twenty-six times. She commands a speaking fee of up to fourteen thousand dollars. In 1997, she obtained her thirteenth honorary degree from the University of Ottawa, describing herself after the ceremony as 'like Minnie Mouse, with a lot of happy students and Moms and Dads getting busy with the flash bulbs'.

A World Wide Web search on Atwood reveals over 6,500 items covering some 3,500 pages. The Margaret Atwood Society Home Page alone averages 1,500 'hits' a month (T. Friedman 1998). In 1997, *Alias Grace* was reviewed in scores of newspapers, magazines, and journals, including the *Christian Science Monitor*, the *Alternative Law Journal* and the *Daily Yomiuri*. Scholarly studies on Atwood included such titles as 'Nomenclatural Mutations: Forms of Address in Margaret Atwood's Novels' (Nischik 1997: 329–51), 'Tales of Beauty: Aestheticizing Female Melancholia' (Restuccia 1996: 353–83), and 'Atwood's *Robber Bride*: The Vampire as Intersubjective Catalyst' (Perrakis 1997: 151–68). The US-based Margaret Atwood Society – of which more later – is classified as an Allied Organization of the (American) Modern Language Association, meaning that it has the right to hold two sessions on Margaret Atwood at the annual MLA Humanities Convention. Over the last few years, there has usually been only one session on Canadian literature other than Atwood. Atwood, the poetic analyst of 'double vision',[2] has thus doubled up on all her compatriots.[3]

Atwood as celebrity

Why begin with such an arbitrary scattering of anecdotes, such a random assortment of facts and figures? Clearly, my intention is not to trivialise the achievements of a highly gifted writer, or to make light of the many academics – including myself – who have found profit in her work. Rather, it is to suggest that neither Atwood nor her work can be seen outside of their requisite material context, both as aspects of a thriving literary/critical industry in North America, Europe and elsewhere in the world and as part of the global image-making machinery that has helped turn Atwood into national icon and cultural celebrity. In order to understand the 'Atwood phenomenon', it is first necessary to ask: what is a celebrity? Accordingly, I will turn very briefly to three studies on celebrity culture and media image-making: Stuart Ewen's *All Consuming Images* (1988), an accessible treatment of 'the prominence, significance and consumption of style … as a modern historical phenomenon' (Ewen 1988: 10); Daniel Boorstin's older but still influential book *The Image*, first published in 1961; and, more recently, David Shumway's work on intellectual celebrity culture, the arguments of which are summarised in his *PMLA* article, 'The Star System in Literary Studies' (1997). I will then turn, in a little more detail, to Pierre Bourdieu's more restricted notion of the consecrated writer to suggest that the prestige attached to Atwood has to do with far more than the perceived quality of her work. Let me begin with Ewen.

Following the historian Lewis Erenberg, Ewen traces the emergence of the phenomenon of celebrity to the rise of mass performance culture and, particularly, the movies in the early part of the twentieth century. As Ewen puts it,

> Audience identification with emerging 'stars,' along with a growing apparatus of press agentry, combined to produce a public display of personal life that was intricate and enveloping in its detail, vernacular in its expression. In a society where everyday life was increasingly defined by feelings of insignificance and institutions of standardization, the 'star' provided an accessible icon to the significance of the personal and the individual.
>
> (Ewen 1988: 92–3)

Celebrity came into being, that is, through the merging of private processes of sympathetic identification – the star as 'object of emulation' (Erenberg 1981) – with public processes of repetition that allowed the 'individual life of the celebrity [to achieve] an aura through mass reproduction' (Ewen 1988: 93). The merchandising of the celebrity and of celebrity culture followed later, with the desired effect of media machinery being to manufacture a naturalised image of the celebrity as an embodiment of 'every consumer's dream of what it would be like if money were no object' (Ewen 1988: 99). For Ewen, celebrities' lives 'provide a vernacular depiction of wealth [while also tending] to mask the relation between wealth and power' (Ewen 1988: 100). But equally important to the notion of celebrity is what Daniel Boorstin calls 'the self-deceiving magic of prestige' (Boorstin 1961: 247). For Boorstin, prestige is generated through the multiplication of media images. Prestige, says Boorstin testily, originally meant deceit or illusion. ... The new favorable sense is probably an American invention [but] in common parlance the merest hint of the old unfavorable sense still remains. A person who has prestige has a kind of glamor: he [or she] momentarily blinds or dazzles us by his [or her] image.

(Boorstin 1961: 247)

There is a huge gap, one would have thought, between the wealth and prestige of the adulated film-star and the much more limited celebrity status that accrues to even the most admired and canonised literary figures. But as David Shumway argues, focusing not so much on creative writers as on university-based critics and theorists, the star system within the academy is a function of a larger consumer culture in which 'celebrities are presented as produced images that are endlessly discussed and manipulated in public' (Shumway 1997: 88). Unsurprisingly, Shumway sees the academic star system as privileging style over substance, and as surrendering to a mediatised view of personal intellectual performance that 'inhibits the production of collectively held knowledge and has weakened public confidence in the profession' (Shumway 1997: 86).[4]

But what of the *literary* star system? How are literary celebrities made? Here, as throughout this book, the work of the sociologist Pierre Bourdieu proves useful. A fairly brief rehearsal of Bourdieu's ideas, already discussed elsewhere (see, especially, Introduction) should suffice. For Bourdieu, the literary text exists within a wider field of cultural production. The evaluation of a text, as of its author, will therefore depend on several factors: on the specific material circumstances under which the text is produced, disseminated and consumed, but also on the symbolic assessments provided by the text's various 'agents of legitimation' – publishers, critics and reviewers, individual readers and reading publics, and so on. The value of a text or its writer is thus negotiated by symbolic, as well as material, means. The text or writer accumulates symbolic capital – recognition, prestige and, occasionally, celebrity – through a cumulative process of legitimation that may eventually culminate in what Bourdieu calls 'consecration'. The 'consecrated' text, like the 'canonised' writer, presents a simulacrum of scriptural authority. But both are obvious products of *secular* institutional processes – processes that effectively mask the historical contingencies and shifting power relations underlying cultural production, either by appealing to transhistorical continuities that might have the potential to shore up consecrated/canonical status (e.g. the myth of universal or transcendent value) or by using the logic of scriptural closure to present the consecrated text or canonical writer as a quasi-permanent presence, a *fait accompli*.[5] While consecration, in Bourdieu's sense of the term, describes the end-effect of an accumulation of symbolic, rather than material, capital, it also mystifies the material conditions under which symbolic forms of recognition and legitimation are sought, acquired and negotiated. 'Euphemises' might be a better term than 'mystifies'; for as Bourdieu says, in describing the various symbolic investments through which the multiple producers of the literary/ artistic work are brought into what he calls 'the cycle of consecration',

> [e]ntering the field of literature is not so much like going into religion as getting into a select club: the publisher is one of those prestigious sponsors (together with preface-writers and critics) who effusively recommend their candidate. Even clearer is the role of the art dealer, who literally has to 'introduce' the artist and his work into ever more select company (group exhibitions, one-man shows, prestigious collections, museums) and ever more sought-after places. But the law of this universe, whereby the less visible the investment, the more productive it is symbolically, means that promotion exercises, which in the business world take the overt form of publicity, must here be euphemized. The art trader cannot serve his 'discovery' unless he applies all his conviction, which rules out 'sordidly commercial' manoeuvres, manipulation and the 'hard sell,' in favour of the softer, more discreet forms of 'public relations' (which are themselves a highly euphemized form of publicity) – receptions, society gatherings, and judiciously placed confidences.
>
> (Bourdieu 1993: 77)

Bourdieu's somewhat Olympian view of the machinations of the bourgeois literary/art world seems in need of modification, not merely in terms of its overdetermined class hierarchies and distinctions,[6] but also in view of the increasing difficulty of distinguishing between a 'euphemistic' realm of artistic promotion and public relations and the unashamedly profit-driven world of modern corporate commerce.[7] Bourdieu's work is valuable, still, in showing how specific processes of literary/artistic evaluation belong to a general symbolic economy in which consecrated writers, among other credentialled 'agents of legitimation', are able both to receive and transmit legitimacy, recognition and prestige (see also Introduction). As Bourdieu suggests, consecration is the culmination of a sometimes lengthy legitimising process that effectively entitles the consecrated writer to confer a similarly privileged status on others: 'The consecrated writer is the one who has the power to consecrate and to win assent when he or she consecrates an author or work – with a preface, a favorable review, a prize' (Bourdieu 1993: 42; see also Introduction and the discussion of inter-writer endorsement in the last chapter). But if consecration is a culminating moment, that moment is likely to be repeated; for as Bourdieu suggests, consecration is a cumulative, but also a *self-perpetuating* process by which recognised writers and/or literary works are able to acquire, maintain and reproduce the prestige that accrues to their consecrated status.

The seemingly guaranteed position of Atwood atop the leader-board of Canadian writers clearly owes to a process of consecration in which Atwood herself continues to play an active role. (Atwood's name-recognition alone may be enough to send prospective readers scurrying in search of her latest novel, or to stimulate discussions of her work in literary circles, possibly irrespective of whether or not it has been read.) But in Atwood's case, we are talking not just about a consecrated writer but about a *cultural celebrity*. What is it that makes Atwood a celebrity? Several, to some extent interrelated, factors can be cited here. First, Atwood is a tireless and by all accounts extremely powerful performer; coveting media attention in numerous well-timed interviews, talk-shows and public readings, she is flexible enough to be called upon as an authority on many different subjects. Second, she has benefited from the multiplication of her own media image: as a writer and critic, of course, but also as a Canadian commentator, a nationalist, an environmentalist, a feminist. Needless to say, it matters little whether these images are accurate; what matters is how effectively they circulate – how viable they are as a currency of symbolic authority. Third, she has helped enhance her status as a national cultural icon by speaking out on national issues, editing national anthologies, and even – in one celebrated instance – using literary criticism to diagnose national ills.[8] Fourth, Atwood's national image as a no-holds-barred cultural commentator has been augmented by her international image as a translator and interpreter of Canadian culture. These images, when taken together, have fuelled the common (mis)perception of Atwood as a 'representative', or even 'quintessential', Canadian and Canadian writer.[9] Fifth, this representative status has been enhanced by the wrong-headed view – sometimes inside as well as outside Canada – that Atwood is one of the few Canadian writers who really matter; and that Canada's, after all, is only a 'minor' litera-ture/culture in terms of world standards (a judgement less obviously indicative of Canadian provincialism than of the ignorance of those who make the claim). Atwood herself has contributed, as usual, to this controversy, asserting for example in an essay adapted from her acceptance speech for the National Arts Club Medal that Canada is 'a country in which you [are] relegated to a minor literary subcategory just by being a citizen of it' (qtd in *The Margaret Atwood Society Newsletter* 20, Spring/Summer 1998). Sixth, Atwood has been touted, despite her own occasional qualifiers and disclaimers, as a global spokesperson-activist for feminist issues, while her work has been seen as a barometer of changing emphases in Euro-American feminist debates.[10] The timing of Atwood's work, particularly her early work, is important here, coinciding with the so-called 'second wave' of North American liberationist feminism in the 1960s and 1970s, and then again with the 'post-feminist' debates of the 1980s and on into the 1990s (Howells 1995: chap. 3). Seventh, Atwood has profited from her reputation for quotability – from the soundbite quality of many of her public utterances, as well as from the epigrammatic witticisms that are scattered throughout her writing. And eighth, Atwood, both in her public performances and in her writing, has successfully bridged the gap between academic and popular perceptions of her personality, as well as her work; she is thus seen, with the help of the media, as an intellectually astute but also highly approachable public figure, able to satisfy her wide international audience as well as her restricted academic readership, and not averse to pleasing the crowds by putting academics in their place. (If I can be allowed another illustrative anecdote, this time from *M2 Presswire*, 13 October 1997: Atwood on deconstruction – 'Nobody was able to explain to me clearly [what deconstruction was]. The best answer I got was from a writer who said, "Honey, it's bad news for you and me" ' (qtd in *The Margaret Atwood Newsletter* 20, Spring/Summer 1998).) Soundbites like this can only endear Atwood, not only to other writers, but also to a general, mostly middle-class readership quite likely to be suspicious of academics' self-serving theoretical games and hyperintellectualised 'dirty tricks'. Needless to say, this type of comment is also lapped up by the mainstream press – for whom it is largely intended – where it can be used as mildly anti-intellectual gossip for Canada's (and other countries') literary-minded chattering classes.

All in all, then, Atwood's celebrity status owes to the careful management of multiple images that ensures that she and her work will generate maximum public appeal, both in Canada and elsewhere in the world. Atwood herself participates of course – and very skilfully – in this global mediatising process. Most writers like publicity, even if some profess to feeling uncomfortable under the spotlights; it would be churlish in the extreme to suggest that a celebrity writer like Atwood is simply 'selling out'.[11] Rather, she is highly aware of herself, and of her writing, as a commodity; and she is conscious, too, of the role she plays in the image-making industry that surrounds her work. Atwood has taken the responsibilities that come with her status as a public figure very seriously;

and although she might not see herself, in Edward Said's restricted sense of the term, as an 'intellectual', she has certainly done her part to generate the controversy and disturbance of the *status quo* that, for Said, are integral to the intellectual's vocation. Indeed, some of Said's definitions of the oppositional intellectual in his Reith Lectures of 1993 seem almost tailor-made for Atwood. Here are two examples:

> One task of the intellectual is the effort to break down the stereotypes and reductive categories that are so limiting to human thought and communication.
>
> (Said 1994: xi)

> To be an intellectual involves a sense of the dramatic and the insurgent, making a great deal of … one's opportunities to speak, catching the audience's attention, being better at wit and debate than one's opponents. And there is something fundamentally unsettling about intellectuals who have neither offices to protect nor territory to consolidate and guard; self-irony is therefore more frequent than pomposity, directness more than hemming and hawing.
>
> (Said 1994: xviii)

Atwood, in many respects, matches these descriptions perfectly, without satisfying Said's – no doubt romanticised – conditions that the price the intellectual often has to pay for generating controversy is to become an isolated, self-marginalising, and possibly unpopular figure.[12] Nothing could be less true of Atwood than this. To come back to the eighth and final point of my checklist of criteria for Atwood's celebrity status: Atwood's success is largely due to her ability to capture and mobilise popular feeling. In this context she can be seen, uncharitably no doubt, as something of an establishment subversive, putting forward controversial views that are all the more popular because they are, or are perceived to be, 'irreverent', 'unorthodox', or 'unofficial'. In this sense, I would suggest – uncharitably again – that there is something of a staged controversiality surrounding Atwood and her work. Her putatively anti-establishment views have always tended to move with the fashions of the moment. Her work operates as a gauge of white middle-class – predominantly female – fears and anxieties; the 'oppositional' views that she likes to articulate arguably represent an orthodoxy for that particular social group. And the trademark self-irony that Said associates with the lonely figure of the intellectual has, in Atwood's work, offered a measure of self-protection, a shared way of looking at the self and its relation to society and the wider world. Similarly, the embattled heroines in Atwood's poems and, especially, her novels elicit sympathy not so much because they are outsiders as because they register readily identifiable forms of middle-class alienation. The dangerous territory that Atwood's work has allegedly explored, the ideological minefields she has uncovered, have mostly been negotiated from the safety of the middle-class family, the middle-class educational system, the middle-class home.[13] This is not to make of Atwood an apologist for patriarchal/bourgeois values; it is merely to reiterate that Atwood's fantasies of marginalisation and female disem-powerment (witness the response of the British MPs!) are possibly enjoyed most by those in situations of relative comfort – and positions of power.

Atwood and the canon

Atwood's position within mainstream culture, and the wide international appeal of her work to middle-class readers, have been consolidated by the canonical status accorded to many of her works, and to her work in general. Here again, it seems worth backtracking a little to consider the question: what is a canon? Canons, according to Barbara Herrnstein Smith, are 'mechanism[s] for the reproduction of cultural value' (Herrnstein Smith 1984: 27): they function, that is, as means not only of ensuring cultural continuity but also of propping up the institutional systems through which 'traditional' cultural values are inculcated and upheld (see also Chapter 4). It is interesting in this context to consider the so-called 'culture wars' in North America – particularly the United States – and to track current debates on the possibility of 'abolishing', or at least radically restructuring, the canon in American schools. The best available study on this subject is John Guillory's *Cultural Capital* (1993), a detailed examination of the reliance of contemporary canon debates at US schools and universities on reductionist models of identity politics in the service of liberal-pluralist critique. As Guillory argues, correctly in my view, current discussions of the canon often elide the very power struggles they imagine themselves to be illuminating; in their insistence on representational rights, liberal-left apologists for canon reformation risk ceding ground to their conservative adversaries by simplistically associating the 'traditional' values allegedly upheld by canonical works with the interests of the cultural élite. By 'yield[ing] canonical works to the right', says Guillory, advocates of diversification 'accept the right's characterization of the canonical syllabus as constitutive of a unified and monolithic Western culture' (Guillory 1993: 47). This results in the following impasse:

Basing its agenda upon such assumptions, a left politics of representation seems to have no other choice than to institutionalize alternative syllabi as representative images of non-Western or 'counter'-cultures. This is finally why the project of legitimizing noncanonical works in the university produces an irresolvable contradiction between the presentation of these works as equal in cultural value to canonical works, and at the same time as the embodiment of countercultural values which by their very definition are intended to delegitimize the cultural values embodied in canonical works. The polarization of the debate into Western culturalism versus multiculturalism must then be seen not as a simple conflict between regressive and progressive pedagogies but as the symptom of the transformation of cultural capital in response to social conditions not yet recognized as the real and ultimately determining context of the canon debate.

(Guillory 1993: 47)

These conditions, according to Guillory, are specifically related to the 'heterogeneous constituency of the university' (Guillory 1993: 47) and, more generally, to the uneven distribution of cultural capital in the US educational system at large. The frame of reference – not always fully acknowledged – for Guillory's analysis (as with several other contemporary diagnoses of liberal-pluralist pedagogy – see, for example, Giroux 1992), clearly emerges as the United States. Needless to say, the social conditions that provide the determining context of the current US canon-reform discussions are not the same in other countries, such as Canada, that are currently pursuing their own no less energetic canon debates.[14] (Likewise, several key terms in the debates, such as, most notably, 'multiculturalism', have entirely different histories in the United States and Canada – see Chapter 5.) The overriding context for the ongoing canon debates in Canada arguably pertains, not so much to contemporary minority issues – important though these are – as to a legacy of cultural colonialism: one in which the United States itself has played, and continues to play, a significant role. Yet as several commentators have pointed out, it would be simplistic to see the Canadian canon as a 'reflection' of oppositional cultural nationalism; rather, it has tended to register historical faultlines in the nation's changing political culture – and still does so today. This point is forcefully made in Leon Surette's opening historical essay in Robert Lecker's *Canadian Canons* (1991), a useful collection replete with suggestions on how to 'deconstruct' the Canadian canon, and how to challenge the specifically Canadian presuppositions of order and continuity on which canon formation has been based. Using theories derived from the history of political philosophy, Surette demonstrates convincingly how tensions have been negotiated in (Anglo-)Canadian political culture between 'two contrary paradigms of our cultural destiny – continuity and breach' (Surette 1991: 18). For Surette, Anglo-Canadian cultural theorising has historically tended to waver between two positions, both of them conservative. The first of these positions involves 'look[ing] to distant Britain as a balance against the cultural pressures of the nearby American juggernaut' (Surette 1991: 20); the second involves 'look[ing] to Ottawa and its cultural institutions – the CBC, the CRTC, the Canada Council, and Canada Pension' (Surette 1991: 21). Both of these positions, according to Surette, are partly motivated by the perception of the United States 'as a threat to [Canadians'] cultural and political integrity, and therefore both support Confederation and the degree of centralization that it entails' (21). But the second of these positions is complicated by the recognition that Canadians 'cannot easily claim some mystical continuity with either [their] "spiritual heritage" or [their] history', since neither of these can ultimately 'protect [them] from … British or American domination' (22). For Surette, the formation of the Anglo-Canadian canon – particularly in fiction – has tended to register such cultural stresses, even if the process of canon formation itself 'has not been generated by [a direct] application of [the foregoing] criteria' (24–5).

Surette then turns to a series of canonical works, including Atwood's poetry cycle *The Journals of Susanna Moodie* (1970), to provide examples of how these stresses are internalised through symbolic figures. In the *Journals*, argues Surette, 'Atwood's vision of Moodie as a vulnerable corpse half-buried in a hostile land is [a] version of the [Anglophile] motif of isolation from a parent culture' (Surette 1991: 25). The *Journals* reflect ironically on the irresolvable tension between the desire for continuity and the mournful recognition that Canadians have 'either [been] abandoned by [their] spiritual heritage or have [had their] memories bulldozed' by their domineering American neighbours (25). Surette posits a view of Atwood's work as darkly elegiac, both mourning a Canadian spiritual past to which it has no imaginative access and contemplating the impossibility of an autochthonous Canadian future. This view seems to me reductive, but it is useful insofar as it suggests that one of the main reasons for the canonical status of Atwood's work is its perceived capacity to explore figuratively – often meaning to allegorise – the constitutive ruptures within Anglo-Canadian culture.[15] (Atwood's work is of course frequently disabused of its own allegorical tendencies; as has been pointed out often enough, her work simultaneously invites and frustrates allegorical interpretation, poking gentle fun at readers who might be tempted to read it in combatively nationalistic terms. Classic examples here would have to include the loutish 'Americans' in *Surfacing* (1972), who turn out to be Canadian, and the schooling of Elaine Risley in *Cat's Eye* (1988), which parodies the enduring British-colonial biases of the Canadian educational system.)

Surette's reading of the *Journals* arguably falls victim to this type of allegorical fallacy in its efforts to find representative examples for what we might call, very loosely, the Canadian cultural imaginary. Such attempts to make canonical works constitutive, however ironically, of national cultural identities is always likely to lead to oversimplified interpretations that mythologise the history on which they presume to draw and comment.[16] Notwithstanding, the *ideological* work performed by the idea of a Canadian canon remains important, not merely because it provides what Donna Bennett calls a mythologised 'narrative of aesthetic values that expresses how a culture locates its writing within its larger history' but, more specifically, because the:

> expansion of the CBC, the creation of the Canada Council and the provincial arts councils, and the commercialization of things 'Canadian' as socially valuable have ... given new and more general immediacy to the questions of what the important works in our literature are and by what standards we make judgments.
>
> (D. Bennett 1991: 149, 147)

The canon is important, that is, because it is bound up in a government-sponsored mission to chart the changing configurations of a national culture through its literary production and to promote that vision of a culture, and of its historical transformation, both within the country and abroad. Many Canadian writers (and obviously not just canonised ones) have every reason to be grateful to agencies like the Canada Council, whose support of Canadians' work has been and remains extremely generous, comparing favourably with the support given to writers in most other Western countries. But such sponsorship also runs the risk of placing an onus on the 'Canadian-ness' of the writing, of co-opting it into a national narrative that it might well wish to resist. This process of co-optation is, in large part, a pedagogic project; as Surette puts it, 'Canadian literary criticism has always been an enterprise in which the central purpose was the discovery of the Canadian-ness of the literature written in this country' (Surette 1991: 17). But why should literature conform, or be made to conform, to such national – or, perhaps more accurately, such cultural nationalist – paradigms? Is it the function of criticism to 'discover' national characteristics in a nation's writing, or are such characteristics better seen as the products of that criticism, as its own enabling myths?

The search for a Canadian canon, as John Metcalf argues in his pugnaciously contrary study *What is a Canadian Literature?* (1988), places a political burden on the nation's writers that several of them – not least Metcalf himself – are not prepared to shoulder. Metcalf states his case bluntly: '[S]uccessive Canadian governments have subsidized the arts in the hope that they will shape and define a national identity … [T]his pervasive identification of art with nationalism is pernicious and stands in the way of critical and artistic maturity' (Metcalf 1988: 7). Metcalf sees continuing attempts on the part of academic critics, as well as govern-ment agencies, to define, locate and (re)invent a central Canadian tradition as a misguided ideological enterprise more likely to do damage to Canada's literary reputation than to enhance it. T.D. MacLulich is treated particularly roughly, offering what Metcalf calls 'a classic exhibition of … [Canadian] nationalist fears and paranoia' (Metcalf 1988: 94). Declaring himself to be mystified by the canonical process of inclusion and exclusion by which MacLulich contrives to find a central Canadian tradition in the bourgeois realist fiction of Grove, Callaghan, MacLen-nan, Buckler, Ross, Mitchell, Wilson, Laurence, Richler, Davies and Munro (significantly, there is no place for Atwood on MacLulich's list), Metcalf delivers a stinging response:

> How *could* anyone yoke together such a disparate crew? Sinclair Ross and Margaret Laurence share a kind of transitional status in terms of their writing, but Alice Munro and Richler write in the international style which MacLulich professes to depise. … What connects Richler and Grove other than that Richler called Grove 'a good speller'? If Richler belongs to any tradition at all it is to a tradition of North American Jewish writing, writing which is firmly set in the decay of North American Yiddish culture. Richler doubtless feels closer to the work of Joseph Heller and Philip Roth than he does to the work of W. O. Mitchell or Hugh MacLennan. He would also doubtless feel amazed to hear his work described as in 'the conventions of the bourgeois novel.'
>
> (Metcalf 1988: 39)

Metcalf accuses MacLulich, among several others,[17] of using a political argument in favour of Canadian unity to create imaginary affiliations between a series of only vaguely compatible writers. As Metcalf asserts, in apparent agreement with Guillory's analysis of the ideological function of canon formation, the creation of a central tradition has less to do with formal processes of representative selection than with the distribution of cultural capital in service of the academic institution – and the state:

> The State desires a literature because it seems to believe that a litera-
> ture is one of the marks of a mature and civilized country and because
> it seems to believe that the possession of a literature will somehow
> unify us as a people and define our national identity.
>
> (Metcalf 1988: 96–7)

For Metcalf, the state's attempt to sanction a national literature smacks of
interference, an argument that inevitably makes him vulnerable to the
counter-accusation that he is biting the hand off which he feeds. Nor is
there much to admire in the *ad hominem* nature of Metcalf's arguments,
which rely on precisely the principles of random selection and ideological
bias he is so keen to discover – and impugn – in other people's work.
Metcalf may be right, however, that there is something parochial about
the continuing need to isolate and celebrate what is 'Canadian' about
Canadian literature. National canons are arguably invested in a view of
narrative literary history that is becoming increasingly outmoded,
suspected more and more of imposing 'false coherence on the incoherent'
(Perkins 1991: 6). As Metcalf points out, the continuing debate on canon
formation in Canada is – for better or worse – inextricably connected
with another ongoing debate, on cultural nationalism; neither debate has
a likely outcome any time in the near future. What is clear when looking
at Atwood's work is, first, that it is integral to *both* debates; and second,
that both debates are included *within* the work, as well as in the evaluative
discourses that surround it. Atwood's work engages actively with questions
of literary and cultural value; it has persistently asked the question, not
just of who or what is a 'Canadian', a 'Canadian literature', a 'Canadian
culture', but also of how we might make such evaluative judgements – and
who 'we' are. In Surette's terms, we might say that Atwood has successfully internalised the conflicts in the self-conducted narrative of Canada's
literary/cultural evaluation. And I believe it is for these reasons, rather
than for that universalist chimera, 'intrinsic quality', that Atwood's place
in the Canadian canon has been, and is likely to remain, secure.

But as I suggested before, to see Atwood merely as a 'Canadian' or
'Canadian writer' is misleading. The multiplicity of images, definitions
and categories that has surrounded Atwood's writing has also led to the
canonisation of her work on several different fronts. A classic example
here is the canonisation of Atwood's novel *The Handmaid's Tale* (1985) as
a seminal work of feminist science fiction to rank alongside the novels of
Doris Lessing and Ursula Le Guin. *The Handmaid's Tale*, in my opinion
one of Atwood's weaker novels, has thus probably become her single most
talked-about and academically analysed book. In a fairly comprehensive
list of recent scholarly studies on Atwood's writing published in the

Margaret Atwood Society Newsletter (no. 20, Spring/Summer 1998), there are ten entries for that year alone on *The Handmaid's Tale*, more than twice the number given to any of Atwood's other works. The collection *Approaches to Teaching Atwood's* The Handmaid's Tale *and Other Works* (1996) also suggests that it is *The Handmaid's Tale*, more than any other Atwood novel, that has the most potential to be inserted into the curriculum and eventually enshrined as a school/university set text.[18] *The Handmaid's Tale* can thus be incorporated into several different canons, as a classic work of feminist polemic, of dystopian literature, of science fiction. As has been mentioned by several of Atwood's critics, her work often plays with generic categories, notably gothic romance (*Surfacing, Lady Oracle*), domestic melodrama (*The Edible Woman*), autobiography (*Cat's Eye*), documentary history (*The Handmaid's Tale*) and the detective novel (*Alias Grace*). One effect that this generic scrambling has had on an institutional level is to multiply the possibilities of Atwood's work, especially her novels, featuring in school curricula, university courses and examination lists. Atwood's work is hardly unique, of course, in its self-conscious play with literary modes and categories; such play is a staple of both modernist and postmodernist novelistic traditions, and is arguably integral to the novel itself as a quintessentially polymorphous genre (see, for example, the work of Bakhtin). What is unique, or at least unusual, is that Atwood's reputation as at once ironic expert and artful populariser has helped produce her canonical status, both as a versatile revisionist specialist and as a wittily amateurish bricoleur. Thus it is that, even as she questions the hierarchical process of canon formation, Atwood has managed to capitalise on the multifacetedness of her own appeal, as well as that of the novel, and has succeeded in securing a place on several different canons at the same time.

The Margaret Atwood Society

It is doubtless appropriate that a celebrity writer and cultural icon like Margaret Atwood should have a literary society dedicated to her, and a fanzine all her own. But the Margaret Atwood Society, in fact, only has a relatively recent history. Founded in 1983 by the American scholar Jan Garden Castro, the Margaret Atwood Society has a current membership of around two hundred, a good two thirds of whom are based in the US (1998 figures; see *Newsletter* 21, Fall/Winter 1998). As described in its second Newsletter (1985), the Society is

> an international association of scholars, teachers, students, and others who share an interest in the work of Margaret Atwood. The Society's

main goal is to promote scholarly study of Atwood's work by providing opportunities for members to exchange information and ideas.

(*Newsletter* 2, 1985: 1)

The Newsletter itself, first published in 1984 and now well past twenty
issues, is a primary – and distinctly useful – source of information for
Atwood Society members. Providing regularly updated checklists on
international (mostly North American) sources for Atwood scholarship,
the Newsletter also offers short items on Atwood's latest publications, her
recent worldwide activities and her upcoming readings and promotional
events. Since 1986, a staple of the Newsletter has been a section on what
might best be called 'Atwood-watching', in which sightings are given and
tips offered – '[i]t might be hard to catch a glimpse of Margaret Atwood
next year' (*Newsletter* 3, 1986). Since 1997, this section has been
expanded to include the categories of journalistic 'news' and multimedia
'ephemera' – essentially a gossip column in which fans can learn that
Atwood shares a birthday with Sir Tasker Watkins, the President of the
Welsh Rugby Union (*Newsletter* 20, Spring/Summer 1998: 13), or that
she contributed a 'light-hearted drawing' to the Uxbridge Celebrity
Doodle Silent Action on 19 April (*Newsletter* 20, Spring/Summer 1998:
18). The current format of the Newsletter thus reconfirms the convergence or, perhaps better, the tension between research-oriented
('academic') and publicity-driven ('popular') perceptions of Atwood and
her work, situating Atwood studies firmly within the context of an
international celebrity culture. (Possibly, this tension is indicative of
wider concerns within the academy as a whole. For example, the
Spring/Summer 1997 issue of the Newsletter, in announcing Atwood's
nomination as Honorary Fellow of the Modern Language Association,
praises her lavishly for her civic, as well as literary, achievements in a
manner that betrays characteristic anxieties about overspecialisation and
the gap between academic research and the public domain: 'Margaret
Atwood is a great artist and a public voice, a model for intellectual
engagement sorely needed in our times of ever-increasing specialization
and social fragmentation' (*Newsletter* 18, Spring/Summer 1997: 4).)

The Newsletter, like the Society itself, thus combines a celebratory
mandate with a desire to bridge the gap between single-author scholarship
and contemporary public debate. The minutiae of the former – 'Sally
Jacobsen thanks Judith McCombs for pointing out that there are ten
boxes, not six, of *Robber Bride* material in the Thomas Fisher library'
(*Newsletter* 14, Spring/Summer 1995) – are balanced by the large-scale
controversies of the latter: the international campaign, for example, to
support the legal appeal of a ninth-grade teacher in Alabama who had lost

her job for assigning an Atwood poem with 'sexually-explicit content' (see *Newsletter* 18, Spring/Summer 1997: 1–2). As is understandable for a literary society with a predominantly American membership, several of these controversies are tied in with the US 'culture wars' over representational rights and freedom of speech. Perhaps more surprising is the view expressed by Kathryn VanSpanckeren as outgoing President in 1992 that the Margaret Atwood Society has a 'role in expanding the old, narrow definition of American literature as something that stops at US borders' (*Newsletter* 9, 1992: 2). 'Focusing on Atwood', says VanSpanckeren, 'has helped make American literature a continental … concern', involving Atwood scholars from both sides of the border in a productive 'hemispheric conversation' (*Newsletter* 9, 1992: 2–3). The assimilative impulse behind such comments, although challenged elsewhere by members of the Society (see, for example, *Newsletter* 15, Fall/Winter 1995), provides a reminder that Atwood's work continues to be received very differently in Canada and the United States. As Sally Jacobsen – herself based in the US – remarks in the Fall/Winter 1995 Newsletter,

> Much scholarship, especially in the United States, reads Atwood almost as a token American, or as assimilated and 'nationless' at best. It thereby ignores those boundaries necessarily established by Atwood's speaking as a woman, an artist, and a Canadian. The point is not necessarily and always to read Atwood as a Canadian; rather, it is to consider precisely what it means not to read Atwood as a Canadian and in what instances her nationality is ignored or merely glossed. What is at work and what is at stake for critics when they read Atwood's generic crossings and how does that bear upon her national crossings into American scholarship?
>
> (*Newsletter* 15, Fall/Winter 1995: 3)

These are important questions; nonetheless, as Jacobsen recognises, '[t]he issue of how to read and teach Atwood in America has long been neglected' (*Newsletter* 15, Fall/Winter 1995: 4). While it would be churlish to accuse US Atwood scholars of treating Atwood as little more than a 'token American', reception patterns suggest that several of her works – notably, *The Handmaid's Tale* – have been assimilated in the United States to North American feminist concerns (Howells 1995: chap. 3). The value-systems through which Atwood's work is read, and which have contributed to her celebrity status, thus indicate a continuing discrepancy between frequently mythologised 'Canadian' and 'US' cultural preoccupations, not least those affecting the criteria for celebrity itself. As previously mentioned, some of Atwood's work reflects ironically on such criteria, drawing attention to the cultural frames of reference in which value judgements about literary/artistic success are made (see section 'Atwood and the canon').[19] Thus, while the Newsletter's primary function has been (and remains) to disseminate information about the current state of Atwood scholarship, its *cultural* contribution to the image-making machinery surrounding the Atwood industry affords as yet untaken opportunities for critical self-reflection. Not that the Society is without a self-referential dimension, as indicated for example in its 1994 decision to issue annual honorific awards for Society members in three ostensibly academic categories: best published essay on Atwood by a graduate student; best essay by an independent/senior scholar; best essay by a junior scholar. (While the Atwood awards remain, the categories have altered slightly, with separate book and essay awards now being offered and a second, undergraduate category having been added for students.) While laudably designed to provide incentives for – particularly younger – Atwood scholars, the awards are an interesting case of the trickle-down effect of celebrity culture, one of whose most visible epiphenomena is the literary prize (see Chapter 4). The Society thus plays an active if minor role, not merely in celebrating Atwood, but in perpetuating the public codes of recognition through which her work and the academic industry that nurtures it accumulate a naturalised prestige.

As the Newsletters' checklists demonstrate, Atwood scholarship is in a boom phase. The number of books and articles listed since 1988, the first year of the annotated bibliography, has rarely fallen beneath fifty, rivalling Atwood's own remarkable output – under 'Atwood's Works', sixty-eight entries are recorded for 1998 alone. In addition, the Society-run Margaret Atwood web site, currently hosted by the University College of the Cariboo in Kamloops, British Columbia, is a thriving information-centre, providing a valuable, up-to-the-minute list of electronic research resources and directing users to other sites where material on Atwood can be found. (The section 'Of Related Interest' provides a further indication of the multiplicity of topical debates into which Atwood's work can be inserted. One of the latest lists, in alphabetical order, reads as follows: Cyberculture, cyberpunk, future, genetic engineering/biotechnology/evolution, identity/persona, postmodern, science fiction, slipstream, utopia, women.) Here, as in the Newsletters, academic information slides imperceptibly into literary gossip, with ephemera ranging far and wide from the latest Atwood soundbites to a description of how the cover-page illustration for *Alias Grace* was found, to – believe it or not – a survey of Canadian attitudes to feet. (Atwood, it appears, has only a 9 per cent vote among Canadian women's preferences for a shoe model, being outscored by Olympic rower Silken Laumann (10 per cent), TV personality Pam Wallin (14 per cent), and singer-songwriter

Alanis Morissette (14 per cent).) The Atwood industry thus combines entertainment and instruction – with a moral. Let me end with the moral. In the Electronic Age, the boundaries are becoming increasingly blurred, not only between the medium and the message – McLuhan, another Canadian – but between the different mediatised ingredients that make up and work toward defining academic research. The standard monograph, as in Coral Ann Howells' informative *Margaret Atwood* (St Martin's Press, 1995), is by no means outdated. And the sheer volume of critical work on Atwood emphasises that conventional single-author study, even with the much-vaunted turn to cultural studies, is far from dead. But we may not have to wait too long for the first virtual book on (or book by?) Atwood, suggesting that media technology might succeed in the end in doing what it does best: turning national icons into global celebrities, into virtual stars.

Conclusion
Thinking at the margins: postcolonial studies at the millennium

The rise of postcolonial studies

In spite – or possibly because – of the debate that continues to rage about the viability of its methods, the position of postcolonial literary/cultural studies has never been so secure as it is today. The institutionalisation of postcolonial studies as a bona fide academic field of research has been consolidated by the glut of distinctly similar introductory primers, anthologies and readers to have appeared in the last half-dozen years. In 1994, two substantial collections with almost identical titles were published on opposite sides of the Atlantic: Francis Barker, Peter Hulme and Margaret Iversen's *Colonial Discourse/Postcolonial Theory* (Manchester University Press) and Patrick Williams and Laura Chrisman's *Colonial Discourse and Post-Colonial Theory: A Reader* (Columbia University Press); while a major reference work also appeared, the Routledge *Encyclopedia of Post-Colonial Literatures in English*, edited by Eugene Benson and L.W. Conolly. A further reader was also published in 1995, Bill Ashcroft, Gareth Griffiths and Helen Tiffin's *The Post-Colonial Studies Reader* (Routledge), along with the first of the new-look primers, Elleke Boehmer's *Colonial & Postcolonial Literature* (Oxford University Press, 1995). (Ashcroft, Griffiths and Tiffin's pioneering, still influential primer, *The Empire Writes Back*, mischievously referred to as the 'Little Green Book' (Schulze-Engler 1998: 31, had previously been published by Routledge in 1989.) In 1996, Padmini Mongia's *Contemporary Postcolonial Theory: A Reader* (Arnold) signalled the expansion of the postcolonial theory market, as did three other theory primers/readers to appear in the following year: Peter Childs and Patrick Williams' *An Introduction to Post-Colonial Theory* (Prentice Hall/Harvester Wheatsheaf), Bart Moore-Gilbert's *Postcolonial Theory: Contexts, Practices, Politics* (Verso) and Bart Moore-Gilbert *et al.*'s *Postcolonial Criticism* (Longman). Then, 1998 yielded three more, Leela Gandhi's *Postcolonial Theory: A Critical Introduction* (Allen and Unwin), Ania Loomba's *Colonialism/Postcolonialism* (Routledge) and Dennis Walder's *Post-colonial Literatures in English: History, Language, Theory* (Blackwell), along with yet another Routledge reference work, Ashcroft, Griffiths and Tiffin's annotated *Keywords in Post-Colonial Studies*. Meanwhile, the fear was allayed that creative writers might be 'in danger of becoming the new subalterns of postcolonial studies' (Thieme 1996: 6) with the publication in 1995 and 1996 respectively of two up-to-date literary anthologies, *Concert of Voices: An Anthology of World Writing in English*, published by Broadview Press and edited by Victor Ramraj; and *Post-Colonial Literatures in English*, published by Arnold and edited by John Thieme. More recently, two 'state-of-the-art' journals have appeared that mark the increasing cross-over between postcolonial theory and transnational cultural studies: *Interventions* (Oxford University Press, ed. Robert Young), and *Postcolonial Studies* (Carfax Publishing, eds Dipesh Chakrabarty, Michael Dutton, Leela Gandhi and Sanjay Seth); while still more recent publications include Sangeeta Ray and Henry Schwarz's 500-page *Companion to Postcolonial Studies* (Blackwell, 1999), Neil Lazarus's *Nationalism and Cultural Practice in the Postcolonial World* (Cambridge University Press, 1999) and Ato Quayson's *Postcolonialism: Theory, Practice or Process?* (Polity Press, 2000).

This flurry of activity – and my list is selective – suggests that the emergent postcolonial critical and theoretical industry might be seen not altogether unreasonably as having taken over where the booming trade in 'explanatory' accounts of postmodernism, peaking in the late 1980s, had left off.[1] Little wonder that conservatively oriented critics, such as Russell Jacoby, have reacted with mock-bewilderment, complaining that the term 'postcolonial' has become 'the latest catch-all term to dazzle the academic mind' (Jacoby 1995: 30, also qtd in Loomba 1998: xi); and little wonder that more sympathetically minded critics, like Barker, Hulme and Iversen, have seen postcolonialism as constructing a new master narrative – one in which the partly postmodernism-inspired 'lowering of the capitals' in philosophy, science, theory and history has been ironically accompanied by the raising of the Postcolonial itself to 'the dubious privilege of the upper case' (Barker *et al.* 1994: 2; see also Slemon 1995: 8).[2] Postcolonial studies, as Gayatri Chakravorty Spivak, R. Radhakrishnan and several other of its leading practitioners have repeatedly reminded us, needs to be alert to its complicities with the capitalist world-system it affects to critique.[3] It seems fair to say, however, that most scholars working within the field are only too aware of these complicities. The history of postcolonial studies, despite numerous well-publicised assertions to the contrary, is one of informed self-criticism – one in which the value of the term 'postcolonial' itself has been continually interrogated, its methodological biases unearthed, the potential applicability of its theories put to the test. Not least, postcolonial studies has frequently challenged and updated its own historical models – noting the confusion that arises, for instance, from the use of the prefix 'post' as a historical marker, or the problems that are likely to follow when evolutionary paradigms are deployed uncritically to account for patterns of cross-cultural development.[4] Arguably, though, postcolonial studies has been less effective in critically analysing its *own* institutional history. Thus, while debates abound as to when the postcolonial moment might have begun (Ashcroft *et al.* 1989; McClintock 1992) – or whether, indeed, it might already have ended (Schulze-Engler 1998) – the historical origins of postcolonial studies itself as an institutional phenomenon have gone largely undiscussed. In this concluding chapter, accordingly, I want to trace a brief institutional history of postcolonial studies, beginning with the formation of the alternative paradigms (Commonwealth Literature, the New Literatures in English) it eventually came, by and large, to replace; continuing with some thoughts on the pedagogical implications of the latest critical and theoretical developments; and ending, as I began, on a note of wilful controversy – a further cautionary parable about postcolonialism's discontents (Slemon *et al.* 1995), but also a possible blueprint for its future.

As I have suggested, a kind of historical amnesia has tended to affect postcolonial debates in the Western – perhaps especially the US – academy, even as those debates have so often centred on a revisionist interpretation of the multiply embedded narratives of imperial history. This amnesia pertains to a history of disciplinary origins. Two histories, to be more precise; for the emergence of contemporary postcolonial studies has followed at least two different trajectories – trajectories I shall call, for simplicity's sake, 'the Anglophone/Commonwealth' and the 'US/minority' paths.[5] The first of these paths traces back to a handful of conferences in England in the early to mid 1960s, probably the most important of these being at the University of Leeds in 1964, whose proceedings were to constitute what we might call Commonwealth Literature's founding volume – John Press's *Commonwealth Literature*, published a year later in 1965. (Technically, this collection, while the most influential, was not the first, being pre-dated by *The Teaching of English Literature Overseas*, also edited by Press, in 1963, and by the American-based Australian Alan McLeod's *The Commonwealth Pen*, published in the US in 1961.) Press's collection contains a set of preliminary, perhaps inevitably sketchy observations on the possibility of comparing the English-language literatures of the Commonwealth across national boundaries. The following quotation, taken from D.E.S. Maxwell's paper 'Landscape and Theme', exemplifies the conference's well-intentioned if old-fashioned attempt to uncover the kinship between disparate things:

> In the first [category of colonial experience], the writer brings his own language – English – to an alien environment and a fresh set of experiences: Australia, Canada, New Zealand. In the other, the writer brings an alien language – English – to his own social and cultural inheritance: India, West Africa. Yet the categories have fundamental kinship. Viewing his society, the writer constantly faces the evidence of impact between what is native to it and what is derived from association with Britain, whatever its form. The Nigerian will respond to it differently from the Canadian. Both, however, are responding to circumstances which, for all their dissimilarities, share an attachment, whether voluntary at the start, to a remote society and culture which is manifesting itself in their immediate surroundings …. [Commonwealth writers' shared problem has been to achieve] a distinctively national tone against the intimidating strength of the parent tradition. … While each of their solutions to it is individual in its particulars … the many premises they share impress a general likeness.
>
> (Maxwell 1965: 82–3)

This likeness has notably failed to impress itself, however, on some more recent commentators. Most conspicuously, Salman Rushdie, in his characteristically acerbic essay ' "Commonwealth Literature" Does Not Exist' (originally published in 1983), lambastes Commonwealth Literature as nothing more nor less than a composite fiction dreamed up by ambitious academics, and lent a spurious literary authenticity in the service of a bankrupt political cause:

> [I]t's possible that 'Commonwealth Literature' is no more than an ungainly name for the world's younger English literatures. If that were true or, rather, if that were all, it would be a relatively unimportant misnomer. But it isn't all. Because the term is not used simply to describe, or even to misdescribe, but also to *divide*. It permits academic institutions, publishers, critics, and even readers to dump a large segment of English literature into a box and then more or less ignore it. At best, what is called 'Commonwealth Literature' is positioned *below* English literature 'proper' … [I]t places Eng. Lit. at the centre and the rest of the world at the periphery. How depressing that

such a view should persist in the study of literature long after it has
been discarded in the study of everything else English.

(Rushdie 1991a: 65–6)

Rushdie is certainly right to see Commonwealth Literature as a British-
based, to some extent closet-imperialist academic creation that has been
regarded with a certain degree of bewilderment, even active resentment,
by the writers it has sought to represent. He is also right to point out the
potentially marginalising institutional effect of comparing the 'younger
English literatures' under a dubious umbrella category that not only
encourages false similarities but also presupposes a literary and cultural
affiliation to the Mother Country that mistakenly confirms 'subordinate'
status. This latter point is arguably borne out in the work of some of the
earliest sympathisers of Commonwealth Literature – A. Norman Jeffares,
Arthur Ravenscroft and, especially, William Walsh – much of which, for
all its promotional enthusiasm, exhibits a tendency to high-handed
generalisations about 'other' cultures; to unexamined value-judgements
that couch European preferences in the language of universal standards;
and to the anachronistic deployment of organic metaphors of affiliation
and development (tree/branch, parent/child, river/tributary, etc.) which,
while not openly cultural-supremacist, at least appears to combine the
generous spirit of cross-cultural inquiry with more than a hint of colonial
condescension.[6]

Still, the suspicion remains that (rather like the narrators of some of
his novels – see Chapter 2) Rushdie has succeeded in turning historical
event into self-serving critical mythology. After all, Commonwealth
literary studies, for all the benevolent paternalism of its celebratory
rhetoric and its obsolescent political associations, needs to be understood
historically as an institutional phenomenon. And within that historical
context, it emerges as a significant academic *innovation*. In the early
1960s, few if any writers from other Commonwealth countries had found
their way onto British university syllabi; while the Commonwealth-based
academic organisations that might allow writers and scholars, whatever
their differences, to work together did not yet exist. Rushdie conveniently
forgets this; and he also forgets that the ideological impact of the creation
of Commonwealth literary studies was by no means uniformly – or even
primarily – conservative, arising *both* out of latent British cultural
insecurities in the wake of worldwide decolonisation movements *and* out
of the explicit recognition that a more informed global perspective on the
literary and cultural transformations taking place in the English-speaking
world would be needed for the post-independence period.

While the terminology, critical approach and ideological underpinnings of Commonwealth literary studies have long since fallen out of favour, it is as well to register the importance of its initiating moves. Among those moves, for instance, were the creation of *The Journal of Commonwealth Literature*, the first specialist British journal, in 1965 (preceded by a few years on the other side of the Atlantic by the *CBC Newsletter*, founded in 1962 and the forerunner of *World Literature Written in English*); and the establishment in 1964 of ACLALS, the Association for Commonwealth Literature and Language Studies, a sizeable body of writers and scholars that has succeeded in retaining a large international membership, in evolving a number of similarly active satellite organisations, and in hosting a sequence of important triennial conferences worldwide. (Interestingly enough, for reasons which will be explained later in this chapter, ACLALS has been characterised by an eclectic internationalism within which US-based writers and, particularly, scholars are frequently underrepresented.) Since its inception, ACLALS has been instrumental in setting up a network of international literary contacts that has enabled a younger generation of postcolonial scholars – some of whom are prematurely dismissive of the organisation's terminological and methodological anachronisms – to carry on their work today. Still, as even some of the founder members of ACLALS like the formerly Danish-based Australian scholar Anna Rutherford are willing to admit, the 'Commonwealth' label has outlived its usefulness, fostering a falsely inclusive internationalist outlook which glosses over significant linguistic and cultural differences, and which overlooks continuing asymmetries of power and resources in the English-speaking world. Thus, reflecting on her choice of title for a collection of essays drawn from the ACLALS Silver Jubilee conference in 1989, *From Commonwealth to Post-Colonial* (1992), Rutherford confesses that

> we have come a long way since that first meeting in Leeds, with its demands that the Commonwealth writer be an internationalist who, though he might come from Wagga Wagga or Enugu, must also be comprehensible in Heckmondville and Helmsby. I have often wondered how the writer in London or New York would react to the demand that s/he must also be comprehensible to readers in Murrurundi or Kumasi.
>
> (Rutherford 1992: viii)

As Rutherford implies, the 'Commonwealth writer' should be seen as a metropolitan creation, partly designed to reassure English-speaking academics of their often somewhat doubtful cross-cultural competencies while also meeting a variety of emergent institutional and consumer needs. The 'Commonwealth writer', in such a context, is celebrated as an *exotic*, enjoined to represent his or her given region or country, but also to translate it into terms familiar enough to allow for rudimentary cross-cultural analysis and comparative critique. In this sense, the 'Commonwealth writer', required to play the dual role of cultural ambassador and native informant, is submitted to a controlling metropolitan gaze that joins inquisitive – suspiciously colonialist – amateur-anthropological sensibilities to the philanthropically expressed desire for international *détente*.[7] This exoticist scenario, as I have suggested, is by no means the only one surrounding the figure of the 'Commonwealth writer'; and like others of its kind, it comes equipped with its own powerfully deceptive myths. Nonetheless, it might be taken as indicating some – no doubt unwelcome – continuities between the early concerns of allegedly 'reactionary' Commonwealth literary scholars and the much more 'radical' ambitions of the growing legion of postcolonial critics and theorists practising today.

A further point of contact can be established between 'Commonwealth' and 'postcolonial' criticism by way of an intermediary descriptive term, namely the 'New Literatures in English'. The use of the term 'New Literatures' dates back to the early 1970s, where it became associated with the work of such scholars as Dieter Riemenschneider (in Europe) and Bruce King (in the United States). No less than Commonwealth Literature, the New Literatures can be considered as an academic creation, the practitioners of which, however, were arguably more overt about their own political beliefs. As is generally agreed, the New Literatures developed out of the critical attempt to redefine the literary and cultural traditions of the Commonwealth countries – several of which had recently attained political independence as new nations – while evolving a suitably differentiated framework of comparative analysis in which the literary text, set against a global backdrop of (re)emergent cultural nationalisms, might be seen as a significant vehicle for the exploration of cultural and, above all, *national* identity conflicts and concerns. The New Literatures, while rarely more than a fringe term in North America, Africa, Asia and the South Pacific, has continued to prosper in parts of Europe, partly because its surface blandness has been seen as unthreatening by traditionally conservative European academies but also partly for the opposite reason, because its political concerns have been seen as matching the revived interest in nationalist ideologies within Europe itself. Thus, it becomes possible for Dieter Riemenschneider to summarise the methodological and ideological parameters of the New Literatures as late as 1987:

In recent years the organization and institutionalization of research in the field of Commonwealth literature has shown strong tendencies toward replacing attempts at comprehensive and comparative models of investigation into generally structural, linguistic, thematic, and cultural similarities of the 'new' English literatures with microstructural methodological considerations. Among these we notice, first and foremost, political parameters of nation, continent, and region. When we compare this development – which has been clearly noticeable since the mid-1970s – with the debates of the previous decade we note that the term 'Commonwealth literature' is being gradually replaced by designations such as 'Canadian literature,' 'Australian literature,' 'South African literature,' and so on. Although this is not a uniform development – the discussion in other English speaking areas of the world (for example, in Africa or the West Indies) is informed less by considerations of nation than by those of ethnicity – this tendency toward 'nation' reflects a relativization of methodologies which had been considered dated, if not outlived.

(Riemenschneider 1987: 425)

While the New Literatures is now generally recognised as another questionable umbrella category – another inconvenient term of convenience – it is important to acknowledge the political passions behind this most apparently unemotive of defining tags. As Riemenschneider suggests, a discrepancy soon began to emerge between the *comparative* mandate of the strategically pluralised New Literatures and the perceived need to adjust *independent* literary and cultural traditions to the changing political pressures of the decolonisation era. Several advocates of the New Literatures were well aware of the pitfalls of reading literary texts as 'expressions' – however mediated – of national identity, or of commandeering literature as a 'tribute' – however indirect – to the cultural nationalist cause. As Bruce King remarks at the end of his introduction to the collection *Literatures of the World in English* (1974), several of whose contributors had already been closely associated with the 1960s Commonwealth literary enterprise, '[c]riticism must insist that contemporary or local relevance is not always of enduring value' (King 1974: 21). King continues in similarly admonitory vein:

Cultural nationalists can be simplistic and levelling in their taste. Local colour, dialect, and facile optimism are sometimes preferred to the serious and profound. The universities, where modern literary tastes are often formed, will especially need to be responsible for separating what is of value from writing primarily of historical or momentary interest.

(King 1974: 21)

King appears here to hold back from the cautious political optimism of his later volume *The New English Literatures: Cultural Nationalism in a Changing World* (1980), and to endorse instead a broadly internationalist variant of Leavisite criticism, with its emphasis on the cultivation of literary taste and the refined appreciation for cultural artifacts of 'enduring value', which seems more in keeping with the critical sympathies of nearly a decade before. Here, however, a caveat needs to be entered; for as previously suggested, categories like 'Commonwealth Literature', the 'New Literatures in English', and even 'postcolonial literatures' exist to some extent in a continuum – to see the one as arising from the other, or all of them as forming part of a progressivist history, is to ignore significant overlaps in their critical outlook, political sympathies and methodological approach. And significant contradictions *within* them, as emerge in both of King's early books, which might be seen as straddling universalist Commonwealth and local/historical New Literatures approaches while including an anticipatory nod, as well, to the theoretical sophistries of contemporary postcolonial criticism.[8]

Arguably, these contradictions come to the fore in the much-contested term 'postcolonial' itself. As previously suggested (see Introduction), postcolonial criticism has evolved its own formidable definition industry, with little consensus other than that the term, and the literary and cultural field it represents, are inherently conflicted. Much of the conflict centres on the imprecision of 'the postcolonial' as a temporal marker. Ella Shohat, among others, has accused postcolonial critics of wilfully misrecognising the current *neo*colonial climate (Shohat 1992), while Aijaz Ahmad has chided them for showing more interest in 'the colonialism of the past than in the imperialism of the present' (Ahmad 1992: 93; see also Introduction). For Simon Gikandi, the term 'postcolonial' gives the false impression of something finished: 'If postcoloniality has been defined as the transcendence of imperial structures and their histories, such a definition is obviously contradicted by the everyday experiences and memories of the people in the ex-colonies' (Gikandi 1996: 15). Not that the term, properly defined, is beyond rehabilitation; Gikandi accordingly presents his view of postcoloniality – somewhat different from mine (see Introduction) – as occupying a temporal hiatus, a site of 'transition and cultural instability' in which postcolonial critics and theorists are repeatedly made aware of 'how decolonized situations are marked by the trace of the imperial pasts they try to disavow' (Gikandi 1996: 15). This view has much to be said for it; for in truth, the term 'postcolonial' provides less evidence of imperial 'transcendence' than of the attempt to account for *neocolonialism*, for continuing modes of imperialist thought and action across much of the contemporary world (Huggan 1997b). Even so, as Gikandi is forced to admit, much of the confusion surrounding the prefix 'post' has been self-willed and unproductive (see also Introduction). It is hard to believe, after all, that a single postcolonial critic really thinks that the colonial era is over; that a stake has been driven through the heart of Empire, that it might never again return. All the same, the 'post' in 'postcolonial' remains irritatingly cryptic. If it doesn't mean 'after' colonialism, then what exactly does it mean? Like the 'post' in 'postmodernism', does it risk becoming little more than an empty signifier, a perennial open question, even a sign of intellectual fatigue? One way of circumventing these potentially embarrassing questions is to see 'the postcolonial' as occupying a space of discursive, rather than historical, conflict. This might allow, for example, for such wide-ranging definitions of postcolonial criticism as Homi Bhabha's:

> Postcolonial criticism bears witness to the unequal and uneven forces of cultural representation involved in the contest for political and social authority within the modern world order. Postcolonial perspectives emerge from the colonial testimony of Third World countries and the discourses of 'minorities' within the geopolitical divisions of east and west, north and south. They intervene in those ideological discourses of modernity that attempt to give a hegemonic 'normality' to the uneven development and the differential, often disadvantaged, histories of nations, races, communities, peoples. They formulate their critical revisions around issues of cultural difference, social authority, and political discrimination in order to reveal the antagonistic and ambivalent moments within the 'rationalizations' of modernity.
>
> (Bhabha 1992: 437)

Bhabha's definition is more revealing for the highly abstract language it uses than for its grasp of a field whose history it uncertainly designates as a cluster of 'antagonistic and ambivalent moments'. The language, drawing on a mishmash of sociology and political theory, itself displays the historical anxieties Bhabha attributes to modernity's self-justifying myths. No doubt aware of the dangers of broad transhistorical readings of colonialism and/or imperialism, Bhabha chooses the drastic option of removing the latter term altogether. Instead, he turns 'the postcolonial' into a kind of floating signifier for contemporary resistance to hegemonic forms of social and political authority – an authority arguably relocated in his own diagnostic critical discourse. A tension begins to emerge here between the desire to formulate clearly defined political goals for what Bhabha rather mysteriously calls the 'postcolonial critical project' and the inherent amorphousness of the critical discourse, obviously adapted from European poststructuralism, through which that project is announced and initiated.[9]

But the historical question remains: *when* did this tension begin to emerge? The search for dates here proves elusive; for in many ways the provenance of postcolonial criticism, and its later transformation into a kind of radical intellectual orthodoxy, are as difficult to pinpoint as the historical origins of the term 'postcolonial' itself. The emergence of the constellation of sometimes only vaguely compatible critical and theoretical positions for which the term 'postcolonial' serves as untidy shorthand is perhaps best charted through a series of parallel developments in the Western academy in the 1980s. Among these we might include the increasing theoretical self-consciousness of literary and other humanities studies; the convergence, at times confusion, of theoretical experimentation with political critique; and, above all, the increasing dominance of relativistic, transdisciplinary modes of intellectual inquiry – the postmodernism boom and the indirect critiques it generated of self-ingratiating Western metropolitan societies and worldwide patterns of uneven development; the politically inflected poststructuralisms of Lacan and Althusser, Derrida and, particularly, Foucault. Much ink has been spilt – and not without cause – in debating the appropriateness of a European intellectual heritage to the critical analysis of the literatures and cultures of non-European societies.[10] Much has also been made of the divergences between postcolonial criticism and postmodern theory, with acrimonious exchanges being enacted between perceived apologists for the two allegedly incommensurable causes (e.g. Brydon versus Hutcheon in *Past the Last Post* (1990)), and rhetorical battles being staged in which the situated knowledge of the one is pitted against the totalising prescriptions of the other. While some of these debates have either strayed into the paths of (self-) righteousness or degenerated into dialogues of the deaf, many others have been productive; the fact remains, as Ania Loomba points out in her introductory study *Colonialism/Postcolonialism* (1998), that the recent development of postcolonial criticism and, particularly, theory at Western universities throughout the 1980s and up to the present is partly the result of the dispersal and necessary transformation of intellectual trends and movements (Marxism, psychoanalysis, etc.) that formerly emanated from the metropolitan centres of Europe.

Loomba's sensible conclusion is that postcolonial studies has inherited 'the burden of a Euro-centric past, even as so much of its energy and revisionist power is derived from its provenance within anti-colonial and progressive political movements' (Loomba 1998: 256). This uneasy balance is skilfully negotiated in one of postcolonial studies' founding texts, Ashcroft, Griffiths and Tiffin's aforementioned *The Empire Writes Back: Theory and Practice in Post-Colonial Literatures* (1989) – a study often seen somewhat unfairly as reinscribing the European norms its authors strive so vigorously to resist.[11] Ashcroft, Griffiths and Tiffin's book, for all its methodological inconsistencies, remains a pioneering analysis; a corrective both to the Leavisite complacency of Commonwealth Literature and the political naivety of the New Literatures in English, it also combines some of the more positive aspects – comparative ambition, historical awareness – of these two precursor approaches. Ashcroft, Griffiths and Tiffin's next major work, the collection of excerpted essays *The Post-Colonial Studies Reader* (1995), is less ambitious in its scope but might also be seen as marking a transition – from the literature-based approaches of the 1960s and 1970s and, to a lesser extent, the 1980s to the increasingly inter- or transdisciplinary emphasis of the most recently favoured academic category, 'Postcolonial Studies'. Although Ashcroft, Griffiths and Tiffin's reader takes care to include essays by creative writers as well as academic theorists and critics, its selections arguably consolidate the dominant position of postcolonial *theory* in the field.[12] The place of literature, according to some (see, for example, Thieme 1996), has become increasingly imperilled, with the latest generation of postcolonial scholars more likely to see themselves as philosophers or social scientists than literary critics. While it would be easy enough to read this argument as both reactionary and reductive, it is true that some of the most recent work in the field gives the impression of having bypassed literature altogether, offering a heady blend of philosophy, sociology, history and political science in which literary texts, when referred to at all, are read symptomatically within the context of larger social and cultural trends. In addition, postcolonial theory, for all its historical self-reflexivity, appears at times to view postcolonial literary criticism as little more than an anachronism – a symptom of the nostalgic desire to return to the earlier, over-aestheticised formations of Commonwealth Literature, the New Literatures and (more important in the United States) Third World Literatures in English. A version of this view is presented here by Loomba:

> If postcolonial studies is to survive in any meaningful way, it needs to absorb itself far more deeply with the contemporary world, and with

the local circumstances within which colonial institutions and ideas are being moulded into the disparate cultural and socio-economic practices which define our contemporary 'globality'. This globality is often reduced to discussions of literatures written or translated into English, reminding us that in many ways postcolonial studies is simply a reworking of the older concepts of 'Commonwealth literatures' or 'Third World literatures'. But even these literatures cannot be adequately discussed outside of the difficult interplay between their local and global contexts, an awareness that is all too often erased as we celebrate the hybridity or polyphony or magic realism of these texts!

(Loomba 1998: 256–7)

As Loomba implies, the emergence of postcolonial studies in the 1990s is partly the offshoot of a wider institutional phenomenon – the so-called turn to cultural studies in an increasing number of English (among other humanities) departments at Western universities. Thus, while previous paradigms like Commonwealth Literature had aimed to further metropolitan consciousness of the *internationalisation* of English-language literature, postcolonial studies might better be seen as an analytical attempt to *globalise* the already wide scope of cultural studies. The objectives are relatively clear: historically situated anti-imperialist critique is to be joined to the interdisciplinary analysis of mostly contemporary sociocultural movements and phenomena to produce a blueprint for the re-exploration of political questions of authority, autonomy and agency in an era of cultural globalisation.[13] A further connection exists here in the broadening of 1980s colonial discourse analysis – often though not necessarily focusing on canonical literary/cultural narratives of the nineteenth century, and associated with probably the most famous of postcolonial studies' founding texts, Edward Said's *Orientalism* (1978) – to include the disciplinary objects of a contemporary imperial gaze: the 'exotic' merchandise of tribal/ethnic cultures; the ubiquitous products spawned by a globalised consumer culture; the manufactured scenarios of a Western tourist industry bent on selling the latest version of the cultural other to consumers – while stocks last.

One effect of the latest trend has been a renewed vigilance to capitalist strategies of appropriation, not least the attempted commodification of the marginal discourses of the postcolonial field itself. Another has been the co-optation of postcolonial approaches and methods by disciplines other than that of English literary studies: examples here can be cited in geography (Gregory 1994; Jacobs 1996) and anthropology (Steedly 1993; Taussig 1993), and the disciplinary range is showing every sign of expanding further still. A third, to my mind less salutary effect has been what we might call the *Americanisation* of the postcolonial. The development of postcolonial studies in the United States, as previously suggested, has taken a rather different route to that of other mainly Anglophone settler-immigrant societies (obvious cases for comparison here are Canada and Australia). The crucial difference has been the assimilation of broad-based postcolonial methodologies to current debates on minority cultures within the context of the *nation*. The deployment of postcolonial theoretical models as tools for the analysis of minority discourse has produced some startling critical insights, both in the United States and elsewhere, for instance in 'multicultural' Britain.[14] But it has also arguably produced, particularly in the US, new forms of cultural parochialism – the oddly insular concentration on gauging the effects of changing patterns of immigration and cultural hybridisation on the national self-image; the self-congratulatory desire to assume and analyse 'American' models of globalisation and/or diasporisation elsewhere. These tendencies are then exacerbated by further, apparently shortsighted assumptions: that the United States has cornered the market in postcolonial studies by bringing the cream of the Third World's intelligentsia to the nation's leading research universities (Dirlik 1994); that the best work in the field is almost inevitably produced by those who enjoy the signal advantages of American academia; and that the global scope of postcolonial studies is paradoxically enabled by the dispersal of its brightest scholars, not across the world at large but across a restricted number of US metropolitan sites. Finally, a potential side-effect of the narrow focus on national minority cultures is a skewed perception of the global dimensions of postcolonial studies as little more than a spatial extension of prevailing national racial/ethnic concerns. Thus, while the putatively 'non-hegemonic' literatures and cultures of Africa, Asia and the Caribbean are welcomed for the insights they provide on diasporic patterns of racial/ethnic identity, history and self-empowerment, the more ostensibly privileged, predominantly white literatures and cultures of former settler colonies like Canada, Australia or New Zealand are quite likely to disappear from view.[15]

A further reason for this emphasis has been the emergence of post-colonial studies in the United States as a perceived modification of approaches applied in the 1960s and 1970s to 'Third World Literatures'. This latter term is now recognised as suspect both for its homogenising tendencies and for a hierarchical taxonomy that 'sets up the third world as a vacuum to be filled by the economic and political maneuverings of the first two worlds' (Mohan 1992: 32). With the disintegration of the Cold War, the political situation that led to the creation of a three-world schema has irreversibly altered. The *literary* label, however, has proved rather harder to dislodge, resurfacing in essays such as Fredric Jameson's much-criticised 'Third World Literature in the Era of Multinational Capitalism' (1986) and in Timothy Brennan's work on the global reach of contemporary cosmopolitan culture (see, for example, the first chapter of *At Home in the World* (1997)). (Needless to say, the label has rarely been used in the 'non-Western' locations it claims to represent. Not that the term 'postcolonial', by and large, has proven to be any more popular, providing an ironic reminder of precisely the tyranny of metropolitan definition that postcolonial critics, the majority of whom are located in the Western metropoles, have made it their business to address.)[16]

The oversimplified tendency to see postcolonial studies as having emerged more or less directly out of earlier US approaches to Third World Literatures, or even as having replaced them (Dirlik 1994), lends strength to those who see the politics of postcolonial resistance as a natural development of American minority concerns. Rajeswari Mohan, for example, suggests that 'the political context for the study of postcolonial literature was created in the American academy by feminist and Afro-American critiques of the literary canon, critiques *that were echoed in the international scene* by writers such as Chinua Achebe and Ngugi wa Thiong'o' (Mohan 1992: 30, my emphasis). The idea that the world should conveniently 'echo' the liberation struggles of America is implicitly supported by – of all people – Aijaz Ahmad, for whom postcolonial writing:

> refers simply [*sic*] to literary compositions ... of non-white minorities located in Britain and North America – while efforts are now under way also to designate the contemporary literatures of Asia and Africa as 'postcolonial' and thus to make them available for being read according to the protocols that metropolitan criticism has developed for reading what it calls 'minority literatures'.
>
> (Ahmad 1995a: 8)

As Peter Childs and Patrick Williams point out, Ahmad gets his history back to front here: '[I]t was the literatures of former colonies which were originally designated postcolonial, and the current "efforts" are to examine ways in which the "minority" literatures in Britain and the United States are locatable within the postcolonial paradigm' (Childs and Williams 1997: 20). While Ahmad's mistake should not necessarily be seen as a symptom of the 'Americanisation' of postcolonial studies, it is certainly indicative of the worryingly dehistoricising effect of its institutionalisation as a (trans)disciplinary field. This effect, as I have been suggesting throughout this book, is tied in with an uncritical approach toward cultural difference that freezes products regarded as belonging to the cultural margins within the semiotic field of fetishised representation I have chosen to call the 'postcolonial exotic'. The postcolonial exotic is not a simple *result* of the relatively recent institutionalisation of postcolonial studies, nor does it simply *coincide* with the current entanglement of postcolonial representations of cultural difference within a global-capitalist alterity industry (see Introduction). Rather, the postcolonial exotic, like postcolonial criticism itself, registers continuities with the earlier historical paradigms it believes itself to have outgrown. The exotic, we might then say, is the ghost that comes back to haunt the corridors of postcolonial critical history. It is there in the 'Commonwealth writer' (who *does* exist) and in the celebration of 'other' English-language literatures. And it is there in the rise of postcolonial studies, which can be read both as a record of successive disciplinary transformations and as the accumulated sum of its inevitably unsuccessful attempts to resolve the problem of cultural otherness – one it must repeatedly confront because it is one it continually recreates.

Postcolonial studies and the pedagogic imaginary

Theory and practice

One of the central theses behind this book has been that while 'the postcolonial' is unthinkable outside of the academic debates surrounding the other 'posts', poststructuralism and postmodernism, nor can it be divorced from the more immediate material contexts in which representations of cultural difference are circulated within the global economy – and consumed. As I have repeatedly suggested, the postcolonial field of production has developed at a time of renewed interest in the cultural other, and at a moment when cultural difference has become a valuable consumer item. The widespread recognition that academic discourses of the other are caught in global circuits of cultural consumption might help account for what often appears to be a constitutive insecurity within the postcolonial field. Hence the embattled realisation that postcolonialism, however defined, 'is situated within the ambit of a continuing neo-colonialism, which means that … its politics are interventionary at best, never simply expressivist, and never fully arrived' (Slemon 1993: 159). Continuing doubts about the political effectiveness of postcolonial studies surface at the level of *pedagogic practice*. Thus, while educational theorists like Henry Giroux or Peter McLaren have been able to assert the centrality of emancipatory postcolonial discourses to the formation of a critical pedagogy that allows 'educators to transform the languages, social practices, and histories that are part of the colonial inheritance', and that creates the conditions 'in which students become border crossers in order to understand Otherness in its own terms' (Giroux 1992c: 23–4), university-based teachers of postcolonial studies like Arun Mukherjee or Aruna Srivastava have documented their experiences of a conflict between the anti-racist ideals of postcolonial pedagogy and those institutional relations, practices and processes that replicate 'the [discriminatory] structures on which colonialism and imperialism were based and on which they thrived' (Srivastava 1995: 13; see also Mukherjee 1994a). Stephen Slemon, similarly, notes a continuing mismatch between the utopian proposals of radical educational theory and the 'front-line exigencies of postcolonial literary teaching at the level of immediate classroom engagement' (Slemon 1993: 153). Although Slemon will not go so far as to accuse the academy of perpetuating structural racism, he points out several factors that limit the political effectiveness of postcolonial teaching: namely, the absorption of postcolonial studies into *English* literary studies, often though not necessarily resulting in a dilution of the former's political content or a restriction of its global reach; the rapid emergence of the postcolonial field as an opportune site for professional advancement, helping produce such epiphenomena as the 'postcolonial convert', the 'career postcolonialist', and the 'instant postcolonial expert'; and, not least, 'the positioning of the whole enterprise of pedagogical research … at the "soft option" end of disciplinary engagement', leading to a remarkable division of labour in which pedagogical matters, 'discursively in the feminine, [are placed within] the "service" ranks of [the profession], beneath the purview of intellectual advancement, and far from the rugged masculinity of the theoretical frontier' (Slemon 1993: 154).[17] This bifurcation of theory and practice, while perhaps less dramatic than Slemon indicates, can not only be found in (trans)disciplinary fields like postcolonial studies but also in educational institutions at large like the university, where the pressure to publish continues to outweigh the demonstrated ability to teach. A closer inspection of theoretical essays like Giroux's or McLaren's with more practically oriented ones like Mukherjee's or Slemon's suggests, however, that both types of essay claim a largely prescriptive moral authority from the attempt to reunite theory and practice in the service of transformational social critique. As McLaren says, following his mentor Freire, a critical pedagogy 'makes clear that theory and practice work in concert; it is counterproductive for teachers to view critical pedagogy as essentially a theoretical and descriptive exercise' (McLaren 1992: 11). Yet in a sense this is exactly how his essay views it, relying, like Giroux's, on a rhetoric of exhortation to set out what 'critical educators', their students and the institutions in which both sets of 'cultural workers' operate should, ideally, do. Giroux, in particular, in exploring the 'post-colonial ruptures and democratic possibilities' inherent in what he calls a radical 'border pedagogy', adopts a hectoring tone supplemented by the prevalent use of modal constructions:

> If an anti-racist pedagogy is to have any meaning as a force for creating a democratic society, teachers and students *must* be given the opportunity to put into effect what they learn outside of the school. In other words, they *must* be given the opportunity to engage in anti-racist struggles in their effort to link schooling to real life, ethical discourse to political action, and classroom relations to a broader notion of cultural politics. The school curriculum *should* make anti-racist pedagogies central to the task of educating students to animate a wider and more critically engaged public culture; it *should not* merely allow them to take risks but also to push against the boundaries of an oppressive social order.
>
> (Giroux 1992c: 33, my emphasis)

Mukherjee's catalogue of complaints in her influential essay 'Ideology in the Classroom', first published in 1986, exhibits similarly authoritarian tendencies. After noting the lack of connection between scholarly research and pedagogic practice in the Western (more specifically, Canadian) academy, Mukherjee devotes much of her essay to attacking her own students for their naive insistence to read Canadian texts in universalising humanist terms. While Mukherjee is undoubtedly right to draw attention to the formalist/structuralist hegemony in Canadian literary studies in the mid 1980s, her personal crusade for politicising readings of literary texts appears self-righteous in the extreme. 'I was thoroughly disappointed', says Mukherjee, 'by my students' total disregard for local realities treated in [Margaret Laurence's African-based short story] "The Perfume Sea" ' (Mukherjee 1994a [1986]: 31); then again later, 'I was astounded by my students' ability to close themselves off to the disturbing implications of *my interpretation* and devote their attention to expatiating upon "the anxiety and hope of humanity," and other such generalizations as change, people, values, reality, etc.' (Mukherjee 1994a [1986]: 34, my emphasis). Notwithstanding the advantages of using literature to situate *different* ideological readings (e.g. those of the students), it seems necessary to point out the dangers of an oppositional postcolonial pedagogy fixated on replicating a *particular* ideological reading (i.e. Mukherjee's own). A postcolonial approach thus runs the risk of replacing the ethical imperative of anti-colonial literary/cultural criticism with the moral presumption of an individual teacher self-appointed as custodian-transmitter of the text's allegedly oppositional value.

Elsewhere in her large body of critical work, Mukherjee's emphatic claim to inside knowledge about South Asian cultures ironically reconfirms Gayatri Spivak's complaint that Third World-born teachers, as well as writers, of postcolonial literatures are frequently interpellated as native informants for the societies and cultures they imaginatively represent.[18] Mukherjee's self-consciously provocative stance as oppositional instructor thus suggests a potential double bind in the teaching of postcolonial literary/cultural studies. On the one hand, postcolonial studies sets up a 'pedagogy of resistance' (Giroux 1992a) that aims both to de-exoticise (formerly) colonised cultures and to 'question the very categories through which the history and narratives of the colonized have been written' (McLaren 1992: 25). On the other, postcolonial teachers, in arrogating the authority that derives from knowledge or, still better, experience of these or similarly embattled cultures, risk merely reconfirming the irreducible otherness of the places from which they themselves, like the texts they explicate, are perceived to spring. Needless to say, not all teachers of postcolonial literary/cultural studies are interested in doing this or, for that matter, are in a position to do this; it seems fairer to say that most would be inclined to disavow, or at least question, the cultural authority attributed to them as 'postcolonials' in a Western institutional setting. Ironically enough, the fundamental category-mistake of assuming that a postcolonial teacher must also *be a 'postcolonial'* is precisely the kind of error that a critical pedagogy centring on a nuanced examination of the politics of cultural difference is best designed to reveal. Yet as Timothy Brennan among others has argued, institutional pressures to diversify the faculty body have been allied, particularly in the US context, to a form of racial essentialism through which minority and/or Third World teachers are effectively identified with their 'non-Western', and thus putatively 'non-canonical', subjects. A narrowly conceived identity politics has therefore helped create the contradictory conditions in which 'the defense of teaching non-Western literatures is widely perceived as being made in the language of civil rights (inclusion, equality of representation) rather than on the grounds of what those literatures offer: a humanist knowledge pushing beyond European provincialism' (Brennan 1997: 115). The net effect of this may be that postcolonial studies, for all its globalising impulses, may end up being seen as an aggregate of highly specialised knowledges, cultural competencies and intradisciplinary fields. These fields, represented by those thought best qualified to teach them (i.e. black scholars for black literatures, South Asian scholars for South Asian studies, etc.), create the further misperception of postcolonial teaching as an autoethnographic exercise in cultural translation (see also Introduction). At worst, theory and practice part company again in what Brennan describes as a form of 'liberal racism', whereby the institutional policies designed to enhance diversification serve only to reproduce forms of social exclusion, and the 'value of what is taught [is marginalised and diminished] by [being made] to appear particular and special, [meanwhile] loudly proclaim[ing] to white students that this is not their field' (Brennan 1997: 115).

Brennan's argument, while overstated, has some validity for US universities caught in the liberal conundrum of wishing to support the ideal of greater cultural inclusiveness while remaining bound to a pluralist ideology that compartmentalises and reifies cultural differences, ensuring that these remain dimly understood.[19] To some extent, Brennan's diagnosis of the blatant contradictions within, say, university hiring and curricular policies are a function of what I called in the last section the 'Americanisation' of postcolonial studies; both sets of policies are linked, that is, to the perceived instrumentality of postcolonial theories and methodologies for the purpose of addressing national minority concerns and discourses, and to the assimilation of a supposedly emancipatory postcolonial pedagogy to the democratic ideals of a nation that seeks social redress by appealing to its own tradition of civil rights (see also Giroux 1992c). To locate, as Giroux does, a postcolonial pedagogy within a predominantly US history of anti-racist struggle is to risk forgetting that the institutionalisation of postcolonial studies, in the US and elsewhere, has emerged in response to differentiated sets of local (not necessarily national) conditions. A detailed comparison of set texts, syllabi, instructional aims and teaching methods across the various countries and regions of the world where postcolonial courses are offered at university level would no doubt reveal as wide a spread as that which attends definitions of 'the postcolonial' itself – these being themselves locally inflected (see Harsono below). Naturally enough, a postcolonial pedagogy founded on a theoretical understanding of anti-imperialist resistance will need to evolve specific practices of resistance in response to local institutional contingencies, social and historical circumstances, and cultural needs. But it will also have to address a number of conspicuously *trans*local issues – changing configurations of power within the global economy, for instance – which have an inevitable impact on the ways in which postcolonial literatures and cultures are taught and studied and the discipline of postcolonial studies itself is seen.

Syllabus and canon

One of the most obvious effects of changing local/global pressures on the study of the humanities in Western (higher) educational institutions has been the thought given, particularly in the last two or three decades, to 'opening up the canon' to non-Western literary texts. Postcolonial studies has played a significant role in this alleged democratisation of literary/cultural values, in part by exposing what John Docker calls 'neocolonial assumptions' behind the teaching of traditional English literary works.[20] However, in challenging critical orthodoxies within the mainstream tradition of English literary studies, postcolonial studies risks merely substituting one set of approved standards and guidelines for another. Thus, while it has historically aimed to instil a counter-hegemonic knowledge that heightens awareness of the power-struggles behind canonical processes of inclusion and exclusion, postcolonial studies has also succeeded in evolving – as is perhaps inevitable within an institutional context – literary and critical canons of its own. Few university courses in postcolonial studies fail to find a place for the 'star' theorists and critics; while in those courses, apparently a diminishing number, that give greater weighting to what might problematically be called 'aesthetic matters', the acknowledged celebrity authors are overrepresented, often at no less talented but less globally recognised (and commercially available) writers' expense. As previously explained, one reason for this imbalance is the entanglement of postcolonial studies within a global celebrity culture in which self-perpetuating processes of legitimation and consecration, regulated by the academy but created by the consumer society at large, have the broad effect of manufacturing and to some extent maintaining the mystique surrounding a restricted number of talismanic figures (see Introduction; also previous chapter). Another reason, however, is tied up with what John Guillory has called the 'pedagogic imaginary', a utopian belief-system that he describes as having the capacity to 'organize the discursive and institutional life of teachers in excess of the simple function of disseminating knowledge by projecting a unity of the "profession" in the ideality of its self-representation, the discourse of its own being as a kind of community' (Guillory 1993: 35). The pedagogic imaginary, as Guillory himself admits, is something of a nebulous concept. But this concept is made visible in a quantifiable series of institutional practices, the most obvious of these being the fetishistic attachment to the syllabus as *list*. While a syllabus, on the purely pragmatic level, represents the necessary – and necessarily provisional – outcome of curricular planning, it may also adhere to the ossifying logic of the reproducible list. While the fetishised list, according to Guillory, is primarily a 'symptom of what [François] Lyotard has described as … "the postmodern condition of knowledge" ' (Guillory 1993: 36) – the breaking down of the imagined totality of things-known into an arbitrary sequence of atomised units – recent attempts by Allan Bloom, E.D. Hirsch and others in the US to conflate the *syllabus* with the *canon* represent a rearguard effort to restore an imagined totality on the institutional level: in this case, through the listing of 'great' literary and cultural works. But as Guillory argues, liberal-left critiques of the canon have tended to be bound to a similarly contradictory logic. Thus it is that:

> [a] nostalgia for community pervades the debate about the canon on both the right and the left sides of the debate – on the one side as the unity of Western culture, and on the other as the unity of its individual countercultures, represented by canons of 'noncanonical' works. Both unities contend with the actual dominance of mass culture by projecting an imaginary totality out of mass culture's image of cultural diversity – the form of the list. There is no question that cultural unities, especially unities in opposition, have political effects, that the concept and experience of 'solidarity' is essential to any struggle. But the pedagogic imaginary within which the critique of the canon has been advanced is at once in excess of that solidarity, because it constructs out of its alternative canon/syllabus/list a culture [of, say, 'oppositional' and/or 'marginalised' writers] more homogeneous than it actually is, and in defect of that solidarity, because the image of cultural homogeneity it disseminates is only an image for those who consume it in the university, where it is consumed *as* an image.
>
> (Guillory 1993: 36–7; see also previous chapter)

Guillory is referring primarily here to the ambivalent status of so-called 'noncanonical' literatures in a US academic context. Postcolonial literature, as much as the other modes of 'noncanonical' writing to which it is so often assimilated in the US academy, is clearly a test-case for Guillory's critique of the institutional levelling-out of putatively marginal cultural forms. As Guillory suggests, the multiplication of marginal discourses in the US (and, by extension, the Western) academy opens the way for a productive coalition politics through which the overlapping needs and desires of socially disadvantaged groups can be collectively expressed. At the same time, these groups are inadequately served by a representation-based identity politics that co-opts highly disparate literary/cultural texts for a largely *imaginary* pedagogic agenda, and in which such texts are primarily deployed as forms of cultural capital within an institutional context – in this case, that of the university – while failing to compensate for the *real* social inequalities their deployment is apparently designed to redress (Guillory 1993: 37–8). In this sense, Guillory's concept of the pedagogic imaginary might possibly be seen as a further point of intersection for the contending regimes of value – what I have been calling 'postcolonialism' and 'postcoloniality' – through which postcolonial studies has been constructed at Western universities as both oppositional academic discipline and attractive object of consumption (see also Introduction).[21]

   That postcolonial texts have been incorporated over time into a series of recognisable 'canons of the noncanonical' (Guillory 1993) is apparent from a recent worldwide survey of postcolonial syllabi and course-lists conducted by Yukun Harsono, an undergraduate student at Harvard University.[22] The survey, while by no means comprehensive, reveals several instructive patterns. First and foremost, it demonstrates the extraordinary disciplinary range of postcolonial studies. Courses engaging, to a greater or lesser extent, in postcolonial debates and methodologies can be found in history, geography, anthropology, sociology, psychology, philosophy, architecture, political science, comparative literature, education, dance and music, and the visual arts; while postcolonial approaches are also currently being explored in more specialised fields such as African, South/East Asian, Native/Aboriginal, Subaltern, Feminist, and Gay and Lesbian Studies. Many of these courses are pointedly inter- or multidisciplinary, reflecting the shift away from a literary focus noted in the previous section. Graduate programmes in postcolonial studies like the MA at the University of Essex, co-taught by members of three different departments, are also keen to bill themselves as interdisciplinary:

> Much of the work [in postcolonial studies] has been produced from within the disciplines of literature, history and anthropology, although the field has at its centre a growing body of theory which is essentially non-disciplinary and which can therefore best be addressed in an academic context by a combination of disciplines.
>
> (Advertising blurb, the University of Essex)

Like the composite MA at Essex, several individual courses turn to postcolonial theory, often in tandem with its postmodern equivalent, as a means of contesting disciplinary boundaries and of conceptually reframing traditionally conceived fields and areas of study. An interesting example here is Michael Dutton's course 'An/Other China: Postcolonial Concerns, Postmodern Theory', offered by the Politics Department at Melbourne University. Dutton lists the objectives of the course as being:

- to understand the usefulness and importance of postmodern and postcolonial concerns;
- to discuss questions of social transition in a broader, more theoretically informed manner;
- to understand the limits of area studies and applied theory approaches to the construction of knowledge;
- to analyse the limits to a select body of recent social, political and cultural theory;
- to advance an alternative way of formulating the idea of mainstreaming Asian studies.

(http://miriworld.its.unimelb.edu.au/HB/Arts/166/166–445.html,
compiled by Harsono 1996)

Dutton's course, characteristically ambitious, reflects the predominantly *culturalist* approach of postcolonial studies and its bold attempt to engage with a whole raft of social and political issues within the wider context of a world in transition. Equally characteristic is the free-ranging use of the term 'postcolonial'. Dutton – perhaps wisely – chooses to forego definition, but elsewhere 'postcolonial' is defined as a 'literary genre' ('Introduction to Postcolonial Literature', Wesleyan University); as a combination of 'the colonizer's discourse … and colonized dilemmas' ('Postcolonial Francophone Autobiography', UCLA); as a mechanism for the retrieval of 'alternative histories … and stories that were once suppressed' ('Postmodernism and Postcolonialism: Rewriting History', University of Utrecht); and as a critical medium for the investigation of 'ethical issues involved in geographical inquiry' ('Geographic Thought and Practice', University of British Columbia).

Harsono's survey reaffirms the instrumentality of postcolonial theories and methods – their availability for addressing specific issues of institutional and pedagogical self-reflexivity, as well as for conducting often highly generalised debates within the abstract realm of cultural critique. The survey also confirms the global dispersal of postcolonial studies itself, with courses, modules, or programmes currently on offer in Hong Kong, Brazil and Cyprus, as well as in the more established centres for postcolonial research, notably in Britain, Canada, Australia and, above all, the United States. The global scope of postcolonial studies should not, however, be overestimated; it is surely significant, for example, that the term 'postcolonial' only rarely surfaces in the offerings of universities located in so-called Third World societies, providing further ammunition for those who claim that postcolonial theory and criticism are the latest *translatio imperii* for the overdeveloped Western world.[23] Meanwhile, the availability of books also has an inevitable say in materials selection for postcolonial courses, particularly in countries or regions comparatively isolated from the major Western metropolitan publishing centres.[24] Thus, it is no surprise to find that the best-known authors, whose books are widely and cheaply available, dominate both 'literature' and 'theory' listings for postcolonial studies' syllabi, even though in some cases the wider implications of mass-market publishing are also critically discussed. In a graduate seminar at the National University of Singapore, for example, the blurb draws attention not just to the publishing industry but to Western business practices at large, asking if

> postcolonial theory can survive outside the metropolitan centres of academic influence in the West, and whether it has a complicit ally in the continued dominance of the West, especially in relation to the attempt by Western business establishments to improve their knowledge of the Third World with a view to enhancing their production capabilities and widening their markets.
>
> (http://www.nus.sg/Courses/ELL/rec-poco.html,
> compiled by Harsono 1996)

Financial constraints also dictate the increasing popularity of anthologies and readers as pedagogic tools with which to introduce students to a wide array of postcolonial literary and critical/theoretical texts. Patrick Williams and Laura Chrisman's *Colonial Discourse and Postcolonial Theory* features on several lists, particularly in the United States, where it was initially published, while the Routledge *Post-Colonial Studies Reader*, edited by Ashcroft, Griffiths and Tiffin, is also a popular choice. (The astonishing output of Routledge, which has cornered the market in certain areas of contemporary cultural theory, surely merits a sociologically inflected case study of its own.) Anthologies and readers obviously fulfil an ideological as well as an informative function in disseminating knowledge to both students and teachers about the postcolonial field. This function may be analysed by looking in a little more detail at the three bestselling postcolonial readers currently on the market – Williams and Chrisman's (Columbia University Press), Ashcroft, Griffiths and Tiffin's (Routledge), and Mongia's (Arnold).

The role of the reader

Readers may be provisionally – also provocatively – defined as aggregates of decontextualised knowledge that aim at providing introductory insights into a disciplinary field. In the case of fields as broad as postcolonial studies, the customary problems of partiality and decontextualisation are likely to be accentuated. Hence the editors' efforts in all three readers to acknowledge the limitations of their own collections, to the extent that they sometimes appear slightly disabused of either their own or – not the same thing of course – their publishers' intentions. Williams and Chrisman address the problem by choosing expansive framing categories that allow them to accommodate diverse material while recognising that 'postcolonialism is far from being a unified field' (Williams and Chrisman 1994: 5). Ashcroft, Griffiths and Tiffin go further, issuing the somewhat sniffy prefatory disclaimer that, while:

> the publishers [Routledge] insisted that the title of *The Post-Colonial Studies Reader* be congruent with the other readers which they publish … the authors are equally at pains to insist … that the title is not meant to claim some kind of completeness of coverage or absolute authority.
>
> (Ashcroft *et al.* 1995: xv)

Mongia, meanwhile, contents herself with cocking a snook at other readers, including by implication Ashcroft, Griffiths and Tiffin's:

> Unlike other Readers on the market, this one is not so much interested in a comprehensive mapping of all the areas of debate and discussion as it is in making available a selection of key articles which deal with issues central to an exploration of contemporary postcolonial theory.
>
> (Mongia 1996: 15)

In each case, the implication is that the reader cannot do what its publishers, if not its editors, have designed it to do or that its more modest aim is to make available a number of not always readily accessible sources. Significantly, however, none of the readers engages fully with the important issue, already raised in Mongia's introduction, of how to understand the 'simultaneous disagreement regarding the … validity of postcolonial theory *and* the growth of work that attaches itself to it' (Mongia 1996: 2). Of how to understand, in other words, the *institutionalisation* of postcolonial theory and, more generally, of postcolonial studies as an increasingly consecrated metalanguage – one whose demand is partly dependent on its capacity to produce new definitions of itself and internal frictions, and whose appeal is partly linked both to its supposed pedagogic effectivity (Ashcroft, Griffiths and Tiffin describe their reader explicitly as a 'text to assist in the revision of teaching practices within literary studies in English' (1995: 4)) and to its ability to mystify as well as instruct,

holding out the illusory promise of intellectual mastery while simultaneously announcing its impossibility (Culler 1997).

All three readers can be seen as products of a bargain struck between
influential metropolitan publishers and academic editors alert to changing
patterns of commercial opportunity as well as current institutional needs.
Within this nexus of commercial and institutional contexts, the readers
perform, however, rather different kinds of ideological work. In Williams
and Chrisman's reader, a lengthy introduction carefully sets out the
editors' agenda of postcolonial studies as a cultural-materialist analysis of
changing forms of imperial domination and anti-imperial resistance, both
in the colonial past and the neocolonial/globalist present. The editors'
materialist emphasis leads them to forge some unexpected philosophical
and methodological alliances (such as that between Spivak's deconstructive Marxism and the Frankfurt School critique of Benjamin and Adorno)
while casting a less favourable eye on the type of discourse analysis
inspired by Foucault, one of whose 'unfortunate by-products' has been to
obscure 'the precise relations between [differentiated] forms of power'
(Williams and Chrisman 1994: 18). Postcolonialism, for Williams and
Chrisman, emerges clearly as a mode of critical intervention that revolves
around historically situated colonial/imperial moments but is equally
firmly located within the wider context of post-Enlightenment debates
about the ideological function of modernity and the dialectical nature of
progress. While this approach is certainly fruitful, it arguably twists several
of the collection's essays, conscripting non-European thinkers into the
service of European philosophical projects and tending, for all its
materialist sympathies, to see postcolonial criticism as a cocktail of highly
intellectualised debates. The reader, in fact, despite the useful explanatory
prefaces to its different sections, can hardly be construed as 'introductory',
and may well prove baffling for those not already conversant with at least
some of the broader critical/theoretical arguments that currently define
the field. Thus, while little quibble can be made with the selections
themselves, the organisational frame removes them to a level of
abstraction that many users of the reader, particularly initiates to the field,
might well find offputting. (Some of the frames themselves are somewhat
cryptically entitled, such as Part Five, 'Discourse and Identity', and,
particularly, Part Six, 'Reading from Theory', which contains some
interesting essays which appear to have little, if anything, in common.)

Even more mystifying are the divisions of material in Padmini Mongia's *Contemporary Postcolonial Theory: A Reader*, a collection which post-
dates Williams and Chrisman's but replicates much of its material, if in a
different contextual form. The titles for the three main frames, 'Shifting
Terrains', 'Disciplining Knowledge' and 'Locating Practice', give the

uninitiated reader little indication of what material, subject-matter or critical approach he or she might expect to discover in the essays. Nor does the introduction provide much help, although Mongia does undertake a rather cursory attempt to clarify postcolonial theory's methodology and object of study, tracing its development in terms of a series of recent sociohistorical processes (e.g. globalisation) and as a collective response to the growing awareness that 'the political concepts that have shaped modern history – democracy, the citizen, nationalism – no longer seem adequate for coping with contemporary realities' (Mongia 1996: 5). Mongia's reader is perhaps most useful for the ways in which it reflects on the increasing self-referentiality of postcolonial discourse (see also next section), and on the metropolitan 'success story' of contemporary postcolonial products – of which her own reader is another example – whose effective marketing depends on strategies of domestication and the selective monitoring of intellectually fashionable goods (Mongia 1996: 9). None of these goods is more fashionable, of course, than 'theory' itself as a commodified marker of the academy's alleged engagement with its own institutional methods and critical tools. Mongia's reader, although lacking the range and analytical depth of Williams and Chrisman's, provides the valuable service of turning postcolonial theory on its own institutional axis, showing how postcolonial texts work both to certify their own political engagement and to validate forms of intellectual inquiry that risk becoming complicit in the perpetration of a new academic authoritarianism or, as Gayatri Spivak has called it, a 'new orientalism' (Spivak 1993a: 56, qtd in Mongia 1996: 9; see also Introduction).

Mongia's reader might be seen as marking the bifurcation between postcolonial *theory* and postcolonial *literature* that has accompanied the emergence of postcolonial studies as an institutionalised cultural field. Williams and Chrisman's reader – with some exceptions – pays little more than lip-service to literature; Mongia's reader barely mentions it at all – save the essay by Ahmad, which in any case raises the admittedly problematic category of 'postcolonial literature' only to dismiss it, and reductively at that as an unwanted analogue of those variegated designations of cultural otherness ' "multiculturalism" and "minority literature", even "Third World literature", [which suggest that] in at least one of the many nuances, "postcolonial" is simply a polite way of saying not-white, not-Europe, or perhaps not-Europe-but-inside-Europe' (Ahmad 1995a: 8, also qtd in Mongia 1996: 282).

Given increasing if perhaps exaggerated claims that literary studies is being marginalised within postcolonial criticism, it is good to encounter a reader like Ashcroft, Griffiths and Tiffin's which recognises explicitly that theory and literature are not mutually exclusive. While showing a certain degree of suspicion toward the reification of postcolonial theory in the Western academy – '*The Post-Colonial Studies Reader* is not a collection of theorists, but of ideas; it is not interested in establishing a canon of theories or theorists but in indicating something of the great scope, the rich heterogeneity and vast energy of the field of postcolonial studies' (1995: xvi) – Ashcroft, Griffiths and Tiffin produce a suitably wide-ranging selection of excerpted pieces by creative writers as well as professional critics, and by writers who in many cases double as critics (Wilson Harris, Kamau Brathwaite and Chinua Achebe, among several others), and whose imaginative work converges with their 'non-fictional' criticism in devolving theoretical precepts and political goals.[25]

Ashcroft, Griffiths and Tiffin's reader is undoubtedly well organised, accessible to readers of different competencies and particularly well designed to engage postcolonial students and teachers interested in exploring interdisciplinary approaches to the field. It shows greater geographical range than either of its rival contemporary readers, finding ample space for the contributions of 'settler discourse' – largely missing from Williams and Chrisman's reader – to the postcolonial field. Like Mongia's reader, it is alert to the constitutive role played by educational ideology and institutional practice in the perpetuation of imperial power, arguing in its final section (as I have throughout this book) that the:

> wider sociological dimension of postcolonial … studies [is] urgently in need of address at the present time, and the pieces we reproduce here are intended as much to stimulate the production of more current assessments of the material conditions of cultural production and consumption in post-colonial societies as they are authoritative accounts of the present situation.
>
> (Ashcroft *et al.* 1995: 463)

The decision to use excerpts, however, is likely to prove frustrating for many of the reader's users, merely reinforcing the potential for decontex-tualisation of which the editors are aware, and for which the field itself has become – I would still say unfairly – known. The excerpting of key texts reinforces editorial authority while fostering the 'metonymic fallacy' (see also Chapter 2) that persists within the field. Bite-sized chunks of knowledge substitute for larger arguments; the reader thus risks standing in for what it intends to stimulate – further research – plying a trade instead in aphoristic position-takings within the context of a self-ingratiating postcolonial citation cartel (Schulze-Engler 1998). In a sense, however, it is hardly fair to blame the editors for encouraging intellectual condensation when it is one of the primary functions of the reader as genre to provide the type of abbreviated insights that are more likely to promote citational fluency than they are to inculcate disciplinary knowledge. The reader's 'culturalist' approach aids and abets the condensation process by implying that the texts it reproduces are symptoms of the larger sociopolitical dilemmas they address. Meanwhile, the consecrating function of the reader helps generate further cultural capital for those fortunate enough to be included in it, creating precisely the kind of sanctioned hierarchy – the 'noncanonical canon' of approved representative figures – that practitioners of postcolonial studies, in their critical analyses of imperialism's self-perpetuating mechanisms of justification and legitimation, have made it their business to contest. It is the genre of the reader, perhaps, that most clearly illustrates the contradictions in postcolonialism's own particular conception of the pedagogic imaginary. On the one hand, texts and writers from different countries and different historical periods are gathered together as a representative corpus pressed into the service of an explicitly politicised, anti-authoritarian 'pedagogy of the oppressed' (Freire 1973); on the other, these texts and writers, sampled as it were for quickfire consumption, circulate as commodities within a symbolic economy that replicates the strategies of mastery and exclusion that are the field's primary pedagogic objects of address.

The question of theory

The consumer appeal of postcolonial studies is enhanced, meanwhile, by the scope the field apparently allows for methodological eclecticism – an eclecticism nowhere more apparent than in that seemingly random assemblage of philosophical insight, political analysis and cultural critique that falls under the rubric of 'postcolonial theory'. 'Theoretical' questions concerning the conceptual boundaries as well as practical limits of imperial power, agency and authority have been acknowledged for some time now as being at the centre of the postcolonial field. At the same time, postcolonial scholars have recognised the need to question 'theory' itself as an instrument of intellectual mastery and as a paradoxical medium for the maintenance of institutional hierarchies, even as it posits a challenge to critical standards and the academic *status quo*. Too much has been made, perhaps, of the allegedly obfuscatory rhetoric of some of the leading exponents of postcolonial theory,[26] not enough of the specific institutional effects that the development of postcolonial theory has produced. Two overlapping effects can be briefly recapitulated here: *self-referentiality* and the reduplication of theoretical precepts, and the development of *critical orthodoxies* mediated through celebrity figures.

As previously suggested, a certain defensiveness on the part of post-colonial theorists and critics has been part of the price the field has paid for achieving increasing institutional visibility. This defensiveness has manifested itself in the recourse to theoretical self-reflexivity, of which the most extreme example is the placing of the term 'postcolonial' itself under erasure; in a somewhat self-righteous insistence on the emancipatory pedagogic implications of postcolonial studies; and in the dependence on a small number of what might uncharitably be described as postcolonial guru-figures, who are enjoined to provide intellectual leadership for an emergent cultural field. This last effect has arguably led, at best, to the uncritical acceptance of such politico-theoretical configurations as the Third Space (Bhabha 1994c) and Orientalism (Said 1978), or to the mystification of such historically specific representational processes as cultural 'othering' (Spivak 1987). At worst, it might be said, it has encouraged the creation of a kind of theoretical hall of mirrors where the self-perpetuating manoeuvres of the field risk collapsing into elaborate self-parody, with the familiar names and terms being chanted mantra-like in support of the latest critical arguments, and innovative thought taking second place to an expedient, and potentially endless, rehearsal of intellectual rehearsals. Potted summaries of the work of the three leading-lights of postcolonial theory – Homi Bhabha, Edward Said and Gayatri Spivak – have by now become a staple in the type of introductory survey designed to provide coverage of the major issues in the field (see, for example, Childs and Williams 1997; Gandhi 1998; Moore-Gilbert 1997). Ania Loomba wryly notes that one of the results of the recent boom in postcolonial studies has been 'that essays by a handful of name-brand critics have become more important than the field itself – students feel the pressure to "do" Edward Said, Gayatri Spivak or Homi Bhabha or to read only the very latest article' (Loomba 1998: xv). She blames this state of affairs in part on what Barbara Christian has called the 'race for theory', the unseemly scramble for intellectual legitimacy that has accompanied the widespread commodification of theory at Western universities, resulting in a specialised 'language of control' that is 'as hegemonic as the world which it attacks', and that ironically emerged at precisely the moment 'when the literature of peoples of color, of black women, of Latin Americans, of Africans began to move to "the center" ' (Christian 1990: 41).[27] Loomba identifies a further cause in the blandishments of the Western – particularly the US – academic star system, which conveys the impression that rewards can be reaped from the superficial consumption, rather than critical comprehension, of the theoretical work of a small number of (self-)appointed celebrity critics – work all the more readily accepted because it is seen, often appealingly so, as mystifying or intimidatingly difficult, and which students may be reluctant to challenge 'because they … lack expertise in colonial and postcolonial histories and cultures' (Loomba 1998: xvi).[28]

It is difficult not to be sympathetic to Loomba's and Christian's arguments, particularly given the frequent mismatch between broad theoretical ambition and specific cross-cultural competence that has legitimately been seen as compromising postcolonial studies, both as university teaching subject and as academic research field (Suleri 1992a). As I have suggested in this book, a link can be traced between the fetishised appreciation for famous authors and celebrity critics and the development of a global alterity industry in which the commodified signs of cultural otherness become a currency to be negotiated and traded by metropolitan interest groups (see Introduction). Postcolonial theory, in this context, risks mystifying not only the social, historical and economic circumstances of imperial encounter it seeks to abstract from, but also the specific material conditions underlying its own institutional development – the very conditions of its own existence. The metalanguages of 'theory' might thus be seen as providing a measure of ideological self-protection, even as the insights they devolve work toward eroding the authority of established critical practices and historical truths. Protection is sought in the creation of a self-enclosing affiliative network in which the intellectual validity of any given theoretical project consists in its ability to cross-reference other, preferably canonical, theoretical works. Stephen Slemon and Helen Tiffin, in scorning the craven 'citational obedience' of Euro-American high theory, are remarkably charitable in seeing *postcolonial* theory as having largely avoided such 'filiative footnoting enterprise', and as having refused to 'surrender the agency of resistance to the power of Western intellectual systems' (Slemon and Tiffin 1989: xii, xix). But even they are forced to admit that postcolonial theory has not always been innocent of 'turn[ing] its travelling eye towards the Others of Empire and baldly appropriat[ing] their cultural labour to its own cognitive uses' (Slemon and Tiffin 1989: xvi). Postcolonial theory, seen this way, contributes toward the further exoticisation of 'non-Western' peoples and cultures whose material disadvantages are converted into symbolic capital under theory's imperialist sway. However, to see postcolonial theory *only* in this way is to underestimate its capacity to open up new epistemological horizons, thereby 'open[ing] the door to an enormously enabling critique of power in all of its social locations' (Slemon and Tiffin 1989: xiv). After all, postcolonial theory – theory in general – serves as an effective, if somewhat incalculable, unsettling agency; as Jonathan Culler remarks in the opening chapter of his introduction to *Literary Theory* (1997),

The nature of theory is to undo, through a contesting of premises and postulates, what you thought you knew, so the effects of theory are not predictable. You have not become master, but neither are you where you were before. You reflect on your reading in new ways. You have different questions to ask and a better sense of the implications of the questions you put to works you read.

(Culler 1997: 17)

Culler's definition – not surprisingly given his deconstructionist sympathies – appears to gesture toward a form of politicised poststructuralism in which the potential to 'undo' theoretical postulates is linked to the capacity for anti-authoritarian critique. Postcolonial theory, similarly, might be seen as the provisional attempt to forge a working alliance between the – often Marxist-inspired – politics of anti-colonial resistance, exemplified in the liberationist tracts of Fanon, Césaire and Memmi, and the disparate, allegedly destabilising poststructuralisms of Derrida, Lacan, Althusser and Foucault.[29] This alliance, perhaps understandably, has not always proved particularly successful, prompting widespread criticism of the incompatibility of Marxism's and poststructuralism's respective modes of analysis (Ahmad 1992; Larsen 1995; San Juan 1998; Lazarus 1999), as well as the occasional, more virulent outcry against pampered academics' methodological preference for 'poststructuralist ... language games, few of which recognize the political struggles of real peoples outside such discursive frontiers' (Tapping 1990: 58, also qtd in Slemon and Tiffin 1989: xi). Poststructuralism, at worst, has been accused of favouring a thoroughly Western 'postmodern problematic [which then] becomes the frame through which the cultural products of the rest of the world are seen' (Sangari 1987: 183–4). As Kumkum Sangari points out, 'the postmodern preoccupation with the crisis of meaning is not everyone's crisis' (Sangari 1987: 184); while the 'suspension of the referent', another postmodern/poststructuralist axiom, has arguably succeeded only in occluding worldwide struggles for political agency, and in legitimising 'a wholesale retreat from geography and history into a domain of pure "textuality" in which the principle of indeterminacy smothers the possibility of social or political "significance" for literature [as a whole]' (Slemon and Tiffin 1989: x).

Such critiques, while by now familiar, have by no means lost their legitimacy, even if several of them share a tendency toward strategically reductive interpretations of either poststructuralism, or postmodernism, or both, that has ironically become one of the major 'space-clearing gestures' (Appiah 1992: 149) by which postcolonial studies has claimed validity *for itself* as a politically engaged academic field.[30] Like many postcolonial critics, I see the tension between – broadly speaking – Marxist and poststructuralist theories in postcolonial studies less as a sign of methodological incoherence than as further evidence of the field's unresolved attempt to reconcile political activism and cultural critique. This attempt comes to the fore in manifesto-like declarations of the *ethical* grounding of postcolonial criticism: in Kwame Anthony Appiah's unfashionable, but moving, assertion of postcolonial writers' humanist concern in the face of global suffering (Appiah 1992: 155); in Robert Young's endorsement of postcolonial critique as an embodiment of international accountability in the face of global injustice (Young 2000). This defence of the ethical purchase of postcolonial studies is naturally of vital importance in the continuing attempt to secure the field for radical cultural critique. Nonetheless, the (meta)level at which the claim is made suggests that the field is to some extent held ransom by its recurrent need for self-justification – its need to rethink, as well as refine, its own political aims and objectives; to critically analyse, as well as consolidate, its own institutional alliances and affiliations.[31] A constitutive tension thus exists within postcolonial theory, as within the postcolonial field itself, between 'revisionary force' and 'institutional containment' (Bhabha 1994c); between the stated aims of a radical criticism that seeks, in Patrick Williams' words, to 'understand ... and enable opposition to the globalizing operations of capitalism' (Williams 1999: 284) and the underlying recognition that the field is condemned to inhabit, and to a degree sustain, the system it sets out to critique.

In this section, I have tried to suggest that postcolonial studies is situated within the context of a utopian pedagogic imaginary that simultaneously recognises that the institutional constraints placed upon its political effectiveness may in fact form part of the field's attractiveness – and its wider commercial appeal. Hence it seems impractical to suggest, as Arif Dirlik has done recently, that the field should be divided between 'a critical postcolonialism that is heir to radical legacies of the past' and 'a postcolonialism that is barely distinguishable from the contemporary ideologies of power and represents the hijacking of alternatives for the social imaginary of globalization' (Dirlik 1999: 287). Such Orwellian distinctions – 'critical' postcolonialism good, 'ideological' postcolonialism bad – risk merely replicating the binary patterns of some earlier anti-colonial criticism, displacing these on to a new set of global conditions in which 'the postcolonial' is more likely to be construed as 'post-national and post-revolutionary'; as 'locat[ing] itself in diasporic formations rather than settled societies'; and as 'nourish[ing] itself from the globalization both of capital and culture' (Dirlik 1999: 289). The idea of wresting a revolutionary 'critical' postcolonialism from the clutches of global-capitalist enterprise is perhaps no more than a saving illusion. But as I have suggested throughout this book, anti-imperialist resistance is not necessarily diminished when 'resistance' itself is inserted into global-capitalist networks of cultural consumption. Rather, at least two different regimes regulating the *value* of resistance enter into mutual conflict. The postcolonial exotic, as a semiotic field, exists at the intersection of these regimes of value; and as in other such fields, the signs it generates are subject to a struggle for regulation and control. This struggle, while it takes place at the level of symbolic exchange, is obviously influenced by material factors, some of which I have sought to analyse in previous chapters of this book. The cultural capital generated and accumulated within the postcolonial field of production is clearly subject to market forces, forces largely responsible for producing the effects of the exotic mentioned in the previous pages (mystification of the cultural other; fetishisation of cultural difference; collapsing of the field into those who are seen as controlling, or being controlled by, global interests; and so on). Yet it is equally obvious, first, that the global market is by no means the only market; and, second, that the market itself may be a valuable source of creative cross-cultural ferment. As Amitava Kumar has recently argued, there is 'a logic of the marketplace that is able to contest both the limits of the nation-state and the global hegemony of the World Bank and the interests it represents' (Kumar 1999: 202). Regional markets, in particular, are loci of 'cross-cultural fertilization [that] pose a serious challenge to globalization and to the structural adjustments advocated by the World Bank and other multinational corporations vying to recolonize Africa [and other postcolonial regions]' (Diawara 1998: 142, qtd in Kumar 1999: 202). Such markets arguably hold the balance between local needs and global interests that Kumar sees as providing a more profitable future, both for postcolonial studies and for the neocolonial world in which it functions and which it seeks, however indirectly, to transform. If the postcolonial exotic is – in some ways – the stifling product of homogenising market forces, it also needs to be seen, like the market itself, as an agent of productive destabilisation and welcome change. And if postcolonial studies is – to some degree – constrained by the exoticist machinery of representations in which it is made to operate, it still has the potential to turn that machinery against itself, adapting it for future use.

Coda: postcolonial Tintin

The popularity of Tintin appears to have reached new levels in Europe, culminating in the recent consecration of the globe-trotting Belgian cartoon-character as 1999 European Icon of the Year. No doubt more surprising is to discover the cult of Tintin in Black Africa – the stereo-typical 'Dark Continent' derided in Hergé's colonialist fictions. Yet by all accounts Tintin is alive and well in this unlikeliest of places. A friend of mine, recently returned from Senegal, brought back a clutch of two-foot 'Tintins', purchased from a store in Dakar that specialises in reproductions of the pint-sized hero. One of these he gave to me, and it stands, colonial sentinel, on my desk as I sit writing my latest academic treatise on the 'postcolonial condition'. It stands looking at me now, its eyebrows arched in mock-inquiry. What, the figure seems to be saying, do *I* have to do with 'the postcolonial'? Surely, my presence here is proof that colonialism has never been 'posted' (Aidoo 1972); that Europeans have never tired of seeing their own reflected image, or of collecting trophies of their own world-beating, native-dominating past? Surely I, 'Tintin', am a sign of the durability of colonial fantasy; and of its *profitability*, its continuing usefulness to all those new imperialists who are currently manipulating the resources of the global tourist industry? But, says my snub-nosed friend, look at my face; look at my colour. Consider who made me. Who is it that my mimicry empowers: is it you, white man, white tourist; or is it perhaps my makers, who understand the symbolic profits to be gained from fashioning likenesses – but *different* likenesses – of me?

My African 'Tintin' (see cover photograph) affords an unusual example of what Christopher Steiner calls African 'tourist art' (Steiner 1994) – the kind of art, often mass-produced, that ostensibly caters to white colonialist sensibilities, but that sometimes subtly undercuts them, turning the stereotypes on their heads.[32] The language of African tourist art is wilfully exotic; it trades for the most part in primitive tropes and in a hypercommodified 'native authenticity'. While simulating a regional distinctiveness, African tourist art is clearly geared to the global market. As such, it is symptomatic of the convergence between 'postmodern' and 'postcolonial' moments; it is caught between the demands of a transna-tional consumer public and the need to decolonise cultural production in a post-independence (not 'post-imperial') age. It is the hybrid semiosis generated by this convergence that constitutes the symbolic field I have been referring to throughout this book as the 'postcolonial exotic'.

By examining distinctive features and discursive effects of the post-colonial exotic, this book has attempted to show the inextricable connection between the production of 'the postcolonial' and the globalisation of consumer society. The postcolonial exotic represents the interface between two apparently incompatible systems – the oppositional system of postcolonial resistance and the profit-driven system of the transnational culture industries and global trade. Arising from the clash between these two contending systems is a series of exotically hybridised or, perhaps better, 'transculturated' products.[33] These products, as with 'Tintin', are either outrightly commercial or, as with the novels of Rushdie and Roy (see Chapter 2), well aware of their commercial viability. The postcolonial exotic is an effect of commodification, but it is not simply reducible to the cultural logic of consumer capital (Jameson 1991). In a sense, it might be seen as a congeries of strategic exoticisms, designed to show the workings of the globalised alterity industry and to repoliticise exotic categories of the cultural other as an unsettling force. Still, the postcolonial exotic suggests in the end that attempts to create or maintain a categorical distinction between the 'postcolonial' and the 'postmodern' are likely to be ill-fated. The language of resistance is entangled, like it or not, in the language of commerce; the anti-colonial in the neocolonial; postcolonialism in postcoloniality. What remains – in this context at least – is to lay bare the workings of commodification; for the postcolonial exotic is both a form of commodity fetishism *and* a revelation of the process by which 'exotic' commodities are produced, exchanged, consumed; it is both a mode of consumption *and* an analysis of consumption. Cultural products operating under the sign of this 'exotic' are likely to raise the challenging question: what really is exotic about me? My 'Tintin' asks that question, eyebrows raised in obvious mischief: 'so, you find me exotic; and what does that say, my friend, about *you?*'

Notes

Introduction: writing at the margins

1 See, for example, Stephen Slemon's 1994 essay 'The Scramble for Postcoloni-alism', in which he admits that postcolonialism is often now seen as

> an object of desire for critical practice: as a shimmering talisman that in itself has the power to confer political legitimacy onto specific forms of institutionalized labour, especially on ones that are troubled by their mediated position within the apparatus of institutional power.
>
> (Slemon 1994: 17)

For Slemon, however, this is only one possible view of postcolonialism, which might equally well be seen as

> a way of ordering a critique of totalizing forms of Western historicism; as a portmanteau term for a retooled notion of 'class'; as a subset of both postmodernism and post-structuralism (and conversely, as the condition from which those two structures of cultural logic and cultural critique themselves are seen to emerge); as the name for a condition of nativist longing in post-independence national groupings; as a cultural marker of non-residency for a Third World intellectual cadre; as the inevitable underside of a fractured and ambivalent discourse of coloni-alist power; as an oppositional form of 'reading practice'; and ... as the name for a category of 'literary' activity which sprang from a new and welcome political energy going on within what used to be called 'Commonwealth' literary studies.
>
> (Slemon 1994: 16)

Further perspectives still could be offered; the important point here is that there is a link between the heterogeneity inherent in the concept of the 'postcolonial' and its instrumentality for a variety of institutional and, no less, commercial purposes.

2 As Terry Eagleton has noted recently in the journal *Interventions*, dissatisfaction with the term 'postcolonial' has become a *sine qua non* of postcolonial criticism,

to the extent that postcolonial critics often feel obliged to make elaborate disclaimers in order to protect the integrity of their work (Eagleton 1999: 24).

3 For the case both for and against poststructuralism, see Stephen Slemon and Helen Tiffin's useful introduction to the collection of essays *After Europe: Critical Theory and Post-Colonial Writing* (1989); for more recent, also more critical views, see the work of Ahmad (1992, 1995a) and Dirlik (1994, 1999).

4 For detailed critiques of Bourdieu, see Robbins (1993) and, particularly, Frow (1995).

5 The difference between these two terms has itself often been narrowed into intangibility. For my purposes here, I will maintain the – admittedly tenuous – distinction between postmodernism as both a particular, self-consciously derivative style and a periodising concept linked to late multinational capitalism, the society of the spectacle and Western consumer culture (Jameson 1983), and postmodernity as a global condition characterised by the increasing power of the market over all facets of everyday life (Harvey 1989).

6 A similar argument is made in the context of Native American writing by Julia Emberley in her book *Thresholds of Difference* (1993). For Emberley, postcolonial discourse is of a piece with a postmodern society of the spectacle in which 'images, re-presentations, "authenticities", and "the experience of marginality" circulate as the currency of exchange' (Emberley 1993: 163). For further thoughts on Emberley's work, see below; see also Chapter 6.

7 In his most recent work, Dirlik seems to have backtracked slightly from his previous hard-line position, allowing (at least conceptually) for the possibility of distinguishing between a 'critical postcolonialism' that applies the radical lessons of a previous generation of anti-colonial thinkers (Fanon, Césaire, James, etc.) to the neo-imperial present and an 'ideological postcolonialism' that continues to produce 'a de-historicized, de-spatialized form of knowledge that is readily available for appropriation into contemporary institutions of power' (Dirlik 1999: 288). For a critique of this position, see the Conclusion to this book.

8 The problem of *location* remains central, as it must, to postcolonial criticism. The ubiquitousness of 'travelling theory' in postcolonial criticism – and its appearance in a good deal of postcolonial literature – sometimes suggests a romanticisation of such terms as 'exile', 'migrancy' and 'diaspora' that flies in the face of contemporary socioeconomic realities. For an excellent critique of the occluded privilege in some versions of postcolonial 'travelling theory', see Krishnaswamy (1995); for a balanced view of the advantages, as well as dilemmas, experienced by modern postcolonial intellectuals, see also Brennan (1997).

9 See also a fairly recent essay in the journal *Postcolonial Studies* by Simon During (1998), in which he argues convincingly for a more nuanced understanding of globalisation and of its dialectical relation to a variety of contemporary postcolonial resistance movements. And as Amitava Kumar argues, equally convincingly, in an essay in *College Literature* (1999), the future of postcolonial studies itself may be contingent on a closer understanding of how globalising (market) forces act both to constrain and to enable the type of critical work for which the field is known and with which it seeks to engage in the wider world (see also Conclusion).

10 On the conflicting ideological agendas of exoticism, see Arac and Ritvo (1991), Bongie (1991), Rousseau and Porter (1990) and Todorov (1993). As Rousseau and Porter argue in their introduction to a collection of essays, *Exoticism in the Enlightenment* (1990), exoticist discourses have alternately served as critical weapons directed against 'universal monopolies in religious

truth and legitimate authority' (1990: 12) and as alibis for the colonial interventions of a civilisation – Enlightenment Europe's – that 'increasingly assumed the right to define [and differentiate] human values and conduct in their highest expression' (1990: 6). On the capacity of exoticist discourses to disguise the violence toward which they have historically, if indirectly, contributed, see Mason (1996), Todorov (1993) and, particularly, Arac and Ritvo (1991); see also below.

11 The apparent interchangeability of 'exotic' merchandise on the contemporary world market might be taken as signifying the 'end of exoticism' *per se* as a historically specified system for the articulation of cultural difference. But in fact, as Todorov (1993) shows, exoticism has always been as much about creating likenesses as it has been about identifying differences; in addition, as Bongie (1991) suggests, exoticist discourses have tended to emerge at moments of extreme historical anxiety, partly as a means of gesturing back toward a time or place simultaneously recognised as lost. Exotica thus flourished at around the time when it was feared that the Empire might have ceded its authority; and it is perhaps no surprise that a new wave of (generic) exotica has appeared at the turn of the millennium (Gallini 1996). 'End-of-exoticism' arguments abound (see, for example, Roberts, forthcoming) as symptoms of the fear of increasing global-cultural homogenisation; in fact, it might be more accurate to say that exoticism has *reinvigorated* itself in response to the latest – by no means 'post-imperial' – global conditions.

12 Suleri comes close here to subscribing to what Edward Said has called 'cultural insiderism' (Said 1986): the often mistaken assumption that, say, South Asian (or even South Asian-*born*) critics necessarily know more about South Asian literatures and cultures than Anglo-Americans who batten onto such fields out of a mixture of curiosity and professional interest. Suleri is justifiably worried about the lack of cultural and, above all, historical knowledge displayed by many postcolonial critics; ironically, her self-exemption here – like that of Arun Mukherjee (see Conclusion) – risks merely reinforcing the view, *itself exoticist*, of 'postcolonials' as privileged disseminators, spokespersons as it were, of local cultural knowledge.

13 For a lucid discussion of the connections between exoticism, colonialism and fetishism, see Bongie 1991: esp. 99–106; see also Bhabha's Lacanian approach to the construction of the colonial stereotype in several of his essays, notably 'The Other Question' (Bhabha 1994e).

14 The famous lines in *Capital* have attracted enough commentary for me to forego further explication here. For a recent, helpful attempt to combine psychoanalytic and Marxist approaches to the fetish, see the Introduction to Brantlinger (1996). For a series of brilliant analyses of the implications of commodity fetishism in the contemporary world order, see also Appadurai (1986), esp. Appadurai's own Introduction.

15 See, for example, Sangari's passionately argued view that postmodernism, in alliance with poststructuralism, contracts the world into a narrowly Eurocentric perspective, so that 'the postmodern problematic becomes *the* frame through which the cultural products of the rest of the world are seen' (Sangari 1987: 183; see also Conclusion). As Sangari justifiably complains, the commonly accepted view that 'late capitalism muffles the globe and homogenizes (or threatens to) all cultural production' is 'one "master narrative" that is seldom dismantled as it needs to be if the differential economic, class, and cultural formation of "Third World" countries is to be taken into account' (1987: 184).

16 For different perspectives on the postmodernism/postcolonialism debate, see the essays in Adam and Tiffin (1990), particularly the testy exchange between Brydon and Hutcheon, in which each appears to misread the other. For a time, particularly in the late 1980s and early 1990s, dissociation from post-modernism became a defining move of postcolonial criticism (see Conclusion); this time is now arguably over, although the debate continues, inevitably unresolved.

17 'Third Space' theories have become by now irritatingly prevalent in postcolonial theory, in part as a result of Bhabha's consecration as a (or even *the*) postcolonial thinker. There are other reasons: the instrumentality of the 'Third Space' as a metaphorical medium – a *tertium quid* – for oppositional criticism; the continuing appeal of poststructuralist approaches to literary analysis and cultural critique; the scope the 'Third Space' allows for despatial-ised arguments centring on the culturally hybridised *city* both as a privileged locus of sociopolitical transformation and, no less important, as the predomi-nant (some might say hegemonic) site of literary and critical production. For further thoughts both on 'Third Space' theory and Bhabha's function as a celebrity theorist/critic, see Conclusion.

18 There is no denying that the autobiographical streak in Spivak's writing is one of its most interesting facets; it is not surprising, in this context, that the collection of interviews, *The Post-Colonial Critic* (1990b), is perhaps Spivak's most helpful (and certainly most accessible) contribution to current postcolo-nial debates. While Spivak's much-imitated tendency to take up positions that reflect, as well as react against, her own institutional privilege is both salutary and honest, it does not seem coincidental that she and her work, as the aforementioned title implies, have often been taken as symptomatic. Spivak – or perhaps more accurately, the Spivak industry – has thus subscribed to the very phenomenon against which she herself has been ritually warning: the collapsing of the postcolonial field into a handful of exemplary interpret-ers/informants/spokespersons, and the metonymic association of these institu-tionalised figures with the 'postcolonial condition' as a whole. For further thoughts on this phenomenon, see Conclusion; see also Chapter 2 for a brief analysis of the 'metonymic fallacy' in postcolonial texts.

19 English remains, of course, the primary – some would see it as the exclusive – language of postcolonial studies, prompting numerous arguments that post-colonial critics have failed to practise what they preach. This type of argu-ment, ominously well founded, has resurfaced in the most recent postcolonial journals, notably in Harish Trivedi's polemical accusation (in *Interventions*) that 'the postcolonial has ears only for English' (1999: 272). For a further consideration of the Anglocentric biases of postcolonial theory and criticism, see Conclusion; see also Chapter 2 for a discussion of Salman Rushdie's astonishing assertion that the English-language literature produced by (mostly diasporic) Indians in the post-independence period is superior to that pro-duced in India's other languages – most of which Rushdie himself cannot read.

20 For useful discussions of this dilemma, see Brennan (1997: 36–63) and, particularly, Ahmad (1992: 78–81).

21 On the demand for authenticity, see Root (1996: 69–70); Minh-ha (1989) and, in the more specific context of the reception of Aboriginal writing, Chapter 6 of this book.

22 On the ironies that accrue to construction as a postcolonial 'native informant', see Spivak (who of course has to some extent constructed herself

as one). Spivak's ironic deployment of the anthropological trope is, as ever, strategic; for further thoughts on the instrumentality of anthropological terminology for postcolonial studies, see Chapter 1 of this book.

23 It could, and probably will, be argued that that is precisely what this book is doing. However, I see one of the aims of this book as being to show the effects of metropolitan mediation both on the reception of postcolonial literary/cultural products and on the development of postcolonial studies as an institutionalised academic field. To argue this, as I do, from a Western (if not a major) metropolitan location is to risk being accused of merely perpetuating the phenomenon I am critically analysing (see also Preface). On one level, this is of course true. On another, however, it is never enough simply to admit one's own, or others', complicity; nor is it enough simply to imagine that by dealing, say, with less well-known writers and critics that one has 'escaped' the self-replicating commodity circuits within which postcolonial writers and critics are undeniably caught. Postcolonialism's involvement with global commodity culture is, after all, the subject of this book; the contention that the project is entangled in this entanglement, while in itself legitimate, does not seem particularly useful in this context.

1 African literature and the anthropological exotic

1 Recent and not-so-recent attacks by African writers on censorship and the systematic state repression of writers and other artists indicate a further, internally generated reason for the underdevelopment of the arts in many post-independence African nations. Wole Soyinka, for example, has written that:

> [t]here must be few independent African countries today that have not experienced the truncation of their artistic and intellectual potential in the process of nation building. Some governments have been merely episodic in their execution of cultural repression ... [while others] have been more systematic, their mechanics built into the very definition of government, into the relationship between the ruler and the ruled.
> (Soyinka 1990: 112)

As a prime example of the latter, Soyinka points to the case of Malawi, which has banned so many African literary works that it becomes impossible to know 'what African books are actually read' there (1991: 113), and which has installed a pseudo-British public educational system 'in order to create a British-educated elite to administer the nation along the manners of the old colonial masters' (1991: 113). Meanwhile, Soyinka himself has been among the victims of state repression in Nigeria, which temporarily lost its Commonwealth status after the execution of one of its premier writers, Ken Saro-Wiwa.

2 An exception to the general rule is the relatively large body of work on the publishing industry in Nigeria: see, for example, Bello and Augi (1993) and, most recently, Griswold (2000).

3 The pages of the *African Book Publishing Record*, edited by Hans Zell, do not make for particularly happy reading. Despite the periodic announcement of new (often foreign-funded) initiatives in the African publishing industry, the journal's entries tend to return to the same overriding issues and concerns: the

continuing stranglehold of the multinationals; the chronic lack of resources and the incompatibility of existing materials with local needs and interests; the poor quality of book production; the ambivalent role of international sponsors – 'Northern co-publishers', development agencies and, above all, the World Bank – in supporting local projects; and the premium placed by African writers on publishing abroad.

4 For a recent perspective on this dilemma, see di Leonardo (1998: 306–7). As di Leonardo, an American anthropologist, suggests, the discipline is in crisis because it has 'failed to communicate to the public how the understanding that there *are* no "people without history" utterly changes how we envision Others' (1998: 307). Contemporary anthropologists are hindered by a popular perception of their work as reconfirming the 'timeless essences' of the peoples/cultures they study – a perception fuelled, in some cases, by the work of anthropologists of earlier generations. Ironically, it is not just that anthropology is often viewed as being in league with exoticism, but that anthropologists themselves are correspondingly dehistoricised, seen (as in the title of di Leonardo's book) as 'exotics at home'. Di Leonardo's passionate diagnosis deserves to be quoted at length:

> At every turn, the dead hand of the ethnographic present constrains progressive anthropologists from articulating intelligent perspectives on Others' – everyone's – lives. Attempting to counter the horrors of the 'raiders of the lost ark' frame, we are forced into unwitting impersonations of technicians of the sacred, and thus into complicity with an essentializing, ahistorical perspective that leads us right back into the global pool hall with the (often sociobiological) human nature experts. Schooled by American Anthropology past, the public sphere cannot 'read' scholarly commentators' careful historicizations of Others' lives, and so popular representations of Samoa parallel the 'timeless' Kalahari and other fictions of 'primitive' human lives. ... What anthropologists have done to the !Kung San and Samoans and so many others has been brought home, deservedly, to anthropology. We are Difference, Otherness, Essence, the Once and Future Anthropologists. ... Anthropology is always the same, and primitives have no history. We are all Stone Age Nisa, all timeless Samoans – exotics at home.
>
> (1998: 307)

5 For a more detailed discussion of the case against anthropology in colonial Africa, see Adotevi (1972); for a partial rehabilitation, see Falk Moore (1993) and, particularly, James (1972). For other useful discussions of the ambivalent role of anthropology in both supporting and critiquing colonial authority in Black Africa, see Mudimbe (1988) and the essays in Asad (1972); see also the work of Said (1989) and Minh-ha (1989) – neither of whom has any formal anthropological training – for their influential, if somewhat tendentious, critiques of anthropological 'master narratives'. See also Note 7 below.

6 For an example of *bolekaja* criticism, so named after Nigeria's system of aggressive transport touting, see Chinweizu *et al.*'s memorable tirade in their book *Toward the Decolonization of African Literature* (1983) against interfering Western critics, who are told in no uncertain terms to 'keep [their] hegemonic hands off African literature' (Chinweizu *et al.* 1983: 302).

7 Just how new the New Anthropology is is a matter of some contention within the discipline (see, for example, Marcus and Fischer 1986). The New Anthropology, which is arguably marked by a greater degree of disciplinary self-reflexivity and by an attention to the textuality – the rhetorical constructed-ness – of ethnography, is no doubt open to misunderstanding partly because it has become the object of attention for literary/cultural studies' scholars from *outside* the field. For a blistering response to ill-conceived, but increasingly fashionable, attacks on anthropology from outside the discipline, see di Leonardo (1998: 43–50). See also Note 4 above.

8 On the damaging cumulative effect of several centuries of distorted European representations of Africa, see Hammond and Jablow (1977); see also Mudimbe (1988), who argues convincingly that European discourses of/about Africa, including those derived from anthropology, contributed to nothing less than the *invention* of a 'Dark Continent' that served European psychosexual desires and expansionist needs.

9 The notion that postcolonial literatures devolve both deconstructive and recuperative readings is taken from Ashcroft *et al.* (1989), particularly the opening chapter. The tension between deconstructionist theories and the politics of indigenous self-empowerment is central to continuing debates on the political effectiveness of postcolonial criticism: for further reflections on these debates, see the concluding chapter of this book.

10 For both the theory and the practice of 'contrapuntal' modes of critical reading, see Said (1993). My use of the word 'counter-discourse' here is derived in part from Helen Tiffin, who uses it (via Richard Terdiman) to examine the ways in which postcolonial writers have responded to and creatively transformed the canonised work of their European precursors (Tiffin 1987). For an attempt to apply this term to anthropological, as well as literary, 'classics', see also Huggan (1994a). The notion of 'counter-discourse' remains useful in postcolonial studies, even if it has spawned a whole school of 'writing-back' interpretations, including my own, that began some time ago to follow all-too-predictable lines. 'Counterdiscursive' approaches to postcolonial literatures have arguably fallen out of fashion (see Introduction); but not so much because they are seen, unfairly I think, as reinstalling the European dominant but rather because literature-based approaches have themselves lost ground during the institutional turn to postcolonial cultural studies (see Conclusion).

11 Pratt uses 'autoethnography' in her book *Imperial Eyes* (1992) to refer to 'instances in which colonized subjects undertake to represent themselves in ways that engage with the colonizer's terms' (Pratt 1992: 7). Autoethnography thus necessarily implies a dialectical relationship between 'foreign' codes of representation and 'indigenous' experiences – a dialectic maintained, often for ironic purposes, in several contemporary African literary works.

12 For an explanation of Du Bois's term and its applicability to literary works intended for reception by both 'in-group' and 'out-group' audiences, see Sollors (1986).

13 For supplements to Marcus and Cushman's list, see Marcus and Fischer (1986); see also Geertz's considerations of ethnographic rhetoric, particularly in *Works and Lives: The Anthropologist as Author* (1988). For a useful discussion of possible areas of overlap between literature and ethnography, see also Krupat (1992), esp. the first chapter.

14 The classic essay here is 'The Novelist as Teacher' (1989b, first published in 1965); see also Achebe's own contribution to *Teaching* Things Fall Apart (Lindfors 1991).

15 See Clifford's explication of the trope of 'ethnographic salvage' in his essay 'On Ethnographic Allegory' in Clifford and Marcus (1986). As Clifford suggests, the idea of rescuing putatively 'vanishing' cultures is best seen as a romantic popularisation of an anthropological paradigm that has itself arguably vanished. But the idea, nonetheless, has retained its ideological force, especially outside the discipline:

> The rationale for focusing one's attention on vanishing lore, for rescuing in writing the knowledge of old people, may be strong … I do not wish to deny specific cases of disappearing customs and languages, or to challenge the value of recording such phenomena. I do, however, question the assumption that with rapid change something essential ('culture'), a coherent differential identity, vanishes. … Such attitudes, though they persist, are diminishing … [b]ut the allegory of salvage is deeply ingrained.
> (Clifford 1986: 112–13)

16 For a useful historical essay explaining some of the reasons for Senghor's misplaced enthusiasm for Frobenius, see Ita (1973).

17 For an overview of Frobenius's deluded conception of (pan-)African culture and aesthetic philosophy, see the opening two essays in the *Frobenius Anthology* (1973), 'The Nature of Culture' and 'Reflections on African Art'. For a more recent essay which further punctures the myth of Frobenius's benevolent Afrophilia, see Fabian (1992).

18 For the prosecution, see Sellin (1971); for the defence, Miller (1985).

19 In other, non-fictional works, Head herself arguably occupies this intermediate position. See, for example, her sociological/anthropological portrait of village life in *Serowe: Village of the Rain Wind* (1981).

20 For different, but equally impassioned, diagnoses of this dilemma, see the essays by Soyinka (1991) and Omotoso (1975); in the wider context of literary publishing in the Third World, see also Altbach (1975).

21 A more detailed treatment is urgently needed of the ideological function of 'the paratextual apparatuses' (Genette 1987) surrounding postcolonial literary works. Introductory studies like Ashcroft *et al.*'s make occasional mention of paratextual devices like glossaries, arguing that these may serve both to inform the reader and, by drawing attention to what s/he otherwise would not understand, to install cultural difference into the text (Ashcroft *et al.* 1989: 56–7, 61–4). Equally, however, glossaries and other translational mechanisms might be seen as ways of *domesticating* the text, making it available for what might be euphemistically called 'general consumption'. To date, the only essay that I have come across that deals in any detail with the ideological effects of the paratextual is Wendy Waring's (1995); for a discussion of this essay in the context of the metropolitan packaging of contemporary Aboriginal writing, see Chapter 6 of this book.

22 See, for example, Adewale Maja-Pearce's unabashedly celebratory overview of the first three decades of the AWS: 'In Pursuit of Excellence: Thirty Years of the Heinemann African Writers' Series' (*RAL* 1992), in which he lauds 'the increasing diversity of voices that have emerged from the continent in recent years' (Maja-Pearce 1992: 130). As Maja-Pearce – who has himself played an

important editorial role within the Series – suggests, 'The genesis of the African Writers' Series has become part of the mythology of modern African literature itself' (1992: 125). While this is true, it may also be – as Lizarríbar suggests – part of the problem. The constitutive role played by the AWS in the creation of 'the mythology of modern African literature' is itself in need of critical analysis, precisely the kind of analysis Lizarríbar – however provocatively – presents.

23 See Achebe's eponymous essay in the collection *Hopes and Impediments* (1989a). The question of colonialist biases in Western criticism of African literature is far from resolved, even though the angriest exchanges – often *ad hominem* – probably belong to the period from the late 1960s to the early 1980s.

2 Consuming India

1 On the Orient as exhibition, see Said (1978) and, particularly, T. Mitchell (1992). See also Chapter 4.

2 The term 'Indo-chic' is taken, via the media, from Padmini Mongia's paper on Arundhati Roy (1997). See also below.

3 On Said's own conception of 'imperial geography', see Said (1978: chap. 1). For Ahmad's ironic adaptation of it, see the chapter on Said in *In Theory* (Ahmad 1992: chap. 5); see also the Introduction to this book.

4 'Raj nostalgia', as Rushdie explains in his essay 'Outside the Whale' (originally published in 1984, see also Chapter 4), has been a growth industry in late twentieth-century Britain, partly as the result of loosely defined (post-) Thatcherite longings which have translated into a variety of cultural products, or repeats of cultural products, that look back with mixed affection at Britain's imperial past. 'Raj nostalgia' is not without its own nuances and ironies; for a suitably balanced range of critical responses, see the essays in Greet *et al.* (1992).

5 According to Sugnet, *Granta*'s travel articles are designed:

> to restore the lost dream of empire in a way that allows young-fogey readers to pretend that they're still living in the nineteenth century. … A curious fusion of the 1880s and the 1980s is what keeps all those *Granta* travel writers up in the air, their luggage filled with portable shards of colonialist discourse.
>
> (Sugnet 1991: 85)

For definitions of colonial(ist) discourse, see Said (1978), Spurr (1993) and, particularly, Hulme (1986).

6 Once again, the key text here is Said's *Orientalism*; but see also T. Mitchell (1992) and, especially, Inden (1990).

7 The atmosphere of resentment continues; for a recent, no less vitriolic response, complete with obligatory analogy to Macaulay, see Trivedi (1999).

8 For a summary of Rushdie's self-confessedly romanticised attitude toward the figure of the 'literary migrant', see the title essay of *Imaginary Homelands* (1991c); for a critique of Rushdie's (among others') use of the migrant metaphor, see also Krishnaswamy (1995).

9 See, particularly, Ahmad's chapter on 'Indian literature' in *In Theory* (Ahmad 1992: chap. 7); for further considerations of the marketability of Third World literature in English, see also Brennan (1997: chap. 1) and the Introduction to this book.

10 The term 'Anglo-Indian' is still applied to Indian-born writers (like Rushdie himself) with distressing prevalence, thereby conflating their work with that of the writers from whom they often wish most to distance themselves (Kipling, Forster, etc.). 'Indo-Anglian', while hardly felicitous, at least makes clear that the writer concerned is using *English* – by no means a 'natural' choice, as Rushdie sometimes seems to imply, and certainly not a fact to be elided, as in *The Vintage Book of Indian Writing [in English]*. On the extremely complex issue of the different languages of 'Indian literature', see Ahmad (1992: chap. 7), who also stresses that such labels – and not only in India, of course – carry ideological weight.

11 During deserves to be quoted at greater length from his important essay 'Postcolonialism and Globalisation' (1992). It seems, he says, as if

> almost everyone, almost everywhere, loves the global popular and some-times consumes it: it produces a mood in which exoticisim, normality and transworld sharedness combine, and in which consumption warmly glows. The global popular's humanism cannot be dismissed, precisely because it is so openly commercial. Its 'general magic' relies on the trick by which global markets, technologies and information flows fuse into a humanism transcending national boundaries at the same time as, in its clear dependence on marketing, it leaves in tatters the idealism and naive appeal to human nature so integral to older humanisms.
>
> (During 1992: 343)

For an equally important update to this earlier piece, in which During makes clear that the relationship between postcolonialism and globalisation should properly be understood as dialectical, see his more recent essay in *Postcolonial Studies* (1998); see also the Conclusion to this book.

12 On Rushdie's status as a 'cosmopolitan celebrity', see Brennan, esp. his first book, *Salman Rushdie and the Third World* (1989); on the ambivalent position occupied by the diasporic intellectual, see also Radhakrishnan (1996).

13 See, for example, the travelogue *Days and Nights in Calcutta* (1986), co-authored with Blaise's wife, Bharati Mukherjee.

14 For a more detailed treatment of the implications of Rushdie's Booker success, see my articles in *Transition* (1994b) and *Studies in the Novel* (1997a); see also, in a wider context, the discussion of Booker plc as a 'postcolonial patron' in Chapter 4.

15 Rushdie is of course well aware of this: see, for example, some of the stories in his collection *East, West* (1994), which play, like *Midnight's Children*, on the media-tion of the East–West encounter through the process of commodity exchange.

16 The 'touchstone effect' is characteristic of the metropolitan mediation of postcolonial literary/cultural products as a whole. See the discussion below of another touchstone work, Vikram Seth's *A Suitable Boy* (1993), and of another bestselling Indo-Anglian novel, Arundhati Roy's *The God of Small Things* (1997), which is highly likely to be a touchstone work in the future. Commercial success is not, of course, the only criterion for a literary work to be canonised in this way; nor, for that matter, is unanimous critical acclaim, though both of these factors are obviously important. The touchstone effect is related, rather, to what I describe throughout this book as a postcolonial 'metonymic fallacy' – the decontextualising tendency, ironised of course in

touchstone works like *Midnight's Children*, to take single literary works or literary figures as synecdochic of a nation's literature as a whole.

17 Dalrymple neglects to mention that there might be a connection between the faddishness of the Indo-Anglian novel and the success of his own Indian travelogues. It is interesting to note how often travel writers are favoured by the media, not only as reviewers of 'Indian' (and other 'Third World') material, but also as expert commentators on 'Indian' (and other 'Third World') societies and cultures. A famous if perhaps anomalous example is V.S. Naipaul, whose wildly polemical travel accounts (India, the Caribbean, Africa, etc.) have sometimes been treated as if they were *the* authoritative source. A further connection exists between travel writing – and several of the best-known Indo-Anglian writers are themselves practitioners – and a genre that might best be described as the 'postcolonial tourist novel'. The 'tourist novel' not only introduces the country or countries in which it is set to an unfamiliar readership, but also displays that country or countries as object(s) of metropolitan consumption. For a discussion of the links between travel writing and tourism, see Holland and Huggan (1998); for a more detailed treatment of the tourist novel – if in a different context – see Chapter 7 of this book.

18 See Introduction; see also Chapter 8 (on the celebrity writer) and Conclusion (on the celebrity critic).

19 It is perhaps worth noting in passing that another form of media hype is the manufactured literary *rivalry*, such as that which accompanied the publication of Rushdie's and Seth's most recent novels (*The Ground Beneath Her Feet*, *An Equal Music*, both 1999). It is surely no surprise that the novels were bracketed together for marketing purposes, with numerous 'competitive' events (pre-release readings, interviews, etc.) being hailed as evidence of the writers' – more likely their agents' – desire to outdo one another.

20 Romance is a privileged genre for the retailing of exotic myths and stereotypes, particularly with respect to ethnicity and gender and the relations between them. Not least, romance provides a reminder of the connection between the *exotic* and the *erotic*, a connection explored more fully in other chapters in this book (see, particularly, Chapters 5 and 7).

21 For further thoughts on the class affiliations of these writers, see Brennan (1989, 1997); also Iyer (1993), whose uncritical celebration of the new 'transcultural writing' sidesteps complex issues of class privilege and diasporic affiliation, merely subscribing to the media myth of a global 'happy family' of roving cosmopolitan writers – a myth he is perhaps only too eager to subscribe to, since he sees himself as one. (For further discussion of Iyer's piece, see Chapter 4.) For a recent, spirited defence of the cosmopolitan writer, see the two-part article by Chandra (1999). While irritated by Rushdie's (and his diasporic colleagues') condescension toward Indian-based writers, Chandra is more angered still by an Indian critical establishment seemingly intent on fetishising 'local authors' and 'the regional voice'. However, while Chandra joins others – including Rushdie himself – in debunking the myth of a homegrown 'Indian authenticity', his studied indifference to the impact of the market on Indian writers, especially Indo-*Anglian* writers, seems almost wilfully naive.

3 Staged marginalities: Rushdie, Naipaul, Kureishi

1 For Deleuze and Guattari, a minor literature 'doesn't come from a minor language; it is rather that which a minority constructs within a major

language' (1986: 59). Three main characteristics of minor literature are (perhaps over-simplistically) identified, namely 'the deterritorialization of language, the connection of the individual to a political immediacy, and the collective assemblage of enunciation' (Deleuze and Guattari 1990: 60–1).

2 On the recuperability of 'minor' writing, see Lloyd, 'Genet's Genealogy'; Ferguson's introduction to *Out There* (1990: esp. 9–18); and Brennan, *At Home in the World* (1997: esp. chap. 1).

3 Both writers, it must be said, have also contributed to the myth of their own rootlessness, Rushdie by deploying the figure of 'the migrant' and Naipaul by persisting in seeing himself as an 'exile'. For Rushdie, the 'migrant writer' occupies a space in between cultures; for Naipaul, the 'exile' is a victim of 'originary displacement' (Porter 1991; see also below). Both writers have sought rhetorical advantage from their sense of non-belonging: for a critique of Rushdie's position, see Krishnaswamy (1995); for a critique of Naipaul's, see Nixon (1992).

4 For conflicting perspectives on Naipaul's work, see Hamner (1973), Cudjoe (1988) and Nixon (1992); for a more balanced view, see Hughes (1988).

5 Nixon perhaps goes too far in seeing Naipaul as – in effect – a colonial lackey, buttering up a reactionary metropolitan audience by telling them what he thinks they want to hear. However, it is certainly true that he has been constructed by the First World media as a Third World expert, and that his words carry an ideological weight far beyond their capacity to reveal uncomfortable truths.

6 On the subversive potential of mimicry, see also Scott (1990: 28–44) and Huggan (1997/8). It seems necessary to point out that Naipaul's own conception of mimicry is very different; that he sees the deference of the 'mimic man' as a marker of his own frustrated impotence or even despair. Mimicry, for Naipaul, is a characteristic of colonial cultures (such as Trinidad's) that feel obliged to aspire to – or, perhaps more accurately, have been coerced into looking for – cultural models and values elsewhere. Or such is the *general view* of Naipaul's conception of colonial mimicry – a view that has obviously provided further ammunition for his critics. In fact, I would argue that Naipaul's view on mimicry, like mimicry itself, is inherently unstable; as is the case with Rushdie, conflicting, even contradictory perspectives may be gleaned from his various short stories and novels, and it is unwise, as he himself would surely admit, to take his 'non-fictional' works on trust.

7 On the function of myths of displacement in Naipaul's work, see Nixon (1992) and Porter (1991).

8 Attributions of 'marginality' often fly in the face, of course, of social and cultural realities. Recent figures suggest that whites may well be a minority in Greater London by 2025 (Howe 2000: 29); while in some boroughs in London and other British inner-city areas, this has been the case for some time.

9 There is an uncanny similarity between Bhabha's heady 'Third Space' rhetoric and Rushdie's defence of *The Satanic Verses* as 'a love-song to our mongrel selves' (Rushdie 1991d: 394), even if – as I am suggesting here – Rushdie's novel also seems to parody the allegedly liberating potential within the concept of cultural hybridity. Hybridity, as I argue elsewhere (see below and, particularly, Conclusion) has become a standard commodity of postcolonial discourse: an enactment of the slippage that critics need to open up a space for their own arguments; a means of pre-empting others' criticisms, often peremptorily labelled as 'essentialist'; and – potentially – a mask to hide behind that ob-

scures, but also maintains, one's own critical authority. The idea of hybridity, as Robert Young demonstrates so clearly in his book *Colonial Desire* (1995), can be manipulated in different ideological interests; this is surely true on the (meta)level of critical discourse as well as on the level of social interaction. 'Hybridity' is a key term in the vocabulary of the postcolonial exotic (see also Conclusion). If the postcolonial exotic can be seen, in part, as describing the mechanism by which the term 'exotic' is conscripted to the cause of cultural commodification, the commodities it highlights are less likely to be 'pure' products than the hybridised effects of global processes of mediation and transculturation (in the realm of literature, these might include 'African literature', the 'Indo-Anglian novel', 'multicultural' anthologies, and so on). Hybridity, within the context of the postcolonial exotic, may be less indicative of the potential for cross-cultural creativity and transformation than of the processes by which postcolonial products, and the critical discourse surrounding those products, divert attention away from the institutionalised and/or commercialised circumstances under which they are produced. This is not to deny that hybridity can be a highly enabling concept; what is needed is to gauge more carefully *who exactly* is enabled by it, and to better understand the dialectical relationship between hybridity as a strategy-for-resistance and hybridity as a discursive commodity that disguises continuing hierarchies of power.

10 See, particularly, the sustained attack on Naipaul by a series of fellow Caribbean-born writers/thinkers, including George Lamming, Derek Walcott and Selwyn Cudjoe. It is understandable that Naipaul should be seen by some as having turned his back on the Caribbean; his attitude toward the Caribbean is, however, deeply ambivalent rather than fundamentally antagonistic – even if there are numerous instances, particularly in his 'non-fictional' writing, when he lets his cultural snobbery get the better of him.

11 Theories of performance and performativity, despite their obvious usefulness, have yet to stake a serious claim in postcolonial criticism, despite promising work by Dash, McDougall, Kanneh and, particularly, Gilbert (for an overview, see the 'Body and Performance' section of Tiffin *et al.*'s *Post-Colonial Studies Reader*, 1995). The increasing body of work emerging from an intersection of postcolonial and queer theory suggests, however, that performativity may yet become a central concept for the understanding both of colonial strategies of physical oppression/regimentation and postcolonial identity formation. For a recent, highly suggestive use of performance theory in postcolonial criticism, see S. Fischer (1999).

12 For a more detailed treatment of 'native authenticity', see Chapter 6 of this book.

13 For a fine study of the ideological malleability of 'Englishness', see Gikandi (1996). The fetishisation of 'Englishness' has recently reached hysterical (post-millennial?) levels; for a postcolonially inflected analysis of this literary/cultural phenomenon, see Wachinger (2000).

14 See Hebdige's minor classic *Subculture: The Meaning of Style* (1979); Hebdige's analysis, in particular, of the subcultures of 1970s Britain is of obvious relevance to Kureishi's work.

15 For excellent, theoretically informed readings, see Mohanram (1995), Quart (1992) and Spivak (1993b).

16 This point is emphasised in Quart's reading – the most convincing of the three – which rightly sees the films (*Sammy and Rosie* particularly) as undermining the shibboleths of both Thatcherite autocracy and left-wing community

action. In this sense, they seem much more in keeping with Kureishi's anarchic egotism than with Frears' righteous anger (see interview below).

17 Heterotopias, in Foucault's definition, are both contestatory 'counter-sites', challenging the established spaces of the dominant culture, and multi-level zones that are 'capable of juxtaposing in a single real place several different spaces, several sites that are in themselves incompatible' (Foucault 1986: 22, 25). Both aspects of the definition would appear to apply here, although it is significant in either case that the 'counter-site' is eventually destroyed.

18 On 'carnivalisation' as a temporary overturning of the social order, see Bakhtin (1984).

19 As is the case with Rushdie, Kureishi is much more direct, and more obviously 'political', in his essays: see, for example, the powerful polemic 'The Rainbow Sign' (1986). And as is the case with both Rushdie and Naipaul, a tension emerges between non-fictional 'political' statements and fictional works which seem bent on undermining the 'political' views their protagonists present (see also Note 6 above).

4 Prizing otherness: a short history of the Booker

1 For further critical reflections on Nobel conservatism, see Wai (1985) and, particularly, Winegarten (1994).

2 The Booker shortlist has of course become as much of an institution as the Prize itself. The 'list' has become the site of a veritable media feeding frenzy; it might also be seen as a characteristic of the increasing commodification of cultural knowledge in general, one of whose symptoms, according to Lyotard and, more recently, Guillory is, precisely, 'the list' (see Guillory 1993: 36–7; also Chapter 8 and Conclusion).

3 A good example of this was the simultaneous appearance of Salman Rushdie's and Vikram Seth's latest novels in ideal time for Booker 1999 (see previous chapter for a discussion of the media fabrication of literary rivalries). While the 'rivalry' between Rushdie and Seth was no doubt effective in attracting attention and generating sales, the half-expected 'battle for the Booker' did not materialise, neither novel making it onto the 1999 shortlist.

4 Note, however, Alistair Niven's spirited defence of the Booker's contribution toward fostering what he calls a 'common wealth of talent': qtd in *Booker 30* (1998).

5 Discussions of these differences are integral to my argument in Chapters 1 and 2; see also Brennan (1997: chap. 1) and, especially, Altbach (1975).

6 On the assimilationist tendencies inherent within the category of 'Commonwealth Literature', see the Introduction and, especially, the Conclusion (section one) to this book. For a more detailed discussion of the various connotations of the term 'multicultural', see Chapter 5.

7 The term 'counter-memory' is derived here from Foucault (1977). At its simplest, counter-memory refers to the attempt to narrativise the past in ways that defy, and work toward transforming, official historical records, also presenting alternatives to a linear view of history that favours imperialistic myths of progress. The term is of obvious relevance to postcolonial writers, but it also played a major role in the international wave of 'revisionist' fiction that, beginning in the 1960s, had itself begun to take on an establishment feel by, say, the early 1980s. The consecration of 'historical revisionism' has been completed by such prizes as the Booker, which are testament both to the

enduring energies of the genre and, ironically, to its official approval as one of the hallmarks of exciting new English-language fiction.

8 Two further Booker prizewinners which deal extensively with Indian colonial history, Salman Rushdie's *Midnight's Children* (1981) and Arundhati Roy's *The God of Small Things* (1997), are either treated cursorily here (in the first case) or omitted (in the second), on the grounds that I have already dealt with them in some detail elsewhere: see especially Chapter 2.

9 For alternative, more charitable views on *The Raj Quartet*, see Sharrad (1992) and, particularly, Moore (1992).

10 On the function of *sati* in colonialist discourse, see Newman (1995: 37–42) and, especially, Mani (1990).

11 For different perspectives on the Exhibition, see T. Mitchell (1992) and, in more detail, Richards (1993).

12 For a further discussion of nostalgia in the colonial/exotic context, see Bongie (1991); see also the connection made between colonialism, exoticism and tourism in Chapter 7 of this book.

13 As the distinguished Indian novelist R.K. Narayan has declared frostily, 'the Raj concept seems to be just childish nonsense, indicating a glamorised, romanticised period piece, somewhat phoney' (Narayan, in Greet *et al.* 1992: 151). Fictions of the Raj, for Narayan, are irredeemably shallow, offering marketable Western melodrama 'against a background supposed to represent India' (1992: 151). The term itself is 'meaningless … a vacuous hybrid expression neither Indian nor British, although the O.E.D. (which is a sacred cow for us in India) has admitted it for a definition' (1992: 151).

14 Irony, it could be argued further, functions as an effective alibi for the revival of a decadent, discredited imperial imaginary: see Holland and Huggan (1998: chap. 1).

15 For a more extended treatment of *Midnight's Children*, see Chapter 2. On the question of historical representation, see also Rushdie's essays on *Midnight's Children* in *Imaginary Homelands* (1991c).

16 On ideologies of 'Englishness', see previous chapter. (See also the references in the chapter to the work of Gikandi (1996) and Wachinger (2000).)

17 On the aestheticising and/or dehistoricising effects of multicultural discourses, see the next chapter of this book.

18 See the previously mentioned essays by Wai (1985), Lindfors (1988) and Winegarten (1994). The flurry of media activity surrounding the awarding of the 1999 Nobel to Günter Grass indicates that, while less openly commercial than the Booker, it still has a considerable impact in the public sphere.

19 For further discussion of canon formation within a postcolonial context, see Chapter 8 and the concluding chapter. See also Guillory's indispensable 1993 account of the ambivalent status of 'non' or 'counter-canonical' works within the Western (specifically, US) university curriculum.

20 On the ideological function of 'strategies of containment', see Jameson (1981), particularly the introductory chapter.

21 See Brennan (1997: chap. 1); see also Chapter 2 of this book for a critical response to Brennan's argument.

22 For an elaboration of this argument, see Introduction; for critical responses to Iyer, see also Brennan (1997) and Brydon (1994).

23 These dates – and the procedures in general – have undergone minor changes over time, with the Prize ceremony this year (2000), for example, being delayed until 7 November. Booker plc, meanwhile, is itself in evolution,

having merged in May 2000 with Iceland plc to become the Iceland Group plc. For the latest on the Prize, consult its regularly updated web site at http://www.bookerprize.co.uk.

5 Exoticism, ethnicity and the multicultural fallacy

1 This latter tension is at the centre of Charles Taylor's influential essay (1994, see also below), which attempts to recuperate multiculturalism for community-oriented projects of social transformation. See also the instructive responses to Taylor's paper by Habermas and Appiah in Gutmann (1994).

2 For an overview of some of these arguments, see the essays in Goldberg (1994); for more polemical alternatives, see Schlesinger (1992) and Hughes (1993). It seems worth noting in passing that relatively few of the many books and articles on US multiculturalism mention models deriving from other 'multicultural' societies (Canada, Australia, Britain, New Zealand and South Africa provide the most obvious bases for comparison). While it is tempting to conclude that this is just another example of US self-obsession, it would be more accurate to say that multiculturalism has become the focus in the United States for an emotionally charged debate on the strengths and weaknesses of liberal democracy in general, and more specifically, as I have implied, for attacks from both Left and Right on the loopholes in liberal-pluralist thought.

3 For an historical overview of the issues involved, see Breton (1986).

4 See, for example, Marlene Nourbese Philip's polemical essays 'The "Multicultural" Whitewash' and 'Why Multiculturalism Can't End Racism' in her collection *Frontiers* (1992). For a critique of Nourbese Philip's position, see also below.

5 For differing views on the White Australia Policy and its relation to contemporary redressive multicultural policies, see Castles *et al.* (1988), Jupp (1997) and, particularly, Kane (1997).

6 The equally clichéd term 'mosaic' has arguably served a similar function in Canada. As Evelyn Kallen notes,

> the concept of the [multicultural] mosaic ... implies that many different cultures live within one societal framework, [with] the ethnic groups displaying ... a low level of ethnocentrism and prejudice toward each other. The theory also assumes that no group is dominant and that, therefore, processes of acculturation and assimilation are restricted equally through all groups.
>
> (Kallen 1982: 163–4)

On the mystificatory function of multicultural metaphors, see also Hinz (1996).

7 For a more detailed consideration of the special status of Aboriginals in Australia, see next chapter.

8 See Hutcheon's introduction to the collection *Other Solitudes* (1990); for a similar exploration of the discrepancy between multicultural ideals and ideologies, see also Kulyk Keefer (1996).

9 Thanks to Lynn Lee, who contributed much of the research for this section, for providing this insight.

10 For alternative criticisms of Ondaatje's 'elitism', see Mukherjee (1994c) and Sugnasiri (1992); for a counter-argument, see Verhoeven (1996).

11 On the cultural capital that accrues to ethnic autobiography, see Brennan (1997); see also Chapter 6 of this book.

12 On the need to maintain a critical distinction between literature and sociology, see, however, Hutcheon and Richmond (1990) and Gunew (1994).

13 See Gunew's introduction to *Framing Marginality* (1994) for a discussion of the inadequacy yet, for her, necessity of this much-contested label.

14 On 'minor' writing, see Deleuze and Guattari (1990); also the first section of Chapter 3.

15 See also Begamudre, in Coleman (1996) and Kulyk Keefer (1996) for a defence of their own favoured term, 'transcultural' writing. The term 'transcultural' confers a flexibility arguably missing from the nation-centred multicultural paradigm; however, it may also imply an elision of social and, particularly, class privilege (see the critique of Iyer's conception of the 'transcultural writer' in the previous chapter).

16 See the discussion of the relation between 'marginal' literary forms and material self-reflexivity in the Introduction and Chapters 1 and 2.

17 See, for example, Nourbese Philip (1992).

18 See, for example, Bissoondath's flagrantly contradictory responses to Reform Party policy (1994: 64–5, 200).

19 Loriggio is equally concerned that journalistic treatments of multiculturalism have mostly served to buttress conservative, even reactionary views:

> By and large, journalist critics have defended conservative perspectives. And they have done so with a one-mindedness that has allowed them to out-ideologize the leftist counterparts that they often accuse of being too irredeemably, too blatantly ideological. Less fussy about culture and crowds, right-wing sympathizers have exploited their familarity with television, radio or the popular press with utmost cynicism. Exposure and readability – or vice versa – have been their credo.
>
> (Loriggio 1996: 188)

20 For a deft, if perhaps overly self-congratulatory summary of what he calls the 'Demidenko effect', see Wark (1997: chap. 5); also the useful collection of reviews, interviews and articles in Jost *et al.* (1996).

21 For a defence of the novel's postmodern narrative tactics, see Riemer (1996) and, particularly, Wark (1997); for an attack on their ethical insufficiencies, see Manne (1996) and, in a rather different context, Mishra (1996). For a recent essay examining the exoticist discourses surrounding the production and reception of the novel, see also Longley (2000).

22 For a detailed analysis of this mechanism, see Foster (1982/3) and Bongie (1991); also the Introduction to this book.

23 For a defence of the subversive potential of the drag queen, see Garber (1992); for a critique of Garber, see Holland and Huggan (1998: chap. 3).

24 The gendered coupling of exoticism and eroticism allows Egoyan to explore the disturbing connection between the former's dialectic of attraction and repulsion and the latter's attachment of sexual fantasy to (self-)violation and the death-drive (see also Bataille 1986). The exoticism/eroticism nexus is thus simultaneously a site of *distraction* and *destruction*. For further insights – in a different context – into the destructive tendencies within exoticist discourse, and of their connections to racially and gendered codes of sexual pleasure and lethal power, see the essays in Jolly and Manderson (1997).

6 Ethnic autobiography and the cult of authenticity

1 For definitions of ethnic autobiography, see M. Fischer (in Clifford and Marcus 1986) and Lionnet (1995). The latter draws a connection between 'ethnic' and 'postcolonial' autobiography, arguing that the

> individualistic approach to the genre [of autobiography] contrasts sharply with the one used by most postcolonial writers, male and female. For [these writers], the individual necessarily defines him- or herself with regard to a community, or an ethnic group, and their autobiographical mythologies of empowerment are usually mediated by a desire to revise and rewrite official history.
>
> (Lionnet 1995: 22)

While indigenous autobiographies certainly share some of these characteristics, their assimilation to models either of 'ethnic' or 'postcolonial' autobiography is problematic – not least because the terms 'ethnic', 'postcolonial' and, indeed, 'autobiography' itself have frequently been rejected by indigenous writers (see, for example, Mudrooroo's response).

2 In his important chapter 'On Collecting Art and Culture' (in *The Predicament of Culture*, 1988, see also below), the anthropologist James Clifford argues that authenticity is invariably manufactured to meet a given set of ideological needs. These needs are often – though not necessarily – those of a dominant culture, which labels 'marginal' cultural products, and sometimes minority cultures themselves, as authentic for a variety of ideological reasons: the perceived need to recapture a sense of threatened cultural integrity, often mediated through the vaguely conceived notion of 'spirituality'; the desire to rejuvenate one culture by siphoning off the attributes of another; the repressed wish to save face, or salve conscience, by praising a culture or cultural group that one has previously insulted; and so on. For a more detailed summary of ideologies of authenticity in the historical context of white/Native relations, see Root (1996).

3 For a critique of the applicability of postcolonial theories and paradigms to Aboriginal literature, see Brewster (1995); also Hodge and Mishra (1990).

4 For different versions of this argument, see also Appadurai (1986) and Thomas (1994).

5 On the connection between decontextualisation and individual/state-sponsored collector culture, see also Appadurai (1986) and the Introduction to this book.

6 Examples here might include Thomas' amusing critique of cosmopolitan decor (Thomas 1994: chap. 1) and Appadurai's analysis of globalised ethnic/tribal 'chic' (Appadurai 1986: Intro.); see also the references to Appadurai in the Introduction to this book.

7 See, for example, Terry Goldie's analysis of the various, overdetermined textual *commodities* that mark 'indigeneity' in literary texts – atavistic wisdom, the mystical connection to nature, sexual temptation coupled with the fear of violence, etc. In a sense, this book as a whole is indebted to Goldie's methodology, applying the vocabulary of cultural semiotics – though more loosely than Goldie does – to the wider postcolonial field of production, and critically analysing the 'standard commodities' (Said 1978, also qtd in Goldie 1989: 15) that circulate within the symbolic economy of postcolonial studies in the

context of the global packaging/metropolitan mediation of culturally 'othered' goods. See Introduction for a more detailed breakdown of this mediating process.

8 See, for example, Kurtzer (1998), who more or less accepts Muecke's thesis, and Brewster (1995), who acknowledges it while noting (I would say inaccurately) 'a fundamental contradiction … between Muecke's desire on the one hand to treat literary texts as wholly social … and his invocation on the other of a literary aesthetic' (Brewster 1995: 35).

9 See also Povinelli (1998, also referred to in the previous chapter) for an analysis of the state-monitored narratives of nostalgia, violence and redemption surrounding white/Aboriginal relations in contemporary Australia.

10 For a discussion of authenticity in/and the Enlightenment, see also Taylor (1991).

11 For useful summaries of the main features of indigenous, more specifically Aboriginal autobiographical writing, see Brewster (1995: Chaps 2 and 3) and Longley (1992).

12 See Mudrooroo (1997: chap. 12); the essays by Nettlebeck (1997) and Hughes (1998); and, especially, the discussion of Huggins and Huggins (1994), below.

13 I shall not be entering here into the current debates surrounding Mudrooroo's own (in)authenticity as an Aboriginal/Aboriginal writer. For a recent overview of what is at stake in these debates, see Goldie (1999).

14 For a fairly comprehensive list, see Brewster (1995).

15 See Waring (1995); also Nettlebeck:

> [The] impression of enjoying a ready connection to the speaker [conveyed in several contemporary Aboriginal women's life-narratives] may have the potential to ease the reader into a kind of amnesia about Australia's continuing failures in the arena of Aboriginal rights; to believe, in effect, that the past is released from the present.
>
> (Nettlebeck 1997: 47–8)

16 For a more detailed explanation of the term 'horizon of expectations', see Iser (1980); see also Jauss (1982), in the wider sense of reader expectations that are contingent not only on interpretations of individual texts but also on mediated understandings of literary history.

17 Interethnic endorsement is consolidated in the 1990 First Arcade edition of *My Place*, obviously packaged for an American audience, by a cover reference to the text as 'The Australian *Roots*'. The cover photograph, meanwhile, features *the* touristic icon of Aboriginal spirituality – Uluru/Ayers Rock – thereby facilitating the insertion of the text into a New Age context reaffirmed by Walker's sententious blurb.

18 For Derrida (if I may simplify), the text's lack of an overarching meaning – a 'transcendental signified' – is compensated for by a surplus of signifiers; it is this surplus, whereby the final meaning of the text is forever deferred, that conveys the logic of the supplement. See Spivak's introduction to her translation of Derrida's *Of Grammatology* (1974) for a lucid explanation of the supplement.

19 See the prefatory section, entitled simply 'Writing the Book'; also Nettlebeck's illuminating analysis.

20 As Umberto Eco has suggested, the history of discovered fakes reveals an anxiety over origins (the original artwork, the origins of human life itself, etc.), using a variety of ideological arguments to cover over metaphysical dis-ease (Eco 1990). The unveiling of the fake is, simultaneously, the remystification of

the genuine – a simple truism that lies at the heart of contemporary 'authenticity' debates. On the symbiotic relationship between the genuine and the fake, see also Haywood (1987).

21 See Emberley (1993) for a critique of the imperialist tendencies of postcolonial theory and criticism; also Hodge and Mishra (1990) for their – in my view tendentious – distinction between 'oppositional' (e.g. Aboriginal) and 'complicit' (e.g. white Australian) forms of postcolonialism.

7 Transformations of the tourist gaze: Asia in recent Canadian and Australian fiction

1 An example of this is one of the latest touristic trends, ecotourism. As Joe Bandy has argued, ecotourism attempts to balance the seemingly contradictory agendas of environmental sustainability and industrial development. But while touting itself as a 'caring' alternative to the mainstream tourist industry, ecotourism still remains largely governed by tourism's neocolonial relations of power: 'Ecotourism is a transformative policy of inclusion and democratization, as well as a product of racialized justification for modernization, in which marginalized peoples are subject to a new dependency and a new colonialism' (Bandy 1996: 541; see also Holland and Huggan 1998: 178–9). For other perspectives on the problematic relationship between tourism and development, see MacCannell (1989) and Krotz (1996: esp. chaps. 3–7).

2 On the bogus traveller/tourist distinction, see also Buzard (1993), Holland and Huggan (1998) and MacCannell (1989).

3 See Susan Stewart's interesting discussion of nostalgia in *On Longing* (1984, also referred to in Chapter 4). For analyses of the connections between nostalgia and tourism, see Holland and Huggan (1998) and, especially, Frow (1991).

4 For a rather uncritical treatment of the figure of the spiritual tourist, see Leed (1991).

5 For comparative approaches to literary exoticism, see Rousseau and Porter (1990, for the Enlightenment), Remak (1978, for the Romantics), and Bongie (1991, for the modern period).

6 Hospital's novel can be described, and defended on those grounds, as a *parody* of exotic romance. In this sense, it might be useful to compare it with another novel set in India – Arundhati Roy's *The God of Small Things* (1997) – which is clearly written from a different perspective, but which similarly plays on the conventions of exotic romance as a tale of 'forbidden' cross-cultural love (see Chapter 2). India, of course, and more generally Asia/the Asia-Pacific region remains a favourite backdrop for exotic romances. For the characteristics of (exotic) romance in general, see Beer (1970). For specific perspectives on Asia and the Pacific as privileged sites of exotic/erotic desire, see Jolly and Manderson (1997), particularly the editors' own contributions. For a discussion of European pictorial conventions of the exotic in a Pacific context, see also B. Smith (1985). It could be argued here, no doubt, that the Island Pacific – *the* pre-eminent zone of European exotic reverie – is largely missing from this book: one which, after all, advertises the exotic as its main topic (see also Preface). This argument is acknowledged – but would probably require another book. A more serious lacuna, to my mind, is the treatment of exoticism as a *gendered* discourse of attraction. Note, however, the attention paid in the Introduction, this chapter and, particularly, Chapter 5 to the highly ambivalent politics of race and gender underlying exoticist modes of representation.

7 For an examination of exoticism in Baudelaire's work, see Bongie (1991).

8 The key verses are as follows, in the original French: 'Alors, ô ma beauté! dites à la vermine/Qui vous mangera de baisers/Que j'ai gardé la forme et l'essence divine/De mes amours décomposés!'

9 Both Said (1978) and Inden (1990) note the tendency toward associating India with physiological and/or psychological 'states' as a tell-tale sign of Orientalist representation. This tendency is gently mocked, if also partly upheld, in Hospital's and Rivard's novels; it is loudly derided, of course, in the Menippean satire of Rushdie's novels, especially *Midnight's Children* (1981, see Chapter 2).

10 For a longer version of this argument, see my essay in *Canadian Literature* (1992).

11 On the phenomenon of 'belatedness' in colonial/postcolonial contexts, see Behdad (1994) and Holland and Huggan (1998).

12 On the connection between tourism/travel and camp aesthetics, see Holland and Huggan (1998: chap. 1).

13 'Global culture' is, of course, an amorphous term that rightly elicits suspicion. While Arjun Appadurai, among others, has catalogued the varied effects – and by no means only *negative* effects – of media-generated processes of cultural globalisation (Appadurai 1996), Timothy Brennan has also suggested that 'global culture' functions effectively as an alibi for US-style commercial expansionism and as a universal credo of mass consumption, bolstered by the capitalist myth of the 'free' market, that flies in the face of global poverty and uneven development (Brennan 1997). For varying perspectives on 'global culture', see also During (1992, 1998), Kumar (1999), and the useful collection edited by Wilson and Dissanayake (1996), especially the essays by Dirlik, Featherstone and Miyoshi. All of these essays make clear that 'global culture' (largely a myth) is not to be confused with globalisation (an undoubted reality), and that the operations of the global economy, while by no means identical with 'global culture', produce visible cultural effects. For an exploration of the dialectical relationship between globalisation and postcolonialism, see the two essays on the subject by During and the Introduction to this book.

14 On the exoticist dialectic of the familiar and the foreign, see Bongie (1991), Foster (1982/3) and the Introduction to this book.

15 Tourism and exoticism are, in this sense, symbiotic: for if the tourist industry, as previously suggested, depends on exotic myths to sustain its own commercial interests, contemporary exoticism has arguably become a dominant mode of touristic consumption (see also Introduction).

16 Not just the Australian tourist novel; for the genre has been flourishing elsewhere, notably in Britain and the United States. Whether adapted to the conventions of the postmodern trick-box (Vollmann 1996) or the psychological thriller (Garland 1996), tourist novels are fast becoming the self-fulfilling symbols of a world enveloped and consumed. On the worrying implications of the genre for postcolonial fiction, which sometimes tends to ironise its own touristic propensities, see Chapter 2.

17 It would be unwise to conclude from this that the nation-state has simply surrendered its political relevance, or that we are all marching euphorically into a frontierless 'post-national' future. Apologists for the 'transnational imaginary' (Wilson and Dissanayake 1996) are themselves wary of consigning the nation to the historical dustbin, although they rightly stress the need to form alternative allegiances that transcend the boundaries of the nation-state.

For conflicting perspectives on the nation in a – broadly speaking – postcolonial context, see the essays in Bhabha (1991), particularly those of Brennan, During and Bhabha himself; for a somewhat utopian exploration of the 'postnational' ethos, see also Appadurai (1996).

8 Margaret Atwood Inc., or, some thoughts on literary celebrity

1 It should perhaps not be taken for granted that Atwood is a 'postcolonial' writer at all. My position, however, is similar to that of Coral Ann Howells when she describes Atwood's work – particularly her later fiction – as exploring 'a postcolonial crisis where formerly dominant traditions have been permanently disrupted and where new narratives of cultural difference need to be formulated' (Howells 1995: 37). For a useful essay that further explores the postcolonial dimensions of Atwood's work, see Brydon (1996). For Brydon, 'Atwood invites a combined feminist and postcolonial approach', since her work addresses a nexus of 'cultural, economic, and political oppressions based on ethnicity, nation, and race' as well as gender (Brydon 1996: 49).

2 For an essay examining the insistent doubleness – the 'violent duality' – within Atwood's work, especially her poetry, see Grace in Davidson and Davidson (1981).

3 Most of the facts in the above section are taken from the Summer 1998 edition of *The Margaret Atwood Society Newsletter*, an invaluable source of information – and, often, gossip – for Atwood lovers worldwide. For a more detailed treatment of the Newsletter, see the fourth section of this chapter.

4 See also the concluding chapter for a discussion of the postcolonial academic star system.

5 On the connections between consecration, canonisation and closure, see Herrnstein Smith (1988) and, particularly, Guillory (1993).

6 For critiques, see Frow (1995) and Robbins (1993); also the introductory chapter of this book.

7 An extreme example here would be the blatant commercialism surrounding the annual award of the Booker Prize: see Todd (1996) and, especially, the critical analysis of the Prize in Chapter 4.

8 *Survival* (1972), Atwood's thematic guide to Canadian literature, has arguably done as much as her poetry or fiction to secure her reputation. *Survival* was partly written for, and continues to feature as a set text in, Canadian schools, and has been widely used abroad as a guide (albeit an ironic one) to understanding the 'Canadian victim mentality'.

9 On the phenomenon of the 'representative writer', see also Chapters 1 and 2.

10 While Atwood is frequently dubbed a 'feminist writer', she has shown (as with other critical labels) a certain suspicion toward the designation: 'Some people *choose* to define themselves as feminist writers. I would not deny the adjective, but I don't consider it inclusive' (*Conversations* 139, qtd in Howells 1995: 14). For all her reservations, Atwood has been incorporated into a North American feminist canon, with the arguable result that her nationality and the cultural specificity of her work have been underestimated. (See particularly the packaging of Atwood/Atwood's work in the US, where her Canadian background is rarely mentioned, and she is frequently likened to other 'North American feminist writers'.) For a sensible discussion of Atwood's feminism, see Howells (1995: 14–19). As Howells concludes, 'In Atwood's fiction there are no essentialist definitions of "woman" or "feminism" or even "Canadian",

but instead representations of the endless complexity and quirkiness of human behaviour which exceeds ideological labels and the explanatory power of theory' (Howells 1995: 19). And lest this be interpreted as a humanist catch-all, Howells takes care to add that 'Atwood is a "political" writer in the widest sense, for she is interested in an analysis of the dialectic of power and in shifting structures of ideology' (Howells 1995: 19).

11 Self-promotion is only a part of the multiple mediations that are attendant upon celebrity status: see, by way of comparison, the discussion of Rushdie, Roy and other 'celebrity Indian writers' in Chapter 2.

12 On the figure of the 'marginalised intellectual', see also Chapter 3.

13 It is obviously too easy, though not entirely untruthful, to say that Atwood is a middle-class writer, exploring middle-class attitudes and dilemmas for a mostly middle-class readership. The question of a writer's class affiliation is no less fraught – and, of course, no less potentially reductive – than the identification of a readership with a particular social status. The caveat I issued earlier (via Frow 1995; see introduction and Chapters 1 and 2) applies here as well. For a discussion of class factors in the production and, particularly, the reception of literary works, see also Radway (1991).

14 There is a tacit universalism in many US-based educational arguments – as if the conditions that pertained in the US were automatically extendible to other countries. For a variation on this argument, see the treatment of the US multiculturalism debate in Chapter 5.

15 As Sandra Djwa says in an appreciative essay that clearly owes as much to Frye as to Atwood: 'It is almost as if [Atwood] consciously sets herself down, right in the middle of the Canadian literary landscape, and tries to orient herself by filtering Canadian experience through archetypes of her poetic sensibility' (Djwa 1981: 22). Djwa's essay is remarkable in that it almost completely misses the playfulness – and, frequently, the conspicuous self-irony – with which Atwood has explored this 'literary landscape' and the 'poetic archetypes' that might apply to it.

16 See, by way of analogy, the discussion of metonymic readings of Rushdie's novels in Chapter 2.

17 Metcalf's hit-list is remarkably long, his generosity toward other writers and, particularly, critics remarkably short. Ironically, given that his argument rests on the decontextualised representation of a 'central Canadian tradition', Metcalf's method consists mostly of taking decontextualised quotations from critics and treating them as representative examples of their work.

18 The collection, itself a curious mixture, attributes to the novels' versatility: *The Handmaid's Tale*, as Sharon Wilson confirms in her Preface to the collection, is 'currently the most widely taught Atwood text in the United States, [being] used in economics, political science, sociology, film, business, and other disciplines outside the humanities, and [having been] adopted by several universities … as a required text for all undergraduates' (Wilson *et al.* 1996: 1).

19 Atwood is also acutely aware of the ideological function of the reviewing process, providing a notable parody in her joke-review of her own collection *Second Words*. The parody targets fashionable academic assertions of plural authorship – 'It has long been our opinion that "Margaret Atwood" ("Peggy" to her friends), purported author of some 20 odd books, does not exist … [O]bjective evidence supports the conclusion that this person is merely a front for a committee' (Atwood 1982: 251); the second-hand status of professional literary critics, projected onto the figure of Atwood herself as a self-described

'amateur Victorian fern collector' and fully paid-up member of 'the footnote crowd' (252); the arcane findings of obscure international scholars, including the 'Celtic-Bilgarian ethnologist Gwaemot R. Dratora', the 'noted Transylvanian architect Wode M. Gratataro', and the 'Estonian-Italian postmodernist linguist and expert on metafiction, Trogwate d'Amorda' (251); and, not least, the 'Atwood cult' itself, whose devotees 'will want to add this volume to their T-shirt collection' (253).

Conclusion: thinking at the margins

1 It is deliciously ironic, of course, that the critical/theoretical industry in postmodernism is itself a symptom of the postmodern condition – a condition which, if Jameson is to be believed, has brought about the commodification of consumer society itself (see Introduction).

2 For other well-known critiques of the authoritarian tendencies of postcolonial criticism, see McClintock (1992) and Shohat (1992); see also the Introduction to this book.

3 See, particularly, the work of Spivak (e.g. 1990, 1993a); see also Radhakrishnan (1993) and the Introduction to this book.

4 See, for example, Riemenschneider (1983) for a relatively early series of critical essays on Commonwealth literary history and historiography.

5 While differences may be accounted for, these trajectories should not be understood as wholly separate; see, for example, the recent essay by Watson (2000), which provides evidence of American involvement in the early 'Commonwealth literature' project, while also arguing for the inclusion of the United States within the parameters of contemporary postcolonial studies.

6 For a balanced view of the history of Commonwealth literary studies, which acknowledges its pioneering role while pointing out its conceptual limitations, see Tiffin, 'Commonwealth Literature', in Riemenschneider (ed.) (1983).

7 On the ironic applicability of anthropological metaphors to Commonwealth and, later, postcolonial studies, see Introduction; for an analysis of the fictional treatment of anthropology itself in postcolonial (more specifically, African) literatures, see Chapter 1.

8 Some of the work of the leading figures in what was later to become postcolonial studies represents at once a negotiation between and a self-conscious interrogation of these interrelated approaches. See, for example, the work of Bill New (in Canada) and Helen Tiffin (in Australia).

9 See section two of this chapter for further reflections on the uneasy confluence of postcolonial politics and poststructuralist theory.

10 See, for example, Mukherjee (1990); also the essays in the somewhat optimistically entitled collection *After Europe* (1989, dealt with in more detail later in the chapter).

11 See, for example, Robbins' uncharitable review of the book in *Victorian Studies* (1992); also Hodge and Mishra's still less charitable treatment of it in *Dark Side of the Dream* (1990). Critiques of the book, while by no means unjustified, have become typical of what I identified earlier as the intellectual one-upmanship that casts a shadow over the postcolonial field (see Introduction).

12 For a more detailed analysis of *The Post-Colonial Studies Reader*, see the next section of this chapter.

13 While this global mandate is undoubtedly salutary, one of the effects of the turn to cultural studies has arguably been a *narrowing* of the field's normally

wide-ranging textual base. As Dieter Riemenschneider has remarked, 'cultural' analysis should not be treated as a substitute for wide reading (Riemenschneider 2000). It is possible that the convergence of postcolonial cultural studies with slightly earlier models of colonial discourse analysis (see below) has produced a tendency toward repetition and consolidation: the same 'key' texts, the same 'core' authors, the same 'globally applicable' cultural debates. It is also possible that the current vogue for cultural studies is behind the institutional phenomenon of the 'instant expert' – the born-again postcolonial scholar, jack of all disciplinary trades. While not entirely unsympathetic – nor myself invulnerable – to these arguments, I would also stress the 'positives' in a cultural studies approach: the opening up of the field to interdisciplinary research (whatever the dangers of dilettantism); the linking of politically conscious forms of postcolonial critique with an ideological analysis of contemporary modes of cultural globalisation; and, above all perhaps – a vast territory in which much still remains to be discovered – the exploring of the impact of 'postcoloniality' on globalised *popular* culture, an area which, as I am aware, has been left largely untapped in this book.

14 See, for example, the work of Lloyd and JanMohamed (1990) – for the US – and Gilroy (1987) and Hall (1996a) – for Britain.

15 The frequent coupling of postcolonial literary/cultural studies with US ethnic studies is also reflected in US university hiring policy, often to the extent that the former is officially viewed as little more than a supplement to the latter. This is, as I have implied, an ideological rather than a purely pragmatic decision. In a widely read essay, Dipesh Chakrabarty (1992) draws attention to the impossible but necessary task of 'provincializ[ing Europe] within the institutional site of the university' (Chakrabarty 1992: 22, also qtd in Ashcroft *et al.* 1995: 388). Perhaps a further stage – equally impossible, equally necessary – in the history of postcolonial studies should be the provincialisation of *America* as a self-regarding institutional site.

16 As Anne Brewster has remarked, 'the notion of the post-colonial has only a limited circulation globally. It has little currency in African, Middle Eastern and Latin American intellectual circles, except in the restricted historical sense of naming the period immediately after the end of colonial rule' (Brewster 1995: 22). This formulation seems over-generalised, but it provides a reminder that the global theorising of some postcolonial critics flies in the face of significant local differences and, sometimes, local dissent.

17 For further perspectives on theory and practice within the context of postcolonial pedagogy, see the special double issue of *College Literature* (October 1992/February 1993).

18 See, for example, several essays in the collection *Oppositional Aesthetics* (Mukherjee 1994b). For a wide-ranging discussion of the interpellation and various ideological guises of the postcolonial 'native informant', see Spivak's latest book, *A Critique of Postcolonial Reason* (1999). See also Introduction.

19 See Stanley Fish's analysis of this conundrum in his essay on US multiculturalism (1997, referred to in Chapter 5).

20 See Docker (1978); also the useful 'Education' section of Ashcroft *et al.*'s *Post-Colonial Studies Reader* (1995).

21 For an explanation of the postcolonialism/postcoloniality dialectic, see Introduction.

22 The survey, undertaken over several months in 1996, is far too extensive to be reproduced here in its entirety. It is, of course, in need of updating – my

apologies in advance to those instructors or institutions that find themselves misrepresented here.

23 See, for example, W.J.T. Mitchell (1992); see also the vitriolic response of Harish Trivedi, based at the University of Delhi, to a survey on postcolonial ideologies in the journal *Interventions*, in which he concludes that postcolonialism at best describes 'a little family quarrel between the white peoples of what is now an extended First World' (Trivedi 1999: 271). Such views, though hyperbolic, are enhanced by the fact that the vast majority of postcolonial courses, even in non-English-speaking countries, are held in English, with most though by no means all of them content to rely upon available English-language material and relatively few of them branching out into the comparative *linguistic* fields of, say, African, South Asian or Latin American studies. For further thoughts on the Anglocentric biases of postcolonial criticism, see Introduction; also below.

24 On the negative effects of uneven development in the global publishing industry, see also Chapters 1 and 2.

25 On the capacity of postcolonial literary texts to generate theory, see also Slemon and Tiffin's introduction to *After Europe* (1989, discussed below).

26 For a typically reductive critique, see Jacoby (1995).

27 Nancy Hartsock has made a similar argument for poststructuralist theories, in particular; see her essay in *Cultural Critique* (1987).

28 On the function and implications of academic celebrity culture, see, particularly, Shumway (1997); for its equivalent within the literary field, see Chapter 8 of this book.

29 That all of the above were or are *French*-speakers provides a further reminder that many producers, and still more consumers, of contemporary postcolonial theory are reliant on English translations. On the role of translation – both linguistic and cultural – in postcolonial studies, see Introduction; see also Harish Trivedi's bitterly ironic assertion that 'the postcolonial has ears only for English' – this in spite of the fact that 'the condition of postcoloniality is being experienced by a majority of people in the Third World in local languages distinctly other than English' (Trivedi 1999: 272). English, it bears repeating, is the language of the postcolonial exotic: the privileged language of academic criticism as well as the primary language of multinational commerce, a language whose effectiveness in the global 'marketplace of cultural difference' (Root 1996: 78) is to some extent dependent on other languages not being understood.

30 See, for example, the various, at times ill-tempered attempts to differentiate between 'postcolonial' and 'postmodern' epistemologies and modes of critical analysis in Adam and Tiffin (1990).

31 The nature of this project will of course vary according to location. In Germany, where I currently teach, postcolonial studies is hindered by its marginalisation within a conservative academy in which the New Literatures – as they are persistently called – tend to be seen as little more than an adjunct of English Literature, or as a testing-ground for cultural studies approaches still regarded by many as politically suspect or methodologically weak.

32 See Steiner for a fascinating study of African tourist art, one of several by-products of 'the commoditization of African art in a postcolonial transnational economy' (Steiner 1994: 9).

33 For an application of Ortiz's term in a variety of colonial/postcolonial contexts, see Appadurai (1996) and Pratt (1992).

Bibliography

Achebe, C. (1996) [1958] *Things Fall Apart*, Oxford: Heinemann (African Writers Series: Classics in Context).

—— (1989a) 'Colonialist Criticism', in *Hopes and Impediments: Selected Essays*, New York: Doubleday, 68–90.

—— (1989b) 'The Novelist as Teacher', in *Hopes and Impediments: Selected Essays*, New York: Doubleday, 40–6.

Adam, I. and Tiffin, H. (eds) (1990) *Past the Last Post: Theorizing Post-Colonialism and Post-Modernism*, Calgary: University of Calgary Press.

Adotevi, S. (1972) *Négritude et négrologues*, Paris: Union Générale d'éditions.

Ahmad, A. (1992) *In Theory: Classes, Nations, Literatures*, London: Verso.

—— (1995a) 'The Politics of Literary Postcoloniality', *Race & Class* 36, 3: 1–20.

—— (1995b) 'Postcolonialism: What's in a Name?', in R. de la Campa, E.A. Kaplan and M. Sprinker (eds), *Late Imperial Culture*, New York: Verso, 11–32.

Aidoo, A.A. (1972) 'That Capacious Topic: Gender Politics', in P. Mariani (ed.), *Critical Fictions: The Politics of Imaginative Writing*, Seattle, WA: Bay Press, 152.

Ali, T. (1982) 'Midnight's Children', *New Left Review* 136: 87–95.

Altbach, P. (1975) 'Literary Colonialism: Books in The Third World', *Harvard Educational Review* 15, 2: 226–36.

Altbach, P., Arboleda, A.A. and Gopinathan, S. (eds) (1985) *Publishing in the Third World: Knowledge and Development*, Oxford: Heinemann Educational Books.

Amuta, C. (1989) *The Theory of African Literature*, London: Zed Books.

Ananthamurthy, U.R. (1997) 'Lingua Fracas', *The Sunday Times of India*, 13 July: 19.

Anderson, B. (1983) *Imagined Communities*, London: Verso.

Ang, I. (1996) 'The Curse of the Smile: Ambivalence and the "Asian" Woman in Australian Multiculturalism', *Feminist Review* 52: 36–49.

Appadurai, A. (ed.) (1986) *The Social Life of Things: Commodities in Cultural Perspective*, Cambridge: Cambridge University Press.

—— (1994) 'Disjuncture and Difference in the Global Cultural Economy', in P. Williams and L. Chrisman (eds), *Colonial Discourse and Post-Colonial Theory: A Reader*, New York: Columbia University Press, 324–9.

—— (1996) *Modernity at Large: Cultural Dimensions of Globalization*, Minneapolis, MN: University of Minnesota Press.

Appiah, K.A. (1991) 'Is the Post- in Postmodernism the Post- in Postcolonial?' *Critical Inquiry* 17: 336–57.

—— (1992) *In My Father's House: Africa in the Philosophy of Culture*, New York: Oxford University Press.

—— (1994) 'Identity, Authenticity, Survival: Multicultural Societies and Social Reproduction', in A. Gutmann (ed.), *Multiculturalism: Examining the Politics of Recognition*, Princeton, NJ: Princeton University Press, 149–64.

Arac, J. and Ritvo, H. (eds) (1991) *The Macropolitics of Nineteenth-Century Literature: Nationalism, Exoticism, Imperialism*, Philadelphia, PA: University of Pennsylvania Press.

Asad, T. (ed.) (1972) *Anthropology and the Colonial Encounter*, Atlantic Highlands, NJ: Humanities Press.

—— (1986) 'The Concept of Cultural Translation in British Social Anthropology', in J. Clifford and G. Marcus (eds) *Writing Culture: The Poetics and Politics of Ethnography*, Berkeley, CA: University of California Press, 141–64.

—— (1990) 'Ethnography, Literature, and Politics: Some Readings and Uses of Salman Rushdie's *The Satanic Verses*', *Cultural Anthropology* 5, 3: 239–69.

Ashcroft, B., Griffiths, G. and Tiffin, H. (1989) *The Empire Writes Back: Theory and Practice in Post-Colonial Literatures*, London: Routledge.

—— (eds) (1995) *The Post-Colonial Studies Reader*, London: Routledge.

—— (1998) *Keywords in Post-Colonial Studies*, London: Routledge.

Atwood, M. (1970) *The Journals of Susanna Moodie*, Toronto: Oxford University Press.

—— (1972) *Survival: A Thematic Guide to Canadian Literature*, Toronto: Anansi.

—— (1979) [1972] *Surfacing*, London: Virago.

—— (1980) [1969] *The Edible Woman*, London: Virago.

—— (1982) *Second Words: Selected Critical Prose*, Toronto: Anansi.

—— (1987) [1985] *The Handmaid's Tale*, London: Virago.

—— (1992a) [1979] *Life Before Man*, London: Virago.

—— (1992b) *Margaret Atwood: Conversations*, ed. E. G. Ingersoll, London: Virago.

—— (1993) [1976] *Lady Oracle*, London: Virago.

—— (1994a) [1988] *Cat's Eye*, London: Virago.

—— (1994b) [1993] *The Robber Bride*, London: Virago.

—— (1996) *Alias Grace*, Toronto: McClelland & Stewart.

—— (2000) *The Blind Assassin*, London: Bloomsbury.

Australian Bureau of Statistics (2000) Online source. http://wws.abs.gov.au/Ausstats/ABS%40.ns...eaa80b7187fca2568a900154aac!OpenDocument.

Bail, M. (1980) *Homesickness*, Melbourne: Macmillan.

Bakhtin, M.M. (1981) 'Discourse in the Novel', in M. Holquist (ed.) *The Dialogical Imagination: Four Essays by M.M. Bakhtin*, trans. C. Emerson and M. Holquist, Austin, TX: University of Texas Press, 259–422.

—— (1984) *Rabelais and His World*, trans. H. Irwolsky, Bloomington, IN: Indiana University Press.

Bali Travel News (1999) Online source. http://www.bali-travelnews.com/Batrav/batrav21/cstory.htm.

Bandy, J. (1996) 'Managing the Other of Nature: Sustainability, Spectacle, and Global Regimes of Capital in Ecotourism', *Public Culture* 8: 539–66.

Baranay, I. (1992) *The Edge of Bali*, Pymble, NSW: HarperCollins.

Barker, F., Hulme, P. and Iversen, I. (eds) (1994) *Colonial Discourse/Postcolonial Theory*, Manchester: Manchester University Press.

Bataille, G. (1986) *Erotisme: Death and Sensuality*, trans. M. Dalwood, San Francisco, CA: City Lights.

Beer, G. (1970) *The Romance*, London: Methuen.

Behdad, A. (1994) *Belated Travelers: Orientalism in the Age of Colonial Dissolution*, Durham, NC: Duke University Press.

Bello, S. and Augi, A. (eds) (1993) *Culture and the Book Industry in Nigeria*, Lagos: National Council for Arts and Culture.

Benjamin, W. (1969a) [1968] 'On Some Motifs in Baudelaire', in H. Arendt (ed.), *Illuminations: Essays and Reflections*, New York: Schocken, 155–200.

—— (1969b) [1968] 'The Task of the Translator', in H. Arendt (ed.), *Illuminations: Essays and Reflections*, New York: Schocken, 69–82.

Bennett, B. (1988) 'Perceptions of Australia, 1965–1988', in L. Hergenhan (ed.), *The Penguin New Literary History of Australia*, Ringwood, Vic.: Penguin, 433–53.

Bennett, D. (1991) 'Conflicted Vision: A Consideration of Canon and Genre in English-Canadian Literature', in R. Lecker (ed.), *Canadian Canons: Essays in Literary Value*, Toronto: University of Toronto Press, 131–49.

Bennett, T. (1990) *Outside Literature*, London: Routledge.

Benson, E. and Conolly, L.W. (eds) (1994) *The Routledge Encyclopedia of Post-Colonial Literatures in English, Vols I and II*, London: Routledge.

Berger, J. (1989) G, London: The Hogarth Press.

Bernstein, M. and Studlar, G. (eds) (1997) *Visions of the East: Orientalism in Film*, New Brunswick, NJ: Rutgers University Press.

Bhabha, H. (1983) 'Difference, Discrimination and the Discourse of Colonialism', in F. Barker *et al.* (eds), *The Politics of Theory*, Colchester: University of Essex, 195–211.

—— (1990) 'DissemiNation: Time, Narrative, and the Margins of the Modern Nation', in H. Bhabha (ed.), *Nation and Narration*, London: Routledge, 291–322.

—— (1990) (ed.) *Nation and Narration*, London: Routledge.

—— (1992) 'Postcolonial Criticism', in S. Greenblatt and G. Gunn (eds), *Redrawing the Boundaries: The Transformation of English and American Literary Studies*, New York: Modern Language Association, 437–65.

—— (1994a) 'How Newness Enters the World: Postmodern Space, Postcolonial Times and the Trials of Cultural Translation', in *The Location of Culture*, London: Routledge, 212–35.

—— (1994b) 'Of Mimicry and Man: The Ambivalence of Colonial Discourse', in *The Location of Culture*, London: Routledge, 85–92.

—— (1994c) 'The Commitment to Theory', in *The Location of Culture*, London: Routledge, 19–39.

—— (1994d) *The Location of Culture*, London: Routledge.

—— (1994e) 'The Other Question: Stereotype, Discrimination and the Discourse of Colonialism', in *The Location of Culture*, London: Routledge, 66–84.

Bhardwaj, S.M., Rinschede, G. and Sievers, A. (eds) (1994) *Pilgrimage in the Old and New Worlds*, Berlin: Dietrich Riemer Verlag.

Birch, D. (1991) 'Postmodernist Chutneys', *Textual Practice* 5, 1: 1–7.

Bissoondath, N. (1986) [1985] *Digging Up the Mountains: Selected Stories*, Toronto: Macmillan.

—— (1989) [1988] *A Casual Brutality*, Markham, Ont.: Penguin.

—— (1992) *The Innocence of Age*, Toronto: Knopf.

—— (1994) *Selling Illusions: The Cult of Multiculturalism in Canada*, Markham, Ont.: Penguin.

Blaise, C. (1981) 'A Novel of India's Coming of Age', *New York Times Book Review* Vol. LXXXVI, 16, 19 April: 18–19.

Blaise, C. and Muhkerjee, B. (1986) *Days and Nights in Calcutta*, Markham, Ont.: Penguin.

Bloom, A. (1987) *The Closing of the American Mind: How Higher Education Has Failed Democracy and Impoverished the Souls of Today's Students*, New York: Simon & Schuster.

Boehmer, E. (1995) *Colonial & Postcolonial Literature*, Oxford: Oxford University Press.

Bongie, C. (1991) *Exotic Memories: Literature, Colonialism, and the Fin de Siècle*, Stanford, CA: Stanford University Press.

Boorstin, D.J. (1961) *The Image: A Guide to Pseudo-Events in America*, New York: Atheneum.

Bottomley, G. and de Lepervanche, M. (eds) (1984) *Ethnicity, Class and Gender in Australia*, Sydney: Allen & Unwin.

Bourdieu, P. (1993) *The Field of Cultural Production: Essays on Art and Literature*, ed. R. Johnson, New York: Columbia University Press.

Boyce Davies, C. (1994) *Black Women, Writing, and Identity: Migrations of the Subject*, New York: Routledge.

Brantlinger, P. (1996) *Fictions of State: Culture and Credit in Britain, 1694–1994*, Ithaca, NY: Cornell University Press.

Brennan, T. (1989) *Salman Rushdie and the Third World: Myths of the Nation*, New York: Macmillan/St Martin's.

—— (1997) *At Home in the World: Cosmopolitanism Now*, Cambridge, MA: Harvard University Press.

Breton, R. (1986) 'Multiculturalism and Canadian Nation-Building', in A. Cairns and C. Williams (eds), *The Politics of Gender, Ethnicity and Language in Canada*, Toronto: University of Toronto Press, 27–66.

Brewster, A. (1995) *Literary Formations: Post-colonialism, Nationalism, Globalism*, Melbourne: Melbourne University Press.

Broinowski, A. (1992) *The Yellow Lady: Australian Impressions of Asia*, Melbourne: Oxford University Press.

Brydon, D. (1990). 'The White Inuit Speaks: Contamination as Literary Strategy', in I. Adam and H. Tiffin (eds), *Past the Last Post: Theorizing Post-Colonialism and Post-Modernism*, Calgary: University of Calgary Press, 191–203.

—— (1994) 'Response to Hart', *Arachne* 1, 1: 100–112.

—— (1996) 'Beyond Violent Dualities: Atwood in Postcolonial Contexts', in S.R. Wilson, T.B. Friedman and S. Hengen (eds), *Approaches to Teaching* The Handmaid's Tale *and Other Works*, New York: Modern Language Association, 49–54.

Buford, B. (1997) 'Declarations of Independence: Why Are There Suddenly So Many Indian Novelists?' *The New Yorker*, 23–30 June: 6–8.

Butler, J. (1990) *Gender Trouble: Feminism and the Subversion of Identity*, New York: Routledge.

Buzard, J. (1993) *The Beaten Track: European Tourism, Literature, and the Ways to 'Culture,' 1800–1918*, Oxford: Clarendon.

Caine, Sir M.H. (1998) 'The Booker Story', *Booker 30: A Celebration of 30 Years of the Booker Prize for Fiction 1969–1998*, St. Ives: Booker, 6–12.

Carroll, D. (1990) *Chinua Achebe: Novelist, Poet, Critic*, London: Macmillan.

Castles, S., Kalantzis, M., Cope, W. and Morrissey, M. (1988) *Mistaken Identity: Multiculturalism and the Demise of Nationalism in Australia*, Sydney: Pluto Press.

Célestin, R. (1996) *From Cannibals to Radicals: Figures and Limits of Exoticism*, Minneapolis, MN: University of Minnesota Press.

Chakrabarty, D. (1992) 'Postcoloniality and the Artifice of History: Who Speaks for "Indian" Pasts?', *Representations* 37: 1–24.

Chambers, I. and Curti, L. (eds) (1996) *The Post-Colonial Question: Common Skies, Divided Horizons*, London: Routledge.

Chandra, V. (1999) 'Indo-Anglian Writers: Nowhere and Everywhere', *The Hindu*, 5 December. Online source: http://www.indiaserver.com/thehindu/1999/12/05/stories/130050672.htm.

—— (1999) 'Indo-Anglian Writers: Where the Mind is Without Fear', *The Hindu*, 19 December. Online source: http://www.indiaserver.com/thehindu/1999/12/19/stories/1319067k.htm.

Cheyfitz, E. (1991) *The Poetics of Imperialism: Translation and Colonization from* The Tempest *to* Tarzan, New York: Oxford University Press.

Childs, P. and Williams, P. (1997) *An Introduction to Post-Colonial Theory*, London: Prentice Hall/Harvester Wheatsheaf.

Chinweizu, Jemie, O. and Madubuike, I. (1983) *Toward the Decolonization of African Literature*, Washington, DC: Howard University Press.

Chisholm, K. (1997) 'Incest and Abuse', *Sunday Telegraph*, 1 June.

Christian, B. (1990) 'The Race for Theory', in D. Lloyd and A. JanMohamed (eds), *The Nature and Context of Minority Discourse*, New York: Oxford University Press, 37–49.

Clayton, D. and Gregory, D. (eds) (forthcoming, 2003) *Colonialism, Postcolonialism and the Production of Space*, Oxford: Blackwell.

Clifford, J. (1986) 'On Ethnographic Allegory', in J. Clifford and G. Marcus (eds), *Writing Culture: The Poetics and Politics of Ethnography*, Berkeley, CA: University of California Press, 98–121.

—— (1988) *The Predicament of Culture: Twentieth-Century Ethnography, Literature, and Art*, Cambridge, MA: Harvard University Press.

Clifford, J. and Marcus, G. (eds) (1986) *Writing Culture: The Poetics and Politics of Ethnography*, Berkeley, CA: University of California Press.

Cohen, E. (1973) 'Nomads from Affluence: Notes on the Phenomenon of Drifter-Tourism', *International Journal of Comparative Sociology* 14, 1/2: 89–103.

Coleman, D. (1996) 'Writing Dislocation: Transculturalism, Gender, Immigrant Families. A Conversation with Ven Begamudre', *Canadian Literature* 149: 36–51.

Crick, M. (1991) 'Tourists, Locals and Anthropologists: Quizzical Reflections on "Otherness" in Tourist Encounters and in Tourism Research', *Australian Cultural History* 10: 6–18.

Cudjoe, S. (1988) *V.S. Naipaul*, Amherst, MA: University of Massachusetts Press.

Culler, J. (1988) 'The Semiotics of Tourism', in *Framing the Sign: Criticism and Its Institutions*, Norman: University of Oklahoma Press, 153–67.

—— (1997) *Literary Theory: A Very Short Introduction*, New York: Oxford University Press.

Dabydeen, D. (1994) *Turner: New and Selected Poems*, London: Jonathan Cape.

Dalrymple, W. (1997) 'Type Caste', *Harpers & Queen* 114–15, 169.

Dash, M. (1989) 'In Search of the Lost Body: Redefining the Subject in Caribbean Literature', *Kunapipi* 11, 1: 17–26.

David, D. (1997) 'Notes on Multiculturalism in Canada and Australia', unpublished research paper, Harvard University.

Davidson, A.E. and Davidson, C.N. (1981) *The Art of Margaret Atwood: Essays in Criticism*, Toronto: Anansi.

Deleuze, G. and Guattari, F. (1990) 'What is a Minor Literature?', in R. Ferguson *et al.* (eds), *Out There: Marginalization and Contemporary Cultures*, Cambridge, MA: MIT Press, 59–70.

Demidenko, H. (1994) *The Hand That Signed the Paper*, St. Leonards: Allen & Unwin.

Derrida, J. (1974) *Of Grammatology*, trans. G.C. Spivak, Baltimore, MA: Johns Hopkins University Press.

Diawara, M. (1998) *In Search of Africa*, Cambridge, MA: Harvard University Press.

Dingwaney Needham, A. (1988/9) 'The Politics of Post-Colonial Identity in Salman Rushdie', *Massachusetts Review* 29, 4: 609–24.

Dirlik, A. (1994) 'The Postcolonial Aura: Third World Criticism in the Age of Global Capitalism', *Critical Inquiry* 20: 328–56.

—— (1996) 'The Global in the Local', in R. Wilson and W. Dissanayake (eds), *Global/Local: Cultural Production and the Transnational Imaginary*, Durham, NC: Duke University Press, 21–45.

—— (1999) 'Response to the Responses: Thoughts on the Postcolonial', *Interventions* 1, 2: 286–90.

Djwa, S. (1981) 'The Where of Here: Margaret Atwood and a Canadian Tradition', in A. Davidson and C. Davidson (eds), *The Art of Margaret Atwood: Essays in Criticism*, Toronto: Anansi, 15–34.

Docker, J. (1978) 'The Neocolonial Assumption in University Teaching of English', in C. Tiffin (ed.), *South Pacific Images*, St. Lucia, QLD: SPACLALS, 26–31.

Du Bois, W.E.B. (1990) [1903] *The Souls of Black Folk*, New York: Penguin.

During, S. (1985) 'Postmodernism or Postcolonialism?' *Landfall* 39, 3: 366–80.

—— (1992) 'Postcolonialism and Globalisation', *Meanjin* 48, 2: 339–53.

—— (1998) 'Postcolonialism and Globalisation: A Dialectical Relation After All?', *Postcolonial Studies* 1, 1: 31–47.

Durix, J.-P. (1985) 'Magic Realism in *Midnight's Children*', *Commonwealth Essays and Studies* 8, 1: 57–63.

Eagleton, T. (1999) 'Postcolonialism and "Postcolonialism" ', *Interventions* 1, 1: 24–6.

Eagleton, T. and Fuller, P. (1983) 'The Question of Value: A Discussion', *New Left Review* 142: 76–90.

Eakin, H. (1995) 'Literary Prizes in the Age of Multiculturalism', unpublished research paper, Harvard University.

Easingwood, P., Gross, K. and Hunter, L. (eds) (1996) *Difference and Community: Canadian and European Cultural Perspectives*, Amsterdam: Rodopi.

Eco, U. (1990) *The Limits of Interpretation*, Bloomington, IN: Indiana University Press.

The Economist (1989) 'Who Needs the Booker?', 21–7 October: 101.

—— (1990) 'Old Mammon', 20–6 October: 114.

Egbuna, O. (1974) 'Interview with Obi Egbuna', in B. Lindfors (ed.), *Dem-Say: Interviews with Eight Nigerian Writers*, Austin, TX: African and Afro-American Studies and Research Center, 16–23.

Egoyan, A. (1994) *Exotica*, Toronto: Ego Film Arts.

—— (1995) *Exotica: The Screenplay*, Toronto: Coach House Press.

Eliades, P. (1995) 'Anthologising the Minority', *Hecate* 21, 1: 74–97.

Elliott, S. (1994) *The Adventures of Priscilla, Queen of the Desert*, Sydney: Latent Image Films.

Emberley, J. (1993) *Thresholds of Difference: Feminist Critique, Native Women's Writing, Postcolonial Theory*, Toronto: University of Toronto Press.

Erenberg, L.A. (1981) *Steppin' Out: New York Night-Life and the Transformation of American Culture, 1890–1930*, Westport, CT: Greenwood.

Ewen, S. (1988) *All Consuming Images: The Politics of Style in Contemporary Culture*, New York: Basic Books.

Ezenwa-Ohaeto, A. (ed.) (1995) *Making Books Available and Affordable: Proceedings of the First Annual National Conference on Book Development*, Lagos: New Concept Publishers.

—— (1997) *Chinua Achebe: A Biography*, Bloomington, IN: Indiana University Press.

Fabian, J. (1992) 'White Humor', *Transition* 55: 56–61.

Falk Moore, S. (1993) 'Changing Perspectives on a Changing Africa: The Work of Anthropology', in R.H. Bates, V.Y. Mudimbe and J. O'Barr (eds), *Africa and the Disciplines: The Contributions of Research in Africa to the Social Sciences and Humanities*, Chicago, IL: University of Chicago Press, 3–57.

Farrell, J.G. (1973) *The Siege of Krishnapur*, London: Penguin.

Featherstone, M. (1996) 'Localism, Globalism, and Cultural Identity', in R. Wilson and W. Dissanayake (eds), *Global/Local: Cultural Production and the Transnational Imaginary*, Durham, NC: Duke University Press, 46–77.

Fee, M. (1989) 'Why C.K. Stead Didn't Like Keri Hulme's *the bone people*: Who Can Write as Other?' *Australian and New Zealand Studies in Canada* 1: 11–32.

Feifer, M. (1985) *Going Places*, London: Macmillan.

Felski, R. (1989) *Beyond Feminist Aesthetics*, London: Hutchinson Radius.

Ferguson, R., Gever, M., Minh-ha, T.T. and West, C. (eds) (1990) *Out There: Marginalization and Contemporary Cultures*, Cambridge, MA: MIT Press.

Fischer, M.M.J. (1986) 'Ethnicity and the Post-Modern Arts of Memory', in J. Clifford and G. Marcus (eds), *Writing Culture: The Poetics and Politics of Ethnography*, Berkeley, CA: University of California Press, 194–233.

Fischer, S. (1999) 'Race, Gender and Performance in the Works of Derek Walcott', MA thesis, University of Munich.

Fish, S. (1997) 'Boutique Multiculturalism, or Why Liberals Are Incapable of Thinking about Hate Speech', *Critical Inquiry* 23, 2: 378–95.

Fishlock, T. (1993) 'All Indian Life and Love is Here', *Sunday Telegraph* 21 March.

Foster, S. (1982/3) 'Exoticism as a Symbolic System', *Dialectical Anthropology* 7: 21–30.

Foucault, M. (1977) *Language, Counter-Memory, Practice*, trans. D.F. Bouchard and S. Simons, Ithaca, NY: Cornell University Press.

—— (1986) 'Of Other Spaces', *Diacritics* 16, 1: 22–7.

Francke, L. (1994) 'Review of *The Adventures of Priscilla Queen of the Desert*', *Sight and Sound* 4, 11: 38.

Freire, P. (1973) *Pedagogy of the Oppressed*, trans. M.B. Ramos, New York: Seabury Press.

Friedman, L. and Stewart, S. (1992) 'Keeping His Own Voice: An Interview with Stephen Frears', in W.W. Dixon (ed.), *Re-Viewing British Cinema, 1900–1992*, Albany, NY: State University of New York Press, 221–38.

Friedman, T. (1998) *Internet Resources on Margaret Atwood and Her Works*. Online source. http://www.cariboo.bc.ca/atwood/internet.htm.

Frobenius, L. (1973) *Leo Frobenius: An Anthology*, ed. E. Haberland, trans. P. Crampton, Wiesbaden: Franz Steiner Verlag GMBH.

Frow, J. (1991) 'Tourism and the Semiotics of Nostalgia', *October* 57: 123–51.

—— (1995) *Cultural Studies and Cultural Value*, Oxford: Clarendon.

Furbisher, J. (1993) 'An Indian "Tolstoy" Excites the Literati', *Sunday Times* 21 March: 1–5.

Gallini, C. (1996) 'Mass Exoticisms', in I. Chambers and L. Curti (eds), *The Post-Colonial Question: Common Skies, Divided Horizons*, London: Routledge, 212–20.

Gandhi, L. (1998) *Postcolonial Theory: A Critical Introduction*, Sydney: Allen & Unwin.

Ganguly, K. (1993) 'Something Like a Snake: Pedagogy and Postcolonial Literature', *College Literature* 20, 1: 185–90.

Garber, M. (1992) *Vested Interests: Cross-Dressing and Cultural Anxiety*, New York: Routledge.

Garland, A. (1996) *The Beach*, London: Penguin.

Geertz, C. (1988) *Works and Lives: The Anthropologist as Author*, Stanford, CA: Stanford University Press.

Gelder, K. and Jacobs, J.M. (1998) *Uncanny Australia: Sacredness and Identity in a Postcolonial Nation*, Melbourne: Melbourne University Press.

Genette, G. (1987) *Seuils*. Paris: Éditions du Seuil.

Gikandi, S. (1987) *Reading the African Novel*, London: James Currey.

—— (1996) *Maps of Englishness: Writing Identity in the Culture of Colonialism*, New York: Columbia University Press.

Gilbert, H. (1992) 'The Dance as Text in Contemporary Australian Drama: Movement and Resistance Politics', *Ariel* 23, 1: 133–47.

Gilroy, P. (1987) *There Ain't No Black in the Union Jack: The Cultural Politics of Race and Nation*, London: Hutchinson.

Ginibi, R. Langford (1988) *Don't Take Your Love to Town*, Ringwood, Vic.: Penguin.

Giroux, H.A. (1992a) *Border Crossings: Cultural Workers and the Politics of Education*, New York: Routledge.

—— (1992b) 'Literacy, Pedagogy, and the Politics of Difference', *College Literature* 19, 1: 1–11.

—— (1992c) 'Post-Colonial Ruptures and Democratic Possibilities: Multiculturalism and Anti-Racist Pedagogy', *Cultural Critique* 21: 5–39.

Goff, M. (1989) 'Introduction', in M. Goff (ed.), *Prize Writing: An Original Collection of Writings by Past Winners to Celebrate 21 Years of the Booker Prize*, London: Hodder & Stoughton, 11–23.

—— (2000) 'How the Booker Prize Works'. Online source: http://www.bookerprize.co.uk/site/fact/about/aboutfset_pw.html.

Goldberg, D.T. (ed.) (1994) *Multiculturalism: A Critical Reader*, Cambridge, MA: Blackwell.

Goldie, T. (1989) *Fear and Temptation: Images of the Indigene in Canadian, Australian, and New Zealand Literatures*, Kingston: McGill/Queen's University Press.

—— (1999) 'Who is Mudrooroo?' Unpublished conference paper presented at the 'Compromising Colonialisms' conference, Feb. 1999, University of Wollongong, Australia.

Golding, A. (1995) *From Outlaw to Classic: Canons in American Poetry*, Madison, WI: University of Wisconsin Press.

Golfman, N. (1996) 'Locating Difference: Ways of Reading Multiculturalism', *Mosaic* 29, 3: 175–85.

Gorra, M. (1997a) *After Empire: Scott, Naipaul, Rushdie*, Chicago, IL: University of Chicago Press.

—— (1997b) 'Living in the Aftermath', *London Review of Books*, 19 June: 22–3.

Grace, S. (1981) 'Margaret Atwood and the Poetics of Duplicity', in A.E. Davidson and C.N. Davidson (eds), *The Art of Margaret Atwood: Essays in Criticism*, Toronto: Anansi, 55–68.

Grace, S. and Weir, L. (eds) (1983) *Margaret Atwood: Language, Text and System*, Vancouver: University of British Columbia Press.

Grant, B. (1983) *The Australian Dilemma: A New Kind of Western Society*, NSW, Aus.: Macdonald Futura Australia.

Granta (1997) 'India!': Special Golden Jubilee Issue, 57. 1, ed. I. Jack.

Greenblatt, S. (1991) *Marvelous Possessions: The Wonder of the New World*, Chicago, IL: University of Chicago Press.

Greenway, P., Lyon, J. and Wheeler, T. (1999) *Bali & Lombok*, 7th edn, Hawthorn, Vic.: Lonely Planet Publications.

Greet, A., Harrex, S. and Hosking, S. (eds) (1992) *Raj Nostalgia: Some Literary and Critical Implications*, Adelaide: CRNLE.

Gregory, D. (1994) *Geographical Imaginations*, Oxford: Blackwell.

Griffiths, G. (1994) 'The Myth of Authenticity: Representation, Discourse and Social Practice', in C. Tiffin and A. Lawson (eds), *De-Scribing Empire: Postcolonialism and Textuality*, London: Routledge, 70–85.

Griswold, W. (2000) *Bearing Witness: Readers, Writers, and the Novel in Nigeria*, Princeton, NJ: Princeton University Press.

Grove, V. (1993) 'A Weight for Small Shoulders', *Times* 26 March: 15–16.

Guillory, J. (1993) *Cultural Capital: The Problem of Literary Canon Formation*, Chicago, IL: University of Chicago Press.

Gunew, S. (1990) 'Denaturalizing Cultural Nationalisms: Multicultural Readings of "Australia" ', in H. Bhabha (ed.), *Nation and Narration*, London: Routledge, 99–120.

—— (1994) *Framing Marginality: Multicultural Literary Studies*, Melbourne: Melbourne University Press.

Gunew, S. and Longley, K.O. (eds) (1992) *Striking Chords: Multicultural Literary Interpretations*, Sydney: Allen & Unwin.

Gunew, S. and Mahyuddin, J. (eds) (1988) *Beyond the Echo: Multicultural Women's Writing*, St. Lucia: University of Queensland Press.

Gurnah, A. (1995) 'Displacement and Transformation in *The Enigma of Arrival* and *The Satanic Verses*', in A.R. Lee (ed.), *Other Britain, Other British: Contemporary Multicultural Fiction*, London: Pluto Press, 5–20.

Gutmann, A. (ed.) (1994) *Multiculturalism: Examining the Politics of Recognition*, Princeton, NJ: Princeton University Press.

Habermas, J. (1994) 'Struggles for Recognition in the Democratic Constitutional State', in A. Gutmann (ed.), *Multiculturalism: Examining the Politics of Recognition*, Princeton, NJ: Princeton University Press, 107–48.

Hall, S. (1996a) 'New Ethnicities', in D. Morley and K.H. Chen (eds), *Stuart Hall: Critical Dialogues in Cultural Studies*, London: Routledge, 441–9.

—— (1996b) 'When Was the "Post-Colonial"? Thinking at the Limit', in I. Chambers and L. Curti (eds), *The Post-Colonial Question: Common Skies, Divided Horizons*, London: Routledge, 242–59.

Hammond, D. and Jablow, A. (1977) *The Myth of Africa*, New York: Library of Social Sciences.

Hamner, R. (1973) *V.S. Naipaul*, New York: Twayne.

Harsono, Y. (1996) 'Worldwide Survey of Courses in Postcolonial Studies', unpublished report, Harvard University.

Hartsock, N. (1987) 'Rethinking Modernism: Majority versus Minority Theories', *Cultural Critique* 7: 187–206.

Harvey, D. (1989) *The Condition of Postmodernity: An Enquiry into the Origins of Cultural Change*, Oxford: Blackwell.

Hawkins, F. (1982) 'Multiculturalism in Two Countries: The Canadian and Australian Experience', *Journal of Canadian Studies* 17, 1: 64–80.

Hawthorne, S. (1989) 'The Politics of the Exotic: The Paradox of Cultural Voyeurism', *Meanjin* 48, 2: 259–68.

Haywood, I. (1987) *Faking It: Art and the Politics of Forgery*, Brighton: Harvester Press.

Head, B. (1977) *The Collector of Treasures*, Oxford: Heinemann.

—— (1981) *Serowe: Village of the Rain Wind*, Oxford: Heinemann.

Hebdige, D. (1976) *Subculture: The Meaning of Style*, London: Routledge.

Hergenhan, L. (ed.) (1988) *The Penguin New Literary History of Australia*, Ringwood, Vic.: Penguin.

Higham, C. and Wilding, M. (eds) (1967) *Australians Abroad*, Melbourne: F.W. Cheshire.

Hill, A. (1988) *In Pursuit of Publishing*, London: John Murray in Assoc. with Heinemann Educational Books.

Hinz, E.J. (1996) 'What is Multiculturalism?: A "Cognitive" Introduction', *Mosaic* 29, 3: vii–xiii.

Hodge, B. and Mishra, V. (1990) *Dark Side of the Dream: Australian Literature and the Postcolonial Mind*, Sydney: Allen & Unwin.

Holland, P. and Huggan, G. (1998) *Tourists with Typewriters: Critical Reflections on Contemporary Travel Writing*, Ann Arbor, MI: University of Michigan Press.

hooks, b. (1990) 'marginality as site of resistance', in R. Ferguson *et al.* (eds), *Out There: Marginalization and Contemporary Cultures*, Cambridge, MA: MIT Press, 341–44.

Hosking, S. (1992) 'Lyric and Betrayal: Aboriginal Narrativizing', review of B. Wongar, *The Track to Bralgu* and Ruby Langford Ginibi, *Real Deadly*, *CRNLE Reviews Journal* 1: 14–17.

Hospital, J.T. (1982) *The Ivory Swing*, Toronto: McClelland & Stewart.

Howe, D. (2000) 'We are the Future', *Observer*, 10 September: 29.

Howells, C.A. (1995) *Margaret Atwood*, New York: St. Martin's University Press.

Hryniuk, S. (ed.) (1992) *Twenty Years of Multiculturalism*, Winnipeg: St John's College Press.

Huggan, G. (1992) 'Orientalism Reconfirmed? Stereotypes of East-West Encounter in Janette Turner Hospital's *The Ivory Swing* and Yvon Rivard's *Les silences du corbeau*', *Canadian Literature* 132: 44–56.

—— (1993a) 'Transformations of the Tourist Gaze: India in Recent Australian Fiction', *Westerly* 38, 4: 83–9.

—— (1993b) 'Some Recent Australian Fictions in the Age of Tourism: Murray Bail, Inez Baranay, Gerard Lee', *Australian Literary Studies* 16, 2: 169–78.

—— (1994a) 'Anthropologists and Other Frauds', *Comparative Literature* 46, 2: 113–28.

—— (1994b) 'The Postcolonial Exotic: Rushdie's "Booker of Bookers" ', *Transition* 64: 22–9.

—— (1995) 'Exoticism and Ethnicity in Michael Ondaatje's *Running in the Family*', in W. Siemerling (ed.), *Writing Ethnicity*, Toronto: ECW Press, 116–27.

—— (1996) *Peter Carey*, Melbourne: Oxford University Press.

—— (1997a) 'Prizing "Otherness": A Short History of the Booker', *Studies in the Novel* 29, 3: 412–33.

—— (1997b) 'The Neocolonialism of Postcolonialism: A Cautionary Note', *Links and Letters* 4: 19–24.

—— (1997c) 'Staged Marginalities: Salman Rushdie and V.S. Naipaul', in M. Nadal and M.D. Herrero (eds), *Margins in British and American Literature, Film and Culture*, Zaragoza: Dept. de Filología Inglesa e Alemana, University of Zaragoza, 73–8.

—— (1997/8) '(Post)colonialism, Anthropology, and the Magic of Mimesis', *Cultural Critique* 38: 91–106.

—— (1998) 'Consuming India', *Ariel* 29, 1: 245–58.

—— (2000) 'Exoticism, Ethnicity and the Multicultural Fallacy', in I. Santaolalla (ed.), *New Exoticisms: Changing Patterns in the Construction of Otherness*, Amsterdam: Rodopi, 91–6.

—— (forthcoming, 2003) 'Travel Writing, (Post)colonialism and the Production of Exotic Space', in D. Clayton and D. Gregory (eds), *Colonialism, Postcolonialism and the Production of Space*, Oxford: Blackwell.

Huggan, G. and Wachinger, T. (forthcoming, 2001) 'Can Newness Enter the World? Salman Rushdie's *The Satanic Verses* and the Question of Multicultural Aesthetics', in L. Glage (ed), *Imaginary Homelands: Multicultural Perspectives on Rushdie's Fiction*, Trier: Wissenschaftlicher Verlag Trier (WVT).

Huggins, J. and Huggins, R. (1994) *Auntie Rita*, Canberra: Australian Institute of Aboriginal Studies.

Hughes, M.A. (1998) 'An Issue of Authenticity: Editing Texts by Aboriginal Writers', *Southerly* 58, 2: 48–58.

Hughes, P. (1988) *V.S. Naipaul*, London: Routledge.

Hughes, R. (1993) *The Culture of Complaint: The Fraying of America*, Oxford: Oxford University Press.

Hulme, K. (1983) *The Bone People*, Wellington, NZ: Spiral.

Hulme, P. (1986) *Colonial Encounters: Europe and the Native Caribbean, 1492–1797*, London: Methuen.

Hutcheon, L. (1984/5) 'Canadian Historiographic Metafiction', *Essays on Canadian Writing* 30: 228–38.

Hutcheon, L. and Richmond, M. (eds) (1990) *Other Solitudes: Canadian Multicultural Fiction*, Toronto: Oxford University Press.

Inden, R. (1990) *Imagining India*, Oxford: Blackwell.

Irele, A. (1990) *The African Experience in Literature and Ideology*, Bloomington, IN: Indiana University Press.

Iser, W. (1987) [1980] *The Act of Reading: A Theory of Aesthetic Response*, Baltimore, MD: Johns Hopkins University Press.

Ita, J.M. (1973) 'Frobenius, Senghor and the Image of Africa', in R. Horton and R. Finnegan (eds), *Modes of Thought: Essays in Thinking in Western and Non-Western Societies*, London: Faber & Faber, 303–36.

Iyer, P. (1993) 'The Empire Writes Back', *Time*, 8 February: 46–51.

Jacobs, J.M. (1996) *Edge of Empire: Postcolonialism and the City*, London: Routledge.

Jacoby, R. (1995) 'Marginal Returns: The Trouble with Post-Colonial Theory', *Lingua Franca* 5, 6 (Sept.–Oct.): 30–7.

Jaggi, M. (1997) 'An Unsuitable Girl', *Guardian Weekend* 24 May: 12–18.

Jakubowicz, A. (1984a) 'Ethnicity, Multiculturalism and Neo-Conservatism', in G. Bottomley and M. de Lepervanche (eds), *Ethnicity, Class and Gender in Australia*, Sydney: Allen & Unwin, 28–48.

—— (1984b) 'State and Ethnicity: Multiculturalism as Ideology', in J. Jupp (ed.), *Ethnic Politics in Australia*, Sydney: Allen & Unwin, 14–28.

James, W. (1972) 'The Anthropologist as Reluctant Imperialist', in T. Asad (ed.), *Anthropology and the Colonial Encounter*, Atlantic Highlands, NJ: Humanities Press, 41–70.

Jameson, F. (1981) *The Political Unconscious: Narrative as a Socially Symbolic Act*, Ithaca, NY: Cornell University Press.

—— (1983) 'Postmodernism and Consumer Society', in H. Foster (ed.), *The Anti-Aesthetic: Essays on Postmodern Culture*, Seattle, WA: Bay Press, 111–25.

—— (1986) 'Third World Literature in the Era of Multinational Capitalism', *Social Text* 15: 65–88.

—— (1991) *Postmodernism; or, The Cultural Logic of Late Capitalism*, Durham, NC: Duke University Press.

Jauss, H.R. (1982) *Toward an Aesthetic of Reception*, trans. T. Bahti, Minneapolis, MN: University of Minnesota Press.

Jhabvala, R.P. (1975) *Heat and Dust*, London: John Murray.

Jolly, M. (1997) 'From Point Venus to Bali Ha'i: Eroticism and Exoticism in Representations of the Pacific', in M. Jolly and L. Manderson (eds), *Sites of Desire, Economies of Pleasure: Sexualities in Asia and the Pacific*, Chicago, IL: University of Chicago Press, 99–122.

Jolly, M. and Manderson, L. (eds) (1997) *Sites of Desire, Economies of Pleasure: Sexualities in Asia and the Pacific*, Chicago, IL: University of Chicago Press.

Jost, J., Totaro, G. and Tyshing, C. (eds) (1996) *The Demidenko File*, Ringwood, Vic.: Penguin.

Jupp, J. (1997) 'Immigration and National Identity: Multiculturalism', in G. Stokes (ed.), *The Politics of Identity in Australia*, Melbourne: Cambridge University Press, 132–44.

Jurgensen, M. (1981) *Ethnic Australia*, Brisbane: Phoenix Publications.

Kachru, B. (1986) *The Alchemy of English: The Spread, Functions and Models of Non-Native Englishes*, Oxford: Pergamon.

Kallen, E. (ed.) (1982) *Ethnicity and Human Rights in Canada*, Toronto: Gage Publishers.

Kamboureli, S. (ed.) (1996) *Making A Difference: An Anthology of Canadian Multicultural Writing*, Toronto: Oxford University Press.

Kane, J. (1997) 'Racialism and Democracy: The Legacy of White Australia', in G. Stokes (ed.), *The Politics of Identity in Australia*, Melbourne: Cambridge University Press, 117–31.

Kaplan, C. (1988) 'Michael Arlen's Fictions of Exile: The Subject of Ethnic Autobiography', *A/B: Auto/Biography Studies* 4, 2: 140–9.

Keesing, R. (1989) 'Exotic Readings of Cultural Texts', *Current Anthropology* 30, 4: 459–79.

Kelman, J. (1994) *How Late It Was, How Late*, New York: Dell.

King, B. (ed.) (1974) *Literatures of the World in English*, London: Routledge & Kegan Paul.

—— (1980) *The New English Literatures: Cultural Nationalism in a Changing World*, London: Macmillan.

Kotei, S.I.A. (1981) *The Book Today in Africa*, Paris: Unesco.

Kramer, L. (1967) 'Introduction', in C. Higham and M. Wilding (eds), *Australians Abroad*, Melbourne: F.W. Cheshire, ix–xv.

Krippendorf, J. (1987) [1984] *The Holiday Makers: Understanding the Impact of Leisure and Travel*, London: Heinemann.

Krishnaswamy, R. (1995) 'Mythologies of Migrancy: Postcolonialism, Postmodernism and the Politics of (Dis)location', *Ariel* 26, 1: 125–46.

Krotz, L. (1996) *Tourists: How Our Fastest Growing Industry is Changing the World*, London: Faber & Faber.

Krupat, A. (1992) *Ethnocriticism: Ethnography, History, Literature*, Berkeley, CA: University of California Press.

Kulyk Keefer, J. (1996) 'From Dialogue to Polylogue', in P. Easingwood, K. Gross and L. Hunter (eds), *Difference and Community: Canadian and European Cultural Perspectives*, Amsterdam: Rodopi, 59–70.

Kumar, A. (1999) 'World Bank Literature: A New Name for Postcolonial Studies in the Next Century', *College Literature* 26, 3: 195–204.

Kureishi, H. (1986) *My Beautiful Laundrette and the Rainbow Sign*, London: Faber & Faber.

—— (1988) *Sammy and Rosie Get Laid: The Script and the Diary*. London: Faber & Faber.

—— (1990) *The Buddha of Suburbia*, London: Faber & Faber.

—— (1991) *London Kills Me*, London: Faber & Faber.

—— (1995) *The Black Album*, London: Faber & Faber.

—— (1998) *Intimacy*, London: Faber & Faber.

Kurtzer, S. (1998) '*Wandering Girl*: Who Defines "Authenticity" in Aboriginal Literature?', *Southerly* 58, 2: 20–9.

Lamming, G. (1960) *The Pleasures of Exile*, London: Michael Joseph.

Larsen, N. (1995) 'DetermiNation: Postcolonialism, Poststructuralism, and the Problem of Ideology', *Dispositio/n* 20, 47: 1–19.

Lawson, A. (1995) 'Postcolonial Theory and the "Settler" Subject', *Essays in Canadian Writing* 56: 20–41.

Lazarus, N. (1999) *Nationalism and Cultural Practice in the Postcolonial World*, Cambridge: Cambridge University Press.

Lecker, R. (1991) *Canadian Canons: Essays in Literary Value*, Toronto: University of Toronto Press.

Lee, G. (1990) *Troppo Man*, St. Lucia, Qld.: University of Queensland Press.

Lee, L. (1997) 'Notes on Multiculturalism and Literature in Canada and Australia', unpublished research paper, Harvard University.

Leed, E. (1991) *The Mind of the Traveler: From Gilgamesh to Global Tourism*, New York: Basic Books.

Lefevere, A. (1983) 'Interface: Some Thoughts on the Historiography of African Literature Written in English', in D. Riemenschneider (ed.), *The History and Historiography of Commonwealth Literature*, Tübingen: Günter Narr Verlag, 99–107.

Leonardo, M. di (1998) *Exotics at Home: Anthropologies, Others, American Modernity*, Chicago, IL: University of Chicago Press.

Lévi-Strauss, C. (1984) [1955] *Tristes Tropiques*, trans. J. and D. Weightman, New York: Atheneum.

Lindfors, B. (ed.) (1974) *Dem-Say: Interviews with Eight Nigerian Writers*, Austin, TX: African and Afro-American Studies and Research Center, University of Texas at Austin.

—— (1988) 'Africa and the Nobel Prize', *World Literature Today* 62, 2: 222–8.

—— (1990) 'The Teaching of African Literatures in Anglophone African Universities: An Instructive Canon', *Matatu* 7: 41–55.

—— (ed.) (1991) *Approaches to Teaching Achebe's* Things Fall Apart, New York: Modern Language Association.

—— (1993) 'Desert Gold: Irrigation Schemes for Ending the Book Drought', in D. Riemenschneider and F. Schulze-Engler (eds), *African Literature in the Eighties*, Amsterdam: Rodopi, 27–38.

Lionnet, F. (1995) *Postcolonial Representations: Women, Literature, Identity*, Ithaca, NY: Cornell University Press.

Litvack, L. (1996a) 'Canadian Writing in English and Multiculturalism', in R. Mohanram and G. Rajan (eds), *English Postcoloniality: Literatures from Around the World*, Westport, CT: Greenwood Press, 119–34.

—— (1996b) 'The Weight of Cultural Baggage: Frank Paci and the Italian-Canadian Experience', in P. Easingwood, K. Gross and L. Hunter (eds), *Difference and Community: Canadian and European Perspectives*, Amsterdam: Rodopi, 107–18.

Lizarríbar, C.B. (1998) *Something Else Will Stand Beside It: The African Writers Series and the Development of African Literature*, Ann Arbor, MI: UMI.

Lloyd, D. (1990) 'Genet's Genealogy', in D. Lloyd and A. JanMohamed (eds), *The Nature and Context of Minority Discourse*, New York: Oxford University Press, 369–93.

Lloyd, D. and JanMohamed, A. (1990) (eds) *The Nature and Context of Minority Discourse*, New York: Oxford University Press.

Longley, K.O. (1992) 'Autobiographical Storytelling by Australian Aboriginal Women', in S. Smith and J. Watson (eds), *De/Colonizing the Subject: The Politics of Gender in Women's Autobiography*, Minneapolis, MN: University of Minnesota Press, 370–86.

—— (2000) 'Fabricating Otherness: Demidenko and Exoticism', in I. Santaolalla (ed.), *New Exoticisms: Changing Patterns in the Construction of Otherness*, Amsterdam: Rodopi, 21–40.

Loomba, A. (1998) *Colonialism/Postcolonialism*, London: Routledge.

Loriggio, F. (1996) 'Multiculturalism and Literary Criticism: Comparisons and Possibilities', *Mosaic* 29, 3: 187–203.

Lumb, P. and Hazell, A. (eds) (1983) *Diversity and Diversion: An Annotated Bibliography of Australian Ethnic Minority Literature*, Melbourne: Hodja Educational Resources Co-operative Ltd.

MacCannell, D. (1989) [1976] *The Tourist: A New Theory of the Leisure Class*, New York: Schocken Books.

MacLennan, H. (1945) *Two Solitudes*, Toronto: Macmillan.

MacLulich, T.D. (1988) *Between Europe and America: The Canadian Tradition in Fiction*, Toronto: ECW Press.

Maja-Pearce, A. (1992) 'In Pursuit of Excellence: Thirty Years of the Heinemann African Writers Series', *Research in African Literatures* 23, 4: 125–32.

Manderson, L. (1997) 'Parables of Imperialism and Fantasies of the Exotic: Western Representations of Thailand – Place and Sex', in M. Jolly and L. Manderson (eds), *Sites of Desire, Economies of Pleasure: Sexualities in Asia and the Pacific*, Chicago, IL: University of Chicago Press, 123–44.

Mani, L. (1990) 'Contentious Traditions: The Debate on *Sati* in Colonial India', in A. JanMohamed and D. Lloyd (eds), *The Nature and Context of Minority Discourse*, New York: Oxford University Press, 319–56.

Manne, R. (1996) *The Culture of Forgetting: Helen Demidenko and the Holocaust*, Melbourne: The Text Publishing Company.

Marcus, G. and Cushman, D. (1982) 'Ethnographies as Texts', *Annual Review of Anthropology* 11: 25–69.

Marcus, G. and Fischer M.M.J. (1986) *Anthropology as Cultural Critique: An Experimental Moment in the Human Sciences*, Chicago, IL: University of Chicago Press.

Martin, J. (1978) *The Migrant Presence: Australian Responses 1947–77*, Sydney: Allen & Unwin.

—— (1981) *The Ethnic Dimension: Papers on Ethnicity and Pluralism*, Sydney: Allen & Unwin.

Marx, K. (1978) 'The Fetishism of Commodities and the Secret Thereof', in R. Tucker (ed.), *The Marx-Engels Reader*, New York: Norton, 319–29.

Maschler, T. (1998) 'How It All Began', in *Booker 30: A Celebration of 30 Years of the Booker Prize for Fiction 1969–1998*, St Ives: Booker, 15–16.

Mason, P. (1996) 'On Producing the (American) Exotic', *Anthropos* 91: 139–51.

Maxwell, D.E.S. (1965) 'Landscape and Theme', in J. Press (ed.), *Commonwealth Literature*, London: Heinemann, 82–9.

Mazurek, K. (1992) 'Defusing a Radical Social Policy: The Undermining of Multiculturalism', in S. Hyniuk (ed.), *Twenty Years of Multiculturalism*, Winnipeg: St John's College Press, 17–28.

McClintock, A. (1992) 'The Angel of Progress: Pitfalls of the Term "Postcolonialism" ', *Social Text* 31/2: 84–98.

McDougall, R. (1987) 'Achebe's *Arrow of God*: The Kinetic Idiom of an Unmasking', *Kunapipi* 9, 2: 8–23.

McGee, P. (1992) *Telling the Other: The Question of Value in Modern and Postcolonial Writing*, Ithaca, NY: Cornell University Press.

McGirk, J. (1997) 'Indian Literary Star Faces Caste Sex Trial', *Sunday Times* 29 June: 18–19.

McLaren, P. (1992) 'Critical Literacy and Postcolonial Praxis: A Freirian Perspective', *College Literature* 19, 3: 7–27.

McLeod, A. (ed.) (1961) *The Commonwealth Pen*, Ithaca, NY: Cornell University Press.

McLuhan, M. (1964) *Understanding Media: The Extensions of Man*, New York: Signet Books.

Mehta, G. (1979) *Karma Cola: Marketing the Mystic East*, New York: Ballantine.

Mehta, M. (1996) 'Boom in Germany for Big Indian Novels', *India Abroad* 29 August: 47.

Merivale, P. (1990) 'Saleem Fathered by Oscar: Intertextual Strategies in *Midnight's Children* and *The Tin Drum*', *Ariel* 21, 3: 5–21.

Metcalf, J. (1988) *What is A Canadian Literature?* Guelph, Ont.: Red Kite Press.

Michaels, A. (1996) *Fugitive Pieces*, Toronto: McClelland & Stewart.

Miller, C.T. (1985) *Blank Darkness: Africanist Discourse in French*, Chicago, IL: University of Chicago Press.

—— (1990) *Theories of Africans: Francophone Literature and Anthropology in Africa*, Chicago, IL: University of Chicago Press.

Minh-ha, T.T. (1989) *Woman, Native, Other: Writing Postcoloniality and Feminism*, Bloomington, IN: Indiana University Press.

—— (1991) *When the Moon Waxes Red: Representation, Gender and Cultural Politics*, New York: Routledge.

Mishra, V. (1996) 'Postmodern Racism', *Meanjin* 55, 2: 347–57.

Mitchell, T. (1992) 'Orientalism and the Exhibitionary Order', in N. Dirks (ed.), *Colonialism and Culture*, Ann Arbor, MI: University of Michigan Press, 289–317.

Mitchell, W.J.T. (1992) 'Postcolonial Culture, Postimperial Criticism', *Transition* 56: 11–19.

Miyoshi, M. (1996) 'A Borderless World? From Colonialism to Transnationalism and the Decline of the Nation-State', in R. Wilson and W. Dissanayake (eds), *Global/Local: Cultural Production and the Transnational Imaginary*, Durham, NC: Duke University Press, 78–106.

Mohan, R. (1992) 'Dodging the Crossfire: Questions for Postcolonial Pedagogy', *College Literature* 19, 3: 28–44.

Mohanram, R. (1995) 'Postcolonial Spaces and Deterritorialized (Homo)Sexuality: The Films of Hanif Kureishi', in G. Rajan and R. Mohanram (eds), *Postcolonial Discourse and Changing Cultural Contexts: Theory and Criticism*,Westport, CT: Greenwood Press, 117–34.

Mongia, P. (ed.) (1996) *Contemporary Postcolonial Theory: A Reader*, London: Arnold.

—— (1997) 'The Making and Marketing of Arundhati Roy', unpublished paper presented at the 'India: Fifty Years After' conference, Sept. 1997, University of Barcelona, Spain.

Moore, R. (1992) 'Paul Scott and the Raj as Metaphor', in A. Greet *et al.* (eds), *Raj Nostalgia*, Adelaide: CRNLE, 135–50.

Moore-Gilbert, B. (1997) *Postcolonial Theory: Contexts, Practices, Politics*, London: Verso.

Moore-Gilbert, B., Stanton, G. and Maley, W. (eds) (1997) *Postcolonial Criticism*, London: Longman.

Morgan, S. (1987) *My Place*, Fremantle: Fremantle Arts Centre Press.

Moseley, M. (1993) 'Britain's Booker Prize', *Sewanee Review* 101, 4: 613–23.

Mudimbe, V.Y. (1988) *The Invention of Africa: Gnosis, Philosophy, and the Order of Knowledge*, Bloomington, IN: Indiana University Press.

Mudrooroo (1990) *Writing from the Fringe: A Study of Modern Aboriginal Literature*, Melbourne: Hyland House.

—— (1997) *Milli Milli Wangka: The Indigenous Literature of Australia*, Melbourne: Hyland House.

Muecke, S. (1988) 'Aboriginal Literature and the Repressive Hypothesis', *Southerly* 48, 4: 405–18.

Mukherjee, A. (1985) 'The Poetry of Michael Ondaatje and Cyril Dabydeen: Two Responses to Otherness', *Journal of Commonwealth Literature* 20, 1: 49–67.

—— (1990) 'Whose Post-colonialism and Whose Post-modernism?', *World Literature Written in English* 30, 2: 1–9.

—— (1994a) [1986] 'Ideology in the Classroom: A Case Study in the Teaching of English Literature in Canadian Universities', in *Oppositional Aesthetics: Readings from a Hyphenated Space*, Toronto: TSAR, 30–8.

—— (1994b) *Oppositional Aesthetics: Readings from a Hyphenated Space*, Toronto: TSAR.

—— (1994c) [1984] 'The Sri Lankan Poets in Canada: An Alternative View', in *Oppositional Aesthetics: Readings from a Hyphenated Space*, Toronto: TSAR, 96–111.

Mulvey, L. (1975) 'Visual Pleasure and Narrative Cinema', *Screen* 16, 3: 6–18.

Nadal, M. and Herrero, M.D. (eds) (1997) *Margins in British and American Literature, Film and Culture*, Zaragoza: Dept. de Filología Inglesa e Alemana, University of Zaragoza.

Naipaul, V.S. (1991) [1987] *The Enigma of Arrival*, New York: Knopf.

Nannup, A. with Marsh, L. and Kinnane, S. (1992) *When the Pelican Laughed*, Fremantle: Fremantle Arts Centre Press.

Narayan, R.K. (1992) 'After the Raj', in A. Greet *et al.* (eds), *Raj Nostalgia*, Adelaide: CRNLE, 151–3.

Narayan, S. (1998) Review of S. Rushdie and E. West (eds) *The Vintage Book of Indian Writing 1947–1997*, *Ariel* 29, 1: 263–6.

Nettlebeck, A. (1997) 'Presenting Aboriginal Women's Life Narratives', *New Literatures Review* 34: 43–56.

New, W.H. (1975) *Among Worlds*, Erin, Ont.: Press Porcépic.

Newby, P.H. (1969) [1968] *Something to Answer For*, London: Faber & Faber.

Newman, J. (1995) *The Ballistic Bard: Postcolonial Fictions*, London: Arnold.

New Yorker (1997) Special [Indo-Anglian] Fiction Issue, June 23 and 30.

Niranjana, T. (1992) *Siting Translation: History, Post-Structuralism, and the Colonial Context*, Berkeley, CA: University of California Press.

Nischik, R. (1997) 'Nomenclatural Mutations: Forms of Address in Margaret Atwood's Novels', *Orbis Litterarum: International Review of Literary Studies* 52, 5: 329–51.

Niven, A. (1998) 'A Common Wealth of Talent', in *Booker 30: A Celebration of 30 Years of the Booker Prize for Fiction 1969–1998*, St. Ives: Booker, 40–2.

Nixon, R. (1992) *London Calling: V.S. Naipaul, Postcolonial Mandarin*, Oxford: Oxford University Press.

Nolan, M. (1998) 'The Absent Aborigine', *Antipodes* 21, 1: 7–13.

Observer (1997) 'It's the 50th Anniversary of Our Independence. Reasons to Celebrate Are All Around', 5 October, Travel Section: 10.

—— (1998) 'Visit India at the Millennium!', 8 November, Travel Section: 24.

Okai, A. (1973) 'The Role of the Ghanaian Writers in the Revolution', *Weekly Spectator*, 14 July: 4.

Oluwasanmi, E., McLean, E. and Zell, H. (eds) (1975) *Publishing in Africa in the Seventies*, Ile-Ife: University of Ife Press.

Omotoso, K. (1975) 'The Missing Apex: In Search for the Audience', in E. Oluwasanmi *et al.* (eds), *Publishing in Africa in the Seventies*, Ile-Ife: University of Ife Press, 251–61.

Ondaatje, M. (1982) *Running in the Family*, Toronto: McClelland & Stewart.

—— (1992) *The English Patient*, New York: Vintage.

Ortiz, F. (1998) *Essays*, ed. A. de Fernando Ferrer, Alicante: Inst. de Cultura Juan Gil-Albert.

O'Shaughnessy, K. (1993) 'Seth and the Single Girl', *Vogue*, March: 72, 79.

Ouologuem, Y. (1968) *Le devoir de violence*, Paris: Seuil.

Palling, B. (1993) 'Midnight's Children Come of Age', *Weekly Telegraph*, 22 September: 20.

Papaellinas, G. (ed.) (1991) *Homeland*, Sydney: Allen & Unwin.

—— (1992) 'Exoticism is just a boutique form of xenophobia: writing in a multicultural society', in S. Gunew and K.O. Longley (eds), *Striking Chords: Multicultural Literary Interpretations*, Sydney: Allen & Unwin, 165–7.

Perera, S. (1996) 'Claiming Truganini: Australian National Narratives in the Year of Indigenous Peoples', *Cultural Studies* 10, 3: 393–412.

Perkins, D. (ed.) (1991) *Theoretical Issues in Literary History*, Cambridge, MA: Harvard University Press.

Perrakis, P.S. (1997) 'Atwood's *Robber Bride*: The Vampire as Intersubjective Catalyst', *Mosaic: Journal for the Interdisciplinary Study of Literature* 30, 3: 151–68.

Peterson, J. (1997) 'Le Curry', *The New Yorker*, 23, 30 June, 138.

Pevere, G. (1995) 'Difficult to Say: Interview with Atom Egoyan', in G. Pevere (ed.), *Exoticism: The Screenplay*, Toronto: Coach House Press, 43–68.

Philip, M. Nourbese (1992) *Frontiers: Essays and Writings on Racism and Culture*, Stratford, Ont.: Mercury Press.

Phillips, C. (1997) *The Nature of Blood*, London: Faber & Faber.

Porter, D. (1991) *Haunted Journeys: Desire and Transgression in European Travel Writing*, Princeton, NJ: Princeton University Press.

Povinelli, E.A. (1998) 'The State of Shame: Australian Multiculturalism and the Crisis of Indigenous Citizenship', *Critical Inquiry* 24, 2: 575–610.

Prakash, G. (1994) 'Subaltern Studies as Postcolonial Criticism', *American Historical Review* 99, 5: 1475–90.

Pratt, M.L. (1992) *Imperial Eyes: Travel Writing and Transculturation*, New York: Routledge.

Press, J. (ed.) (1963) *The Teaching of English Literature Overseas*, London: Methuen.

—— (ed.) (1965) *Commonwealth Literature*, London: Methuen.

Price, D.W. (1994) 'Salman Rushdie's "Use and Abuse of History" in *Midnight's Children*', *Ariel* 25, 2: 91–107.

Quart, L. (1992) 'The Politics of Irony: The Frears-Kureishi Films', in W.W. Dixon (ed.), *Re-Viewing British Cinema, 1900–1992*, Albany, NY: State University of New York Press, 241–9.

Quayson, A. (1994) 'Realism, Criticism, and the Disguises of Both: A Reading of Chinua Achebe's *Things Fall Apart* with an Evaluation of the Criticism Relating to It', *Research in African Literatures* 25, 4: 118–36.

—— (2000) *Postcolonialism: Theory, Practice or Process?*, Cambridge: Polity Press.

Radhakrishnan, R. (1993) 'Postcoloniality and the Boundaries of Identity', *Callaloo* 16, 4: 750–71.

—— (1996) *Diasporic Mediations: Between Home and Location*, Minneapolis, MN: University of Minnesota Press.

Radway, J. (1991) *Reading the Romance: Women, Patriarchy, and Popular Literature*, Chapel Hill, NC: University of North Carolina Press.

Rajan, G. and Mohanram, R. (eds) (1995) *Postcolonial Discourse and Changing Cultural Contexts: Theory and Criticism*, Westport, CT: Greenwood Press.

Ramraj, V. (ed.) *Concert of Voices: An Anthology of World Writing in English*, Toronto: Broadview Press.

Ray, S. and Schwarz, H. (eds) (1999) *A Companion to Postcolonial Studies*, Oxford: Blackwell.

Remak, H.H. (1978) 'Exoticism in Romanticism', *Comparative Literature Studies* 15: 53–65.

Restuccia, F. (1996) 'Tales of Beauty: Aestheticizing Female Melancholia', *American Imago: Studies in Psychoanalysis and Culture* 53, 4: 353–83.

Ricard, F. (1985) 'Le berceau de Dieu', *Liberté* 157: 37–43.

Richards, T. (1993) *The Imperial Archive: Knowledge and the Fantasy of Empire*, London: Verso.

Riemenschneider, D. (ed.) (1983) *The History and Historiography of Commonwealth Literature*, Tübingen: Günter Narr Verlag.

—— (1984) 'History and the Individual in Salman Rushdie's *Midnight's Children* and Anita Desai's *Clear Light of Day*', *Kunapipi* 6, 2: 53–66.

—— (1987) 'The "New" English Literatures in Historical and Political Perspective: Attempts Toward a Comparative View of North/South Relationships in "Commonwealth Literature" ', *New Literary History* 18, 2: 425–35.

—— (2000) 'Postcolonial Theory: Introductory Remarks', in B. Reitz and S. Rieuwerts (eds), *Anglistentag 1999 Mainz Proceedings*, Trier: Wissenschaftlicher Verlag Trier (WVT), 227–30.

Riemer, A. (1996) *The Demidenko Debate*, Sydney: Allen & Unwin.

Rimmer, S. (1988) *Fiscal Anarchy: The Public Funding of Multiculturalism*, Perth: Australian Institute for Public Policy.

Rivard, Y. (1986) *Les silences du corbeau*, Montreal: Boreal.

Robbins, B. (1992) 'Colonial Discourse: A Paradigm and Its Discontents', *Victorian Studies* 35, 2: 209–14.

—— (1993) *Secular Vocations: Intellectuals, Professionalism, Culture*, New York: Verso.

Roberts, M. (forthcoming) 'The Global Imaginary', work in progress.

Root, D. (1996) *Cannibal Culture: Art, Appropriation, & the Commodification of Cultural Difference*, Boulder, CO: WestView Press.

Rosaldo, R. (1988) 'Ideology, Place, and People without Culture', *Cultural Anthropology* 3: 77–87.

—— (1993) [1989] *Culture and Truth: The Remaking of Social Analysis*, London: Routledge.

Rouse, R. (1991) 'Mexican Migration and the Social Space of Postmodernism', *Diaspora* 1, 1: 8–23.

Rousseau G.S. and Porter, R. (eds) (1990) *Exoticism in the Enlightenment*, Manchester: Manchester University Press.

Rowse, T. (1993) 'The Aboriginal Subject in Autobiography: Ruby Langford's *Don't Take Your Love to Town*', *Australian Literary Studies* 16, 1: 14–29.

Roy, A. (1997) *The God of Small Things*, New York: Flamingo.

Rushdie, S. (1981) *Midnight's Children*, London: Pan/Picador.

—— (1989) [1988] *The Satanic Verses*, New York: Viking.

—— (1991a) ' "Commonwealth Literature" Does Not Exist', in *Imaginary Homelands: Essays 1981–1991*, London: Granta, 61–70.

—— (1991b) ' "Errata": or, Unreliable Narration in *Midnight's Children*', in *Imaginary Homelands: Essays and Criticism 1981–1991*, London: Granta, 22–5.

—— (1991c) *Imaginary Homelands: Essays and Criticism 1981–1991*, London: Granta.

—— (1991d) 'Is Nothing Sacred?' in *Imaginary Homelands: Essays and Criticism 1981–1991*, London: Granta, 415–29.

—— (1991e) 'Outside the Whale', in *Imaginary Homelands: Essays and Criticism 1981–1991*, London: Granta, 87–101.

—— (1991f) 'The New Empire Within Britain', in *Imaginary Homelands: Essays and Criticism 1981–1991*, London: Granta, 121–38.

—— (1994) *East, West*, New York: Pantheon.

—— (1997) 'Damme, This is the Oriental Scene for You!', *The New Yorker*, 23–30 June: 50–61.

—— (1999) *The Ground Beneath Her Feet*, New York: Random House.

Rushdie, S. and West, E. (eds) (1997) *The Vintage Book of Indian Writing, 1947–1997*, NY: Vintage.

Rutherford, A. (ed.) (1992) *From Commonwealth to Post-Colonial*, Mundelstrup, DK: Dangaroo Press.

Said, E.W. (1978) *Orientalism*, New York: Vintage.

—— (1983) 'Opponents, Audiences, Constituencies and Community', in H. Foster (ed.), *The Anti-Aesthetic*, Seattle, WA: Bay Press, 135–9.

—— (1986) 'Orientalism Reconsidered', in F. Barker *et al.* (eds), *Literature, Politics and Theory*, London: Methuen, 210–29.

—— (1989) 'Representing the Colonized: Anthropology's Interlocutors', *Critical Inquiry* 15: 205–25.

—— (1990) 'Third World Intellectuals and Metropolitan Culture', *Raritan* 9, 3: 27–50.

—— (1993) *Culture and Imperialism*, New York: Knopf.

—— (1994) *Representations of the Intellectual*, New York: Vintage.

Sangari, K. (1987) 'The Politics of the Possible', *Cultural Critique* 7: 157–86.

San Juan, E. (1998) *Beyond Postcolonial Theory*, New York: St Martin's Press.

Santaolalla, I. (ed.) (2000) *New Exoticisms: Changing Patterns in the Construction of Otherness*, Amsterdam: Rodopi.

Satchidanandan, K. (1997) 'The Case of a Wounded Literature', *The Hindu Magazine*, 6 July 1997: ix, xii, xv.

Schlesinger, Jr, A. (1992) *The Disuniting of America*, Knoxville, TN: Whittle District Books.

Schmidt, N. (1981) 'The Nature of Ethnographic Fiction: A Further Inquiry', *Anthropology and Humanism Quarterly*, 8–18.

Schulze-Engler, F. (1997) 'Relocating Resistance: "Postcolonial" Literature and the Politics of Civil Society', *Zeitschrift für Anglistik und Amerikanistik* 45, 3: 208–18.

—— (1998) 'The Politics of Postcolonial Theory', *Acolit* 3: 31–5.

Scott, J.C. (1990) *Domination and the Arts of Resistance*, New Haven, CT: Yale University Press.

Scott, P. (1976) *The Raj Quartet*, London: Heinemann.

—— (1977) *Staying On*, New York: William and Morrow.

Seaton, A. (1996) 'Notes on *Priscilla*', unpublished research paper, Harvard University.

Segalen, V. (1978) *Essai sur l'exotisme, une esthétique du Divers*, Paris: Fata Morgana.

Sellin, E. (1971) 'Ouologuem's Blueprint for *Le devoir de violence*', *Research in African Literatures* 2: 117–20.

Sen, N. Deb (1997) 'An Open Letter to Salman Rushdie', *The Express Sunday Magazine* (New Delhi), 13 July: 4.

Sengupta, S. (1997) 'The New Indo Chic', *New York Times*, 30 August: 13, 19.

Seth, V. (1986) *The Golden Gate*, London: Faber & Faber.

—— (1987) [1983] *From Heaven Lake*, New York: Vintage.

—— (1993) *A Suitable Boy*, London: Phoenix House.

—— (1999) *An Equal Music*, London: Phoenix House.

Sharrad, P. (1992) 'The Books Behind the Film: Paul Scott's *The Raj Quartet*', in A. Greet *et al.* (eds), *Raj Nostalgia*, Adelaide: CRNLE, 123–34.

Shepherd, R. (1985) '*Midnight's Children*: The Parody of an Indian Novel', *SPAN* 21: 184–92.

Shohat, E. (1992) 'Notes on the "Post-Colonial" ', *Social Text* 31/32: 99–113.

—— (1997) 'Gender and Culture of Empire: Toward a Feminist Ethnography of the Cinema', in M. Bernstein and G. Studlar (eds), *Visions of the East: Orientalism in Film*, New Brunswick, NJ: Rutgers University Press, 19–68.

Shumway, D.R. (1997): 'The Star System in Literary Studies', *PMLA* 112, 1: 85–100.

Slemon, S. (1993) 'Teaching at the End of Empire', *College Literature* 20, 1: 152–61.

—— (1994) 'The Scramble for Post-Colonialism', in C. Tiffin and A. Lawson (eds), *De-Scribing Empire: Post-Colonialism and Textuality*, London: Routledge, 15–32.

—— (1995) 'Postcolonialism and its Discontents', *Ariel* 26, 1: 7–11.

Slemon, S. and Tiffin, H. (eds) (1989) *After Europe: Critical Theory and Post-Colonial Writing*, Mundelstrup, DK: Dangaroo.

Smith, B. (1985) *European Vision and the South Pacific*, 2nd edn, New Haven, CT: Yale University Press.

Smith, B. Herrnstein (1984) 'Contingencies of Value', in R. von Hallberg (ed.), *Canons*, Chicago, IL: University of Chicago Press, 5–40.

—— (1988) *Contingencies of Value: Alternative Perspectives for Critical Theory*, Cambridge, MA: Harvard University Press.

Smith, S. and Watson, J. (eds) (1992) *De/Colonizing the Subject: The Politics of Gender in Women's Autobiography*, Minneapolis, MN: University of Minnesota Press.

Sollors, W. (1986) *Beyond Ethnicity: Consent and Descent in American Culture*, New York: Oxford University Press.

Sontag, S. (1984) 'Notes on Camp', in *A Susan Sontag Reader*, New York: Vintage, 105–20.

Soyinka, W. (1976) *Myth, Literature and the African World*, Cambridge: Cambridge University Press.

—— (1990) 'Twice Bitten: The Fate of Africa's Culture Producers', *PMLA* 105, 1: 110–20.

Spivak, G. Chakravorty (1985) 'Three Women's Texts and a Critique of Imperialism', *Critical Inquiry* 12, 1: 243–61.

—— (1987) *In Other Worlds: Essays in Cultural Politics*, New York: Methuen.

—— (1990a) 'Post-structuralism, Marginality, Postcoloniality and Value', in P. Collier and H. Geyer-Ryan (eds), *Literary Theory Today*, Ithaca, NY: Cornell University Press, 219–44.

—— (1990b) *The Post-Colonial Critic: Interviews, Strategies, Dialogues*, ed. S. Harasym, New York: Routledge.

—— (1991) 'Theory in the Margin: Coetzee's *Foe* Reading Defoe's *Crusoe/Roxana*', in J. Arac and B. Johnson (eds), *Consequences of Theory*, Baltimore: Johns Hopkins University Press, 154–80.

—— (1993a) *Outside in the Teaching-Machine*, New York: Routledge.

—— (1993b) '*Sammy and Rosie Get Laid*', in *Outside in the Teaching Machine*, New York: Routledge, 243–54.

—— (1993c) 'The Politics of Translation', in *Outside in the Teaching Machine*, New York: Routledge, 179–200.

—— (1996) 'How to Teach a "Culturally Different" Book', in D. Landry and G. MacLean (eds), *The Spivak Reader*, New York: Routledge, 237–66.

—— (1999) *A Critique of Postcolonial Reason: Toward a History of the Vanishing Present*, Cambridge, MA: Harvard University Press.

Spurr, D. (1993) *The Rhetoric of Empire: Colonial Discourse in Journalism, Travel Writing, and Imperial Administration*, Durham, NC: Duke University Press.

Srivastava, A. (1995) 'Postcolonialism and its Discontents', *Ariel* 26, 1: 12–17.

Steedly, M. (1993) *Hanging without a Rope: Narrative Experience in Colonial and Postcolonial Karoland*, Princeton, NJ: Princeton University Press.

Steiner, C.B. (1994) *African Art in Transit*, Cambridge: Cambridge University Press.

Stewart, S. (1984) *On Longing: Narratives of the Miniature, the Gigantic, the Souvenir, the Collection*, Baltimore, MD: Johns Hopkins University Press.

Stokes, G. (ed.) (1997) *The Politics of Identity in Australia*, Melbourne: Cambridge University Press.

Sugnasiri, H.J. (1992) 'Sri Lankan Canadian Poets: The Bourgeoisie that Fled the Revolution', *Canadian Literature* 132: 60–79.

Sugnet, C. (1991) 'Vile Bodies, Vile Places: Traveling with *Granta*', *Transition* 51: 70–85.

Suleri, S. (1992a) *The Rhetoric of English India*, Chicago, IL: University of Chicago Press.

—— (1992b) 'Woman Skin Deep: Feminism and the Postcolonial Condition', *Critical Inquiry* 18: 756–69.

Surette, L. (1991) 'Creating the Canadian Canon', in R. Lecker (ed.), *Canadian Canons: Essays in Literary Value*, Toronto: University of Toronto Press, 17–29.

Swann, J. (1986) ' "East is East and West is West"? Salman Rushdie's *Midnight's Children* as an Indian Novel', *World Literature Written in English* 26, 2: 353–62.

Tapping, C. (1990) 'Literary Reflections of Orality: Colin Johnson's *Doctor Wooreddy's Prescription for Enduring the Ending of the World*', *World Literature Written in English* 30, 2: 55–61.

Taussig, M. (1993) *Mimesis and Alterity: A Particular History of the Senses*, NY: Routledge.

Taylor, C. (1991) *The Ethics of Authenticity*, Cambridge, MA: Harvard University Press.

—— (1994) 'The Politics of Recognition', in A. Gutmann (ed.), *Multiculturalism: Examining the Politics of Recognition*, Princeton, NJ: Princeton University Press, 25–74.

Thieme, J. (ed.) (1996) *The Arnold Anthology of Post-Colonial Literatures in English*, London: Arnold.

Thomas, N. (1994) *Colonialism's Culture: Anthropology, Travel and Government*, Princeton, NJ: Princeton University Press.

Thwaite, A. (1987) 'Booker 1986', *Encounter* 68: 37–8.

Tiffin, H. (1983) 'Commonwealth Literature: Comparison and Judgement', in D. Riemenschneider (ed.), *The History and Historiography of Commonwealth Literature*, Tübingen: Günter Narr Verlag, 19–35.

—— (1984) 'Asia and the Contemporary Australian Novel', *Australian Literary Studies* 11, 4: 468–79.

—— (1987) 'Post-Colonial Literatures and Counter-Discourse', *Kunapipi* 9, 3: 17–34.

—— (1989) 'Rites of Resistance: Counter-Discourse and West Indian Biography', *Journal of West Indian Literature* 3, 1: 28–45.

The Times (1993) Special supplement on the 'Booker of Bookers', 21 September.

Todd, R. (1996) *Consuming Fictions: The Booker Prize and Fiction in Britain Today*, London: Bloomsbury.

Todorov, T. (1993) *On Human Diversity: Nationalism, Racism, and Exoticism in French Thought*, Cambridge, MA: Harvard University Press.

Trivedi, H. (1993) *Colonial Transactions: English Literature and India*, Manchester: Manchester University Press.

—— (1999) 'The Postcolonial or the Transcolonial? Location and Language', *Interventions* 1, 2: 269–72.

Turner, G. (1986) *National Fictions: Literature, Film and the Construction of Australian Narrative*, Sydney: Allen & Unwin.

Turner, L. and Ash, J. (1975) *The Golden Hordes: International Tourism and the Pleasure Periphery*, London: Constable.

Tutuola, A. (1952) *The Palm-Wine Drinkard*, London: Faber & Faber.

Ubale, B. (1992) *Politics of Exclusion: Multiculturalism or Ghettoism?*, North York, Ont.: Ampri Enterprises.

Unwin, V. and Currey, J. (1993) 'The African Writers' Series Celebrates Thirty Years', *Southern African Review of Books* March/April 1993: 3–5.

Updike, J. (1997) 'Mother Tongues: Subduing the Language of the Colonizer', *New Yorker* 23, 30 June, 156–61.

Urry, J. (1990) *The Tourist Gaze: Leisure and Travel in Contemporary Societies*, London: Sage.

Vakil, A. (1998) [1997] *Beach Boy*, London: Penguin.

Van Herk, A. (1991) 'Post-Modernism: Homesick for Homesickness', in B. King (ed.), *The Commonwealth Novel Since 1960*, London: Macmillan, 216–30.

Veer, P. van der (1997) ' "The Enigma of Arrival": Hybridity and Authenticity in the Global Space', in P. Werbner and T. Modood (eds), *Debating Cultural Hybridity: Multi-Cultural Identities and the Politics of Anti-Racism*, London: Zed Books, 90–105.

Verhoeven, W.M. (1996) 'How Hyphenated Can You Get? A Critique of Pure Ethnicity', *Mosaic* 29, 3: 97–115.

Vickers, A. (1989) *Bali: A Paradise Created*, Ringwood, Vic.: Penguin.

Viswanathan, G. (1989) *Masks of Conquest: Literary Study and British Rule in India*, New York: Columbia University Press.

Vollmann, W.T. (1997) [1996] *The Atlas*, New York: Penguin.

Wachinger, T. (2000) 'Trapped in Between. Postcolonial Englishness and the Commodification of Otherness in British Narratives of Hybridity', Ph.D. dissertation, University of Munich.

Wai, I. (1985) 'The Nobel's Asian Lockout', *World Press Review* June: 59–60.

Walder, D. (1998) *Post-colonial Literatures in English: History, Language, Theory*, Oxford: Blackwell.

Walsh, W. (ed.) (1970) *A Manifold Voice: Studies in Commonwealth Literature*, London: Chatto & Windus.

—— (1973) *Commonwealth Literature*, Oxford: Oxford University Press.

Ward, G. (1988) *Wandering Girl*, Broome: Magabala Books.

Waring, W. (1995) 'Is This Your Book? Wrapping Postcolonial Fiction for the Global Market', *Canadian Review of Comparative Literature* 22, 3/4: 455–65.

Wark, M. (1997) *The Virtual Republic: Australia's Culture Wars of the 1990s*, Sydney: Allen & Unwin.

Wasserman, R. (1994) *Exotic Nations: Literature and Cultural Identity in the US and Brazil, 1830–1930*, Ithaca, NY: Cornell University Press.

Watson, T. (2000) 'Is the "Post" in Postcolonial the US in American Studies? The US Beginnings of Commonwealth Studies', *Ariel* 31, 1/2: 51–72.

Werbner, P. and Modood, T. (eds) (1997) *Debating Cultural Hybridity: Multi-Cultural Identities and the Politics of Anti-Racism*, London: Zed Books.

White, R. (1981) *Inventing Australia: Images and Identity 1688–1980*, Sydney: Allen & Unwin.

Will, C. (1990) 'Canadian Multiculturalism: Policy, Ideology and Reality', in R.-O. Schultze (ed.), *Canadian Studies at the Beginning of the Nineties: Directions and Perspectives in Politics, Literature and Women's Issues*, Augsburg: Institute for Canadian Studies, University of Augsburg, 81–103.

Williams, P. (1999) 'Totally Ideological', *Interventions* 1, 2: 282–5.

Williams, P. and Chrisman, L. (eds) (1994) *Colonial Discourse and Postcolonial Theory: A Reader*, New York: Columbia University Press.

Wilson, J. (1995) 'A Very English Story', *The New Yorker* 6 March: 96–106.

Wilson, R. and Dissanayake, W. (eds) (1996) *Global/Local: Cultural Production and the Transnational Imaginary*, Durham, NC: Duke University Press.

Wilson, S.R., Friedman, T.B. and Hengen, S. (eds) (1996) *Approaches to Teaching Atwood's* The Handmaid's Tale *and Other Works*, New York: Modern Language Association of America.

Winegarten, R. (1994) 'The Nobel Prize for Literature', *American Scholar* 63, 1: 65–75.

Young, R.J.C. (1990) *White Mythologies: Writing History and the West*, London: Routledge.

—— (1995) *Colonial Desire: Hybridity in Theory, Culture and Race*, London: Routledge.

—— (2000) 'The Politics of Postcolonial Critique', in B. Reitz and S. Rieuwerts (eds), *Anglistentag 1999 Mainz Proceedings*, Trier: Wissenschaftlicher Verlag Trier (WVT), 231–44.

Zacariah, M. (1976) 'Sacred Cows, Sexy Sculptures and Starving Millions: Stereotypes and Other Problems in Teaching About South Asia', in P. Wakil (ed.), *South Asia: Perspectives and Problems*, Toronto: CASAS, 131–40.

—— (1985) 'Janette Turner Hospital's Passage to India: A Critique of *The Ivory Swing*', *Toronto South Asian Review* 4, 1: 54–61.

Zell, H.M. (1992) 'Africa: The Neglected Continent', in N. Kumar and S.K. Ghai (eds), *Afro/Asian Publishing: Contemporary Trends*, New Delhi: Institute of Book Publishing.

—— (1993) 'Publishing in Africa: The Crisis and the Challenge.' in O. Owomoyela (ed.), *A History of Twentieth-Century African Literatures*, Nebraska: University of Nebraska Press, 369–87.

Index